Handbook of International Mergers and Acquisitions

Handbook of International Mergers and Acquisitions

Preparation, Implementation and Integration

Edited by

Gerhard Picot

palgrave macmillan

First published 2002 by
PALGRAVE MACMILLAN
Houndmills, Basingstoke, Hampshire RG21 6XS and
175 Fifth Avenue, New York, N. Y. 10010
Companies and representatives throughout the world

PALGRAVE MACMILLAN is the global academic imprint of the Palgrave Macmillan division of St. Martin's Press, LLC and of Palgrave Macmillan Ltd. Macmillan® is a registered trademark in the United States, United Kingdom and other countries. Palgrave is the registered trademark in the European Union and other countries.

ISBN 0–333–96867–0

This book is printed on paper suitable for recycling and made from fully managed and sustained forest sources.

A catalogue record for this book is available from the British Library.

Library of Congress Cataloging-in-Publication Data
Handbook of international mergers and acquisitions: preparation, implementation, edited by Gerhard Picot.
p. cm.
Includes bibliographical references and index.
ISBN 0–333–96867–0 (cloth)
1. Consolidation and merger of corporations. 2. Consolidation and merger of corporations—Law and legislation. I. Picot, Gerhard.
HD2746.5 .H359 2002
658.1′6—dc21

10 9 8 7 6 5 4 3 2 1
11 10 09 08 07 06 05 04 03 02

Printed and bound in Great Britain by
Antony Rowe Ltd, Chippenham and Eastbourne

Contents

List of Figures

List of Tables

Preface

At the beginning of the new millennium, mergers and acquisitions (M&A) worldwide are still radically changing the corporate landscape, owing to their rapid growth in transaction numbers and volume. Managers and M&A advisers have to respond to increasing globalisation and new technological challenges, in particular in the areas of information and communication, as well as to the opening and deregulation of many markets. Driven by a philosophy of shareholder value, they form a new economic, social and cultural environment. It is only by a profound understanding of the factors of success that they are able to improve transaction management and create new economic values.

According to the complex character of the global undertakings – primarily in the case of cross-border transactions – complex economic, legal, technical and social tasks arise, closely interlinked and embracing several sectors and disciplines. At the same time, M&A comprise considerable procedural particularities owing to the varied embodiments they take at an international and national level:

- Corporate sales and acquisitions
- Mergers
- Alliances, cooperations and joint ventures
- Corporate safeguarding and succession
- Management buy-out and buy-in
- Initial public offering (IPO)
- Conversions
- Restructurings.

M&A as well as, in particular, global transactions thus need to be considered in an overall and interdisciplinary manner regarding their three stages: planning, implementation and integration.

For the first time, such an overall and interdisciplinary representation of the subject at the international level is offered in this book. The exposition is particularly clear because it follows the usual course of the transactions in their structure and issue representation, from their planning and implementation to integration at the post-merger stage. With its practical, research-based and concise content, the book addresses primarily entrepreneurs, managers, investment bankers, legal advisers, accountants and other advisers on M&A issues as well as students.

I wish to address special thanks to my co-authors, Messrs Dr Helmut Bergmann, Dr Alexander Dibelius, Dr Stephan Eilers, Stephan A. Jansen, Dr Tomas Koch, Professor Heinrich Pack, Professor Peter Pribilla, Professor Dr. Frank Richter and Dr Rainer Zimmermann for having made the book possible despite their heavy professional workload. As many thanks to Zelah Pengilley of Palgrave for our good and efficient cooperation in editing the book; further, to my assistant,

Ms Sandra Nöhre, from the law firm Freshfields Bruckhaus Deringer, for her substantial support.

October 2001 *Professor Dr Gerhard Picot*

Notes on the Contributors

Helmut Bergmann is managing partner of the Berlin office of Freshfields Bruckhaus Deringer. He specialises in advising multinational corporations in the planning and implementation of M&A. As a member of the Competition & Trade Group of the firm he has filed numerous mergers, acquisitions and joint ventures as well as other agreements to the European Commission and to the German Federal Cartel Office. He frequently handles multinational merger filings to antitrust authorities around the world. He also advises clients in cartel investigations and in ongoing matters concerning the German and European antitrust laws. He has written a number of articles and lectures frequently on German and European competition law.

Alexander Dibelius is co-head of the Investment banking Division of Goldman Sachs & Co. OHG in Frankfurt. His responsibilities include client coverage and transaction management in Germany, Austria and Switzerland. He joined Goldman Sachs in 1993 and became a managing director in 1997. From 1987 to 1992 he was a partner with McKinsey & Co.

Stephan Eilers LL.M (Tax) is a partner in Freshfields Bruckhaus Deringer. He is one of the two heads of the practice group Tax. Before joining the firm, he worked for three years for a major law firm in Munich and Frankfurt advising on commercial law. He specialises in national and international tax law in particular relating to the planning for corporate sucession and capital markets (IPOs, derivatives, bonds and options). He is the author of numerous publications relating to international and national tax issues. He is listed in Euromoney's World's Leading Tax Advisers.

Stephan A. Jansen is founder and General Manager of the Institute for Mergers and Acquisitions (IMA) at the Private University Witten/Herdecke, Germany. He was previously founder and Managing Director of cosinex GmbH, the first public electronic procurement portal in Germany. He has held a visiting scholarship at Stanford University and acted as visiting Professor at Harvard Business School. He is co-editor of *M&A Review* and has published widely in the area of M&A.

Tomas Koch is a principal at McKinsey & Co. in the Global Chemical Practice and a member of the Post Merger Management (PMM) Practice. Besides several PMM projects on corporate and business unit level, he analysed the key factors of success in mergers for the chemical industry in an global knowledge effort at McKinsey.

Heinrich Pack is Chief Commercial & Financial Manager of the Demag Cranes & Components GmbH. He is also visiting professor at the Private University Witten/Herdecke, Germany, in the Institute for Mergers and Acquisitions (IMA).

Gerhard Picot has been a partner in Freshfields Bruckhaus Deringer since 1979. He speciallises in mergers and acquisitions, and has advised on a variety of national and international transactions, including acquisitions and disposals, mergers, IPOs, cooperations and restructrings. He is listed as a lending specialist in the field of corporate and M&A in both Chambers Global 2001/2002 and JuVe 2001/2002. Gerhard Picot is also a professor in Commerical Law at the Institute for Mergers & Acquisitions – IMA – at the Private University of Witten/Herdecke, and is a member of both national and international lawyers' associations as well as German Country Chairman of the Americal Bar Association. He is the author of numerous publications, particularly in the area of mergers and acquisitions (see http://www.picot.de).

Peter H. Pribilla is a member of the Corporate Executive Committee of Siemans AG with responsibility for Corporate Personnel. In the course of his professional career he held various leading positions primarily in the information and telecommunications sector. He is honorary professor of the Munich University of Technology.

Frank Richter joined the Investment Banking Division of Goldman Sachs & Co. OHG in Frankfurt as an Executive Director in July 2000. Previously he worked as a management consultant for McKinsey & Co. He is also Professor of Corporate Finance & Strategy at the Institute for Mergers and Acquisitions (IMA), Private University Witten/Herdecke, Germany.

Rainer Zimmermann completed studies in German, journalism and sociology before starting out as a freelance editor and journalist. He joined ABC/Eurocom in 1988 as consultant, and also lectured in Integrated Communications at the European Business School, Oestrich-Winkel, Germany. In 1991, he was elected to the ABC/Eurocom managing board. Dr Zimmermann was appointed managing director of Kohtes Klewes in 1992, became managing partner in 1993 and company CEO. When Kohtes Klewes Kommunikation GmbH (Holding) was renamed European Communications Consultants GmbH (ECC), Dr Zimmermann assumed the position of ECC managing partner and has been CEO since September 1999. Since January 2000 he has been managing partner and CEO of BBDO Group Germany. He writes and publishes regularly on communications topics, also in his role as joint publisher of the *Manual of Corporate Communications* (first published in 1998), together with Professor Klaus Merten. He is a supervisory board member of start AG and board member of 'GWA', 'Deutsches Werbemuseum e.V.', 'Düsseldorfer Kunstverein', 'Westdeutschen Akademie für Kommunikation e.V. (WAK)'. BBDO Düsseldorf GmbH.

Part 1

Planning of Mergers and Acquisitions

1

Economic and Business Law Parameters for the Planning of Mergers and Acquisitions

Gerhard Picot

1 Introduction

M&A Facts

Advancing into the 21st century, our society and economy are facing entirely new challenges. The rapid technological developments and the accompanying worldwide digital network have led to a necessity for transcontinental, global and frontier-less corporate, competition, production and communications systems. The number and volumes of international and cross-border as well as national Mergers and Acquisitions (M&A), the 'Level' in the business of investment banking and corporate finance, therefore reach new records from year to year.

On a worldwide scale, the volume of corporate acquisitions and mergers reached almost 3500 billion US dollars in almost 37 000 transactions in the year 2000 (Figure 1.1, 1.2). Telecommunications with a transaction volume of 683 billion US dollars was the branch of business with the highest amounts involved; this amount includes the takeover of Mannesmann by Vodafone for some 200 billion US dollars, which broke all financial records in the history of corporate mergers. Second to telecommunications as the branch of business with most M&A internationally, there is the media business in which the merger between Time Warner and AOL led the pack at 184 billion US dollars. This was followed by the financial services branch of business, the most important transaction there being the Chase Manhattan and J. P. Morgan merger.

The increasing globalisation and technological developments, in particular in information and communications technology, as well as the opening of new markets and the associated concentrations are indications, that in principle this development will continue.

The single European market (SEM) and the opening of previously protected markets such as telecommunications and energy have triggered new expectations of a further merger wave among European companies (Figure 1.3).

The number and value of M&A with a European involvement in the year 2000 highlights the fast-track development of the M&A business: whereas the number of transactions rose from 11 050 in 1999 to 12 450, the value was found by Thomson Financial Securities Data to have increased from 1082 billion US dollars

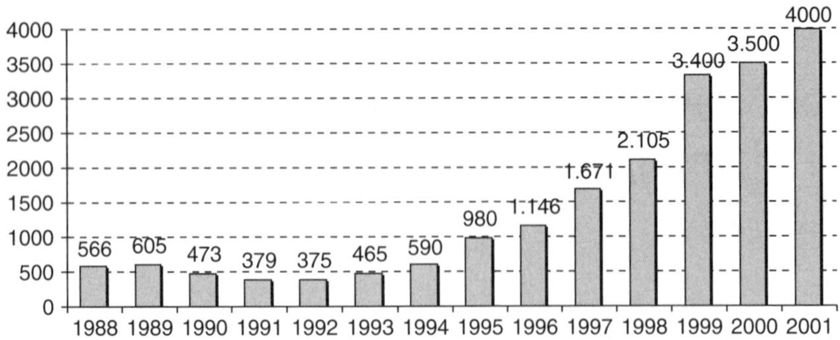

Figure 1.1 Merger wave: transaction volume worldwide, 1988–2001, billion US dollars
Source: Thomson Financial Securities Data.

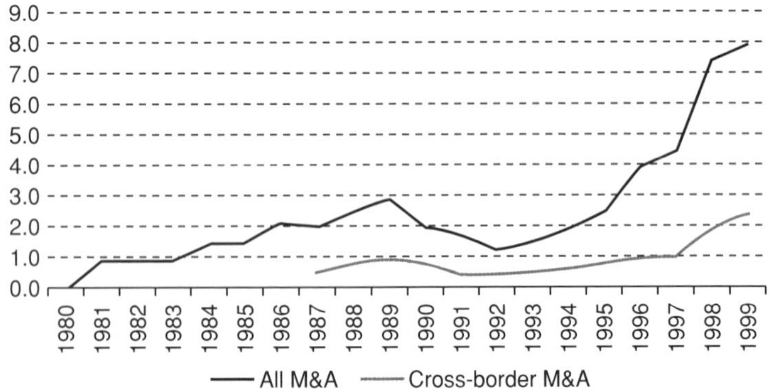

Figure 1.2 Value of worldwide M&A as a percentage of gross domestic product (GDP), 1980–99
Source: UNCTAD, Cross-border M&A database (based on data from Thomson Financial Securities Data Company).

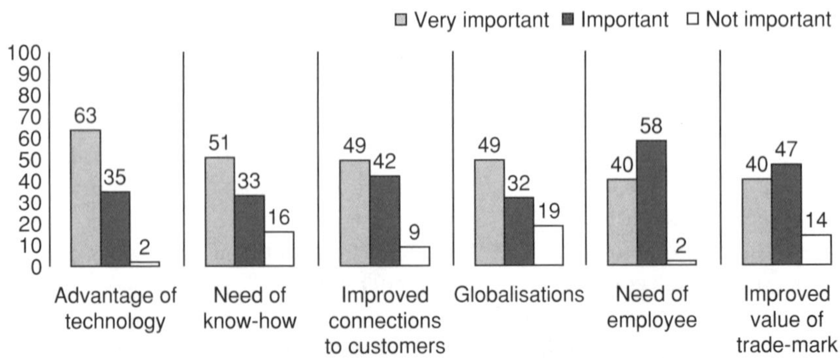

Figure 1.3 Factors driving international M&A, per cent
Source: Arthur Andersen, Questionnaire among 30 leading companies of technology, media and communication worldwide.

in 1999 to 1510 billion US dollars in the year 2000. Of these M&A, 270 were notified to the European Commission in the year 1999.

Especially in the automobile industry, the investment goods industry, the chemical and pharmaceutical industries, the energy business, among banks and insurance companies and in the information, communications and high-tech area, and not least in the transportation business, the European corporate landscape will continue to change fundamentally owing to M&A. As, in addition to the speed of market penetration, it is especially the size of a company which determines its commercial success, about half of all companies in these branches of business are currently planning to take over a competitor or to merge with one (Figure 1.4).

In its *10th World Investment Report* (WIR) the United Nations Conference on Trade and Development (UNCTAD) forecast that foreign investments by companies would in the year 2000 for the first time break through the magical 'sound barrier' of 1 trillion 1000 billion, US dollars (1999: 865 billion) (Figure 1.5).

With more than 85 per cent (1999: 83 per cent = 720 billion US dollars) of all direct investments, cross-border corporate M&A are more than ever becoming the driving force behind globalisation (Figure 1.6).

In this process, the dynamics of the world economy are increasingly concentrating on the industrialised countries. The multinational groups in the European Union (EU) invested about 510 billion US dollars abroad in 1999. Regarding investments abroad, Great Britain (119 billion US dollars) was ahead of the USA and France as well as Germany with 50.6 billion US dollars (1989: 91.2 billion US dollars). Direct investments coming in were absorbed by the industrialised countries in 1999 to the amount of 636 billion US dollars, representing almost three-quarters of the global direct investments (865 billion US dollars). Among the receiving countries, the USA was ahead of Great Britain, Sweden, France, the Netherlands and Germany (21.1 billion US dollars) with 275.5 billion US dollars, which

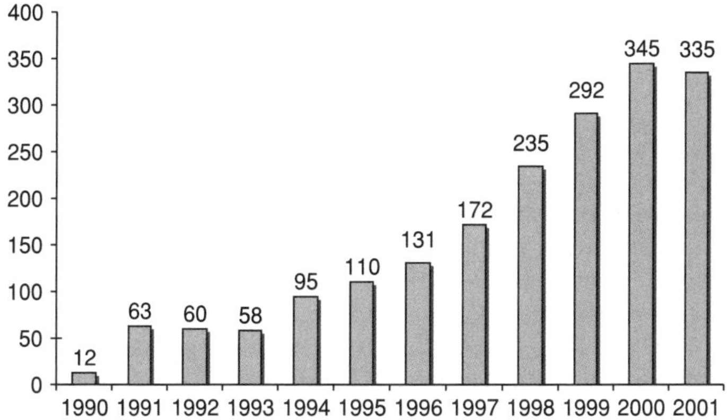

Figure 1.4 M&A in Europe: cases notified in Brussels, 1990–2000
Source: EU Commission.

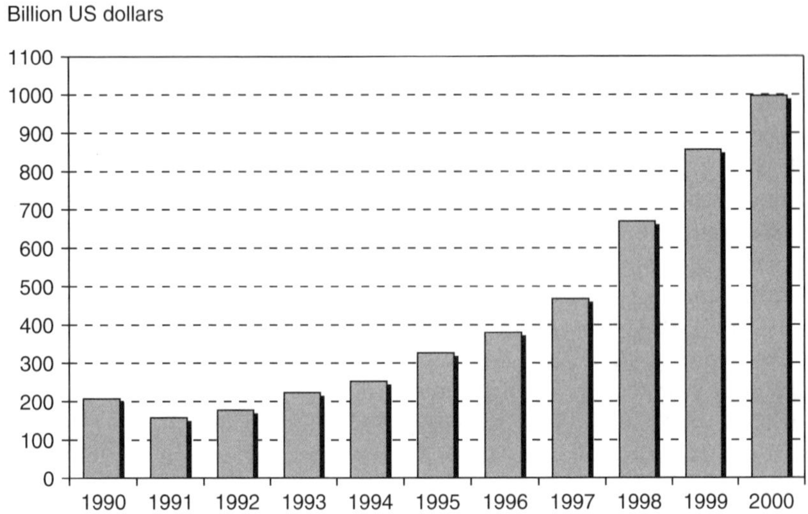

Figure 1.5 Development of foreign direct investments (FDIs) worldwide, 1990–2000, billion US dollars
Source: UNCTAD/Deutsche Bundesbank.

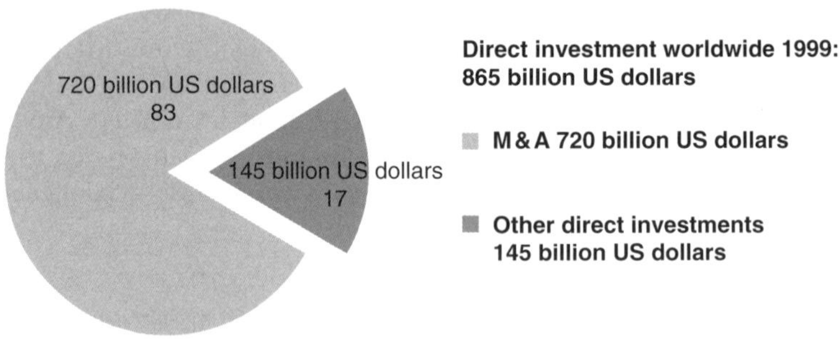

Figure 1.6 Share of M&A in foreign direct investments (FDIs) worldwide, 1999, per cent
Source: UNCTAD.

represents 43 per cent of all direct investments in the industrialised countries. Although foreign direct investments (FDIs) were made in the developing countries in 1999 to the amount of 208 billion US dollars – up from 176 billion US dollars in 1998 – and FDIs thus became the most important external source of financing for the developing countries, these countries fell back in relative terms from 38 per cent in 1997 to 24 per cent in 1999, in spite of the greater absolute amounts. Also in the developing countries, M&A accounted for the lion's share of the direct investments. In terms of the overall national economies and looking at considerations of social policy, an extremely worrying aspect is that, on the one hand, the FDIs now represent the biggest external source of financing for developing

Table 1.1 Cross-border M&A with a value of over 1 billion dollars, 1987–99

Year	Number of deals	% of total	Value (billion dollars)	% of total
1987	14	1.6	30.0	40.3
1988	22	1.5	49.6	42.9
1989	26	1.2	59.5	42.4
1990	33	1.3	60.9	40.4
1991	7	0.2	20.4	25.2
1992	10	0.4	21.3	26.8
1993	14	0.5	23.5	28.3
1994	24	0.7	50.9	40.1
1995	36	0.8	80.4	43.1
1996	43	0.9	94.0	41.4
1997	64	1.3	129.2	42.4
1998	86	1.5	329.7	62.0
1999	109	1.7	500.8	69.6

Source: UNCTAD, cross-border M&A database (based on data from Thomson Financial Securities Data Company).

countries but, on the other, the companies involved in the developing countries generally are those being taken over rather than the acquirers. Therefore, in spite of the direct investments, in most cases no new production capacities or jobs are created in the developing countries. Instead, the M&A dynamics and the emergence of global corporate markets and of worldwide oligopolies seriously regard developing countries in their process of development (Table 1.2).

Increase in Value and Greater Yields Through M&A

In view of the enormous economic significance of the increasing transaction numbers and volumes, it is regrettable that more than 50 per cent of all transactions do not bring the desired increase in values and greater return on investments. The studies made by reputed international management consultants, such as by A. T. Kearney in 1998, all show this clearly (Figure 1.7).

In a new study of all international transactions involving listed companies with a volume exceeding 500 million US dollars between January 1996 and September 1998, McKinsey came to a somewhat more encouraging conclusion. According to this study, every second corporate merger or takeover was successful from the buyer's point of view, and for the sellers 90 per cent of all transactions were profitable. Among the companies which created values through take-overs, 92 per cent performed strongly in their own core business.

Nevertheless, managers and their M&A advisers are called upon not only to more precisely identify the factors determining the success of a transaction. They are especially called upon to optimise the creation of new economic values, on the basis of their expert knowledge of their branch of business and with the help of creative transaction strategies and financing, and at the same time to fulfil their

Table 1.2 The 10 biggest international corporate takeovers, 1996–2000

Rank	Buyer	Target company	Branch of business	Year	Value**	Value*
1	Vodafone Group (GB)	Mannesmann (D)	Telecommunications	2000	400.0	200.0
2	AOL (USA)	Time Warner (USA)	Internet/media	2000	331.7	165.8
3	Pfizer (USA)	Warner-Lambert (USA)	Pharmaceuticals	2000	173.0	86.5
4	MCI Worldcom (USA)	Sprint (USA)	Telecommunications	1999	231.2	115.6
5	Exxon (USA)	Mobil (USA)	Oil	1998	150.9	150.9
6	Travellers (Citigroup) (USA)	Citicorp (USA)	Banks	1998	144.7	72.8
7	SBC Communications (USA)	Ameritech (USA)	Telecommunications	1998	124.6	62.3
8	Vodafone Group (GB)	Air Touch (USA)	Telecommunications	1999	124.6	62.3
9	NationsBank (USA)	Bank America (USA)	Banks	1998	120.6	20.6
10	AT&T (USA)	MediaOne (USA)	Telecommunications/cable TV	1999	116.6	58.3

Notes: *Billion US dollars.
**Billion DM (rate of exchange dollar 2.01, English pound 3.23, French franc 0.3).
Source: FAZ-Archiv, *FAZ* (5 February 2000, p. 18).

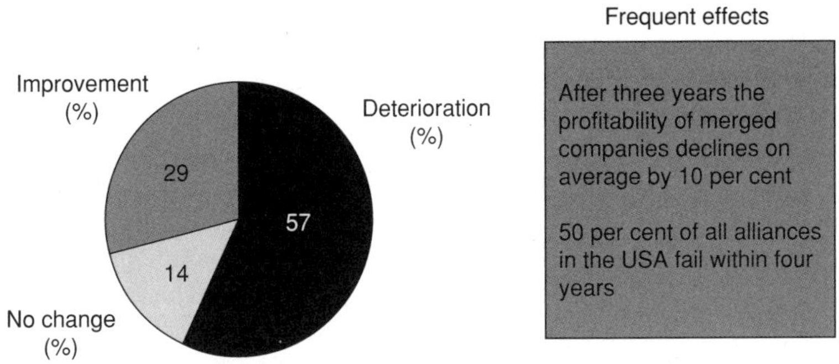

Figure 1.7 Changes in profitability after the M&A transaction, 1998, 100 per cent = 230 companies
Source: A. T. Kearney (1998).

ethical and social responsibility. In view of the increasing transaction volumes, they will be compelled more than in the past to disprove the cliché that the true motive for such a megafusion is not an economic necessity, but megalomania and greed on the part of the managers.

Because of the complex nature of the companies involved as a totality of factual and legal circumstances and relations, these transactions generally involve manifold interdisciplinary tasks. In solving them, the relevant managerial factors and the commercial, technical and social parameters closely linked with them must be defined and taken into account in planning the acquisition. In addition the special procedural requirements must be observed which follow from the manifold forms of national and international M&A, from corporate mergers, the sale and purchase of companies, alliances, cooperations and joint ventures to integration, conversion and restructuring measures.

Transactions successes can be optimised in the long term only if the merger partners are selected and brought together in accordance with modern capital market requirements, and managers and their advisers considerably improve transaction management. They must regard the area of M&A as an independent field of work based on international know-how which requires a comprehensive view and handling.

Especially in the past, it was not duly taken into account that this is true in all three phases of a merger or acquisition, namely with respect to

- Planning
- Implementation
- Integration.

Furthermore, the individuals involved in the transaction processes must have a deep basic interdisciplinary understanding of the aspects, content and problems of the other special fields involved in order to be able to better understand each other and to raise the degree of efficiency of the transaction. In the case of an international transaction, there is in addition the need to be able to communicate the specific content and special features in all of their many facets in the contract language, in most cases English. Only on the basis of a joint language – a joint 'transaction language' as it were – is a close and optimal cooperation possible between the different experts.

This applies, for example, to the businessmen, investment bankers, auditors, technicians and other M&A advisers who, with knowledge of the basic contexts under commercial law, are better able to assess the economic opportunities and risks (e.g. in the due diligence process, in the evaluation of the companies and in view of any restructuring measures which may be necessary). But the same applies inversely, too (e.g. for the commercial lawyers who are able to cast the commercial targets and objects and the contracting parties' concepts into meaningful contracts only if they have a solid basic knowledge of business economics as well as a certain technical understanding).

So far only few institutions, especially in Europe, offer a comprehensive and interdisciplinary scientific concept. The optimisation potential for transactions and the know-how bundled among the M&A experts can, in view of the ever-faster development processes, be recognised and put into effect only with an in-depth scientific approach and basis. The empirical values gained in practice must be ordered systematically, structured, and analysed in order to be able to develop creative scientific models on an empirical basis to improve the transaction successes.

But in addition to scientific research, it is especially academic teaching which is required. In practice a great number of highly qualified M&A specialists are needed for manifold management and consulting tasks. They must all be made familiar theoretically and practically with the tasks and problems specifically involved in such transactions. Specialised knowledge is also needed by medium-sized entrepreneurs when they want to sell, or introduce to the stock exchange, the companies built up by them with all their personal feelings and involvement. To enable the specialised knowledge to be obtained, a teaching and further training programme specifically relating to such transactions in the most interdisciplinary manner possible must be offered, including practical experience. At the same time the necessary social responsibility and competence must be conveyed to the students. In particular, they must learn to be creative and diplomatically skilled and to use their personality and personal trustworthiness to successfully conclude also difficult transactions.

Because of the great economic significance of the transactions, it is therefore necessary to follow the principle of combining local strength with international skills, emphasising the urgent need to create independent national transaction cultures with due regard to international standards.

2 'Fusionitis' or New Management Strategy

In view of the enormous economic significance of the transaction numbers and volumes, it is alarming that about half of all transactions do not lead to the desired increase in value and higher return on investment for the shareholders.

Especially dangerous are transactions based on pure financial considerations or supposedly unique circumstances. As the McKinsey study mentioned above proves, the transactions which are more likely to be successful are those where, before the acquisition, both companies performed well in the same core business or operated in related branches of business.

In recent years many companies largely exhausted their internal optimisation resources by means of restructuring, flexible production processes and modern information systems. Managers who wish to comply with the owners' and shareholders' desire to quickly raise the value of the company or the shareholder value must therefore decide: do they want to achieve further growth potentials through their own time and strength, consuming corporate and product developments; or do they prefer the time-saving purchase or merger with companies in the same or related branches of business, as in the case of DaimlerChrysler (Figure 1.8).

If management decides to acquire a company or to merge, it is beside the point to accuse them generally of having 'Fusionitis' or a pathological fusion euphoria. The challenge of the future is rather to understand that – as Rubens Ricupero, Secretary General of the United Nations Council for Trade and Development put it – a 'corporate market' has come into being throughout the world.

The factors determining the success of M&A are only gradually being practically and scientifically recognised and researched. Companies and their internal and external M&A experts must improve their consultancy instruments and expert knowledge, bundle their experience, and further develop their know-how. Only in this way will they be able in the future to precisely assess and control the economic risks involved in every transaction as an entrepreneurial course of action.

For this purpose they can, on the one hand, make use of the know-how of reputed investment consultants in their search for suitable transaction partners and in developing creative financing models (Table 1.3).

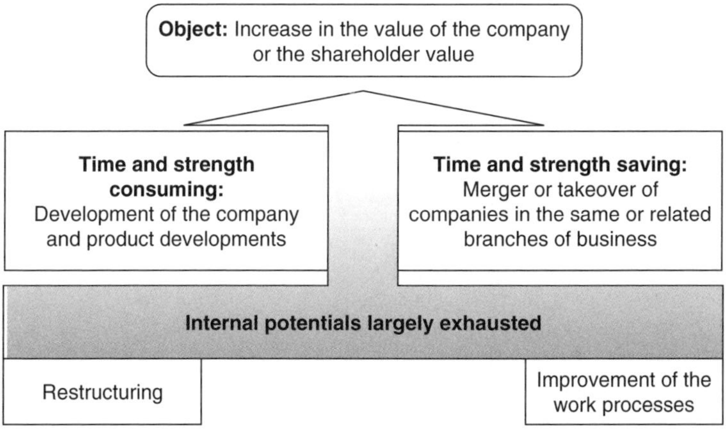

Figure 1.8 Increasing company or shareholder value

Table 1.3 The biggest investment consultants worldwide, 2000

Rank	Consultants	Transaction volumes (billion US dollars)	Number of deals
1	Goldman Sachs	1.05 450	213
2	Morgan Stanley Dean Witter	90 399	232
3	Merrill Lynch	83 739	158
4	Credit Suisse First Boston	51 451	212
5	UBS Warburg	44 454	128
6	J. P. Morgan	38 586	135
7	Schroders Salomon Smith Barney	35 084	199
8	Rothschild	33 703	109
9	Chase Manhatten	29 121	168
10	Deutsche Bank	25 558	123
11	Lazard	24 726	96
12	Bear Stearns	21 544	47
13	Lehman Brothers	20 380	125

Source: Thomson Financial Securities Data.

They can also retain international and national law firms for planning, implementation and integration (Table 1.4).

The same applies to the employment of national and international management consultants, auditors, or advertising agencies (Table 1.5).

In addition, companies must react to the fact that complex transactions suffer considerably if the M&A teams composed of investment consultants, lawyers, auditors, businessmen, technical experts, security experts, environmental advisers and other consultants do not speak a common language because of their focused expert knowledge. Not to mention the difficulties in communicating all facets of

Table 1.4 The biggest M&A law firms in Europe, first half-year 2001

Rank	House	Value (billion Euro)
1	Freshfields Bruckhaus Deringer	156.2
2	Slaughter and May	122.3
3	Linklaters & Alliance	120.4
4	Clifford Chance	113.6
5	Sullivan & Cromwell	98.6
6	Shearman & Sterling	94.3
7	Cleary Gottlieb Steen & H.	79.4
8	Skadden Arps Slate M. & F.	53.6
9	Herbert Smith	48.8
10	Hengeler Mueller W. W.	46.4

Source: *Mergermarket*.

Table 1.5 The biggest management consulting firms in the world, 2000

	Sales (billion dollars)	Employees
Andersen Consulting	8.31	65 134
PriceWaterhouseCoopers	6.00	46 500
Ernst & Young International	3.97	19 050
Computer Sciences	3.50	Not known
Deloitte Consulting/DTT	3.24	19 560
KPMG	3.00	15 240
McKinsey & Company	2.50	Not known
Mercer Consulting Group	1.54	11 034
Arthur Andersen	1.37	9196
A. T. Kearney	1.23	4646

Source: *Management Consultant International* (June 1999).

the necessary specific content in the negotiating language – or, as now common in international deals, in English. In the case of a cross-border international deal it is in addition necessary for the project teams to be composed of representatives of the different nationalities and cultures in order to be able to quickly recognise and react to the different interests of the companies and their employees.

All this makes it necessary to develop national M&A cultures against the background of the many years of international (and especially Anglo-American) transaction experience and customs. At the same time, this is one of the reasons why the big globally operating investment banks and consulting firms can provide outstanding opportunities and prospects to the next generation of international M&A experts in this attractive field of business of investment banking and corporate finance.

Managers and their advisers must be put into a position where they can as precisely as possible examine and analyse, already in the lead-up to a transaction, whether and to what extent the companies fit together in all their parameters and cultures. This also includes the question of what steps are necessary to ensure the commercial success of the transaction in all of its phases while taking into account to the greatest possible extent the interests of the employees and the different production sites. This goes from the planning phase (i.e. the preliminary considerations regarding the decision-making process for the transaction), to the implementation phase (i.e. due diligence), and the evaluation of the companies as well as the negotiation and drafting of the transaction agreement, and finally to the integration phase.

On the whole, the facts described above give rise to the question of how the management of M&A – i.e. of mergers between companies, the acquisition or sale of companies, restructuring, the consolidation of companies, alliances, cooperations and joint ventures as well as stock exchange introductions or IPOs – as well as the search for merger partners and their introduction to each other can be improved with due regard to modern capital market requirements in order to significantly improve the success ratio.

To optimise the success ratio of such transactions, the following basic aspects and 'general' success factors of the transactions must be taken into account:

- Overall consideration of *planning, implementation* and *integration* in every transaction phase
- *Interdisciplinary basic understanding* of the aspects and problems of the other special fields
- Exact determination of the bases of *decisions* and *visions*
- Minimisation of *risks* in the portfolio as well as realistic assessment (and not overestimation) of the synergetic potentials and integration costs
- Development of *systematic and consistent transaction strategies*
- Clear *definition* and *structuring* of the transactions
- Clear definition and arrangement of the structures in the *top and middle management*
- Clear *definition and internal communication* of the transaction as well as outlining clear perspectives for all employees
- Precase *implementation* of the bases of decisions and visions
- *Integration* of the companies and the corporate cultures
- Creation, formation and explanation of a *new corporate identity* and 'sense of solidarity'
- Avoiding '*patriotic*' thinking in cross-border transactions
- Clear *external communication* of the vision and strategy of the transaction
- Consideration of the usual *transaction risks* as a consequence of the general economic requirements.
  - greatest possible speed
  - with the best possible decisions
  - and the least possible expense.

In addition to these 'general' success factors, the study by A. T. Kearney has shown that seven 'special' success factors are crucial in successfully implementing a transaction (Figure 1.9).

The more the parties succeed in recognising, understanding and controlling these factors and in developing strategies to overcome the danger potential, the stronger the M&A success curve will rise and the better an increase in the value of the company will be realised. Empirically it has become clear that more time and effort was invested in the proactive implementation of the post-merger integration (PMI) phase of successful M&A.

3 The Term 'Mergers and Acquisitions': the Concentration of Undertakings and the Purchase and Sale of an Undertaking

In many other languages there is nothing equivalent to the English term 'Mergers and Acquisitions'. As already explained, this concept comprises the field of the concentration of undertakings and the cooperation between businesses; also, for example, the takeover of a business by way of a purchase or barter transaction,

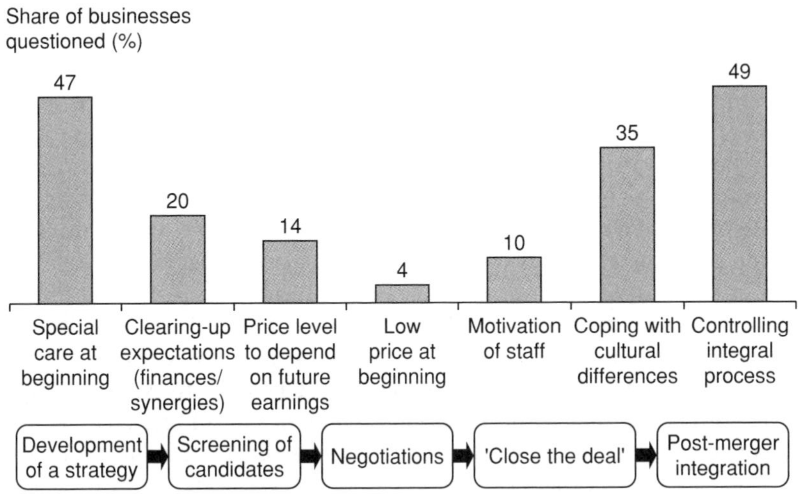

Figure 1.9 Weighted success factors in the entire merger process
Source: *Business International*; A. T. Kearney (1988).

measures to protect undertakings, corporate successions, privatisation as well as management buy-out (MBO), management buy-in (MBI) and 'going public'.

But the term 'purchase of an undertaking' is no more concrete. Given the lack of a definition of 'undertaking' the attempts that have been made correctly to define this term are numerous. Whereas the undertaking in the legal sense is an entity with the institutional and functional features of a business in the traditional sense, the science of business management sees an undertaking as an economic unit of the overall economy which is operated by an undertaking for its own account and at its own risk for the purpose of making a profit. Features such as market shares, resources, business opportunities, contractual relations and employment contracts provide an indication how to understand these terms, but they can also not hide the fact that a comprehensive definition of an undertaking – and thus of the purchase of an undertaking – is not possible. As explained in the introduction to this chapter, the term 'Mergers and Acquisitions' is therefore understood here in the broad Anglo-American sense with its manifold forms:

- Purchase and sale of undertakings
- Concentration between undertakings
- Alliances, cooperations and joint ventures
- Formation of companies
- Corporate succession/ensuring the independence of businesses
- Management buy-out and buy-in
- 'Going public'/IPO
- Change of legal form
- Restructuring.

4 The Planning of Mergers and Acquisitions

Preliminary Work, Studies and Analyses

Each complex transaction begins with internal preparatory work, studies and analyses of the company, its competitive environment, the market and the conceivable development possibilities as well as those being considered. Generally this is initially done by the entrepreneurs, managers and their supervisory bodies, including internal experts, especially in the departments for corporate development and planning as well as the legal and tax departments.

Even at this early stage, these preparatory considerations must consider the question of what external M&A advisers to consult in order to jointly develop creative strategies and financing schemes and to look for suitable transaction partners. This applies especially to advisers in the field of investment, corporate finance, commercial law, and general management consultancy. These advisers must generally not only have the required expertise in their respective fields as well as sufficient experience in M&A, but also special knowledge of the branch of business concerned and, in the case of a cross-border transaction, international competence and a powerful network. The advisers are then hired by means of an engagement letter, if appropriate after a so-called 'beauty contest' or 'pitching'.

The Planning Phase for M&A

In the planning phase for M&A, the entire transaction is first planned in the most interdisciplinary and comprehensive manner possible. This especially concerns the operational and (tax) legal techniques and optimisation with special regard to their implementation and integration.

The planning work relates primarily to the aspects of:

- Whether,
- When, and
- How

a merger or an acquisition is to be put into effect.

The Question as to 'whether'

The question as to 'whether' primarily concerns the identification of the *corporate objects* and which of these objects are to be pursued through organic growth and which through M&A in the form of participations or a full takeover. At the same time, the consequences of the growth strategy and its economic or financial effects in the light of the competition situation and the extension of the value added chain must be carefully examined.

Empirically, in approximately 85 per cent of all concentrations between undertakings and acquisitions, the question as to 'whether' is answered with a view to the object of achieving growth in the core business.

The Question as to 'When'

The answer to the question as to 'when' depends primarily, on the one hand, on the need to strengthen the core business and on strategic considerations specific to the company concerned or on inherent or market necessities and, on the other, on the financial and personnel resources of the company for the proposed M&A activity. This at the same time raises the question of the *priorities*, which can be answered only by classifying different M&A options and opportunities as 'top', 'high', 'medium' and 'low' priority. Then, taking into account the feasibility of the proposed activities (with the available staff), the order in which action is to be taken follows. The decision will also be influenced by the fact that purposeful M&A activities can, after successfully going public, be presented as important price support operations to win investors' favour.

The Question as to 'How'

In examining the question as to 'how' a merger or an acquisition is to be put into effect, the different available forms of M&A must first be examined – i.e. a concentration between undertakings, the purchase or sale of a business, restructuring, measures to ensure the further existence and independence of a company, alliances, cooperation and joint ventures, as well as going public or an IPO.

The classification mentioned above must be reviewed again to determine whether the strategic corporate object can be achieved through a mere cooperation or a strategic alliance, or whether an acquisition of a minority or majority share or a merger should be attempted.

On the basis of this review, suitable *target companies* whose resources or capabilities allow the planned M&A strategy to be put into effect must be identified. The possibilities which are then available must be brought into line with issues of corporate evaluation, the determination of valuable consideration (i.e. the price), and with the integration planning.

The planning activities thus relate in particular to the following points:

- Analysis of the *current economic situation* of the company and the target, and the situation to be expected, in particular any synergies during and after the transaction
- Definition of the *corporate objectives*
- Examination of the *operational, economic and legal framework, parameters and effects* of the transaction
- Examination of the possible *entrepreneurial forms*, especially the possible tax arrangements
- Development of the economically desired or most favourable *transaction strategy* and, if necessary, restructuring or reorganisation strategy
- *Legal planning* of the transaction or restructuring concept
- Recognition of the *management structure* and the (general) structure of the staff possibly affected, especially with respect to seniority and age (so-called 'population')

- Identification of the *employees* who are (possibly) concretely affected, with their social data (e.g. seniority, age, pension situation, severe disability, maternity leave, works council membership), including their functions and qualifications
- Seeking *other employment opportunities* for employees within the company, the group or other companies
- Calculation of the *internal and external costs* necessary for the transfer, integration and restructuring
- Preparation of a three-phase detailed time, process and, if appropriate, lay-off plan for the planning, implementation and integration of the transaction and restructuring measures, with special regard to the provisions of *commercial law*, in particular the most significant national and international legal issues as well as any risk situations (risk management and precautionary or back-up management)
- Fixing of the production, administrative and personnel capacities and processes necessary in the *planning period* and *after* the transaction or restructuring
- Preparation of plausible and comprehensible *reasons, statements and PR* measures necessary to internally and externally communicate the transaction.

In all such planning work, the difficult test of how the future would look for the company *without* the proposed transaction is necessary (Figure 1.10).

Process Planning

The question as to 'how' requires a decision about the desired form of the merger or acquisition, but a further question that arises concerns the *procedure* in such a transaction.

Here it should be noted first that the transaction does not proceed on the basis of any fixed rules. The procedure is as manifold as the companies or parts of companies to be acquired themselves, as the economic and operational issues which arise and the conflicting interests of the buyer and the seller, as well as the various forms of M&A. However, it is possible to distinguish between:

- a *traditional* transaction and
- a transaction by way of a *(restricted) bidding* or *auction* procedure.

A traditional transaction is basically a normal 'shake-hands' deal between the contracting parties. In most cases, it is generally through contacts at a higher or the highest level of the companies concerned or through the services of professional M&A advisers that the contracting parties first come into contact.

The (restricted) bidding or auction procedure is used particularly for bigger transactions and is in principle governed by the same rules as 'ordinary' bidding and auction proceedings. However, certain characteristic features, procedures and terminologies have developed and are being increasingly used. Because of the competition between the bidders or potential buyers, this can result in somewhat traught proceedings. An example of this was the bidding competition between VW and BMW for Rolls-Royce, which considerably pushed up the purchase price.

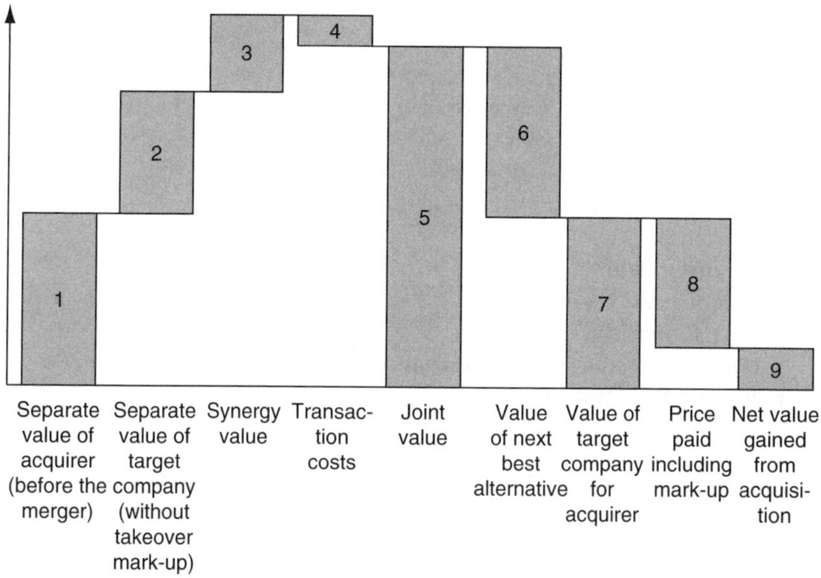

Figure 1.10 Value determination for M&A
Source: Plinke, *Mega-Mergers: Entwicklung, Motive und Herausforderungen* (6 November 1998).

Both types of M&A generally proceed in three phases which have been discussed already in the context of the overall view of M&A:

- Planning
- Implementation
- Implementation and integration.

Process Planning for Traditional Transactions

For traditional transactions the *process planning* takes place in three phases.

1st phase: planning of M&A

- Overall planning for the transaction, in particular the operational and managerial and (tax) legal techniques and optimisation with special regard to the following two phases, namely its implementation and integration.

2nd phase: implementation of M&A

- Confidentiality or non-disclosure agreements
- Minutes of meetings/heads of agreement
- Letter of intent
- Option

- Preliminary agreement
- Due diligence
- Evaluation of the company
- Presentation of a draft transaction agreement prepared by the transaction partners and their legal advisers
- Negotiation for the M&A, especially
  - the subject matter of the agreement
  - the purchase price
  - the transfer date
  - the claims and legal relationships to be transferred, especially the employment relationships
  - liability, representations and warranties
- Conclusion of the contract
- Closure.

3rd phase: integration of M&A

Process Planning for the Transaction by the (Restricted) Bidding or Auction Process

Compared to a traditional corporate transaction, an M&A transaction by way of the so-called (restricted) bidding or auction process is distinctive in that the process is determined primarily by the investment and corporate finance advisers or by other M&A advisers. The potential interested parties or transaction parties are generally advised, solicited or selected and brought together by these M&A experts in accordance with modern capital market requirements.

For an M&A transaction by way of the so-called (restricted) bidding or auction proceedings, the process described below, which varies depending on the requirements in each case, is conceivable. Through this process, the contracting parties are led to the actual contract negotiations and the conclusion of the agreement through an increasingly concrete information process and a bidding competition and offering process which is initially loose and increasingly intensive.

For this purpose a so-called 'information memorandum' with the basic information and data about the target company is prepared first. Then potential transaction partners are identified and contacted to determine their general interest in the transaction, and at the same time their credit-worthiness and trustworthiness is checked.

This is followed by the first round of the bidding procedure, which begins with a letter to the potentially interested parties. This letter describes the bidding procedure and the intended structure of the transaction – e.g. as a share deal with the transfer of the shares or as an asset deal with a transfer of the different assets – and the addressee is requested to make a first non-binding offer. Generally the information memorandum as well as a confidentiality agreement (CA) or a non-disclosure agreement (NDA) is attached to this letter. The CA or NDA must be signed and returned by the bidder. In many cases a draft transaction agreement is also sent to the interested parties together with the first letter, requesting that the bid be made on the basis of this draft and that any (important) amendments which may be desired be put down in writing.

It is then the bidders who make their first non-binding offer, generally in the form of a proposal or letter of intent (LoI). It is advisable for them to point out the non-binding nature of the offer and to reserve the right to change or terminate the proceedings as well as the structure of the transaction at any time without any adverse legal consequences and costs (break-up fees). Furthermore, the bases and assumptions upon which their preliminary evaluation of the company and thus the offer and in particular the purchase price offer are based, should be set out as precisely as possible. This is necessary to be able to subsequently justify a change of the offer if it turns out that these assumptions were incorrect and the company consequently had a lower value. Furthermore, the first bid should already contain the conditions which are indispensable from the bidder's point of view; the same goes for the most important amendments of the draft transaction agreement which are desired. This includes, for example, an in-depth and satisfactory examination of the company (due diligence – for this see in detail Part 2, Chapter 5), clauses for representations and warranties and to the extent necessary the consent or approval of the organs of the company (e.g. general meeting, supervisory board) and the public authorities, in particular the cartel authorities.

The seller will then examine the bids received and choose from among the bidders those candidates who appear to be interesting. Important aspects in this connection for the seller should not only be:

- The *amount* of the offer, in particular the purchase price, but also
- The *seriousness and credibility* of the offer
- Nature of *financing* of the purchase price
- The concept for *future development* and the protection of jobs in the company, as well as
- The reasonable expectation of the most *professional, uncomplicated and speedy conclusion* possible for the contract negotiations.

The second round of bidding begins with a further letter to the preferred bidders. The contents and rules for the use of a 'data room' (data room index and procedure) may also be set out in this letter, together with an explanation. In the data room (certain) documents relating to the company may be made available for an inspection. If this has not already been done, the first draft transaction agreement should in any case be sent together with this second letter.

The bidders are then given the opportunity to conduct at least a limited due diligence examination. This means that no especially sensitive corporate data are disclosed initially. In spite of the confidentiality agreement and statements of non-disclosure signed by the bidder and his advisers, it is not possible to totally rule out the danger that the bidders with whom negotiations are not continued will otherwise use the information received to the seller's disadvantage.

The bidders must now make a legally binding offer if they wish to continue to take part in the bidding procedure. In their offer, they can make use and take account of the information made available to them. In particular, the offer and especially the purchase or barter price will be adjusted and more concretely set out in view of the further information received and the due diligence examination conducted since the first non-binding offer. The same applies, for example, in the case of an intended participation or a necessary adjustment or compensation mechanism if a contractual or equity joint venture is envisaged. Furthermore, the offer contains, if necessary, a clause stating that the approval of the supervisory board or other board is a condition precedent. This provides a certain possibility to withdraw at a later stage. The bidder will make only the amendments and insert the clauses into the draft transaction agreement which are considered to be necessary to safeguard the bidder's interests without seriously impairing its chances in the selection process.

If the proposed acquisition is financed through borrowing, a fee will generally have to be paid when the binding offer is made. This fee is payable to the financing or syndicated banks as a stand-by fee. This is especially inconvenient for a bidder if it is not foreseeable whether it will be chosen at all as a preferred bidder. Not least because of this reason the bidder should demand exclusivity for the further negotiations in case it is selected as a preferred bidder. However, in return, the seller will generally demand a down payment on the purchase price or some other premium which the seller can keep if the negotiations fail for reasons for which the bidder is responsible. Conversely, the bidder should benefit from a contractual penalty in the event of a violation of exclusivity as it would otherwise be a blunt instrument.

After receiving the binding offers, the seller chooses the bidder with which it prefers to negotiate the transaction, or to carry out the transaction, or the seller tries to push up the price offered by the bidders, as in the Rolls-Royce case.

In the decision to select the preferred bidder, not only the criteria described above, but in particular the contents and scope of the amendments of the transaction agreement proposed by the bidder will be decisive. Furthermore, it is naturally advantageous for a seller if a bidder does not demand exclusivity for the final negotiations, as the seller will be interested in not being put under pressure and in 'keeping in' with other bidders, if possible. The more time that passes after the selection of the preferred bidder, the more the seller's negotiating position deteriorates as other less preferred bidders may lose interest in the transaction or bow out of the bidding process, and may be approached, if at all, only after some time has passed, if the bidding process fails, to enquire whether they are still interested in the transaction.

The negotiating teams must then work out the details of the transaction agreement in negotiations. For this, it is necessary first to choose an experienced and also diplomatically skilled chief negotiator. In the negotiations, the main issues then primarily concern provisions relating to valuable consideration (e.g. purchase price payment or stock swap), the contractual warranty and liability system, as well as the entire contract and completion.

If the notarisation of the agreement is necessary to make it legally effective, it may be advisable, to save costs in the case of a major transaction, to have the agreement notarised abroad, especially in Switzerland. However, it must first be ensured in this case that the concrete notarisation abroad is recognised by the national courts as equivalent to a domestic notarisation.

Generally, an employee meeting and a press conference are held immediately after the agreement is signed. For listed companies, a so-called 'ad hoc statement' must be issued promptly. The agreement then enters into force upon the fulfilment of the conditions precedent mentioned above – e.g. approval by the shareholders' assembly, the supervisory bodies and/or the cartel authorities. Depending on the transaction agreement, the shares or the assets pass over to the acquirer in exchange for payment of the purchase price or by way of a barter when the transaction agreement enters into force.

To ensure the proper transfer of the business in cross-border deals, it is advisable to conclude a closing agreement to the effect that the transaction can be completed with a closing. Such an agreement can also include a provision stating that the purchase price or at least a part of the purchase price is to be paid only if certain values are reached in the time after the conclusion of the agreement or the transfer of the business. The fate of the companies concerned and the success of the transaction now depends on successsful integration, as described in Part 3 of this book.

On the whole, the process plan described below is followed for major M&A transactions through the so-called (restricted) bidding or auction process. In each case, a concretely adjusted process plan should be prepared, with a detailed action plan, especially concerning the individual measures to be taken, responsibilities, dates and deadlines, and dates for concrete measures.

5 Business Law Parameters for M&A

National Business Law Parameters

The planning, implementation and integration of the transactions, in particular the purchase or sale of a company, restructuring, cooperation, and measures to preserve the existence of a company (corporate succession, MBO, MBI), depend especially on business law parameters.

Given the manifold forms of M&A, it is not possible to provide independent legal concepts or legal instruments in the general national and international laws of contract for the regulation and implementation of a merger or acquisition. Only certain aspects such as the purchase and sale of a business can be regarded and regulated in a typifying manner. Thus, the law governing purchase contracts in particular provides concrete principles for the purchase and sale of undertakings, from the beginning of the first contact between the contracting parties to the implementation and integration of the corporate transaction.

These principles are supplemented especially by provisions in the following fields of law, which at the same time provide answers to the most significant national and international legal questions arising in M&A:

- Contract law
- Corporate law
- Labour law
- Company pension law

- Tax law
- Cartel law
- Environmental law
- Insolvency law
- International law.

Transnational Corporate Forms

To overcome problems, for example in direct cross-border mergers of undertakings, as well as other obstacles under national law, European law is pushing for a *harmonisation* of the national business and corporate laws and for the creation of *supranational corporate forms*.

Already since the foundation of the European Economic Community (EEC), experts have been working on the creation of a European private company and a European stock corporation. So far this has been unsuccessful, apart from the European Economic Interest Grouping (EEIG), which has little practical legal significance.

The main difficulty in the development of such European corporate forms is especially that the co-determination rights of employees are extremely diverse in the member states of the European Community. The model of employee co-determination as it exists in Germany, in particular, is hardly understood anywhere else in Europe.

'World Stock Corporation'

On the whole, the multinational companies already existing today continue to strengthen their global corporate structures and increasingly display the essential features of a 'World Stock Corporation'. All the same, it is not possible to overlook the fact that a global corporate form is still far in the future, although in practice the national law under which globally operating companies are incorporated is becoming increasingly insignificant.

Practitioners are therefore compelled to create models themselves to make possible the concentration of global corporate units. To do so, they make use of the national legal system which allows the greatest possible leeway for complex transaction structures. An example is the Business Combination Agreement of DaimlerChrysler, which may serve as a model for further supranational corporate concentrations. Although this central agreement dealing with the merger between the two companies dealt to a great extent with measures regarding corporate issues under German law, the contracting parties agreed that this contract should be governed by the more flexible law of the US state of Delaware.

6 M&A Practices as a Source of Law

International Transaction Practices

The internationalisation of the economy and, not least of all, the increasing influence and the special M&A know-how of the investment banks, the international law firms as well as the corporate finance departments of auditing companies and consultants have caused the style, content and proceedings of national and international M&A to be increasingly influenced by the international and especially Anglo-American transaction practices.

The emergence of a uniform international 'transaction law' is accompanied by the increasing use of Anglo-American legal instruments and terminology. This applies increasingly not only to cross-border transactions, but also to national transactions.

Legal authors and practitioners therefore face the task of continuing the development of national, European and international structures of business and company law in the light of the practical requirements and developments as well as Anglo-American legal instruments. On the whole, however, this paves the way for a process which may involve a far greater effort in terms of planning, drafting and implementing transactions than would be necessary from a traditional national point of view.

M&A Practices as a Separate 'Transaction Law'

In practice, it is becoming increasingly irrelevant in drafting transaction agreements what national legal system governs the transaction agreement between the contracting parties.

The reason for this is that it has become the general practice to create complete and comprehensive contracts in order to contractually deal in the most efficient manner with all situations which must be dealt with and with all risks, both recognised and conceivable. The contracting parties no longer rely on the national law chosen by them to provide fair and reasonable rules for their complex respective interests. Instead they are increasingly creating their own comprehensive sets of rules. At the same time these comprehensive contracts often serve as models for further transactions.

The transaction agreement has thus gained the character of an *independent and closed legal system*. A consequence of this is that transaction know-how is becoming increasingly bundled in the heads of M&A specialists and in the ever-more detailed collections of model agreements based on their experience. This development is supported by the practice of international arbitration tribunals, which decide the legal disputes to be settled by them primarily on the basis of economic arguments arising from actual M&A practice.

On the whole, this has created an international uniform 'transaction law' which, as a form of commercial usage, will in the long term be characterised as a binding source of law. This M&A know-how remains largely concealed from scientists and students, except where it is conveyed to them by M&A practitioners.

7 Global Valuation and Accounting Standards

The instruments used for international M&A – not least under the influence of the international capital markets – increasingly also include global valuation and accounting standards, for example the International Accounting Standards (IAS) and the frequently used US Generally Accepted Accounting Principles (US GAAP).

8 The Trend to 'One-Stop-Shop' M&A Advice

Because of the high demand for M&A advice, the international consultancy and investment companies are becoming more interested in advising companies in all phases of national and cross-border transactions, i.e. on the planning, structuring, implementation and integration of the transactions in a comprehensive manner.

At the same time they are trying to offer companies overall concepts, also in complex mega transactions, for the manifold and closely related interdisciplinary economic, legal, technical and social tasks. Therefore, the 'one-stop-shop' offer includes legal M&A advice in addition to economic – financial advice.

This development requires M&A advisers to be increasingly prepared to display in-depth entrepreneurial thinking and action for the strategic and commercial issues in the M&A field. Mere knowledge and skills in one's non special field are no longer sufficient to rise to the complex challenges in practice. M&A lawyers must therefore endeavour to improve their knowledge of business management and finances in order to be able to optimally advise their clients on transactions. Conversely, this applies also to economic advisers who must be offered an interdisciplinary economic and legal M&A course of studies as well as appropriate further training.

It is understandable that especially the mega mergers arouse public interest and create headlines in the economic press. Not only the major M&A, but also the 'smaller' ones will become increasingly international and cross-border transactions because of the increasing globalisation and greater proximity of the markets. Therefore, they will all require more international consultancy competence, i.e. cross-border and highly qualified advice which can so far be provided only by the big international law, investment and corporate finance firms. It is therefore not surprising that these international advisers were able in recent years to handle most deals and also the greatest transaction volumes among themselves.

9 Process Plan for Transactions by Way of the (Restricted) Bidding or Auction Process: Beginning of the Transaction (Kick Off)

1st Phase: Planning of M&A

1.1 Naming and appointing a responsible project manager with an expert project team, if need be additionally a negotiating team (with an experienced and also diplomatically skilled chief negotiator) and M&A advisers

1.2 Analysis and definition of the transaction objects, e.g. cooperation, joint venture, acquisition or sale (including the target and any object of the business to be sold)

1.3 Overall planning for the transaction, in particular the operational and (tax) legal techniques and optimisation with special regard to the following two phases, namely its negotiation and integration
1.4 Preparation of an action and documentation plan
1.5 Preliminary decision, e.g. on an asset or share deal
1.6 Structuring of the transaction object, changes in the target company, the part of the company, the business, the partial business, the business division or the product line, in such a way that – if appropriate under the management of a holding company – an independent, manageable, self-contained and possibly also legally independent unit arises which can be the subject matter of a transaction
1.7 Preliminary valuation of the object of the transaction on the basis of the financial forecast and a business plan
1.8 Preliminary definition of the conditions for the transaction, in particular the sales or barter conditions
1.9 Preparation of the documentation necessary for the M&A negotiations, if appropriate with a draft transaction agreement, e.g. the Sale and Purchase Agreement (S&PA)
1.10 Preparation of an information memorandum
1.11 Preparation of a management presentation
1.12 Draft confidentiality or non-disclosure declaration/statement or agreement for the first bidding process
1.13 Draft first-round bidding instructions

2nd Phase: Implementation of M&A

2.1 Initial marketing approach to contact potentially interested parties or investors
2.2 Provisional (credit) review of the preferred interested parties
2.3 Written confirmation of interest in the transaction by potential partners
2.4 Signing of the prepared confidentiality or non-disclosure declaration/statement or agreement for the information and bidding process
2.5 Delivery of the information memorandum
2.6 Sending of the first-round bidding instructions and request that the interested parties submit a provisional and non-binding offer, if appropriate on the basis of a draft corporate transaction agreement, e.g. the Sale and Purchase Agreement (S&PA)
2.7 Submission of the first non-binding bids by the interested parties
2.8 Preparation of the further and final bidding process (final bidding)
2.9 Draft letter of intent (LoI)
2.10 Preparation of the 'data room' on the basis of the action and documentation plan and an (own) due diligence list of the seller
2.11 Preparation of a new confidentiality commitment/statement of non-disclosure to be signed by each of the potential purchaser's employees involved in the due diligence and by the legal and financial advisers
2.12 Fixing of the 'data room' procedure

2.13 Seller's decision as to which interested parties should take part in the final round of bidding
2.14 Extensive disclosure of detailed corporate data and internal information by way of a management presentation
2.15 Submission of a final binding offer
2.16 Signing of a new confidentiality agreement/statement of non-disclosure by the potential buyers and by all employees and advisers assisting them
2.17 Access to the 'data room' for the selected interested parties and inspection as well as financial and legal review (due diligence) of all documents relevant to the economic and legal evaluation of the object of transaction
2.18 If necessary, additional enquiries with the management, the project team or the M&A advisers
2.19 Inspection of the operating facilities
2.20 Decision and statement by the seller as to which of the remaining potential buyers should begin the decisive contract negotiations
2.21 Beginning of the first contract negotiations, especially concerning.

- The subject matter of the agreement
- Valuable consideration or purchase price
- The transfer date
- The claims and legal/contractual relationships to be transferred, especially:
  - employment relationships
  - liability, representations and warranties as well as any conditions precedent, e.g. required approval by the shareholders' assembly and the supervisory bodies, approval by the cartel authorities

2.22 Summary of the positions taken by the negotiating teams in the first negotiations in so-called 'non-binding position papers'
2.23 Conclusion of the first round of negotiations by confirmation of the intention to conclude the agreement, summarising the so-called milestones in a letter of intent (LoI), an option, a memorandum of understanding, or a provisional agreement
2.24 Press release by the negotiating parties
2.25 (At the latest) delivery of the draft Sale and Purchase Agreement
2.26 Negotiation on the details of the transaction agreement and, if necessary, ancillary agreements such as a contribution agreement, term sheets, etc.
2.27 Conclusion of the transaction agreement in the legally prescribed form

3rd Phase: Integration

2

Mergers and Acquisitions: Interface between Companies and the Capital Markets

Alexander Dibelius

1 Introduction

Mergers and Acquisitions (M&A) are transactions that take place in the capital markets. Hence, in principle the sale or purchase of a company or the merger of two businesses is not much different from purchases or sales of equity or debt instruments on a securities exchange. In addition, apart from several differences there are some interesting interactions between the capital markets and M&A transactions.

So what are the main differences? First, while securities traded on capital markets certify only partial rights, M&A transactions are usually about obtaining control of an entire company. Secondly, in M&A transactions the company – as the object traded – will or is at least able to influence the transaction in the capital market through its management. The developments during the Vodafone–Mannesmann transaction clearly showed this. Mannesmann as the target of a transaction between a buyer (Vodafone) and a potential seller (Mannesmann's shareholders) had significant influence on the outcome of the M&A transaction. The question of control, which ultimately means control over all or at least a majority of the shares of a company, and also the role of the company or its management differentiate M&A transactions from simple purchases and sales of securities in the capital markets. At the same time, M&A transactions cannot escape the capital markets with their codified and non-codified rules and regulations. In the following we discuss in five short sections the key interactions between the capital markets and M&A transactions.

Capital markets evaluate companies and they assess transactions (see 'Democratisation of valuation'), and the parties involved in M&A processes have to take this into consideration. Shareholder value, a buzzword of modern corporate governance, is directly derived from a company's valuation in the capital markets. Likewise, the success of M&A strategies is increasingly measured by the capital markets. The market's immediate and long-term responses to transactions determine how the likelihood that a transaction will be successful is judged ('Acid test for transactions'). Studies in this field have shown that the market's immediate reaction to the announcement of an M&A transaction is a very good indicator of the transaction's success in the long run, measured as long-term return to shareholders. A company's market capitalisation is increasingly seen as a strategic weapon. While among traditional measures of the success of a company size is the only criterion that is still controversial, in particular as far as revenue, asset or headcount levels are concerned. However, a company's market capitalisation is and continues to be one of, if not the key aspect in an M&A transaction where the control over another business is at stake ('Market capitalisation as a strategic weapon'). M&A transactions give corporate management more entrepreneurial freedom. Purchases or sales of companies or parts of companies that would have been impossible or unthinkable in the past are suddenly feasible. Investment bankers, lawyers, auditors, investor relations specialists and other professionals increasingly assume the role of market-makers in the market for corporate control. Ideally, by providing their services they help to ensure that corporate goals can be achieved with the help of the M&A market ('Investment bankers as market agents'). Finally, there is a need for more, and particularly more efficient, regulation in the M&A market relative to the public capital markets. Unlike in Anglo-Saxon and other Continental European countries, Germany is still in its infancy as regards the effective regulation of international or public transactions ('Regulatory deficits in the German market for corporate control').

We now look at these interactions between the capital markets and M&A transactions in more detail.

2 Market Capitalisation as a Strategic Weapon

Since the mid-1990s the market capitalisations of some companies – and of entire stock markets – have soared. In the 1990s the market capitalisations of the world's 100 fastest growing global companies rose by more than 30 per cent per year, whereas that of the market as a whole rose by roughly 17 per cent. Why does the market capitalisation of a company matter at all? Does the widely held belief that what matters is speed rather than size and that size stands in the way of dynamism no longer apply?

Power Through Market Capitalisation

Today, high market capitalisations give companies genuine advantages when it comes to quickly seizing growth opportunities in an expanding world economy. This means that size and growth opportunities should not merely be seen in terms of a trade-off, but may well be mutually reinforcing. Some M&A transactions become possible only because of a company's high market capitalisation. In acquisitions paid with shares having a strong market capitalisation is essential. In more than 80 per cent of transactions with a volume in excess of EUR 1 billion the acquiring company uses its own shares and, thus, its market capitalisation, to implement the transaction. At the same time, high valuations protect companies against being taken over themselves. Hence, companies are confronted with a new paradigm. They have to make sure that their valuations are high in absolute terms and their market capitalisation increases more rapidly than the overall market in order to continue to be or become large and global companies. Otherwise they are at risk of losing control over their own fate. Airtouch, General Electric, Aventis and others have shown how M&A transactions can help to deal with this new paradigm.

Growth of Market Capitalisation

The growth of market capitalisations can be explained in two dimensions: first, in terms of the growth of a company's book equity value as a measure of the sum of its assets and the growth of its retained profits in a given period and, secondly, in terms of the premium the capital market is willing to add to this book value. Interestingly, the premiums ('market over book') of top companies have grown more rapidly than their book equity values.

There is a strong correlation between differences in the growth of companies' market to book ratios and differences in their returns on book equity. Taken together, this means that it is easier for a company to grow its market capitalisation by increasing its return on equity than by increasing its earnings growth in absolute terms. This can be shown by comparing the historical growth of the market capitalisation of global companies resulting from changes in their market to book ratios to growth resulting from changes in their overall book equity values. Therefore, market to book ratios are rather the result of high returns on equity than strong absolute earnings growth. However, the market has rewarded only those companies with huge market capitalisations that try to achieve both high earnings growth and high returns on capital.

In an increasingly global and growing world economy that offers businesses enormous growth potential this means different starting points for companies with respect to their ability to control their strategic future (see Figure 2.1).

No Strategic Control

Companies that are not big enough (measured in terms of their book equity values) and lack the necessary performance (measured in terms of their market to book ratio as a proxy) are vulnerable (lower left-hand quartile in Figure 2.1). Typically, they have little capital and generate low returns on that capital, and operate in mature and primarily national markets. Sooner or later they are taken over by other businesses able to achieve higher returns on their assets.

Control Through Performance

Companies in the upper left-hand quartile generate high returns on relatively little capital. Normally, they operate in rather narrow markets and create value by applying proprietary know-how or technologies. As few of their competitors are able to generate similarly high returns on capital employed, these companies have at least some temporary protection. The challenge for them is that they need to move into new markets or offer new products which can often be accomplished by acquiring other businesses. If these companies fail to apply their

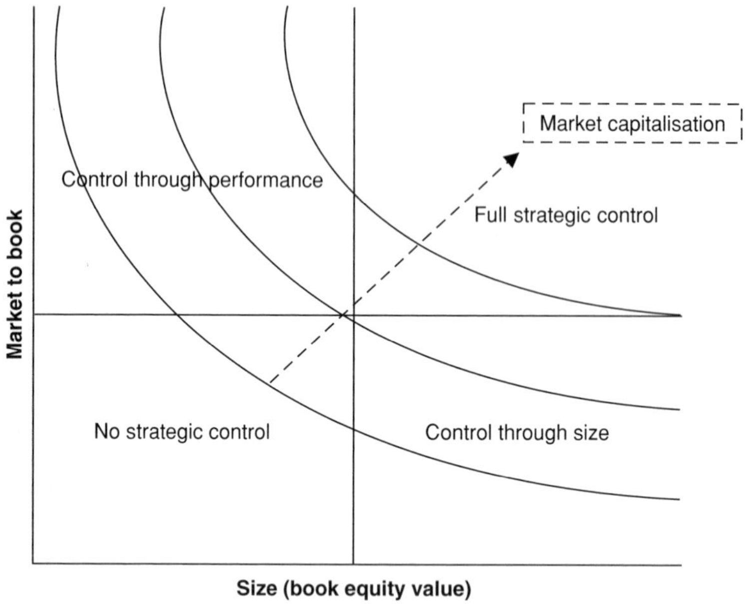

Figure 2.1 Interaction between a company's size and performance

outstanding skills to a larger global asset base, they are at risk of being taken over.

Control Through Size

Companies in the lower right-hand quartile often survive because of their sheer size, even though they generate only low returns. These are mostly established companies in capital-intensive industries which have expanded internationally in the past. If they fail to enhance their returns by divesting those assets that generate the lowest returns and reinvesting the proceeds from these divestitures in higher-return activities, they are at risk of being acquired when their industries consolidate.

Full Strategic Control

Companies in the upper right-hand quartile generate high returns on a large capital base. They are able to determine their strategic future on the basis of their market capitalisations. Typically, these companies operate globally and have skills that set them apart from their competitors. Their high market capitalisations allow them to acquire competitors and, at the same time, protect them against being taken over themselves. Therefore, they are able to determine not only their own fate but, possibly, that of their entire industry. The challenge for them is to defend their position against new competitors and find further opportunities for profitable growth.

3 Democratisation of Valuation

The interaction between capital markets and M&A transactions is particularly evident with regard to company valuations. A transaction will be completed only if the buyer and seller can agree on price.

First of all, the purpose of putting a value on a company is to calculate the amount a buyer would be willing to pay for it. The relevant decisions are made by the management of the acquiring company, which – often with the help of professional advisers – forms an idea of the target's value from the perspective of their own company and its shareholders, and by the target's shareholders who receive the purchase offer. Only if the latter are willing to accept a buyer's offer is it possible to complete a transaction. Ultimately, this willingness is reflected in the reaction of the capital markets. Frequently, the share prices of the companies concerned change substantially when transactions or plans to carry out a transaction are announced. If the target's shareholders receive a cash offer, the investor community's assessment of the control premium offered and of whether or not a proposed transaction makes sense is primarily reflected in the share price of the acquiring company. If, however, a company uses its own shares as an acquisition currency, the capital market will directly determine the purchase price, provided the exchange ratio is fixed.

A large number of different valuation methods have been developed and used to arrive at accurate valuations. These methods differ in terms of their theoretical foundations and practical suitability.

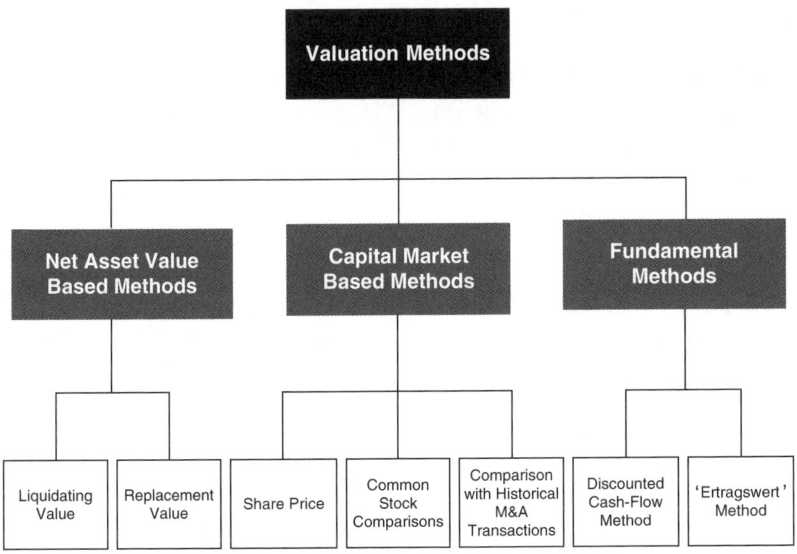

Figure 2.2 Overview of common valuation methods

Methods Focusing on Net Asset Value

Methods focusing on net asset value are based on the assumption that companies should be valued based on the volume and quality of their assets.

Methodology

According to these methods, the price a potential buyer is willing to pay for a target will be equal to the value he or she attaches to the target's assets. If the target is to continue its operations, this value is equal to the replacement value. If it is to be closed down, it is equal to the liquidating value that can be realised within a given time horizon. Intangible assets can also be taken into account by estimating sales prices for them. Therefore, valuation methods focusing on a company's net asset value are based on a buyer's assessment of the target's value. The buyer has the alternatives to obtain the assets he wants either wholesale or gradually (build or buy). This is precisely the greatest weakness of these methods. Other factors determining the target's value such as the possibility to overcome barriers to entry by acquiring a competitor or realising synergies in an M&A transaction are not taken into account. Therefore, application of these methods is typically limited to the valuation of parts of a company or individual assets. They are often used to find a floor for the purchase price.

Assessment

One of the advantages of methods focusing on net asset value is that estimating the value of a company using these methods is relatively straightforward. If a purchase price comes under review in a court of law, it is easy to show how it has been calculated and to defend that price. Nevertheless, these methods have become less important as the capital markets have continued to develop.

Capital Market-Based Methods

Valuation methods that calculate the value of a target on the basis of its current share price or on the basis of the valuations of comparable public companies or transactions are widely used.

Common Stock Comparisons

As a first step pursuant to this method, a universe of companies comparable with the company to be valued is identified. The criteria used to identify these comparables include product range, production methods used, size and geography of markets, revenue levels, etc. As a second step, various multiples relating their market values to certain performance measures are calculated for these comparables. Usually, a company's market value is related to its revenues, EBITDA, EBIT and net earnings. Sometimes a company's net asset value is also used. For young companies – especially in the telecommunications, software and internet industries – that are still in the phase of strong growth and whose earnings multiples are often negative, other yardsticks such as the number of lines, subscribers or highly qualified employees are used instead. In a third step, the resulting multiples are used to put a value on the target of an M&A transaction. In most cases, the average or median of a ratio is multiplied with the corresponding multiple of the target.

Analysis of Comparable Transactions

This method is similar to common stock comparisons. Valuations of companies are derived on the basis of past transactions of sufficient similarity in terms of the type and size of the companies involved. Instead of current market valuations the purchase price is related to relevant historical ratios and the resulting multiples are used to estimate the value of a company. One of the key advantages of this method particularly for M&A transactions is that it also takes account of acquisition premiums.

Assessment

Market value-based methods rely on the capital market's perspective to estimate the value of a company. To take account of the high significance of investors' assessment of transactions, past experience can be used. These methods implicitly take account of all factors influencing the valuations of the companies and transactions concerned. The premiums paid in historic transactions reflect synergies, if any, and barriers to entry overcome.

However, these methods pose some difficulties and have some drawbacks. In the first place, it is often difficult to find a sufficient number of comparable companies. The comparability of companies is often severely limited by differences in size, product range or business models applied. Moreover, the methods are based on the highly restrictive assumptions that capital markets are efficient. According to the Efficient Market Theory, the capital markets are, for instance, able to identify differences in the accounting practices of different companies and reflect these in their valuations. In reality, this assumption does not hold so far. Other drawbacks are that transaction-specific risks are not taken into consideration and, as regards comparisons with similar transactions, the fact that these are not forward-looking. In spite of this, market-based valuation methods are a valuable tool for evaluating M&A transactions. Particularly for conglomerates these methods are used in sum-of-the-part analyses to identify potential undervaluations of an entire conglomerate relative to the value of its individual divisions by comparing these with relevant other businesses.

Fundamental Methods

While market-based methods use external value parameters, fundamental methods focus on the intrinsic value of a company. Pursuant to the net present value method this value is derived by adding the discounted future free cash flows due to shareholders. Fundamental approaches are thus based on forward-looking data.

In Anglo-Saxon countries the Discounted Cash Flow (DCF) method is widely used. In Germany, another method, the so-called 'Ertragswertmethode', is also applied. Both methods differ primarily with respect to the definitions of cash flow figures and discount rates they use.

Discounted Cash Flow Method

Pursuant to the DCF method, forecast cash flows are discounted with the so-called weighted cost of capital (WACC). Depending on the selection of cash flow figures and the corresponding WACC, the total enterprise value or equity value can be calculated directly. While the cost of debt can be computed on the basis of the actual terms and conditions of a company's debt, the cost of equity is estimated with the help of the Capital Asset Pricing Model (CAPM). This theoretical model is based on the assumption that in perfect capital markets investors are able to diversify their risks optimally and, consequently, that only the assumption of company-unspecific risk – the so-called 'market risk' – may be taken into account. This risk depends on the volatility of a company's share price relative to movements of the market portfolio which, for reasons of simplicity, is represented by a stock index. This dependency is expressed with the beta factor which is usually computed from historical volatilities. Thus, in addition to individually projected company data, valuations also reflect market information. This market information which reflects the judgements of the capital markets and, implicitly, of the entire investor community helps to make valuations more objective.

'Ertragswert' Method

The German 'Ertragswert' method uses special cash-flow equivalents ('Ertragsüberschüsse') instead of cash flows. To ensure that valuations are not influenced by differences in accounting policies, these cash flow equivalents must be sustainable. In the 'Ertragswert' method, computation of the discount rate is less well structured. Basically, risk-free market rates are taken which are adjusted by adding risk premiums in order to reflect the actual situation. Auditors use this method to deliver valuation opinions. It is primarily relevant for transactions carried out under German law in connection with merger opinions ('Verschmelzungsgutachten'). The German auditors' association HFA has established guidelines on how this method should be applied.

Assessment

In practice, DCF methods have been gaining ground. One of the main weaknesses of these methods is the limited suitability of the CAPM for practical valuation purposes. As theoretically well-founded methods, they use very restrictive assumptions such as the existence of perfect capital markets. In addition, the computation of the beta factor is often problematic. A number of studies have shown that betas change over time. Therefore, the use of historical series is rather problematic. The main advantages of this method are the simultaneous consideration of both internal and external valuation information and its forward-looking nature. Thus, the subjective forecasts of all relevant monetary variables in M&A transactions can be made transparent and compared in a relatively objective manner. Synergies or perceived risks are also reflected in valuations. If the DCF method results in a higher valuation of a company than market-based methods, the management can obtain indications on how to create additional shareholder value by closing 'value creation gaps' through appropriate M&A transactions. Another positive is the relatively long time horizon of the forecasts used.

What all capital markets-based valuations have in common is that they are derived from the judgements and decisions of many millions of market participants. The ongoing setting of prices by matching demand and supply is a valuable guide. Fundamental methods such as DCF analyses help to make these decisions plausible and take into account future value creation opportunities. It can be shown that the correlation between the development of free cash flows and market values is very high in the medium to long term, although today the immediate EPS impact of a transaction is often seen as an indicator of a company's future share price performance.

4 Acid Test for Transactions

Whether and to what extent a transaction will be successful is a controversial issue. Opinions differ especially as to which criteria should be used to measure the success of a transaction.

Market Judgement vs. Cost of Capital

Typically, the capital market responds to the announcement of a transaction with a rise or fall in the relevant share prices. This is the market's immediate assessment of the likely success and value creation of a transaction. However, analyses of initial share price movements following the announcement of a merger or acquisition have shown that the market is not always right. If a company's ability to generate earnings that, in the long run, are at least equal to the cost of the capital used in an acquisition is taken as a measure for the fundamental success of a transaction, it becomes clear that the capital market's assessment of transactions is not always correct. Only in one out of two transactions is an initial indication of success by the capital market (share price gains of at least 5 per cent for the buyer following the announcement of a transaction) followed by fundamental success. Thus, the market is much more optimistic than reality. The market is much better at forecasting the failure of a transaction. In more than 80 per cent of the transactions surveyed share price declines in response to the announcement of a transaction were followed by fundamental failure, i.e. returns to capital employed below the cost of capital. Taken together, this goes to show that the market is better at spotting failures rather than successes. However, the above data which, at first sight, seem to be compelling (comparison of approximately 50 acquisitions carried out over a period of three years) and the conclusions derived from these should be taken with a pinch of salt.

While the criteria for judging the success or failure of a transaction are easy to understand and – apart from problems relating to capturing these data – can be computed exactly, ultimately they do not provide a sufficient basis for judging the success or failure of M&A transactions. This is owing to the fact that the performance of a company that has carried out an M&A transaction cannot be compared to the performance of that same company if it had not carried out this M&A

transaction. Only such a comparison, which is impossible in practice (even though it is common in science where it is exclusively accepted as proof of the influence of a determinant on a sample relative to a control sample which were absolutely identical at the start of an experiment) would show with a sufficient degree of certainty whether or not a transaction has contributed to the success of a company. As far as the fundamental yardstick for measuring the success of a transaction referred to above ('returns in excess of the cost of capital') is concerned, it can be said that a transaction deemed as a failure on this count could still be regarded as a success as long as one cannot rule out that, without such transaction, the returns generated by the companies involved would not be lower still.

Other Success Criteria

Having said this, some conclusions about the success or failure of transactions can be drawn from studies performed by Goldman Sachs and a number of industry consultants. Many businesses use the actually realised synergies in comparison with those estimated at the time of announcement to measure the success or failure of a transaction. This success criterion is also questionable. If it really applied, this would mean that the success or failure of a transaction is primarily the result of whether a company makes boastful or rather modest announcements.

Factors identified many times as a reason for the failure of M&A transactions primarily include overestimates of revenue and cost synergies and post-transaction integration efforts that are neither fast nor aggressive enough. According to these studies, successful transactions are characterised by a heavy focus on core activities and a correspondingly strong rationale. Transactions carried out with the aim of diversifying into other businesses should be viewed sceptically in the long run.

Moreover, big transactions seem to be less promising than smaller ones. Other success factors are clearly defined and negotiated terms and conditions of a transaction and a fast and radical post-merger integration process.

5 Investment Bankers as Market Agents

Despite the risk of failure of M&A transactions the existence of a functioning market for corporate control is enormously important for an economy. Economic restructuring and adjustment processes are necessary to facilitate research into and the rapid spread of new technologies and, more generally, to match economic activities with real human needs. For companies, a functioning market means a wider range of strategic options. Instead of growing organically and developing new technologies – which is often cumbersome – they can accelerate growth, overcome barriers to entry quickly and sometimes gain fast and cheap access to technological innovations by means of acquisitions or mergers. Assets that no longer fit a company's strategic concept can be sold off with relative ease, rather than having to close them down which is often expensive and time-consuming. For instance, the conversion of Hoechst AG from a broadly diversified conglomerate into a pure life science player within a few years was only possible through a number of acquisitions and divestitures and the merger with Rhône-Poulenc into Aventis.

There are a number of criteria that can be used to assess the efficiency of the market for corporate control. We use the model of a securities exchange where prices are set by means of an auction process to show which criteria are particularly important and how investment banks can contribute to a well-functioning M&A market. The key characteristic of a securities exchange is its liquidity. For prices to be set efficiently, there must be sufficient demand and supply of assets (Figure 2.3). This is particularly important in the M&A market where corporate strategies often need to be implemented under enormous time pressures. It is often attributed to the reduced liquidity of the German M&A market that in the past German corporations have not streamlined their excessively diversified portfolios or have not done so to a sufficient degree.

How can a high degree of liquidity in a market be achieved? As outlined above, a sufficient number of market participants willing to 'deal in' corporate control is crucial. To achieve this, the market must be transparent so that none of the participants feels itself at a disadvantage (transparency/fairness). Moreover, the costs of dealing in the market should be low (cost efficiency). Every market produces information. This should include anything that might influence transactions, thus enabling market participants to make well-informed decisions (information efficiency). Finally, valuation efficiency has to be mentioned. Only if the M&A market is able to find prices that properly reflect the value of the companies traded will these be willing to act as demanders and suppliers in this market

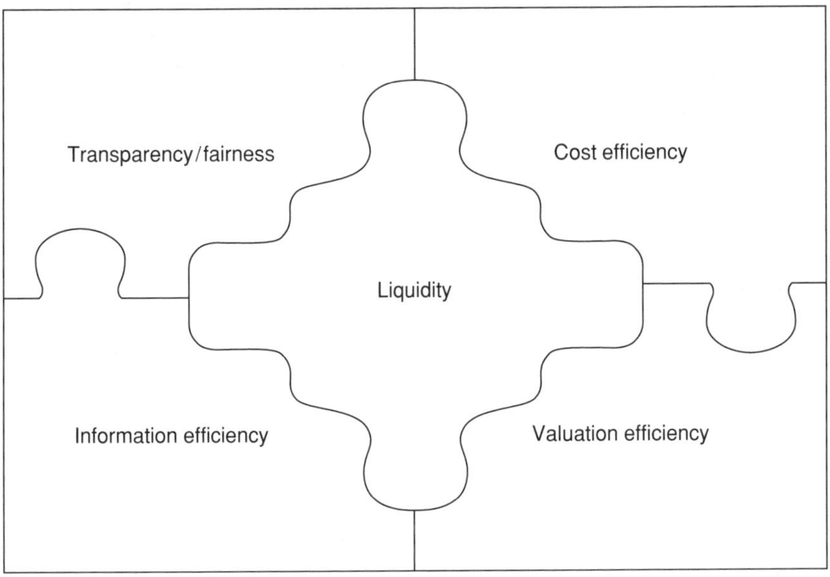

Figure 2.3 Quality criteria for a stock exchange

(valuation efficiency). We will discuss below to what extent investment banks contribute to the liquidity and efficiency of the M&A market. We will show that investment banks perform the role of market-makers. Even though they do not take proprietary positions, they guarantee the M&A market's liquidity.

Information Efficiency

Information is a key element of the business of M&A advisers. As specialists, investment banks initially help to obtain and process information in the M&A market. Many banks are organised in industry groups which regularly screen market segments to identify sound and feasible potential M&A transactions. This screening of markets and industries takes account of economic trends and developments, particularities of individual countries and industries and the market positions and characteristics of individual companies. These analyses are based on market and company research and on the in-house expertise bankers have gathered from transactions carried out in the past.

On this basis, the investment banks develop solid concepts and strategies for individual projects of their clients, communicating to them the requirements of the capital market. Thus, the capital market's views can be 'translated' into individual corporate strategies. Also, during the execution of transactions the investment banks contribute to the quality of the information needed. In buyside and sellside mandates as well as in mergers, M&A advisers play a key role in the due diligence process, the aim of which is to gather all relevant information. In addition to the advice of investment banks, the expertise of lawyers, auditors or tax advisers is often needed in the due diligence process. Investment bankers in many instances assume the role of 'network brokers'. They help their clients select advisers in other fields and act as mediators between the different parties involved. In effect they help to ensure that in each phase of a transaction information is gathered and processed by competent specialists.

Transparency/Fairness

Market fairness is an indispensable requirement for the M&A market to function properly. To provide all participants with a level playing field, a high degree of transparency is needed. As intermediaries in the M&A market, investment banks are often responsible for ensuring that a transaction is executed in a transparent and fair manner.

It is also the job of M&A advisers to help their clients with their internal and external communication efforts. This can be done in many different ways. For instance, in a sellside mandate the advising investment bank may have to structure communications with potential buyers such that all of them get the same information, while simultaneously ensuring that they do not know which other potential buyers are involved. This is the only way to guarantee that none of the market participants gets preferential treatment. Hence, a sufficient degree of transparency is necessary to ensure a fair and efficient sales process.

With respect to communications with investors, the capital market expertise of the investment bankers advising on a transaction is also often a valuable resource.

In takeovers – especially in hostile ones – hardly any press release is published without first being reviewed by the relevant M&A advisers. Often investment bankers take over the public relations efforts of their clients and help them select law firms or other specialists through their networks of contacts.

Especially during the negotiations which are part of any M&A deal it is sometimes difficult to guarantee that all participants are treated fairly. Here, investment bankers have various functions and their reputation is central for their role as advisers that are loyal to their client but at the same time try to promote a fair and constructive negotiation process. The aim of the negotiations must be to achieve the best possible terms and conditions for their clients. At the same time, the investment bankers help to bring about a transaction. With their expertise and experience which enables them to develop appropriate negotiation strategies for their clients and examine the validity of the arguments used by the opposite side and identify the underlying strategies, M&A advisers can help to avoid a situation where negotiations break down and achieve the best possible terms and conditions for their clients.

In addition, investment bankers also have an objectivity-enhancing role in a deal. As external advisers they can help to reconcile opposing interests by creating a negotiating environment that is based on mutual trust between the parties involved. All too often, negotiations are blocked because of personal motives or antipathies between managers. In addition, by heavily insisting on one's own negotiating positions the management of either side can easily kill a deal. Here, investment bankers who are far less involved emotionally can keep the negotiating process afloat and complete it successfully by setting and communicating objective criteria. Ultimately, the credibility of the negotiating parties is the most important success factor. To some extent you simply have to believe the information provided by the opposite side. With its reputation, the advising investment bank signals all parties involved that the negotiating process will be conducted in a professional and fair manner, thus enhancing liquidity in the M&A market.

Cost Efficiency

To persuade investors to use a market, the costs of dealing in that market must be low. This also applies to the M&A market. Here investment banks have an important role to play by ensuring that the transaction costs their clients have to pay remain low. Given the fees which the banks receive for their services, this may seem contradictory at first glance. Similar to purchases and sales of securities, transaction costs are incurred in the different phases of corporate acquisitions and mergers.

Information and Decision-Making Phase

First of all, clients need to obtain sufficient information to be able to decide whether an M&A transaction makes sense economically. As outlined above, in this phase investment banks act as providers of information who greatly facilitate decision-making for their clients by gathering, processing and providing information. Also, during the due diligence process M&A advisers support their clients and, with their expertise and experience, they are able to reduce the transaction costs these have to pay. These savings come not only in the form of time advantages, but above all in lower risk protection costs. Experienced investment bankers are often able to properly assess risks and irregularities in a potential transaction, helping to considerably reduce uncertainties and the related risk protection costs.

Execution Phase

When an investor decides to purchase or sell securities, he places an order with the market maker who then matches supply and demand. Costs are incurred in accepting and processing the order and especially in finding a counterparty. When the market-maker has brought together two parties, they enter into a contract of purchase and sale. In addition to the costs of closing this contract, transaction costs arise from settlement and protection against realisation risks, if any.

Similarly, in M&A transactions several parties need to be brought together. To make this process transparent and cost-efficient, investment banks initially have to develop efficient transaction structures. For purchases and sales of companies this means defining the subject of the transaction and setting the terms and conditions of payment. The subject of a transaction may be shares in the target company ('share deal') or individual assets ('asset deal'). For both the buyer and the seller, these have different tax implications. Investment bankers are responsible for finding and implementing the most cost-efficient alternative for their clients. To complement their own expertise, M&A advisers often seek the help of lawyers specialising in tax law or tax advisers. Sometimes these considerations and analyses result in highly complex transaction structures, as was the case with the merger of Daimler and Chrysler. These may offer the client advantages which he would not have benefited from without the involvement of an M&A adviser.

Consideration in an M&A transaction may be paid in cash ('cash offer') or in shares ('share offer'). Typically, the takeover premium the buyer has to pay is higher in a share deal because of the reduced liquidity and higher risks associated with securities vs. cash. In addition, when using shares as an acquisition currency, a possible dilution of voting rights and dividend payments of existing shareholders need to be taken into account. Often, tax treatment also differs significantly. For instance, the pooling-of-interest method may be applied in a corporate takeover only if structured as a share deal. By carefully balancing out the advantages and disadvantages, M&A advisers can identify the payment structures that best suit their clients.

The same goes for the legal structure of takeover and business combination agreements. As in simple securities purchases, it is the main purpose of the agreements used in M&A transactions to protect the contracting parties against realisation risks. Here it is the investment bank's responsibility to develop alternative structures and select and implement the best possible one for their clients. For instance, formulae are frequently agreed upon to determine the purchase price and the parties are typically granted the right to rescind the agreement under certain circumstances. Representations and warranties may also be used to reduce risks related to information and forecasts provided by the counterparty. While a buyer will seek far-reaching representations and warranties for all information provided by the seller, the latter will prefer very specific guarantees in combination with comprehensive waivers of liability. In cooperation with the legal counsels involved, the advising investment bank will seek to ensure that the agreements match its client's interests as far as possible and, at the same time, do not create incalculable risks with regard to false information or high liability claims. Generally, an investment bank's reputation also serves as a confidence-building signal with respect to the legal structure of a transaction. By referring to the expertise and professional integrity of an advising investment bank, a company may signal its counterparty credibility. This may help to create a more relaxed negotiating climate and avoid transaction costs.

Valuation Efficiency

Companies will enter into M&A transactions only if they feel that the price the counterparty is willing to pay is equal to the value of the asset to be sold. From an economic point of view, this leads to prices that allow an efficient allocation of resources within an economy. As explained above, investment banks play an important role in properly assessing the value of a company in the M&A market.

In an M&A transaction investment banks initially identify issues influencing valuations during the due diligence process. Their expertise enables them to prioritise the relevant information and uncover any risks. Using appropriate valuation methods, investment banks calculate valuation ranges that provide the basis for negotiating a deal, thus helping to ensure the quality of valuations in the M&A market. Given that normally all of the contracting parties in an M&A transaction retain advisers, they use comparable valuations as a starting point. Therefore, the outcome of negotiations will not be totally irrational.

6 Regulatory Deficits in the German Market for Corporate Control

The widespread demands for efficient regulation of the German M&A market may be surprising, given the high degree of regulation and bureaucracy in Germany. Yet, the existing German rules and regulations regarding corporate acquisitions are less efficient than in the USA or the UK. This is probably owing to the relatively small number of transactions in the German M&A market. In Anglo-Saxon countries, an efficient regulatory system has been developed in the past on the basis of the experience gathered in a large number of completed and attempted takeovers.

Generally, the reason for laying down rules and regulations is to achieve benefits for all parties involved through efficiency gains resulting from the compliance by all parties with these rules and regulations. Rules and regulations for the M&A market are ultimately designed to ensure a high level of discipline in the capital markets. The objective is to guarantee investor protection (particularly with respect to minority shareholders), fairness, speed and legal certainty. Rather than suffering from a lack of rules and regulations in quantitative terms, the German M&A environment suffers from a lack of efficiency of the existing regulatory system. The system consists of several subsystems governing the behaviour of the parties involved in M&A transactions. In the following, we explain only the most important components.

Antitrust Law

Both friendly and unfriendly takeovers are subject to supervision by the relevant antitrust authorities. Within the EU, the question that needs to be answered initially is whether EU merger control or national merger control legislation – in Germany, the Act against Unfair Competition ('GWB')– applies. Pursuant to the so-called effects principle[1], the main criterion for answering this question is in which jurisdiction the market and competitive environment is affected. In corporate acquisitions that also affect non-European markets, non-EU antitrust authorities may impose restrictions for a proposed business combination. Cross-border acquisitions, particularly when involving US firms are often delayed considerably and can be completed only after substantial conditions have been met. Examples such as the proposed mergers of General Electric and Honeywell, and of Lagrange and Schneider, have shown that the success of transactions often depends on whether antitrust considerations are taken into account.

Company Law

To date, German company law is the most important legal basis for M&A transactions. The German Stock Corporation Act ('AktG') and, within this act, in particular legislation concerning groups of companies, contains several provisions which define the rights and obligations of a company's corporate bodies and have been designed to protect minority shareholders. German legislation concerning groups of companies governs measures such as mergers, conversions, agreements between companies and integrations. For instance, in an integration according to sections 320 and 321 AktG outside shareholders are entitled to adequate compensation in either cash or shares of the acquiring company. Whether or not such compensation is adequate can be determined by the courts.

According to the general provision of section 93 AktG the members of the management board of a German stock corporation have a general duty of care. They shall act applying the standard of care of a trustee, representing the property interests of third parties. Among other things, this may create the obligation for the management board to inform their own shareholders about the pros and cons of a takeover offer before they accept it.[2] Other obligations of the management board in corporate takeovers result from the Act on Control and Transparency in Business Enterprises (KonTraG)[3] which to a large extent reformed the AktG. Among other things, it is the management's duty to put in place adequate risk management and internal monitoring systems to be able to recognize early 'developments that may endanger the company's future existence'.[4] These include, for instance, the risks involved in the post-take-over integration of the target company. In addition, the KonTraG expands the reporting requirements of the management board *vis-à-vis* the supervisory board. For example, it requires the management board to provide information about its future business policies, including M&A projects which are typically of a strategic nature. In addition, the management board has a duty to provide their own shareholders with background information about a takeover or attempted takeover and give their opinion on a takeover offer.

In a takeover, the target's management board has to observe the principle laid down in section 53a AktG to treat all of the target's shareholders equally. Hence, if the bidder is a shareholder of the company, the management board must make available to the bidder the same information the other shareholders get (section 131, paragraph 4, sentence 1 AktG).

So far the German Stock Corporation Act does not explicitly provide for the possibility of a squeeze-out. Thus, unlike in the USA, an acquirer in Germany cannot purchase the shares of minority shareholders remaining after a successful takeover offer, if any, against their will.[5] This outdated regulation may constitute a very serious obstacle for corporate takeovers and severely restricts the efficiency of the market for corporate control. The existence of minority shareholders results in expenditures related to the compliance with regulations designed to protect minorities and the ability of minority shareholders to hold up a takeover, for instance by lodging unjustified complaints. It is primarily for this reason that the instrument of a squeeze-out is to be created in connection with the planned introduction of a law regulating corporate takeovers.[6] According to the draft of the new takeover law a shareholder who owns at least 95 per cent of the shares of a company shall be given the option of lawfully squeezing out minority shareholders against payment of cash compensation.

Securities Trading Act

In the context of Germany's 2nd and 3rd Laws for the Promotion of the Financial Markets, several provisions to be observed in any M&A transaction have been introduced in the Securities Trading Act (WPHG). First, these include the obligation to disclose shareholdings above 5 per cent which makes it much more difficult for a potential acquirer to buy a company gradually and unnoticed. Secondly, under ad hoc disclosure requirements the target's management must not keep secret for too long substantial corporate actions that influence the target's share price, including an attempted takeover. Thirdly, the WPHG contains provisions regarding insider trading which restrict the spreading of sensitive information and strictly prohibit the trading of securities which are the subject of a takeover offer. Compliance with the WPHG is monitored by the Federal Supervisory Office for Securities Trading (BAWe) which has at its disposal a powerful set of sanctions to enforce the law. For instance, management board members who fail to comply with this law may be fined amounts of up to DM 3 million.[7]

Takeover Code

Although M&A transactions in Germany are subject to a large number of rules and regulations covering different areas, for a long time there was no single systematic set of regulations to establish a clear legal framework for corporate acquisitions and mergers. In 1979 the Stock Exchange Expert Commission (BSK) presented guidelines for corporate takeovers. According to these guidelines, a system of self-regulation was to be set up for public take-over offers, which were relatively little known at that time in Germany. However, compliance with this code of conduct was not monitored as there was no authority responsible for its enforcement. As a result of this, the code of conduct had little practical relevance.[8]

Development and Structure of the Takeover Code

Therefore, the BSK published on 14 July 1995 a takeover code (the Takeover Code) that is closely modelled on London's City Code. With the Takeover Panel and its executive bureau at the Deutsche Börse AG in Frankfurt am Main, a body has been created to monitor compliance with and to further develop the provisions of the Takeover Code. To ensure that the code is interpreted and adjusted in the light of practical experience, the members of the Takeover Panel are selected from different sectors of the economy. At present (Autumn 2001), it has 15 members from the following areas:

- Stock exchanges
- Banking
- Industry
- Insurance
- Retail investors
- Institutional investors
- Science.

The code has been designed as a dynamic set of rules and regulations that meet the practical needs of the M&A business. Hence, corporate takeovers in Germany are not regulated by law. Rather, the Takeover Code is a set of recommendations by an independent commission of experts, the BSK, which the companies concerned may volunteer to sign and to comply with. The provisions of the Takeover Code are thus subsidiary to the provisions of the laws described above. The Takeover Code becomes legally binding only if in its public takeover offer the bidder enters into a contractual obligation to comply with the Code's provisions. In this case, the target's shareholders have contractual rights which they may exercise.[9]

Content

The primary purpose of the Takeover Code is to protect minority shareholders from unfair treatment in the context of corporate takeovers. This protection rests on four main pillars:

(1) The principle of equal treatment
(2) The duty of transparency
(3) The target's duty to refrain from actions that influence its share price
(4) Mandatory public offers.

The basic idea is to enable the shareholders concerned to make a free and well-informed decision to accept or reject a takeover offer. In addition, the Takeover Code tries to ensure above all the fairness and efficiency of the capital market by prohibiting manipulations of the market.

Specifically, the code recommends bidders to retain a financial services company, usually an investment bank, to help it prepare and implement a takeover (Article 6) and to consult with the target's management before launching a public takeover offer (Article 4). All of the target's shareholders have to be provided with the same accurate and adequate information (Article 2). The minimum contents of the offer document to be sent to the holders of securities of the target are clearly defined and include, among other things, information about the bidder, its shareholding in the target, if any, the purchase price offered and the deadline for accepting the offer, information about the bidder's intentions with respect to the target and about the possible consequences of a successfully completed takeover (Article 7). Also, the acquirer must inform the Federal Supervisory Office for Securities Trading, the Executive Bureau of the Takeover Panel, the German stock exchange on which the securities of the target and, where applicable, the securities offered in exchange are listed, about the contents of the offer prior to its publication in a national journal for mandatory stock exchange notices.

The core provisions of the Takeover Code are those regarding mandatory public offers (Articles 16 and 17).[10] These provisions require anybody who obtains control over a target to make an offer, without undue delay, to all other shareholders of the target to acquire their securities. In this context, 'control' is not merely defined in quantitative terms. On one hand, control is achieved by obtaining the power of disposal over more than 50 per cent of the voting rights in the target. If, at the last three annual general shareholders' meetings of the target three-quarters of the voting rights present were on average equivalent to less than 50 per cent of total voting rights, it is sufficient for an acquirer to exceed the correspondingly lower threshold of voting rights to achieve control over the target, as defined by the Takeover Code. Moreover, a bidder who has the right to appoint or remove the majority of the members of the administrative, management or supervisory body of the target is deemed to have control over the target. In addition to the threshold of control, the Takeover Code also defines the level of the purchase price stated in the mandatory offer. The purchase price must not be lower than either the highest share price during the three months prior to achieving control or, if higher, the weighted average share price at which it has purchased additional shares after having achieved control (Article 17).

The mandatory offer adds protection of the wealth position of minorities to the protection of their legal position granted under the provisions of the AktG and the laws concerning groups of companies. It ensures equal treatment of outside holders of securities and those that have decided earlier to exchange their shares.

The target's management also has the duty to provide all holders of securities, which are the subject of the takeover offer, with the same information required to assess the offer. In addition, at the latest within two weeks after publication of the offer, the target shall publish a reasoned statement of its position in relation to the offer (Article 18).

As a counterpart to the mandatory offer, the Takeover Code requires the target's management to refrain after the announcement of a public offer from measures that may obstruct a takeover, unless expressly authorised to carry out such measures by the general meeting (Article 19). This provision is not only in the best interest of the bidder, but it is also to prevent the target's management from protecting its own position at the expense of the target's shareholders.[11]

Criticism of Takeover Code

Against the background of increasing M&A activity in the German and European markets, the Takeover Code has become the subject of lively debate. International institutional investors in particular have complained in the past about the lack of a generally applicable and binding set of rules for corporate takeovers in Germany. Another trigger of this debate has been the draft '13th Directive of the European Parliament and the Council in the Area of Company Law on Takeover Offers', which aims for a minimum of harmonisation in the EU member countries of legislation regarding corporate takeovers. As the contents of the EU proposal differ little from those of the Takeover Code, demands to reform the Takeover Code are due to the success of similar regulations in other countries rather than to the obligation to implement the EU directive. Criticism of the Takeover Code focuses primarily on two aspects.

One of them is that acceptance of the Takeover Code is voluntary as a result of which it does not offer legal protection and is not enforceable by the courts.[12] By 11 April 2001, only 755 of Germany's 1016 exchange-listed companies, including 86 DAX 100 firms, had signed the Takeover Code.[13] In addition, there has been a growing number of incidents in the past where acquirers have failed to comply with the duty to submit mandatory offers.[14] In such cases the Takeover Panel is unable to enforce the provisions of the Code by means of appropriate sanctions. For instance, in the initially hostile bid for Mannesmann by Vodafone, both parties and their respective advisers had explicitly accepted the German Takeover Code. However, the press announcements with which both companies tried to influence the target's shareholders, did not always comply with the provisions of Article 2 of the Code pursuant to which the information provided must be accurate and stated in an appropriate manner. Following a reprimand by the Executive Bureau, both companies agreed to stop using certain phrases criticised by the Executive Bureau and to strictly adhere to the requirement of stating the information in an appropriate manner. Although both parties gave in, this example shows how shaky the foundations of the regulation of corporate takeovers in Germany still are. The second point of criticism regarding the German solution is certainly to do with the success of regulations in other countries, primarily the USA and the UK. The German Takeover Code was modelled on the London City Code. The latter is also based on voluntary self-regulation and is enforced primarily through public reprimands issued by the Takeover Panel. Similar to Germany, this supervisory body is comprised of representatives from various industrial and trading companies, banks and financial services institutions. The City Code has been very successful, as all takeovers carried out so far have been executed in compliance with its provisions. However, a comparison with the UK regulations is not really adequate. On one hand, many of the provisions of the City Code relate to rules and regulations fully enforceable by the courts. On the other hand, the UK Code is a system that has been continuously developed in the light of a large number of precedents. While the UK Takeover Panel has constantly refined the City Code in the process of handling more than 6000 takeover offers, the German Take-over Panel has dealt with less than 70 takeover offers during the short period of its existence.

The German Takeover Act

In view of ongoing demands to regulate takeovers by law, the Federal Government presented on 11 April 2001 a draft takeover bill.[15]

In principle, the draft law contains rules and regulations similar to those of the Takeover Code. However, there are some meaningful amendments. The Federal Supervisory Office for Securities Trading (BAWe), where a takeover council (§ 5) and an objections council (§ 6) will be set up, will be given responsibility for the supervision of corporate takeovers (§ 4). Another change relates to the documentation required in a takeover, which is to be more comprehensive than at present. For instance, the offer document to be submitted by the bidder shall include information about the impact of the proposed takeover on the target's employees (§ 11). Questions of liability for inaccurate or incomplete information in the offer document have been clearly answered (§ 12). The proposed threshold for achieving control over the target as defined by the Takeover Code is 30 per cent, simplifying the present regulation. The provisions regarding the determination of the offer price will also be changed. For instance, the minimum price offered in a mandatory offer must not be lower than the weighted average share price during the last six months prior to public announcement of the intention to launch a takeover offer (§ 16). Block purchase premiums will not be taken into account. To enforce the take-over law, the BAWe will have at its disposal a set of coercive legal measures (§ 60 ff). In addition to barring takeovers, these include fines of up to EUR 500 000. The management board's obligation to refrain from frustrating actions is to be eased by allowing them, in addition to seeking competing offers from friendly bidders ('white knights'), to take certain defensive measures after publication of a takeover offer, provided a corresponding resolution has been adopted by 75 per cent of the target's share capital represented at a general meeting of shareholders. These measures include – as is common in the USA – capital increases (poison pills) and sales of certain assets (so-called crown jewels) which can considerably complicate matters for a hostile bidder.

To complement the Takeover Act, the possibility of a squeeze out is to be incorporated in the Stock Corporation Act, allowing the acquiring company to compensate the remaining outside shareholders once it has acquired at least 95 per cent of the target's shares.

Criticism of the Draft Act

The main criticism regarding the Federal Government's plans for regulating corporate takeovers voiced particularly by mutual fund companies and bankers is undoubtedly that defensive measures will be permitted. The Federal Government's strong lobbying to allow such measures was one of the reasons why the EU Takeover Directive was rejected by the European Parliament on 4 July 2001. However, it remains to be seen whether German managers will be able to use resolutions by general shareholder meetings to shield themselves from the performance pressure in the market for corporate control.

Generally, the proposed law shows the Federal Government's intention to make trading of corporate control more efficient. For example, the planned squeeze-out will allow private equity funds to act more flexibly. In addition, many large corporations could use this provision to achieve a delisting of exchange-listed subsidiaries. Examples include VW (Audi), Vodafone (Mannesmann), Intermarché (Spar preference shares) or Nestlé (Nestlé Germany).

Thus, it seems certain that a takeover regulation will be enshrined in law. It remains to be seen what this law will finally look like and how well it will work in practice. At the end of the day, any statutory regulation must be practicable and increase the power of the shareholders concerned in order to enhance the quality of Germany as a financial centre and as a 'democracy of shareholders'.

7 Conclusions

In conclusion, it is safe to say that the influence which the capital markets exert indirectly through Mergers and Acquisitions on corporate governance is immensely important. Mergers and Acquisitions do not only expand the set of strategic tools available to successful companies, but, through hostile takeovers, they also perform an important control function with respect to a company's management.

In Germany too recent developments suggest that managers will increasingly have to comply with the strictly performance-oriented demands of the capital markets lest their companies become takeover candidates. Examples such as FAG Kugelfischer, Commerzbank or mg technologies have confirmed this. After FAG Kugelfischer, following several years of poor share price performance, has become the victim of a well-prepared takeover by INA, the pressure has increased considerably on companies which are in a situation similar to FAG.

Generally speaking, Germany is a good example of how important a large number of successful M&A transactions is for the efficient functioning of the market for corporate control. Only a sufficiently large number of Mergers and Acquisitions can create the necessary experience and resultant know-how among all parties involved, from management to consultants, to politicians, the press and the general public. Especially in terms of the number and size of deals, Germany has for a long time lagged considerably behind the US and the UK. However, the last several years have shown that major M&A transactions can be done in Germany as well and there has been a significant increase in the number of hostile takeovers.

This development has made it necessary for many executives to take into account their companies' market capitalisation both in terms of shareholder value and as a strategic instrument when making management decisions. At the same time, the importance and the degree of professionalism in the capital markets in Germany have increased considerably. For instance, in recent years investment banks have significantly broadened the range of M&A advisory services they offer and enhanced the professional quality of these services. This development has been facilitated especially by the fact that reputable US securities houses have discovered Germany as an attractive market and built up sizable capacities in Germany. Of course this has gone hand in hand with a corresponding increase in applied valuation know-how as relevant transactions are now typically prepared and executed by more and, above all, more experienced bankers. On the investor side there is also a growing number of professional market participants such as arbitrageurs or institutional investors who deal with M&A activities. The general public is also increasingly paying attention to M&A activities. Thus, more and more retail investors are eager to hear the opinions of experts, particularly TV reporters and research analysts. This has had a positive influence on the quality of company valuations and on the assessment of the likelihood that proposed M&A transactions will be successful, as these are normally based on a broader consensus. As recent legislative initiatives have shown, politicians are also acknowledging how important the market for corporate control is for the economy and have tried to create the necessary efficient regulatory systems.

Notes

1 In Germany defined in section 130 paragraph 2 of the GWB.
2 Cf. Beckmann (1995, pp. 2407ff.).
3 Gesetz zur Kontrolle und Transparenz im Unternehmensbereich (1998).
4 Cf. section 91 paragraph 2 AktG in conjunction with Hirte, *Kapitalgesellschaftrecht*, 2nd edn (1999, p. 61).
5 Cf. Than (1997, pp. 405ff.).
6 Bundesministerium der Finanzen, Bonn, last amended September 2001 (pp. 52–5, and 75–8).
7 Claussen Schwark (1997, p. 7).
8 Schuster and Tschocke (1996, p. 17f.).
9 More detailed information in Diekman (1997, pp. 897ff.) and Groβ (1996, pp. 1909ff.).
10 More detailed information in Hopt (1997, pp. 368 384ff.).
11 Loehr (1999, p. 12).
12 Cf. Kirchner and Ehricke (1990, pp. 105–16).
13 Until 17 June 1999, the Takeover Panel knew of 25 cases where no mandatory bid was submitted although the control threshold had been exceeded. All companies concerned had not accepted the Takeover Code.
14 Caspari (2000).
15 Bundesministerium der Finanzen 1 September 2001.

Bibliography

Achleitner, A.-K. (1999) *Handbuch des Investment Banking* (Wiesbaden).
Beckmann, R. (1995) Der Richtlinienvorschlag betreffend Übernahmeangeboten auf dem Weg zu einer europäischen Rechtsangleichung, *DB* 48, pp. 2407ff.

Börsensachverständigenkommission (1999) *Standpunkte der Börsensachverständigenkommission zur künftigen Regelung von Unternehmensübernahmen* (Frankfurt am Main).

Bundesministerium der Finanzen (2001) *Entwurf eines Gesetzes zur Regelung von Unternehmensübernahmen* (Bonn, last amended September 2001).

Caspari, K.-B. (2000) Übernahmesegen kommt in 2001, Börsen – Zeitung (1 December).

Claussen, C. P. and Schwark, E. (1997) *Insiderrecht für Finanzanalysten* (Frankfurt am Main)

Diekman, H. (1997) Hinweise zur Anwendung des Übernahmekodexes der Börsensachverständigenkomission, *Wertpapier Mitteilungen IV, Zeitschrift für Wirtschafts-und Bankwesen*, pp. 897ff.

Gesetz zur Kontrolle und Transparenz im Unternehmensbereich (KonTraG) (1998) (21 April).

Groβ, Wo. (1996) Übernahmekodex für öffentliche Übernahmeangebote: Anerkennung und Rolle des begleitenden Wertpapierdienstleistungsunternehmens, *DB*, 38, pp. 1909–14.

Hirte, H. (1999) *Kapitalgesellschaftrecht*, 2nd edn, (Frankfurt am Main).

Hopt, D. (1997) Europäisches and deutsches Übernahmerecht, *ZHR* 161, pp. 368–420.

Kirchner, C. and Ehricke, U. (1998) Funktionsdefizite des Übernahmekodex der Börsensachverständigenkommission, *Die Aktiengesellschaft*, 3, pp. 105–16.

Loehr, H. (1999) *Drei Jahre Übernahmekommission*, Bericht der Übernahmekommission.

Schuster, S. and Tschocke, C. (1996) *Übernahmerecht* (Frankfurt am Main).

Than, J. (1997) Zwangsweises Ausscheiden von Minderheitsaktionären nach Übernahmeangebot?, *Festschrift für C. P. Claussen*, pp. 405ff.

Von Rosen, R. and Seifert, W. G. (cos) (1999) *Die Übernahme börsennotierter Unternehmen*, (Eschborn).

3

Global Tax Planning and Global Tax Structuring

Stephan Eilers

Tax planning and tax structuring are the most important elements in the preparation of M&A transactions. They apply to domestic/national transactions and, to a large extent, to cross-border transactions. This chapter attempts to address elements of tax structuring which appear – generally – in every tax planning and tax structuring situation. We summarise these issues in the following ten recommendations on proper tax planning, which might not apply in every M&A situation, but which reflect our experience.

1 Start Early

Tax planning for M&A situations can never start too early. It could be quite risky if business decisions on M&A transactions are made without proper reflection of possible tax consequences of the transactions. Special attention – across all jurisdictions – must be given to holding periods, namely periods in which shares or assets may not be sold tax free despite general tax exemptions which might otherwise be applicable in the relevant jurisdiction.

- *Retrospective 'timing' limitations* which might make transactions difficult or aggressive from a tax perspective if one were to combine the effect of the planned transaction with a previous one.
- *Legislative changes*, as tax legislation is developing rapidly in many jurisdictions and could offer new opportunities or disadvantages if timing differences in the application of various tax regimes are not exploited.[1]
- Planning considerations and tax risk assessments are normally subject to the results of a possible *tax due diligence*.[2]
- Tax planners have to use their skills to get involved early on in the transactions even if that might be difficult in view of the confidentiality arrangements which normally apply. Only the *timely involvement of tax planning capacity* avoids the very well-known situation (on the advisory side as well as on the corporate side) in which the tax department gets to review the transaction only shortly before signature/closure of the deal, with the usual negative implications.

2 Know the Tax Position

The transactional partner's knowledge of the current tax position is an important ingredient of all tax structuring. Only if one takes that position into account can the proposals be effective and lead to consensus. In this process the tax due diligence should not only be directed at identifying potential tax *risks* in the target or in the proposed business combination but also in identifying *opportunities* within the context of the acquisition such as 'tax synergies' by grouping activities in one jurisdiction. Taxes are also an important factor in the identification of the purchase price. Only if the buyer, for example, knows about the applicability of capital gains exemptions on the seller's side (or equivalent deferral possibilities) can it factor that position into the identification of a purchase price which could, for example, constitute a successful offer in an auction of the target. The buyer, however, must also clearly define its tax objectives such as the possible depreciation of goodwill acquired or hidden reserves which are just as significant elements of the purchase price as software developed inhouse, for example. The tax structuring partners in a transactional process always have to keep in mind that M&A transactions in their broadest sense combine *by coincidence*, and that for a short but decisive moment, two or more tax payers which have acted independently from each other up to that moment are working in concert.

3 Avoid One-Sided Structuring

Tax structuring should not unilaterally put the interest of one side to the fore. In many cases this will lead to a contradictory process ('share versus asset transaction') which could eliminate creativity from the structuring process. The same might be true of the endless discussions at the famous 'holdco' or 'topco' of business combinations which are very often debated without a clear view of the shareholder structure of the combined entities. Only knowledge of the shareholder structure, however, can determine whether a location is detrimental to a certain group of shareholders (such as to pension funds which might be hit in a credit system if dividends suffer a withholding tax burden and no tax credit is available to the respective pension fund). In the process of the tax structuring one has always to be aware of the changing nature of tax laws. One should not build a structure on a specific feature in a specific jurisdiction (unless it is a very reliable jurisdiction such as the Netherlands). Furthermore, one should not structure transactions so inflexibly that future transactions might be precluded by domestic tax provisions, such as the imposition of overlong holding periods, as a condition for a capital gains exemption.

4 No Taxes in the Creation of the Structure

The main focus of tax structuring in transactions should be on two aspects: the mitigation of possible tax burdens in the creation of the new structure and the proper review of possible tax burdens in the future. Tax burdens which occur in the creation of a structure could deter interested parties from implementing the transaction at all or could give disadvantaged parties an 'appetite' for compensation mechanisms in the structure. Those compensation measures normally do not make economic sense and make the transaction less appealing into the bargain.

Tax hurdles on the way into a structure could include in particular capital gains taxes for selling shareholders. This is especially true in situations in which a tax authority qualifies a transaction, such as a share for share exchange, as a taxable transaction which then leaves the taxpayers without the necessary liquidity for the tax liability incurred. The tax planner has then to look for deferral mechanisms which may facilitate the transaction. The other area in which taxes could be incurred in the course of setting up the structure is in relation to transfer taxes which could also impose substantial burdens on transactional planning.

5 Look at the Tax Situation After Implementation

Tax planners must provide the parties to a transaction with a realistic view of the likely tax landscape after the transaction. The inevitable question which must be answered is: 'Are we better off with this transaction than without it?'. There are numerous factors which influence the answer to that question. Issues such as a change in the source of the taxpayer's income or a possible change in the qualification of that income as a result of a change in the legal format of the income sourcing entity are of primary significance. Sometimes it is too simplistic just to look at a tax burden comparison even though that document normally stands at the beginning of a post-transaction analysis. The analysis must also take into account the opportunities to optimise a tax situation of, for example, a combined entity by moving profits out of highly taxed jurisdictions so that the overall tax burden of the newly combined group might be lowered.

6 Know the Timing of the Transaction

Tax planning should not be finalised ahead of the transaction to such a degree that the tax planner then abandons the transaction once the initial job is done. It is essential to stay in close contact with the dynamics of the transaction and to be able to react swiftly and flexibly to dangers which might occur. It is also important to keep in touch with the timing of a possible transaction as tax issues might have a decisive influence on that timing. This could be either through delays in obtaining the necessary ruling or because of clearing processes which might depend on different tax authorities (some of which may be in different jurisdictions). Timing also means that tax law might permit certain steps in the transaction to be implemented only after a certain time period (i.e. holding periods for assets), or that the transaction itself is not allowed to be implemented prior to the granting of rulings.[3]

7 Be Aware of Transfer Taxes

Transfer taxes which are normally incurred in the transfer of certain assets include most importantly VAT, special share transfer taxes or stamp duties and real estate transfer tax. All three aspects require special tax attention. Whereas in intra-European transactions VAT on asset transactions could normally be mitigated either through a VAT exemption[4] or a corresponding deduction of the amount of VAT paid, it becomes much more difficult in the case of inbound or outbound European/non-European country transactions. Other transfer taxes such as real estate transfer taxes could be avoided/lowered through proper structuring, but this takes more time and needs the focus of the tax planning teams of the transaction.

8 Care over Documentation

For the drafting of documentation the same rules apply as to timing. The tax team should monitor the documentation continuously and review the core documents. This is especially true in situations where the transaction is 'ruling controlled'. In those situations documents, implementation, prospectuses and other materials available to tax authorities upon audit must mirror the facts, intentions and financial implications as they are presented in documentation submitted for the ruling. In a non-ruling-controlled transaction the documentation should be adapted to reflect the particular business needs which underlie a specific tax purpose or specific tax structure. On the other hand the tax planners have to make the negotiating team aware of specific risks which need to be covered in the documentation.

9 Proper Communication

Another rule of successful tax structuring is the proper communication of the tax ideas into the transaction. First of all the tax structuring concept must be made known and integrated into all aspects of the transaction such as financing (which must also be reviewed from a tax perspective) and legal work (including the antitrust work). Those responsible for tax structuring must ensure that the other participants in the transaction are absolutely clear on the tax requirements for ruling approval/ruling control. Deviations from the agreed structure which ensue from ruling negotiations, for example, must also be properly communicated to the transactional teams. The requirement for proper communication is also valid for the ruling/tax authorities so that they are aware of possible changes/difficulties and are not surprised to hear that the transaction is contemplated, or surprised to be asked at the 'last minute' for concessions which (perhaps because of the timing pressure of the request) they might otherwise not be prepared to give.

10 Prepare for Potential Audit Situations

Once a transaction is completed the tax team should step back and review the situation on an ongoing basis. One might discover (even very shortly afterwards) that not all potential tax risks have been excluded through proper (and safe) planning mechanisms nor through ruling processes. Again, a proper assessment of uncovered or only partly covered tax risks can only help the business to go forward. It might be advisable for the tax department to monitor continuously, on a regular basis, how the risk situations develop and what financial consequences these might have on the business. No transaction is without tax risks but if one looks at the ten issues we have outlined above one can go a long way to substantially reducing those exposures.

11 The German Tax Reform 2001 and its Influence on Tax Planning and Structuring

A recent example of the strong and immediate influence of legislative changes on M&A tax planning and structuring is the German Tax Reform 2000/2001. Due to the growing 'tax competition' between the different countries especially trying to attract multi-national corporations, Germany felt the necessity to improve the tax situation of corporations and their shareholders. The old corporation tax imputation system with its problems for foreign shareholders was abolished and replaced by a new system[5]. The most important changes in the taxation of corporations were:

- The corporate tax rate was reduced to 25 per cent as of 2001. This rate applies to both retained and distributed profits.
- Corporate shareholders could receive dividends from other corporations fully tax exempt as of 2002.
- Capital gains from the disposal of shares in corporations are generally fully tax exempt for corporate shareholders as of 2002. On the other hand, losses from these disposals are no longer deductible as of 2002.

M&A transactions in Germany have been immediately influenced by these changes. Of course, corporate sellers have been highly interested in realising a tax exempt gain . Instead of postponing the transaction to 2002 – when the tax exemption would have come into force – certain deferral structures (e.g. stock loan scheme, capital increase scheme, mutual call and put options, change of fiscal year) have been developed in order to achieve the economic results (cash for the seller, management control for the buyer) in 2001 while deferring the realisation of a taxable gain to the future. On the other hand, shareholdings which had lost part of their value had to be sold before 2002 in order to realise the loss from a tax point of view – either by way of sale to a real third party or, if no third party was interested, within a group of affiliated companies.

The new tax regime has lead to many other changes in relation to M&A transactions, their tax preparation or post-acquisition measures. Just to mention a few:

- In general, the tax exemption for dividends and capital gains of corporation has made Germany much more attractive as a jurisdiction for holding companies[6] (e.g. as a location of the common holding of a new business combination). On the other hand, the deduction of shareholding-related expenses has been legally restricted, so that ways to mitigate that problem (e.g. by way of a fiscal unity between the corporations) have to be implemented.

- In order to mitigate a 'misuse' of the new capital gains exemption by individuals, certain legal time restrictions and holding periods have been introduced, e.g. after tax-free conversions or the transfer of businesses into corporations. This requires a thorough review of the 'history' of the shares if they should be sold tax-exempt.
- The thin capitalisation rules have been tightened so that the financing of acquisition needs a thorough review from the tax side in order to achieve the full deductibility of interest expenses.

This brief overview shows just a part of the tax implications related to an M&A transaction and the possible changes of the basic conditions due to new legislation.

Notes

1 See for example on the different timing application schemes in the 2001 German tax reform Eilers and Wienands (2000, pp. 957f., 1229f.).
2 On tax due diligence see Eilers (2000, p. 103f.).
3 On ruling processes in Germany see Schießl and Eilers (2000).
4 See Article 5 para 8 of the 6. council directive and (e.g. in Germany) see para. 1a of the German VAT Act.
5 For detailed information on the tax reform see Freshfields Bruckhaus Deringer (2000).
6 See Eilers and Schmidt (2001), p. 8.

Bibliography

Eilers, S. (2000) 'Tax due diligence', in Schaumburg, H., *Unternehmenskauf im Steuerrecht*, 2nd edn (Stuttgart/Germany).

Eilers, S. and Wienands, H.-G. (2000) 'Steuersenkungsgesetz: Besteuerung der Dividendeneinnahmen von Körperschaften nach der Neufassung von § 8b Abs. 1 KStG', in *GmbH-Rundschau 2000*, pp. 957 ff.

Eilers, S. and Wienands, H.-G. (2000) 'Steuersenkungsgesetz: Anteilsveräußerungen durch Körperschaften nach der Neufassung von § 8b Abs. 2 KStG', in *GmbH-Rundschau 2000*, pp. 1229 ff.

Eilers, S. and Schmidt, R. (2001) 'Der Holdingstandort Deutschland nach der Steuerreform', in *Finanz-Rundschau 2001*, pp. 8 ff.

Freshfields Bruckhaus Deringer (2000) 'Unternehmenssteuerreform – Die Neuregelungen des Steuersenkungsgesetzes für Kapitalgesellschaften und ihre Anteilseigner', in *NJW*, 51/2000.

Schießl, M. and Eilers, S. (2000) 'Germany', in *IBFD, The International Guide to Advance Rulings* (Amsterdam).

Part 2

Implementation of Mergers and Acquisitions

4

The Implementation of Mergers and Acquisitions under Business Law Aspects: the Formation of the Transaction Agreement

Gerhard Picot

1 General Aspects of the Implementation of M&A under Business Law

Companies are complex subjects of M&A transactions:

- Purchase and sale of companies
- Mergers of companies
- Joint ventures and alliances
- Corporate succession
- Management-Buy-Out (MBO) and Management-Buy-In (MBI)
- Going public/Initial Public Offerings (IPO)
- International (cross-border) M&A
- Integration, conversion and reorganisation.

This requires very careful planning and implementation and, in particular, negotiation.

The mere entering into negotiations on agreements gives rise in most legal systems to a relationship of trust and good faith similar to that under contract that imposes obligations on the parties to the agreement for mutual consideration, care and loyalty and demands from them the diligence of debtors. This also results in a liability similar to that under contract, thus hypothesising wilful intent or negligence. Therefore, in principle the mere breaking off of negotiations on agreements does not lead to an obligation to pay damages.

Already at the beginning of entering into an agreement, numerous legal details of the national and international legal systems[1] must be observed, that are important both for the formation and implementation of the agreement or the transaction as well as for possible claims or defences against such claims in the event of failure of the negotiations.

In the case of larger mergers and acquisitions, the drafting of a Letter of Intent (LoI) or Memorandum of Understanding (MoU) is regularly followed by negotiations and agreements on the details and terms of the transaction. It is then extremely important that all these preliminary talks and the results of the subsequent due diligence examinations are reproduced in legal terms as exactly as possible in the transaction agreement. The transaction agreement is thus the cornerstone for optimal formation and implementation of mergers and acquisitions as well as for their integration.

An important object of negotiation and contractual regulation is always the law concerning warranty and liability. In the case of corporate takeovers, to begin with essential differences between an *asset deal* and a *share deal* must be observed. In addition the general rules of default in performance of an obligation as well as liability for fault and liability based on principles of reliance are particularly important.

Internationally, in this respect, it has become usual to a large extent to include, according to the model of case law, substantial assurances and guarantees (so-called representations, warranties and guarantees) of the seller with concrete terms for the consequence of liability and the scope of the liability or its limitation in the transaction agreement. In this case, the seller regularly ensures that the company demonstrates certain conditions or properties on a certain due date (e.g. signing date or closing date) and that, for example, the production facilities are in a condition conducive to the continuation of operations with certain quality standards, production volumes, etc. The liability framework is, at the same time, a certain reflection of the conditions/circumstances and data of the company that the buyer had already or ought to have observed within the due diligence examination in the 'data room'.

The transaction agreement or the Sales and Purchase Agreement (S&PA) has, thus, to regulate or take into consideration the following:

- The *subject matter* of the agreement (e.g. transfer of companies, businesses, parts of businesses)
- The *consideration*, in particular the purchase and/or (shares) exchange price
- The point in time of the *transfer* of the business
- The assumption of *rights and obligations* from contractual relationships, in particular from employment relations
- The *warranties* and *guarantees*
- The liability for *previous obligations*
- Agreements *restricting competition*
- Possible *restraints on disposal*
- *Reservations* of consent and authorisation
- Terms according to *national, European* or *international cartel law*
- The *formal* aspects
- The *closure*
- *Miscellaneous*.

2 Pre-Contractual Negotiation Stage

Confidentiality Agreements

If an intended transaction becomes publicly known too early, this can have repercussions for all concerned. Already in view of the pre-contractual obligations, the parties involved must in a series of legal systems treat the negotiations as confidential and not use the knowledge obtained to the disadvantage of the party to negotiations. The extent of such pre-contractual confidentiality may be uncertain in the individual case. Such obligations should thus be strengthened and made more precise by way of confidentiality/non-disclosure agreements or contractual statements of non-disclosure.

Negotiation Protocols

During the first stage of lengthy contractual negotiations, the parties may compile and exchange position papers, negotiation protocols or so-called 'preliminary contracts'. Thereby, points of negotiation which had already been (conclusively) negotiated are put down in writing in order to include them as part of the prior negotiations in the further course of contractual negotiations.

Letter of Intent

The instrument of the Letter of Intent (LoI), which originates from the Anglo-Saxon legal tradition, cannot be defined in general terms in other legal systems. The most common form is the declaration of an intention to reach a particular legal result with the other party, i.e. the transfer of the company.

In principle, according to the various legal systems the letter of intent has no legally binding effect. All the same, describing a declaration as a 'Letter of Intent' is not decisive in the legal evaluation of whether it is legally non-binding or (already) binding. Rather, this question is to be decided in accordance with the intention of the parties. According to this, an LoI does not yet, in principle, bind the negotiating party within the meaning of a (pre)-contractual obligation, but only contains the legal but not-yet-binding stipulation of his or her *negotiating position*. Even in the case of a legally non-binding LoI, violation of the duty of care can give rise to liability if this foundation for conduct is deviated from without good cause. An LoI can, however, be binding if the wish for legal commitment of one party is expressly or conclusively given by the contents of the LoI. In order to avoid unclear points, it is in any case advisable to state in the LoI an exact ruling as to which of the given statements shall be legally binding and what legal consequences and liabilities are to ensue from them.

Option

Options give a party to an agreement the unilateral right to form a contract with regard to the subject matter and consideration offered and (as a rule) limited in time, i.e. to buy or sell the company (so-called call- or put-option). By exercising such an option, the party makes an agreement that is concluded subject to a condition precedent and is fully effective.

Preliminary Agreement/Memorandum of Understanding

Preliminary agreements create an obligation to conclude the main agreement which, under certain circumstances, cannot yet be finalised because certain points considered by the parties as requiring clarification are still open. In order to be effective, a preliminary agreement must set out all *essential points* with sufficient precision. The sufficient certainty is, as a rule, given if the subject matter of the transaction and price and the ancillary points deemed essential by the parties have been stipulated or can be determined by interpreting the agreement. If the main agreement requires notarial form, a preliminary agreement is not effective if merely concluded in writing.

Since the sufficient precision of the essential points required for concluding an agreement is enough for a preliminary agreement and – in contrast to a LoI – the right to performance has already been given, without the parties to the agreement having agreed to all the details in the agreement, extreme restraint should be exercised with this legal instrument.

The instrument of the 'Memorandum of Understanding' (MoU) used above all in the Anglo-Saxon legal tradition is, similar to the LoI, unable to be given a universally valid definition in other legal systems. In order to avoid uncertainty whether the parties to the agreement merely want to give the MoU the character of a mutual LoI or already that of a legally binding preliminary agreement, precise settlement in the MoU of what legal consequences and liabilities should result from it is in any case advisable.

Due Diligence and Pre-Acquisition Audit

In order to establish clearly the content and scope of the subject matter of the transaction as well its value, in practice it is customary and advisable, as early as possible in the stage of negotiation proceedings and before submission of a binding offer, to carry out a careful inspection of the company (so-called 'due diligence'), in particular a:

- *Commercial* due diligence
- *Financial* due diligence
- *Legal* due diligence
- *Tax* due diligence
- *Technical* due diligence
- *Scientific* due diligence
- *Environmental* due diligence
- *Human Resources* due diligence
- *Cultural* due diligence

and with a view to the chances and risks to make a detailed analysis, a so-called 'Pre-Acquisition Audit'. The results of this preparatory examination are, as a rule, summarised by legal and other experts separately in a so-called *Due Diligence*

Report and together with an Executive Summary submitted to the decision-making body of the company interested in the acquisition. In exceptional cases such an examination can, (for example, for timing reasons) only be carried out as a Post-Acquisition Audit, after conclusion of the transaction agreement; relevant reservations should be included in the transaction agreement in the form of legal assumptions, conditions, etc.

Since the subject matter of the due diligence will be treated in detail later, at this point for a better understanding of its legal importance, only the three different functions of the due diligence examination will be emphasised:

- First the due diligence examination provides an opportunity for the party to the agreement to obtain information on the *subject matter* of the transaction
- Further, the examination serves to reveal to the buyer *chances*, *risks* and *weaknesses* of the target company
- Finally the due diligence serves to reveal and document the *target object* also for purposes of evidence.

Nobody knows the company as well as the previous owner or the former management. For the party to the transaction, in particular the buyer of the company and joint venture partner, careful inspection of the target company is thus not only a basic prerequisite for the success of a deal but necessary for appropriate assessment of the target company, the stipulation of a binding offer of consideration and the contractual negotiations, especially also with regard to the warranty and liability system to be agreed upon. A certain limitation of the due diligence may be considered if, for example, a competitor appears as a party interested in buying, who already has certain ideas about the subject matter and the environment of the transaction. The same also applies for a Management buy-out (MBO) or Management buy-in (MBI), in which the investors utilise the insider knowledge of the internal or external managers on the target company, the value of the company, the development resources and the market through an economic participation of the managers in the company.

Between the due diligence on the one hand and the legal and contractual warranty, guarantee and liability obligations of the seller on the other there is a close interplay that has to be meticulously observed in the contractual negotiations. At the same time, the rule applies: the less data and information made available by a party to the agreement, the greater the scope and detail of the demands of the other party to the agreement will have to be for contractual promises of guarantees, warranties and liability. Conversely, the seller will, after an extensive due diligence, regularly point out to the buyer that he now has the same level of knowledge as the buyer himself. Accordingly, the seller will make the effort to rule out his liability for disclosed risks in the purchase and sale agreement, or at least to limit them.

3 The Purchase and Sale Agreement: Negotiation, Conclusion and Implementation

Owing to the standardised structure of the purchase agreement, it appears useful to first of all represent the formation, conclusion and implementation of M&A using the example of the purchase and sale agreement. Subsequently the special forms of M&A will be explained:

- Hostile takeover
- Mergers of companies
- Joint ventures and alliances
- Corporate safeguarding and succession of companies
- Management buy-out and Management buy-in
- Going public/Initial Public Offerings (IPO)
- International (cross-border) M&A.

Types of Corporate Acquisition: Asset Deals and Share Deals

Purchase and sale agreements contain a whole assortment of special rights and obligations.

The corporate acquisition can take place by way of an *asset deal*, i.e. transfer of the entirety of the assets and liabilities of the company. This is known as acquisition by way of singular succession or asset deal.

The purchase of a company can also occur by way of transfer of the corporate body through the acquisition of *shares or interests*, i.e. through purchase of a company or an interest in a company. The corporate body of a company can be a legal entity, a partnership or an individual company. In the cases of the corporation and the partnership, the assets belonging to the company are clearly separated from the private assets of the partners. The participation of the seller under corporation law directly represents the legal purchase object so that the identity of the company remains unchanged. This form of corporate acquisition is known as a *share deal*.

General Comments on the Formation of Purchase and Sale Agreements

In view of the increasing internationalisation and globalisation of the transaction processes, as well as by virtue of the powerful influence of international investment banks and law firms, one cannot evade the trend of drafting transaction agreements according to international and, in particular, Anglo-American models as well as (predominantly) in the English language.

As already mentioned above, for forming transaction agreements in practice, it is thereby more and more insignificant under what legal system the parties to the agreements place a transaction agreement. International M&A experts no longer rely on the legal system they have chosen as having suitable rulings at disposal for the complex structure of their interest. Rather, to an increasing degree, they create their own self-contained sets of contractual rulings which, in turn, serve as a pattern for further transactions and more and more take on the character of *independent legal systems*. In these contractual rulings, to an increasing degree according to the model of the Anglo-Saxon common law or case law, all known and recognisable situations and risks in need of adjustment are settled. These rulings appear instead of the civil law and contractual (fundamentally) generalised methods of settlement used in numerous legal systems, in which instead of concrete examples in case law, abstract generalised terms are used that allow an indefinitely large number of cases of application to be covered. Without general-clause-type abstract legal terms or generic terms the matters for settlement are defined and agreed as conclusively as possible in the transaction agreement through the written description and listing of all matters and applications.

On the whole, the outcome of this is that know-how of transactions is accumulating more and more in the heads of the M&A specialists as well as in their detailed and experience-oriented pattern collections. In this way a uniform international 'Transaction Law' is evolving that, as a commercial custom, will in the longer term increasingly assume the character of a self-binding legal source.

In spite of the standards and patterns emerging in practice for the formation and contents of the transaction agreements, owing to the complexity of the companies as an entirety of objects and rights, actual relations and experiences as well as entrepreneurial activities on the one hand and branch-specific characteristics on the other, it is nevertheless not possible to deal with and master the multiple facets of a transaction with a 'good' standard agreement. Since the subject matter of the transaction agreement deals with the living company as a living organism with all its internal and external relations, it is, on the contrary, advisable, against the scenario of this agreement technique, to settle all important legal and economic aspects for the parties to the agreement in such detail that surprises can be ruled out. In particular, known and recognisable risks and risk situations such as, for example, urgent reorganisation measures of the target company must be limited and distributed as clearly as possible through consents or guarantees or relevant agreeing on waivers amongst the parties to the agreement or taken into account in the consideration and, above all, in the purchase price.

At the same time, at the beginning of more comprehensive transaction agreements:

- A detailed *table of contents*
- An *index of appendixes*

should be included for a better overview.

Depending on the desired structure from the legal and above all fiscal law point of view, the transaction can be carried out in line with the previous comments as:

- A transfer of individual assets (so-called *asset deal*) or as
- A transfer of shareholdings in a company (so-called *share deal*).

Subject Matter of a Purchase and Sale Agreement

The subject matter of the purchase and sale agreement is to be considered differently with regard to the acquisition of individual assets (asset deal) than with respect to the acquisition of a company or a participation in a company (share deal).

The Acquisition of Individual Assets (Asset Deal)

If the acquisition of a company as an asset deal deals with the purchase of individual assets, then the seller binds himself to surrender the object to the buyer and gain ownership of the object. The seller of a right is obliged to procure the buyer the right and if the right is to the possession of an object, to transfer this object. Since the acquisition of a company involves the acquisition of an entirety of objects and rights, actual relations and experiences as well as entrepreneurial actions, special consideration must be taken into account for the transfer of the company to the acquiring party. The transfer of a company involves at the same time the transfer of the entire 'company' as organism, so besides the transfer of objects and rights, there is also an obligation to introduce the acquiring party into the field of activity.

The purchase and sale agreement relates to a company as an entirety of objects and rights. Since according to numerous national legal systems, a company as such cannot be the subject of a transfer operation, in an asset deal the individual assets and liabilities that are to be transferred have to be regularly determined individually and in specific and concrete terms, taking into consideration the peculiarities of the various legal systems. For this reason, it must be clearly and unambiguously resolved which individual component parts of the company are to be transferred. At the same time, peculiarities arise with respect to the transfer of claims, contractual positions and legal relations. If the seller of a company wishes to transfer his obligations arising from current agreements with the effect of legal release to the buyer, it is usually necessary to obtain the agreement of the third party to the agreement or to create a so-called 'trilateral legal transaction' between all parties concerned. Problems can, in particular, arise with respect to the transfer of rights and obligations from continuing obligations.

For the purchaser who is unfamiliar with the company to be acquired, this procedure is not without risk. If the company to be transferred has drawn up a balance sheet in order to determine and transfer the objects and rights reference can be made to the balance sheet and inventory. In order to exclude any doubt, it is recommended to include 'all-transfer' or 'catch-all' clauses. A mere provision referring to the value or number is not sufficient.

Likewise, depending on the national legal system (cf. the contribution of a 'business' under Italian law) the contractual relations with suppliers and customers or with other third parties – as, for example, leasing companies, etc. – have to be named and transferred individually, taking into consideration so-called 'change-of-control' clauses. In the event that such an agreement existing with a third party should become without legal effect because of the asset transfer, or the third party to the agreement should refuse his consent to the transfer of the agreement to the purchaser of the company, in the internal relationship of the parties to the agreement among each other such respective party requires provisions that particularly protect him.

Other rulings can apply depending on the national legal system as regards employees. If a business or part of a business is acquired from another owner through legal transaction, according to the European Council Directive 98/50/EC of 29 June 1998 amending Directive 77/187/EEC, owing to the transfer of business, the acquiring party automatically assumes the rights and liabilities from the employment relations existing at the point in time of the transition (cf. in detail subsequently under Item 3 g). This can concern a binding ruling that can neither be alterable by mutual consent through an agreement between employer and employee nor through a contractual agreement between employer and the party acquiring the company. In this way, the employees remain in principle connected to the business or part of the business to which they are to be objectively assigned according to the focus of their activity, provided they do not oppose the transfer of their employment relations to the new employer.

The Acquisition of a Company or a Participation in a Company (Share Deal)

In the share deal the acquiring party, by way of the participation in the company, directly achieves an interest in the assets of the company. In such a share deal, a description of the individual component parts of the company is unnecessary. The acquisition of membership rights under the law relating to corporations is an acquisition of rights.

Since merely a change of owner takes place at the company and the company remains the contracting party, the contractual relations with third parties do not need to be individually transferred with their consent. The same applies with regard to employees for whom no change of employer occurs. It must admittedly be considered that often particular agreements with banks, suppliers and licensors also contain so-called 'change of control' clauses for the case of a share deal, which in the event of a change in ownership of the company of the party to the agreement make provision for a cessation of the business base or a right of termination; in these cases, even before signing the purchase and sale agreement, if possible a statement should be obtained from the third party that he adheres to the agreement and will not exercise his right of termination.

If the transaction agreement is to safeguard that the value embodied in the company is transferred, it must bind the seller in a lasting way to transfer precisely the very assets and rights that constitute this value at the point in time of concluding the agreement. At the same time, for the formation of the purchase and sale agreement it can make a considerable difference if, for example, a service provider company in the telecommunications sector or a production company in the automotive sector is acquired. In this respect, it will have to be borne in mind to a differing degree that the employees, the basis for rendering services, production facilities, machines and fixtures, immaterial assets, industrial property rights, business records, customer lists, know-how and goodwill, as well as the supply terms and customer relations, actually pass into ownership within the scope of the transaction.

Ancillary Agreements, Supply and Service Agreements, Term Sheets and Special Clauses to the Purchase and Sale Agreement

When acquiring a corporation, it must be further taken into consideration that the individual corporation may, for example, be dependent on other companies of the corporation, in particular for energy and raw materials. The sale and purchase agreement is then at least for a transitional period to be supplemented by ancillary agreements, in particular supply and service agreements or so-called 'term sheets' with the corporate companies in question, so that a continuation of the company under the previous terms of reference is guaranteed. This particularly applies if the acquired company is located in a so-called 'industrial park', demonstrating a certain infrastructure at the location which cannot, or only to a slight extent, be influenced by the purchaser of the company.

Structuring of the Purchase Object

Often it is in the interest of the seller to structure the purchase object – i.e. the company or part of the company, the establishment or part of the establishment, the business area or the product line – in such a way that, independently of the corporate acquisition model actually intended, such sale is made possible or at least simplified. This structuring of the purchase object is intended to reform or adjust it, for example with respect to legal structure, organisation or relationship to the remaining part of the company (e.g. administration, finances, supplies, services, energy supply, safety facilities or social services) in such a way that a clear, compact, possibly also legally independent entity capable of being sold comes into existence. In this way, the seller can offer the purchase unit as a 'package deal' and at the same time give structure to and simplify the purchase negotiations in its own interests. At the same time, as a consequence of the concentration of the company on its own core areas, it often becomes necessary to close down production operations or to pass these on together with the operational infrastructure and working premises, for example by the creation of so-called 'industrial parks', to third companies by way of sale or exchange (so-called swap), against establishments relating to the core area. In total, the companies aim to create cost saving and flexible structures for production, distribution and organisation which optimise their customer-oriented innovation, quality of performance and efficiency within the scope of global corporate strategies.

Moreover, the transfer agreement will have regularly to contain terms that guarantee the acquiring party the keeping of the company's value for the period after the transfer. To this end, agreements restricting competition can be made that forbid the seller and possibly also his members to conduct activities in the business area of the company that has been sold for a certain period of time.

In mergers or acquisitions of companies, there can be a considerable period of time between the date of the first evaluation of the company, the conclusion of the transaction agreement and the actual transfer of the business (closure). For larger-scale acquisitions this is often contingent on the consent of the Cartel

Office having to be obtained for the acquisition and that up to then a ban on accomplishment exists. Up to the transfer qualifying, the effective date or the closure, the value of the company can be subject to considerable fluctuations. For this reason, the parties to the agreement frequently agree on compiling a 'transfer-day balance sheet'. Should it ensue from the transfer day balance sheet that the agreed minimum values for the equity capital, the working capital, etc. have not been achieved, then an adjustment of the purchase price or compensation payment has to take place.

Purchase Price/Shares as Acquisition Currency

A central problem of the purchase and sale agreement is often the determination of the *purchase price*. A differentiation must be made between the purchase price and the corporate value (reference is made in detail in Part 2, Chapter 6) which, however, as a rule is of decisive significance for the fixing of the purchase price. The purchase price is determined by the parties to the agreement on the basis of estimations of value by both parties which are formed according to their level of knowledge at the time of formation of the contract. The parties must at the same time pay regard to the difficult circumstance that in forming such evaluation, it is almost always necessary to take future trends into consideration. The same applies if instead or in addition to a cash payment, shares of the acquiring company are transferred as consideration.

Often the parties agree that the final purchase price is to be established on the basis of an accounting balance sheet to be drawn up on the day of transfer. Diverging from this, the parties may determine other – also global – evaluation and accounting standards in an agreement as for example the 'International Accounting Standards – IAS' and the frequently used 'US – Generally Accepted Accounting Principles – US GAAP'.

In connection with corporate alliances, in particular in the form of joint ventures, the question arises of whether the corporate evaluation should exclude or take into account the advantages of affiliation and synergetic effects on the basis of the so-called 'stand-alone principle' or upon application of the so-called 'affiliation consideration principle'.

In view of the volume of international transactions, which are often in the region of billions, companies are tending more and more to use the share as 'purchase price currency' for mergers and acquisitions. In the transfer of shares the burdensome nature of the liquidity of companies and the negative accounting effects connected with external financing can be discounted – as, for example, the regular considerable goodwill depreciations – occur on the balance sheet. Also the acquiring party to the agreement can possibly – given corresponding evaluation of his share – be able to offer the other party to the agreement with his share as acquisition currency an attractive purchase or exchange price.

As acquisition currency, the share has advantages especially in the event of a hostile takeover (Figure 4.1). If the target company was evaluated highly on the stock market, this was formerly considered as good protection against a hostile takeover because of the high takeover cost that ensued. The example of the

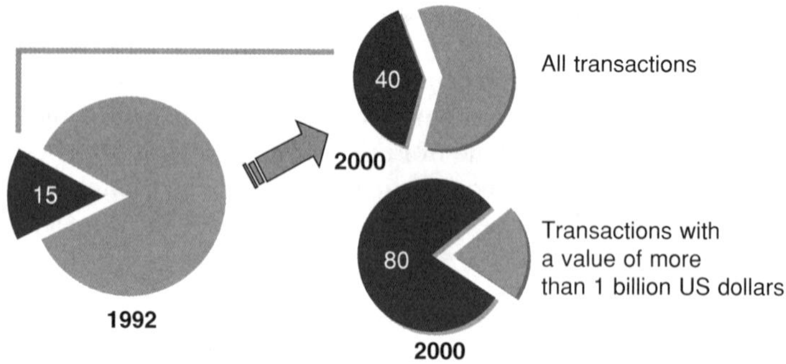

Figure 4.1 Shares as currency, per cent

hostile takeover of Mannesmann AG by Vodafone has, however, shown that this difficulty can be overcome by an exchange of shares. The value of the share as transaction currency is, in fact, decisively determined by the degree of probability of success of the hostile takeover considered by the market and how high it rates the value of the merged company. If the market rates both factors positively, usually the value of the share of the company taking over increases from the point in time when the takeover activities become known, and it receives a strong currency that enables it to acquire highly rated companies through a hostile takeover.

Against this scenario, it is not surprising that at present more than 80 per cent of corporate mergers with values in excess of DM 2 billion are financed through the vehicle of exchange of shares. Above all, the acquisition of the media giant Time Warner by America Online (AOL) as well as the equally spectacular takeover of Cable & Wireless HKT by the start-up company Pacific Century CyberWorks (PCCW), which was not even one year old, show that by using the share as acquisition currency, relatively young firms with comparatively low sales and profits can take over traditional, large companies.

In a 'common' acquisition of a company, in which the purchase price is effected in cash, the transaction agreement is to be qualified as a purchase agreement. If, on the other hand, the 'purchase price' is effected in shares it is, in principle, an exchange agreement or in the case of a combined cash/share payment it is a mixed purchase/exchange agreement. However, in the complete or partial use of shares as currency basically there are no differences in the legal character of the transaction agreements.

Admittedly the course of the transaction, if shares are used as means of payment, does have some particularities, since on the one hand the buyer first has to procure the shares for the transaction before he can offer them as 'purchase price' and on the other the seller – similar to the case in a self-conducted purchase of company – possibly has to procure information through a self-conducted due diligence on the value of the company whose shares he is to receive as purchase price.

For the acquiring company, there are various possibilities of procuring the necessary self-owned shares for an acquisition.

To begin with, a share offer can be financed with shares that are acquired in the market from the cash flow earned. The largest advantage of a share offer, the considerate treatment of self-owned liquidity can, of course, not be utilised here since the buyer has first of all to acquire the shares with cash, which could also be used directly to pay the purchase price.

In practice, the shares are thus procured by means of a capital increase. At the same time, there are various possibilities of carrying out a capital increase:

- Capital increase from company means
- Capital increase against contributions
- Conditional capital increase
- Authorised capital.

A capital increase from company means would encumber the liquidity and balance sheet in the results, just as the cash payment of the purchase price. This form of capital increase is thus not expedient for M&A.

Capital increase against contributions and conditional capital increase avoid this disadvantage. Admittedly, the shareholders' meeting is in principle responsible for the decision on an increase of capital and implementation of this is expensive and time-consuming. Precisely in the case of companies quoted on the Stock Exchange, it is necessary in the case of transactions to be able to react immediately to the situation on the capital market and to procure counterpayment in the form of shares for the sellers of the target company as quickly as possible. Both the capital increase against contributions and the conditional capital increase, without exception, presuppose a resolution of the shareholders' meeting. For this reason, these forms of capital increase are not very suitable for a short-range flexible acquisition strategy.

In consequence, shares for acquisitions in closer accordance with national legal systems are mainly procured through utilising authorised capital. Periodically, the board of directors can be empowered through the Articles of Association for at most five years after registering the stock corporation to increase the basic capital up to a nominal amount by issuing new shares against contributions. The same can, of course, also take place by means of a change to the Articles of Association later on. In contrast to the capital increase against contributions and the conditional capital increase, the management board can already procure its share currency long before a transaction – have it in stock, so to say – without designating a definite transaction proceeding. The management board then decides, inasmuch as the empowerment does not contain any particular stipulations, on the content of the share rights and the terms of the issue of shares. The decision of the management board as a rule requires the consent of the supervisory board. In the event of the use of authorised capital, the board of directors thus needs only to obtain the consent of the supervisory board and can, in this way, react quickly and flexibly to the situation in the M&A market.

In the case of takeovers and mergers of companies, the capital increase takes place against contributions in kind. These consist of partnership interests in the target company that are contributed to the company to be taken over. With the entering of the capital increase in the Commercial Register, the new shares are created that the partners of the target company receive as counter-payment for the contribution of their partnership shares.

The prerequisite for the issue of the newly created shares is the exclusion of the subscription right of the shareholders of the company that is taking over. Basically every shareholder has a subscription right to the new shares corresponding to his previous shareholding ratio. Only an exclusion of this subscription right renders the use of the shares as acquisition currency possible, since otherwise the newly acquired shares cannot be transferred to the partner to the transaction. In principle, an exclusion of subscription right can be carried out in the following way within the scope of the authorized capital:

(1) Exclusion of subscription right through the decision of the shareholders' meeting
(2) The decision of the board of directors.

If the aforementioned resolutions and the consent have taken place, for implementation of the capital increase subscription of the new shares by the seller is required, as well as an examination of the value of the contribution in kind.

The seller or shareholder of the target company receives as counter-payment for the transfer of his shares, the shares in the acquiring company. He would like to be regularly assured that he will receive this counter-payment in a proper way. This interest in being assured can be taken into account in that the seller first contributes all his shares in the target company as contribution in kind to the acquiring company. From the seller's point of view, it is advisable to place this contribution under the condition precedent that the increase is actually carried out and with legal effect. Because if for any reason the capital increase should fail, through the condition precedent it is avoided that he has too rashly relinquished his shares in the target company. If and when the capital increase is carried out effectively depends on circumstances mainly to be found in the realm of the acquiring party and is not able to be influenced by the seller or shareholder of the target company. At this point, the resolutions of the board of directors and the supervisory board, as well as the examination of the value of the contribution in kind, should be mentioned. For the seller or shareholder of the target company, it is therefore advisable to agree to effect the entry of the capital increase for procuring the new shares himself. For this, all necessary original documents for the capital increase signed by the relevant bodies of the acquiring party have to be handed over to him by the acquiring party with which he can then initiate the entry in the Commercial Register.

If the seller insists that the purchase price is made wholly or in part not with shares but in cash, and if the purchaser does not have the necessary cash means, a solution can be found by means of a loan on securities. In this case, the former shareholders of the acquiring company appear first as lenders on securities toward the sellers as borrowers. The lenders assign their already existing shares to the borrowers in order to render them in a position to immediately sell these shares to third parties and convert them into cash, even before the capital increase has been entered in the Commercial Register. In return, the borrowers obligate themselves to transfer (back) to the lenders a corresponding number of new shares that they receive as purchase price after the capital increase. In order to achieve that the proceeds from the sale of the old shares are not paid to the borrowers before the borrowers have transferred the new shares to the lenders, the lenders can, on their part, ensure through an agreement that the sales proceeds from the old shares remain in an escrow account and are not paid out until the procurement and transfer of the new shares to the borrowers has taken place.

To safeguard against loss of value in the case of payment of the purchase price by installment, the instruments of index or escalation clauses are at disposal.

Particular Forms of Agreement

Given gross deviation from performance and counter-performance, a purchase and sale agreement can, according to some national legal systems, be contrary to public policy and void.

The inventory and value of the company can be subject to considerable fluctuations during the period extending from the start of negotiations via the point of conclusion of the sale and purchase agreement until the day of transfer (effective date). Particular significance is thus attached to the determination of the transfer date.

Claims to profit are usually due to the party who is the shareholder at the time of the resolution relating to the distribution of profits, insofar as this is not excluded in the shareholders' agreement. Shares in corporations are thus usually transferred together with the rights relating to profits. Deviations from these agreements are admittedly possible. A loss occurring before the transfer date reduces the assets of the shareholders. The buyer thus has a possibility of claiming a reduction of the purchase price. It is advisable for the parties to the agreement to reach definitive agreement on the claim to payment of the profit.

The transfer of shares in partnerships is, in principle, treated in the same way as the transfer of shares in corporations. However, it can be doubtful whether, and if so, to what extent, further rights and obligations from the partnership beside the capital interest should be transferred – for example, loan accounts, capital reserve accounts or general clearing accounts, voting rights, notification rights, termination rights, rights to profits and the credit resulting from settlements. For this reason, detailed contractual ruling is recommended. In case the partnership participation is transferred only in part it is also justifiable to assume only a proportionate transfer of the rights and obligations. Profits gained up to the date of transfer are, in principle, due to the seller. Losses which arise before the date of transfer can be taken into account by reducing the purchase price. If the time of conclusion of contract and the date of transfer do not coincide, the right of the seller to make cash withdrawals should in any case be contractually regulated for the interim period.

Takeover of Rights and Liabilities from Employment Relations (Transfer of a Business)[2]

Experience in mastering national and international integration tasks within the scope of mergers and takeovers has heightened awareness of the fact that for the success of transactions, not just the so-called 'hard factors' such as, for example, management, organisation, finance and capital expenditure, are decisive but also the so-called 'soft factors' such as, for example, communication and culture of companies (self-image, social structure, working climate) as well as, last but not least, human resources.

The legal framework of the necessary integrative measures that must already be taken into consideration when drafting the transaction agreement offer in Europe above all the provisions in European and national law for safeguarding the rights of the employees. Numerous national legislators in Europe have settled the rights and obligations of the employers and employees in the case of transfer of ownership and implemented the European Directive 77/187 EEC (European Economic Community) of 14 February 1977 on the safeguarding of claims of employees upon the transfer of companies, businesses and parts of businesses into national law. The European Commission modified this directive in part on 29 June 1998 through the European Directive 98/50/EC (both Directives were replaced by the Council Directive 2001/23/EC of the European Union of 12 March 2001, published in the *Official Journal* L 82, 22/03/2001 p. 0016–0020). The primary purpose of this Directive is the protection of employees in case of a change in owner of the company and, in particular, a safeguarding of their claims. The Directive stipulates that the owner of a business or part of a business automatically enters into the rights and obligations of the existing employment relationships. The Directive cannot be applied to all forms of transaction of companies but only to those for which the ownership changes. The employment relations should remain connected to that business or part of a business to which they are to be objectively allocated according to the focus of their activity.

In the case of an asset deal, such a change of ownership is present since the economic assets and liabilities are transferred to the new acquiring party by way of singular succession. Also, with the reorganisation of companies by merger, division and transfer of assets, the Directive is, in principle, applicable. The distinctiveness of the reorganisation consists in the fact that the transition – in contrast to the normal asset deal – takes place by means of universal succession or partial universal succession and not by singular succession. Only with a change of legal form can the protective ruling to the benefit of the employee not be used, as in this case a transition is missing and thus there is no change of ownership.

A share deal, on the other hand, does not comprise a transfer of a business within the meaning of the directive. This is because in a share deal it is not all, or certain, assets and liabilities that are transferred, but the participation as such. At company level there is thus no change in contractual party for the employees and thus no change of owner.

The Council Directive 98/50/EC of 29 June 1998, amending Directive 77/187/ EEC on the approximation of the laws of the member states relating to the safeguarding of employees' rights in the event of transfers of undertakings, businesses or parts of businesses, as published in the *Official Journal* L 201, 17/07/1998, pp. 0088–0092 (replaced by the Council Directive 2001/23/EC of the European Union of 12 March 2001, published in the *Official Journal* L 82, 22/03/2001 p. 0016–0020), is shown below.

THE COUNCIL OF THE EUROPEAN UNION,
Having regard to the Treaty establishing the European Community, and in particular Article 100 thereof,
Having regard to the proposal from the Commission, (1)
Having regard to the opinion of the European Parliament, (2)
Having regard to the opinion of the Economic and Social Committee, (3)
Having regard to the opinion of the Committee of the Regions, (4)

(1) Whereas the Community Charter of the fundamental social rights of workers adopted on 9 December 1989 ('Social Charter') states, in points 7, 17 and 18 in particular that: 'The completion of the internal market must lead to an improvement in the living and working conditions of workers in the European Community. The improvement must cover, where necessary, the development of certain aspects of employment regulations such as procedures for collective redundancies and those regarding bankruptcies. Information, consultation and participation for workers must be developed along appropriate lines, taking account of the practices in force in the various member states. Such information, consultation and participation must be implemented in due time, particularly in connection with restructuring operations in undertakings or in cases of mergers having an impact on the employment of workers';
(2) Whereas Directive 77/187/EEC (5) promotes the harmonization of the relevant national laws ensuring the safeguarding of the rights of employees and requiring transferors and transferees to inform and consult employees' representatives in good time;
(3) Whereas the purpose of this Directive is to amend Directive 77/187/EEC in the light of the impact of the internal market, the legislative tendencies of the Member States with regard to the rescue of undertakings in economic difficulties, the case-law of the Court of Justice of the European Communities. Council Directive 75/129/EEC of 17 February 1975 on the approximation of the laws of the Member States relating to collective redundancies (6) and the legislation already in force in most Member States;
(4) Whereas considerations of legal security and transparency require that the legal concept of transfer be clarified in the light of the case-law of the Court of Justice; whereas such clarification does not alter the scope of Directive 77/187/EEC as interpreted by the Court of Justice;
(5) Whereas those considerations also require an express provision, in the light of the case-law of the Court of Justice, that Directive 77/187/EEC should apply to private and public undertakings carrying out economic activities, whether or not they operate for gain;

(6) Whereas it is necessary to clarify the concept of 'employee' in the light of the case-law of the Court of Justice;

(7) Whereas, with a view to ensuring the survival of insolvent undertakings, Member States should be expressly allowed not to apply Articles 3 and 4 of Directive 77/187/EEC to transfers effected in the framework of liquidation proceedings, and certain derogations from that Directive's general provisions should be permitted in the case of transfers effected in the context of insolvency proceedings;

(8) Whereas such derogations should also be allowed for one Member State which has special procedures to promote the survival of companies declared to be in a state of economic crisis;

(9) Whereas the circumstances in which the function and status of employee representatives are to be preserved should be clarified;

(10) Whereas, in order to ensure equal treatment for similar situations, it is necessary to ensure that the information and consultation requirements laid down in Directive 77/187/EEC are complied with irrespective of whether the decision leading to the transfer is taken by the employer or by an undertaking controlling the employer;

(11) Whereas it is appropriate to clarify that, when Member States adopt measures to ensure that the transferee is informed of all the rights and obligations to be transferred, failure to provide that information is not to affect the transfer of the rights and obligations concerned;

(12) Whereas it is necessary to clarify the circumstances in which employees must be informed where there are no employee representatives;

(13) Whereas the Social Charter recognizes the importance of the fight against all forms of discrimination, especially based on sex, color, race, opinion and creed,

HAS ADOPTED THIS DIRECTIVE:

Article 1 (of the Council Directive 98/50/EC of 29 June 1998)
Directive 77/187/EEC is hereby amended as follows:

1. the title shall be replaced by the following:

'Council Directive 77/187/EEC of 14 February 1977 on the approximation of the laws of the Member States relating to the safeguarding of employees' rights in the event of transfers of undertakings, businesses or parts of undertakings or businesses';

2. Articles 1 to 7 shall be replaced by the following:

SECTION I

Scope and Definitions

Article 1

1. (a) This Directive shall apply to any transfer of an undertaking, business, or part of an undertaking or business to another employer as a result of a legal transfer or merger.

(b) Subject to subparagraph (a) and the following provisions of this Article, there is a transfer within the meaning of this Directive where there is a transfer of an economic entity which retains its identity, meaning an organized grouping of resources which has the objective of pursuing an economic activity, whether or not that activity is central or ancillary.
(c) This Directive shall apply to public and private undertakings engaged in economic activities whether or not they are operating for gain. An administrative reorganization of public administrative authorities, or the transfer of administrative functions between public administrative authorities, is not a transfer within the meaning of this Directive.

2. This Directive shall apply where and insofar as the undertaking, business or part of the undertaking or business to be transferred is situated within the territorial scope of the Treaty.
3. This Directive shall not apply to sea-going vessels.

Article 2

1. For the purposes of this Directive:
   (a) 'transferor' shall mean any natural or legal person who, by reason of a transfer within the meaning of Article 1(1), ceases to be the employer in respect of the undertaking, business or part of the undertaking or business;
   (b) 'transferee' shall mean any natural or legal person who, by reason of a transfer within the meaning of Article 1(1), becomes the employer in respect of the undertaking, business or part of the undertaking or business;
   (c) 'representatives of employees' and related expressions shall mean the representatives of the employees provided for by the laws or practices of the Member States;
   (d) 'employee' shall mean any person who, in the Member State concerned, is protected as an employee under national employment law.
2. This Directive shall be without prejudice to national law as regards the definition of contract of employment or employment relationship.

   However, Member States shall not exclude from the scope of this Directive contracts of employment or employment relationships solely because:
   (a) of the number of working hours performed or to be performed,
   (b) they are employment relationships governed by a fixed-duration contract of employment within the meaning of Article 1(1) of Council Directive 91/383/EEC of 25 June 1991 supplementing the measures to encourage improvements in the safety and health at work of workers with a fixed-duration employment relationship or a temporary employment relationship (*), or
   (c) they are temporary employment relationships within the meaning of Article 1(2) of Directive 91/383/EEC, and the undertaking, business or part of the undertaking or business transferred is, or is part of, the temporary employment business which is the employer.

SECTION II

Safeguarding of Employees' Rights

Article 3

1. The transferor's rights and obligations arising from a contract of employment or from an employment relationship existing on the date of a transfer shall, by reason of such transfer, be transferred to the transferee.

   Member States may provide that, after the date of transfer, the transferor and the transferee shall be jointly and severally liable in respect of obligations which arose before the date of transfer from a contract of employment or an employment relationship existing on the date of the transfer.
2. Member States may adopt appropriate measures to ensure that the transferor notifies the transferee of all the rights and obligations which will be transferred to the transferee under this Article, so far as those rights and obligations are or ought to have been known to the transferor at the time of the transfer. A failure by the transferor to notify the transferee of any such right or obligation shall not affect the transfer of that right or obligation and the rights of any employees against the transferee and/or transferor in respect of that right or obligation.
3. Following the transfer, the transferee shall continue to observe the terms and conditions agreed in any collective agreement on the same terms applicable to the transferor under that agreement, until the date of termination or expiry of the collective agreement or the entry into force or application of another collective agreement.

   Member States may limit the period for observing such terms and conditions with the proviso that it shall not be less than one year.
4. (a) Unless Member States provide otherwise, paragraphs 1 and 3 shall not apply in relation to employees' rights to old-age, invalidity or survivors' benefits under supplementary company or inter-company pension schemes outside the statutory social security schemes in Member States.

   (b) Even where they do not provide in accordance with subparagraph (a) that paragraphs 1 and 3 apply in relation to such rights, Member States shall adopt the measures necessary to protect the interests of employees and of persons no longer employed in the transferor's business at the time of the transfer in respect of rights conferring on them immediate or prospective entitlement to old age benefits, including survivors' benefits, under supplementary schemes referred to in subparagraph (a).

Article 4

1. The transfer of the undertaking, business or part of the undertaking or business shall not in itself constitute grounds for dismissal by the transferor or the transferee. This provision shall not stand in the way of dismissals that may take place for economic, technical or organizational reasons entailing changes in the workforce.

Member States may provide that the first subparagraph shall not apply to certain specific categories of employees who are not covered by the laws or practice of the Member States in respect of protection against dismissal.

2. If the contract of employment or the employment relationship is terminated because the transfer involves a substantial change in working conditions to the detriment of the employee, the employer shall be regarded as having been responsible for termination of the contract of employment or of the employment relationship.

Article 4a

1. Unless Member States provide otherwise, Articles 3 and 4 shall not apply to any transfer of an undertaking, business or part of an undertaking or business where the transferor is the subject of bankruptcy proceedings or any analogous insolvency proceedings which have been instituted with a view to the liquidation of the assets of the transferor and are under the supervision of a competent public authority (which may be an insolvency practitioner authorized by a competent public authority).
2. Where Articles 3 and 4 apply to a transfer during insolvency proceedings which have been opened in relation to a transferor (whether or not those proceedings have been instituted with a view to the liquidation of the assets of the transferor) and provided that such proceedings are under the supervision of a competent public authority (which may be an insolvency practitioner determined by national law) a Member State may provide that:
   (a) notwithstanding Article 3(1), the transferor's debts arising from any contracts of employment or employment relationships and payable before the transfer or before the opening of the insolvency proceedings shall not be transferred to the transferee, provided that such proceedings give rise, under the law of that Member State, to protection at least equivalent to that provided for in situations covered by Council Directive 80/987/EEC of 20 October 1980 on the approximation of the laws of the Member States relating to the protection of employees in the event of the insolvency of their employer (**);

   and, or alternatively, that

   (b) the transferee, transferor, or person or persons exercising the transferor's functions, on the one hand, and the representatives of the employees on the other hand may agree alterations, insofar as current law or practice permits, to the employees' terms and conditions of employment designed to safeguard employment opportunities by ensuring the survival of the undertaking, business or part of the undertaking or business.
3. A Member State may apply paragraph 2(b) to any transfers where the transferor is in a situation of serious economic crisis, as defined by national law, provided that the situation is declared by a competent public authority and open to judicial supervision, on condition that such provisions already exist in national law by 17 July 1998.

The Commission shall present a report on the effects of this provision before 17 July 2003 and shall submit any appropriate proposals to the Council.

4. Member States shall take appropriate measures with a view to preventing misuse of insolvency proceedings in such a way as to deprive employees of the rights provided for in this Directive.

Article 5

1. If the undertaking, business or part of an undertaking or business preserves its autonomy, the status and function of the representatives or of the representation of the employees affected by the transfer shall be preserved on the same terms and subject to the same conditions as existed before the date of the transfer by virtue of law, regulation, administrative provision or agreement, provided that the conditions necessary for the constitution of the employees' representation are fulfilled.

   The first subparagraph shall not apply if, under the laws, regulations, administrative provisions or practice in the Member States, or by agreement with the representatives of the employees, the conditions necessary for the reappointment of the representatives of the employees or for the reconstitution of the representation of the employees are fulfilled.

   Where the transferor is the subject of bankruptcy proceedings or any analogous insolvency proceedings which have been instituted with a view to the liquidation of the assets of the transferor and are under the supervision of a competent public authority (which may be an insolvency practitioner authorized by a competent public authority), Member States may take the necessary measures to ensure that the transferred employees are properly represented until the new election or designation of representatives of the employees.

   If the undertaking, business or part of an undertaking or business does not preserve its autonomy, the Member States shall take the necessary measures to ensure that the employees transferred who were represented before the transfer continue to be properly represented during the period necessary for the reconstitution or reappointment of the representation of employees in accordance with national law or practice.

2. If the term of office of the representatives of the employees affected by the transfer expires as a result of the transfer, the representatives shall continue to enjoy the protection provided by the laws, regulations, administrative provisions or practice of the Member States.

SECTION III

Information and Consultation

Article 6

1. The transferor and transferee shall be required to inform the representatives of their respective employees affected by the transfer of the following:

- the date or proposed date of the transfer,
- the reasons for the transfer,
- the legal, economic and social implications of the transfer for the employees,
- any measures envisaged in relation to the employees.

The transferor must give such information to the representatives of his employees in good time before the transfer is carried out.

The transferee must give such information to the representatives of his employees in good time, and in any event before his employees are directly affected by the transfer as regards their conditions of work and employment.

2. Where the transferor or the transferee envisages measures in relation to his employees, he shall consult the representatives of his employees in good time on such measures with a view to reaching an agreement.
3. Member States whose laws, regulations or administrative provisions provide that representatives of the employees may have recourse to an arbitration board to obtain a decision on the measures to be taken in relation to employees may limit the obligations laid down in paragraphs 1 and 2 to cases where the transfer carried out gives rise to a change in the business likely to entail serious disadvantages for a considerable number of the employees.

   The information and consultations shall cover at least the measures envisaged in relation to the employees.

   The information must be provided and consultations taken place in good time before the change in the business as referred to in the first subparagraph is effected.
4. The obligations laid down in this Article shall apply irrespective of whether the decision resulting in the transfer is taken by the employer or an undertaking controlling the employer.

   In considering alleged breaches of the information and consultation requirements laid down by this Directive, the argument that such a breach occurred because the information was not provided by an undertaking controlling the employer shall not be accepted as an excuse.
5. Member States may limit the obligations laid down in paragraphs 1, 2 and 3 to undertakings or businesses which, in terms of the number of employees, meet the conditions for the election or nomination of a collegiate body representing the employees.
6. Member States shall provide that, where there are no representatives of the employees in an undertaking or business through no fault of their own, the employees concerned must be informed in advance of:

- the date or proposed date of the transfer,
- the reason for the transfer,
- the legal, economic and social implications of the transfer for the employees,
- any measures envisaged in relation to the employees.

SECTION IV

Final Provisions

Article 7

This Directive shall not affect the right of Member States to apply or introduce laws, regulations or administrative provisions which are more favorable to employees or to promote or permit collective agreements or agreements between social partners more favorable to employees.

Article 7a

Member States shall introduce into their national legal systems such measures as are necessary to enable all employees and representatives of employees who consider themselves wronged by failure to comply with the obligations arising from this Directive to pursue their claims by judicial process after possible recourse to other competent authorities.

Article 7b

The Commission shall submit to the Council an analysis of the effects of the provisions of this Directive before 17 July 2006. It shall propose any amendment which may seem necessary.

(*) *OJ L* 206, 29. 7. 1991, p. 19.

(**) *OJ L* 283, 20. 10. 1980, p. 23. Directive as amended by Directive 87/164/EEC (*OJ L* 66, 11. 3. 1987, p. 11).

Article 2 (of the Council Directive 98/50/EC of 29 June 1998)

1. Member States shall bring into force the laws, regulations and administrative provisions necessary to comply with this Directive by 17 July 2001 at the latest or shall ensure that, by that date, at the latest, the employers' and employees' representatives have introduced the required provisions by means of agreement, Member States being obliged to take the necessary steps enabling them at all times to guarantee the results imposed by this Directive.
2. When Member States adopt the measures referred to in paragraph 1, they shall contain a reference to this Directive or shall be accompanied by such reference on the occasion on their official publication. The methods of making such reference shall be laid down by Member States.

   Member States shall inform the Commission immediately of the measures they take to implement this Directive.

Article 3 (of the Council Directive 98/50/EC of 29 June 1998)

This Directive shall enter into force on the day of its publication in the Official Journal of the European Communities.

Article 4 (of the Council Directive 98/50/EC of 29 June 1998)

This Directive is addressed to the Member States.

Done at Luxembourg, 29 June 1998.
For the Council
The President
R. COOK

(1) *OJ* C 274, 1. 10. 1994, p. 10.
(2) *OJ* C 33, 3. 2. 1997, p. 81.
(3) *OJ* C 133, 31. 5. 1995, p. 13.
(4) *OJ* C 100, 2. 4. 1996, p. 25.
(5) *OJ* L 61, 5. 3. 1977, p. 26.
(6) *OJ* L 48, 22. 2. 1975, p. 29. Directive as amended by Directive 92/56/EEC (*OJ* L 245, 26. 8. 1992, p. 3).

The prerequisites for the transfer of an undertaking, business or part of an undertaking or business

According to this Council Directive 98/50/EC of the European Union of 29 June 1998 in every case of an asset deal or the reorganisation of an company, it must be checked whether the factual prerequisites of a transfer of an undertaking, business, or part of an undertaking or business have been complied with.

The prerequisite is that an undertaking, business or part of an undertaking or business is transferred to another owner. If a business or part of a business is not the subject matter of the transfer operation, a purchase of rights and assets is present that has no impact on employment relationships.

The definition of a transfer of an undertaking, business, or part of an undertaking or business

The Council Directive 98/50/EC of the European Union of 29 June 1998 now contains a legal definition of a transfer of an undertaking, business, or part of an undertaking.

According to the amended Article 1 (1) of the Council Directive 77/187/EEC of 14 February 1977 this Directive shall apply to any transfer of an undertaking, business, or part of an undertaking or business to another employer as a result of a legal transfer or merger, if there is a transfer of an economic entity which retains its identity, meaning an organised grouping of resources which has the objective of pursuing an economic activity, whether or not that activity is central or ancillary.

This definition is closely based on the decisions of the European Court of Justice (ECJ) on the business concept. According to this, for the existence of a transfer of a business it is of significance whether an economic entity, while retaining its identity, is transferred to a new owner in such a way that it can actually be managed or operated by the new owner with the same or similar business operations. For the assumption of a transfer of a business, therefore, according to the opinion of the ECJ, a transfer of operational means is not necessary if the substantive essentials of an economic entity is nevertheless transferred while retaining its identity.

On the question as to which factors are essential for determining the identity, the characteristics of the businesses have to be taken into account. Accordingly for production operations the – mobile – operating resources such as machines and equipment can be essential. For commercial and service operations for which the operating assets mainly consist of legal and contractual relations, in contrast, it is primarily the immaterial assets which are essential – e.g. industrial property rights, business documents, customer lists, supply and delivery agreements with third parties, the know-how and goodwill, i.e. the launch of the company on the market.

If only particular functions or areas of competence are transferred to a third party by so-called outsourcing, without it constituting a transfer of the economic entity to a new owner while retaining its identity, no business transfer is present.

Also the question of whether the main workforce – i.e. a significant part of the personnel in terms of number and expertise – is assumed or not can have particular importance for determining whether a business transfer has taken place, according to the ruling of the ECJ. Assuming personnel is only indicative of a business transfer when considering other matters with equal regard. Thus, especially in branches in which human labour is of particular importance, employees who are bound together by their activities on a long-term basis can represent an economic operational entity. This is in particular the case if the employees assumed include those with considerable operational know-how or members of management, and the assumption of these employees is of major importance for the continuation of the business.

Considering the current ruling of the ECJ, the following indications are thus to be observed when deciding whether an economic entity has been transferred to the new owner while retaining its identity:

- The transfer of material operating resources such as buildings, production means, machines, stock materials, etc.
- The assumption of the established clientele or the provision of access to the customer market
- Transfer of patent and user rights, know-how and goodwill
- Taking over existing agreements
- The value of the intangible assets
- Assuming the main workforce – i.e. a group of employees of considerable importance in terms of number and expertise and bound in an economic unit by a common activity
- Continuation of a business under the same trade name
- the degree of similarity between the activities before and after the transfer.

Transfer to another employer as a result of a legal transfer or merger

The criterion of a transfer to another employer as a result of a legal transfer or merger is merely a question of definition compared to cases in which the transfer is based on law (legal succession) or sovereign act (allocation of land and appurtenances in forced sale). Every legal transfer is sufficient that leads to a transfer of organisational and managerial power via the business in question to a new owner. Examples are purchase, rent, lease, donation, usufruct, partnership agreement and agreement under public law.

Time of the transfer

For the time of the transfer, it is not a question of when the relevant agreements are concluded or the working funds transferred. The decisive time is when the acquirer is in a position to exercise organisational and managerial power. If the transfer depends on the consent of the creditors or banks, this prerequisite is fulfilled if the consent is granted. In the case of a graduated take-over, it depends on when the significant working funds necessary for continuation of operation were transferred.

Transition of the Individual Rights and Liabilities According to Employment Contracts and Industrial Law; Right of Objection

The amended Article 3 of the Council Directive 77/187/EEC of 14 February 1977 stipulates that the transferor's rights and obligations arising from a contract of employment or from an employment relationship existing on the date of a transfer shall, by reason of such transfer, be transferred to the transferee. The Member States may provide that, after the date of transfer, the transferor and the transferee shall be jointly and severally liable in respect of obligations which arose before the date of transfer from a contract of employment or an employment relationship existing on the date of the transfer.

Following the transfer, according to the amended Article 3(3) the transferee shall continue to observe the terms and conditions agreed in any collective agreement on the same terms applicable to the transferor under that agreement, until the date of termination or expiry of the collective agreement or the entry into force or application of another collective agreement.

Member States may limit the period for observing such terms and conditions with the proviso that it shall not be less than one year.

The transfer of the rights and liabilities is not dependent on the consent of the acquirer or the employee. The legal consequences can thus not be severed to the detriment of the employee. This also applies for agreements with the employee himself.

However, the employee is granted a right of objection that basically must be exercised within a number of weeks as of when the notification of the transfer of ownership is made. The timely objection results in the employment relationship not being transferred to the new owner but remaining with the former owner of the business. As a rule, in such a situation a notice of dismissal for operational reasons is justified since the workplace has ceased.

Protection of All 'Employees'

According to the amended Article 2 (1) of the Council Directive 77/187/EEC of 14 February 1977 all 'employees' are protected. 'Employee' shall mean any person who, in the member state concerned, is protected as an employee under national employment law. This Directive shall be without prejudice to national law as regards the definition of contract of employment or employment relationship.

However, member states shall not exclude from the scope of this Directive contracts of employment or employment relationships solely because:

(a) of the number of working hours performed or to be performed,
(b) they are employment relationships governed by a fixed-duration contract of employment within the meaning of Article 1(1) of Council Directive 91/383/EEC of 25 June 1991 supplementing the measures to encourage improvements in the safety and health at work of workers with a fixed-duration employment relationship or a temporary employment relationship, or
(c) they are temporary employment relationships within the meaning of Article 1(2) of Directive 91/383/EEC, and the undertaking, business or part of the undertaking or business transferred is, or is part of, the temporary employment business which is the employer.

In principle all employees – i.e. white-collar workers, blue-collar workers, trainees and also the executive staff – are thus covered.

If a part of a business is transferred, it depends on whether the focal point of the employee's work was in the part of the business that has been transferred. Members of the executive body are not employees. Their employment contracts are thus not transferred to the new owner. The same applies for employees that have already left the company at the time of transfer.

Although according to the amended Article 3(1) of the Council Directive 77/187/EEC of 14 February 1977 the transferor's rights and obligations arising from a contract of employment or from an employment relationship existing on the date of a transfer, by reason of such transfer, are transferred to the transferee, according to the amended Article 4 (a) paragraphs 1 and 3 shall not apply in relation to employees' rights to old-age, invalidity or survivors' benefits under supplementary company or inter-company pension schemes outside the statutory social security schemes in member states, unless member states provide otherwise. Even where they do not provide in accordance with Article 4 subparagraph (a) that paragraphs 1 and 3 apply in relation to such rights, according to Article 4 (a) member states shall adopt the measures necessary to protect the interests of employees and of persons no longer employed in the transferor's business at the time of the transfer in respect of rights conferring on them immediate or prospective entitlement to old age benefits, including survivors' benefits, under supplementary schemes referred to in subparagraph (a).

Closure of a Business

The assumption of a business transfer and a closure mutually exclude each other.

A closure requires the serious and final decision to discontinue the business and production operations for a significant period of time in economic terms. If the business soon becomes operational again, there is no factual presumption of the intention of closure. In this case, the rights of the employees continue to be protected.

Given a considerable geographical relocation of the business (and not a business transfer) a closure is then assumed if the old business organisational entity is factually and lawfully dissolved and the business is carried on at the new location with an essentially new workforce. Frequently, however, this will materialise only after the fact, once it is clear how many employees will be relocating to the new site.

Information and consultation

According to the amended Article 6 of the Council Directive 77/187/EEC of 14 February 1977 (see pp. 82–3) the transferor and transferee shall be required to inform the representatives of their respective employees affected by the transfer of the following:

- the date or proposed date of the transfer,
- the reasons for the transfer,
- the legal, economic and social implications of the transfer for the employees,
- any measures envisaged in relation to the employees.

The transferor must give such information to the representatives of his employees in good time before the transfer is carried out. The transferee must give such information to the representatives of his employees in good time, and in any event before his employees are directly affected by the transfer as regards their conditions of work and employment. Where the transferor or the transferee envisages measures in relation to his employees, he shall consult the representatives of his employees in good time on such measures with a view to reaching an agreement. Member States whose laws, regulations or administrative provisions provide that representatives of the employees may have recourse to an arbitration board to obtain a decision on the measures to be taken in relation to employees may limit the obligations to cases where the transfer carried out gives rise to a change in the business likely to entail serious disadvantages for a considerable number of the employees.

The information and consultations shall cover at least the measures envisaged in relation to the employees. The information must be provided and consultations taken place in good time before the change in the business as referred to above is effected.

Dismissal by the Transferor or the Transferee

According to the amended Article 4 (1) of the Council Directive 77/187/EEC of 14 February 1977 the transfer of the undertaking, business or part of the undertaking or business shall not in itself constitute grounds for dismissal by the transferor or the transferee. This provision shall not stand in the way of dismissals that may take place for economic, technical or organisational reasons entailing changes in the workforce. Member States may provide that this shall not apply to certain specific categories of employees who are not covered by the laws or practice of the member states in respect of protection against dismissal.

If the contract of employment or the employment relationship is terminated because the transfer involves a substantial change in working conditions to the detriment of the employee, according to the amended Article 4(2) the employer shall be regarded as having been responsible for termination of the contract of employment or of the employment relationship.

The Warranty and Liability System

Elation over the merger, rash behaviour, inattentiveness and insufficient control set by the transaction agreement can quickly turn a successful-seeming transaction into a nightmare.

Largely unnoticed by the public and the press, former contractual partners end up tangled in possibly lengthy and costly partisan disputes under due process of the law or with national or international courts of arbitration. At the forefront of these disputes are issues such as non-fulfilment of individual obligations and poor or delayed performance by a contractual party. Quite often the parties to the contract argue over the fact that false information about significant aspects of a company was given or necessary explanations or advice was not given – such as, for example, information about the turnover and earnings of the target company. In such situations not only the seller is liable, possibly also the managers of the company selling and perhaps even the managers of the company being sold may be held personally liable if they have reprehensibly breached their duties to inform.

General Information on Warranty and Liability Law

The rules of warranty and liability law belong to the most difficult and controversial legal questions in relation to M&A.

Already during the negotiation process and the drafting of the transaction agreement the parties to the contract must consider whether the warranty and liability law of national legal systems offers them sufficient control mechanisms or whether they must reach additional agreements in order to reach an adequate balance of opposing interests in conflict situations.

This is particularly significant in regards to the rescission given to the seller upon mistakes by the company or absence of warranted features, seeing that the transferring back of the company, in particular following integration or implementation, is in many ways not in the interest of those involved owing to its ongoing changes and developments. The applicability of the legal liability for material defects can lead to problems, because the liability consequences intended for a material defect, such as:

- Rescission of the purchase through the return of the purchase item in exchange for the return of the consideration
- Lowering of the purchase price
- Indemnity
- Avoidance of the purchase and sale agreement

often do not match the specific requirements of a purchase of the company.

Owing to the seller's desire for a contractual limitation of his warranty and guarantee liability, the opposing interests in the negotiation process regularly clash heavily. An extensive warranty exclusion benefiting the purchaser can be acceptable to the seller if company relations are transparent and orderly enough. With complicated and unclear company relations, for his protection the purchaser needs, in contrast, a contractual warranty and guarantee liability of the seller that is as extensive as possible and that in the end reflects the results of the due diligence examinations.

The content of the guarantee agreement can be expanded or moderated through a guarantee of completeness by the seller that before the closing of the purchase and sale agreement he provided the purchaser all business documents for careful examination by a thorough, open due diligence process; moreover, the seller guarantees that no further business relations, business obligations or other substantial circumstances exist.

The comprehensive compendium of contractual guarantees, as has become the standard for transaction agreements, can, however, lead to the liability not only of the selling company, rather also to the personal liability of the managers of the seller and/or – for a share deal – of the managers of the target company.

It is part of the expected responsibility and due diligence of a good manager not to accept a contractual guarantee without an internal audit. Should a manager breach this duty and assume contractual guarantees 'at random', then, if necessary, he is liable to his company to pay for the resulting damages – i.e. he must exempt the seller from the buyer's claims stemming from the breach of the guarantees. The managers of the target company are, within the framework of a share deal, regularly commissioned to conduct such an examination of the negotiated guarantees before the closing of the contract. Given an insufficient audit, this can lead to the seller's claims for damages against the target company and can establish the personal liability of the managers. In the end a liability of the participating managers comes into consideration also directly against the buyer if the managers stop a particular position of confidentiality with respect to the buyer and also profit personally from the company purchase, as is the case, for example, with the warranty of a so-called 'stay-bonus'. Such an obligation of indemnity of the managers can really only be first established upon consciously false information and can lead to their criminal responsibility.

Therefore it is urgently recommended that the managers of the seller and/or the target company examine thoroughly which contractual guarantees the seller can sensibly assume. In practice it is common to submit to the respective directors of the different company departments compendia of questions regarding these topics, which are then resolved during the development of the contract negotiations up to the execution of the contract. In this way it is also documented in writing that the managers have acted carefully during negotiations and the execution of the company purchase and sale agreement.

Independent Guarantee Commitments

The national requirements about the warranty and liability law on the purchase of the company can be greatly mitigated through the agreement of independent guarantee commitments. The assumption of an independent guarantee commitment requires that the seller, beyond the legal warranty, accepts responsibility for the presence or absence of certain circumstances, and will indemnify the purchaser if a risk develops. Whether an explanation in a purchase and sale agreement contains a guarantee commitment is to be determined by interpretation. Because expressions such as 'warranty' or 'guarantee', also in a notarised document, do not necessarily suggest an independent guarantee, it is recommended that respective provisions in the agreement expressly are identified, as 'guarantee commitment' or 'guarantee agreement' and to insert these separately from the simple warranties in the agreement's text.

A guarantee commitment can refer not only to characteristics within the meaning of the liability for material defects, but also to all present or future conditions. Moreover, it can refer to all sorts of information.

There are many possible kinds of guarantee commitment. Basically, the guarantee compendium organised according to the respective interests of the parties to the contract is a reflection of the due diligence checklist (see p. 65) and therefore does not need to be enumerated here. As a rule the parties to the contract will agree to only such guarantees that are substantial and necessary for an appropriate distribution of risks.

For a performance guarantee the seller takes responsibility for the onset of a certain economic success. Through an instability guarantee he guarantees that a precisely described risk does not have a negative effect for the purchaser. A subcategory of the instability guarantee is the balance sheet guarantee that refers to the correctness of the information on the balance sheet. As a rule only the observance of the principles of proper bookkeeping is promised. Moreover, the guarantee should also include the exercise of accounting and valuation options. Instead of or in addition to balance sheet guarantees the parties to the contract can also incorporate a guarantee concerning shareholders'/stockholders' equity. Through this, the seller promises the presence of a certain amount of shareholders'/stockholders' equity at a certain period of time. The amount of the shareholders'/stockholders' equity is reported in a balance statement. This guarantees, however, only against depreciation. The capability interest above and beyond the pure value interest can therefore possibly be protected by a special holdings/inventory guarantee. Holdings/inventory guarantees can also refer to the type and location of real estate, company facilities, holdings and relations to companies as well as to inventory and personnel status.

Upon execution of the purchase and sale agreement, should a future closing date be agreed upon that occurs only after the closing of the contract, as a rule it is recommended that the purchaser protect the non-existence of liabilities guaranteed by the seller on the signing date also for the time of the transfer, in order to narrow the risk of unfavourable changes. Such a rule for the closing date can be observed, for example, in the form of a contractual guarantee or warranty consent of the seller, by which the seller commits to indemnify the sold company from all liabilities still existing upon the closing date. If the company, despite this sole internal indemnification, still has to fulfil old requirements of third parties, the purchaser can activate a corresponding claim for reimbursement against the seller.

In particular with regard to the balance sheet guarantee, but also regarding all other guarantees, the question arises:

- Whether the seller should accept *unlimited responsibility* for the objective correctness of the guaranteed facts (so-called 'hard guarantee' statements)
- Or whether the whether the seller should only accept *limited responsibility* for the subjective correctness of the guaranteed facts, depending on his personal knowledge (so-called 'soft guarantee' statements).

If the seller's guarantee commitment is restricted to 'according to his knowledge' or 'to the best of his knowledge', for example that certain features of the company exist or do not exist, from the purchaser's perspective the question of the burden of proof should be settled considering that the burden of proof for the seller's knowledge in principle and without a deviating contractual rule rests with the purchaser. If the purchaser would like to avoid this, a reversal in the burden of proof must be incorporated into the agreement so that the seller is liable, given that he proves that he had, in fact, no knowledge of the questionable circumstance.

The legal consequence of an independent guarantee commitment to be agreed upon contractually and also applicable according to the law in numerous legal systems is above all the claim for performance of the purchaser. The seller must create the conditions that would exist if the guarantee commitment had been fulfilled. For a balance sheet guarantee, this means that the conditions must be created that would have existed if from the start the balance sheet had corresponded to the law and the principles of proper bookkeeping. Only if the creation of the guaranteed conditions is not possible does the purchaser have a right to indemnity. Considering that these legal consequences often show themselves not to be feasible and not of great interest, it is recommended that along with the independent guarantees, their legal consequences should be determined in detail. On the whole an independent guarantee, including the contractually determined legal consequences, grants the parties to the contract the opportunity to form the purchase and sale agreement according to their individual interests and needs and to distribute the approximate risks appropriately.

Also in regard to the legal consequences and the level of liability given a breach of the contractual guarantees, following the practice of international contracts, a certain standard materialises. Normally only rights to damages are granted to the purchaser, in particular a rescission – i.e. a reversed transaction and/or return of performances – is excluded. Furthermore, as a rule the level of the liability is contractually limited to a percentage of the purchase price, and individual claims are allowed beyond a minimum level of damages per individual case and on the whole starting only from a certain level of damages.

Last but not least, the limitation period for the individual warranty claims should also be determined in the contractual guarantee agreements in consideration of the respective situation of the party to the contract. These can be configured differently according to the type of guaranteed conditions, for example, for old liabilities and taxes.

The Liability of the Consultant

Consultants to the parties to the contract of a purchase are liable to their contractors fundamentally according to contractual principles from the respective contractual relationship. Under the strict condition of a 'contract with protective effect favouring third parties' the consultant can be liable to a formal non-participant in the contract. Moreover, the liability of the consultant can result from the breach of obligations under public law, if, for example, the obligation under cartel law to notify the merger is breached with fault or negligence during the handling of a merger, that must be notified. These liability principles are also applied in the area of consulting for company purchases.

Legal Responsibility for Old Liabilities

The purchase of a company – depending on the precise formation – has the result that the acquirer enters into the seller's existing legal status at the time of the transition. With the reservation of diverging contractual agreements a liability of the purchaser for the responsibility of the acquired company or an on-going liability of the seller from legal regulations of national legal systems can result.

If the purchase of a company takes place through an asset deal, a liability of the purchaser comes into consideration also for such liabilities of the seller that are not explicitly contractually transferred.

In the case of the purchase of a company through a share deal, the purchaser will become the new holder of the company, including its liabilities to third parties. In this situation more penetrating questions of liability under business law arise, however – when, for example, the current shareholder had not fulfilled his contribution debt or remained obligated from the perspective of the liability for balance. Special legal responsibility for old liabilities with the purchase of private companies or holdings results above all from the acquisition of a limited interest and the purchase of corporations or interests, in particular shares in limited liability corporations (share deal).

Non-Competition Agreements

The agreement on a prohibition against competition can assist the buyer of the enterprise in preventing the seller from endangering the economic profitability of the enterprise after its transfer by unfair competitive practices, in particular by using its know-how, customer relations, etc. elsewhere. In the case of a corporate acquisition, a prohibition of competition already arises for the seller as an (unwritten) auxiliary duty, if such duty to refrain from competition is necessary for the due and proper transfer of the enterprise to the buyer. Depending on the individual circumstances, it may be advisable to include an unambiguous agreement relating to competitive practices, including a concrete description of, for example, the protected know-how, etc. In so doing, a range of statutory provisions must be observed. It must also be realised that a prohibition of competition undertaken by the seller does not have any binding effect on family members or on an associated enterprise, as these are not parties to the competition agreement. In this connection, it is also a problem whether, and if so in how far, the seller must make clear to the buyer that, for example, his wife intends to open a competing enterprise in the near future.

Owing to their primary effect of restricting competition, prohibitions of competition can fall under the prohibition set out in Article 81 I of the Treaty establishing the European Community. According to this provision, all agreements between enterprises, decisions by associations of enterprises and concerted practices which serve to affect trade between member states and have as their object or effect the prevention, restriction or distortion of competition within the common market are incompatible with the common market, prohibited, null and void. A contravention against Article 81 I EC Treaty is deemed to have occurred only if the prohibition against competition, in terms of duration, territorial application or material content, exceeds the measure necessary to achieve the specific purpose of a prohibition of competition, i.e. to ensure the transfer of the enterprise, including the good will associated with the enterprise, the know-how and other immaterial values.

On the basis of its notification regarding collateral agreements to mergers under Regulation 4864/89, the Commission stated that a prohibition of competition is justified by the purpose of the merger if, with respect to its duration, its territorial application and its purpose, it does not exceed the limits of what can reasonably be regarded as necessary. The permissible duration of a prohibition of competition cannot be determined in an abstract sense, as is the case with the permissible extent of territorial and material restrictions. Rather, the permissible duration depends on the competition situation in the individual case. In the case of a corporate acquisition, the Commission has declared a five-year prohibition of competition as permissible if the good will and know-how are transferred with the enterprise. If the transfer only extends to the good will, the Commission has judged a prohibition of merely two years as compatible with Article 81 I EC Treaty.

Of particular practical importance for the contractual agreement on a prohibition of competition with a view to European antitrust law is the possibility provided by EC procedural law of obtaining a negative clearance of the EC Commission for a prohibition of competition. Such negative clearance has the effect that a fine cannot punish an impermissible prohibition on competition.

Restraint on Disposal, Consent and Approval Requirements

Should the company transfer take place effectively and without disruptions, it can be necessary to take third parties' restrictions and rights to participate into account. Such restraints on disposal and consent requirements can result in particular from the legal form of the company to be sold as well as from conditions under public law, labour law, family law, or guardianship law, as well as laws of succession. In company purchase and sale agreements the control of a so-called 'committee proviso' is often necessary.

Further, restrictions under public law are to be taken into account because they can prevent the purchaser of a company from practising the business of the company. The exercise of a trade can be tied to a personal licence of the operator (e.g. to operate a TV or telecommunication company, security company, conduct brokerage activities, building contracting or care activities) or to a relevant authorisation (e.g. of a production facility). In contrast to the personal licence the relevant authorisation issued to the seller can be transferred by the purchase agreement.

National and European Cartel Law

Larger transactions can be subject to national and/or European merger control rules. In addition, an approval of a merger by other national cartel authorities can be required if an international transaction is subject to other ruling laws on merger control. Numerous merger control laws at the national and supranational levels rule that all related agreements and transactions are rendered null and void until the final approval of the cartel authorities. Furthermore, because of the unauthorised execution of transactions which are subject to a reporting requirement before the merger, substantial fines can be ordered against the company as well as against its managers. In order to avoid difficulties with these conditions it is necessary to incorporate a 'merger control clause' into the transaction agreements.

As a result, before the closing or the final execution of the merger each transaction must be carefully examined as to whether it is subject to reporting requirements. Because of the considerable significance of this topic, the remarks in Part 2, Chapter 7, focus on the details of merger controls.

Form of the Contract

The purchase and sale agreement as such requires no particular form to be effective.

A particular form, however, needs to be taken into account according to national rules of law because with the purchase of a company through the purchase of individual assets (asset deal) through individual legal successions (singular succession), a variety of individual assets, rights and obligations, are transferred, whereas with the purchase of a company through an acquisition of interest the company shares are transferred (share deal).

If real estate or inheritance rights belong to the sold company during an asset deal, the purchase and sale agreement, according to national law, frequently requires notarisation. This applies fundamentally to the transaction as a whole and thereby also for these agreements which would not, of themselves, require any form.

For the purchase of a company with real estate through an acquisition of shares (share deal) the real estate itself is not a subject of the agreement so that the agreement does not regularly require notarisation. The obligation to transfer and the transfer of shares to corporations, in particular to prohibit speculative activities with shares and to protect the investor, frequently requires notarisation within the country or in a foreign country.

With the execution of a framework agreement a Directive concerning the form of contract pertaining to one of the individual agreements is also regularly to be complied with in terms of the framework agreement.

In order to spare costs, in practice foreign notarisations are frequently accepted.

Closing

The concept of a closing originates from the Anglo-American contract practice. Predominantly the transfer date marks the closing. Individually it also means the summary description of the legal transactions to take place on this transfer date.

If the company acquisition takes place through an asset deal, i.e. singular succession, the closing includes the transfer of a variety of assets, rights and intangible good-will of the business. Because the company should be transferred as a whole, the time of the transfer in regards to the different components should if possible be combined. The transfer date is frequently postponed until the future. Because of tax and balance sheet technical reasons, the end of the fiscal year can be recommended. However, as an exception, a backdated transfer date can be considered.

Reporting of the Acquisition of Shares in a Corporation

With the acquisition of shares in a corporation it must be taken into account that, according to several national provisions, the purchaser can activate the rights and obligations in respect of the company that are connected to the shares only after the acquisition is reported to the company.

4 The Hostile Takeover

Takeover Regulations

The decision on the question of who holds the shares in a target company lies fundamentally in the legal system of the shareholders and not in the competence of the managers. Nevertheless, transactions take place regularly by way of a friendly takeover, meaning through a certain tacit agreement with the management of the target company. This applies above all also in cases of cooperative transactions which, for example, have the foundation of joint ventures as an object. In contrast, cases exist by which a company attempts to assume the shares of another company against its will or against the will of the management.

In the USA and Great Britain hostile takeovers are not unusual and do not have a negative image. Whereas the US investment bank J. P. Morgan in Continental Europe from 1990 to 1998 registered a total of only 52 hostile takeover attempts with a value of US dollars 69 billion, in 1999 it listed 34 hostile takeover offers with a total value of about US dollars 408 billion: the acquisition of Mannesmann by Vodafone came to US dollars 203 billion alone. In 1999, however, no more hostile takeovers took place; the unwanted purchasers were also more successful than in earlier years. In 54 per cent of all cases they reached their goal; only 25 per cent of the companies assailed succeeded in remaining independent (Figure 4.2).

The bidders must often pay high premiums with an average of 44 per cent. With the increasing premiums the analysts note also the growing success of the hostile takeovers and the availability for sale of almost every company. For the shareholders of the hostile bidders the takeover struggle in contrast ends mostly with

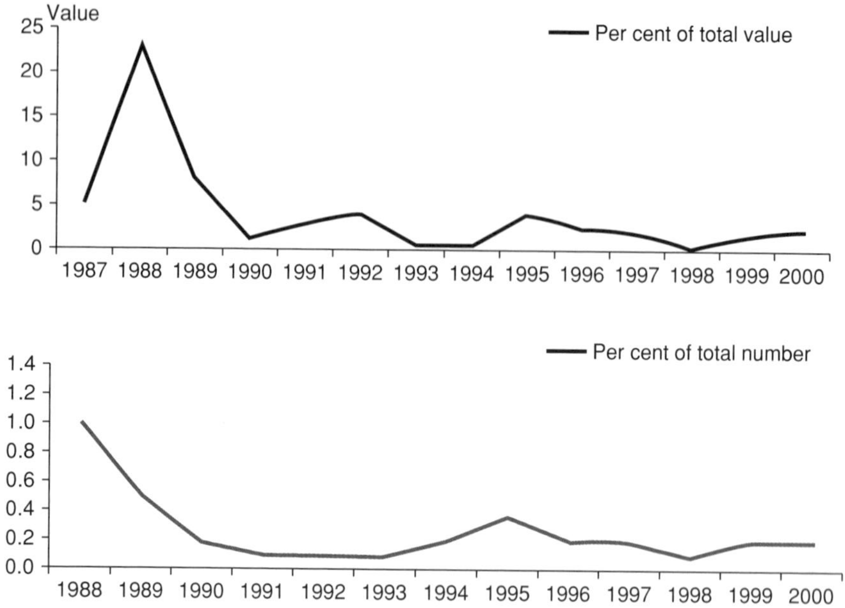

Figure 4.2 Share of hostile takeovers in cross-border M&A, 1987–2000 per cent of total
Note: Defined as deals in which the acquirer is a finance company (buyout firm, venture capital company, merchant bank, commercial bank, etc.), acquiring a target firm whose main activity is non-financial. However, target firms of industrial combinations that are considered as aiming at operational rather than financial objectives are excluded. These involve financial companies with SIC codes as follows: 16, 44, 65, 83, 106, 107, 150, 151, 176, 183, 195, 201, 247, 310, 330, 334, 363, 439, 55 and 8. Furthermore, deals whose target firms engage in information retrieval services are also excluded.
Source: UNCTAD, Cross-border M&A database (based on data from Thomson Financial Securities Data Company).

disappointment. The share price of the aggressor, on the basis of the (too) high purchase price paid, regularly develops much less favourably than the respective market as a whole. The development of the share price of the thirteen companies listed on the stock exchange that conducted a successful hostile takeover in 1999 lay, according to calculations by J. P. Morgan, on average 18 per cent under the performance of the market as a whole.

The target subjects of hostile takeovers are most companies the price development of which could not convince the shareholders. Therefore, ten of the thirteen acquired companies in the two years before the offer developed 23 per cent below the market average.

Anglo-American corporation law on the purchase of the company attempts to protect the shareholders against the results of such a hostile takeover. Correspondingly, the USA as well as Great Britain maintain comprehensive, if differing, takeover rules. In Continental Europe, above all, Austria and Switzerland possess detailed legal takeover regulations. Germany has passed a takeover code (WpÜG) in November 2001 which came into force in January 2002.

The 'City Code on Takeovers and Mergers,' which in 1968 originated as the initiative of the Governor of the Bank of England and Chairman of the London Stock Exchange, reflects the Anglo-Saxon self-understanding of 'fair play' with takeovers and mergers. This does not consist of a material examination, but rather compliance with the 'rules of the game'. Currently 38 rules have been derived from the ten principles of the City Code. The City Code has no legal power, but represents the 'collective opinion of those who are professionally active in the areas of takeovers and mergers'; it has been effectively applied in thousands of cases. The fair and equal treatment of the shareholders stands at the centre. A 60-day time limit applies to the offer. The announcement does not initiate day one, rather the delivery of the takeover documents to the shareholders. During the on-going offer the participating companies the participating companies are subject to a standstill obligation. In order to guarantee the shareholders the possibility of withdrawing, a bidder must make a cash offering to the shareholders, as long as the bidder holds more than 30 per cent of the voting rights of the target company. According to this rule, that has currently been seldom used, the level of the offer must be based on the highest share price of the target company in the previous 12 months.

On the European level, it has been attempted for over 25 years to regulate company takeovers by passing guidelines. For the protection of the shareholders facing the takeover offer, the EU members, at the beginning of March 2000, after numerous drafts of guidelines over previous years and a fundamental agreement in 1999 'in principle' agreed upon a compromise for the guidelines. The final resolution on the draft, however, failed in June 2001.

Techniques of the Hostile Takeover

Different possibilities exist for the aggressor to create a hostile takeover. The potentially most promising possibilities are the so-called 'tender offer' and the so-called 'dawn raid'.

A tender offer concerns a public offer for a takeover to the shareholders of the target company. Provisions exist in numerous legal systems for regulating the tender offer which stipulate the rules for the takeover of companies listed on the Stock Exchange.

In contrast to the tender offer with a dawn raid the aggressor attempts secretly to take control of the target company, in that through the acquisition of larger blocks of shares he changes the minority relationships in his favour. In some countries this course of action is prevented with companies listed on the Stock Exchange because if the voting rights are exceeded by 5 per cent, 10 per cent, 25 per cent, 50 per cent and 75 per cent it is to be reported to the regulatory authority as well as to the target company. Because of this report, however, stock prices usually rise, whereby a takeover is made more difficult. In order to avoid this – and circumvent the Stock Exchange – large financial investors must simultaneously acquire blocks of shares.

Defence Against Hostile Takeovers

The neutrality obligation of the target company's board of directors during the offer time limit means that neither according to the Takeover Code nor according to the guideline recommendation of the Commission can the board of directors develop any kind of defence mechanisms. On the one hand, this is because the Takeover Code and the guideline recommendation of the Commission do not (yet) comprise legally binding rules. Furthermore, in consideration of the Takeover Code numerous possibilities exist, above all in the realm of prevention, to defend against an attempt at a hostile takeover.

The Dual System of the Board of Directors and the Supervisory Board (Two-Tier Board)

In some countries the dual system of a board of directors and a supervisory board builds a natural wall of protection against a hostile takeover. In order to achieve actual control over the company the aggressor must determine the members of the board of directors who, however, are appointed by the supervisory board. The board of directors can be dismissed before the expiration of its period in office only for significant reason. The voting out of a member of the supervisory board, however, is possible only with the agreement of a (qualified) majority of the shareholders. In relation to the usual five-year period in office of a member of a board of directors and a supervisory board this leads to the aggressor requiring possibly numerous years until he achieves control over the business operations of the target company, even though he may have acquired the qualified majority.

Poison Pill

The poison pill is conceivable in many forms. The variant most commonly used in the USA is options, which allow the shareholders of the company to acquire shares well below market price on a takeover attempt.

White Knight

In addition, a capital increase comes into consideration with an exclusion of the shareholders' option within the framework of authorised capital for the purpose of issuing new shares – approximately to an allied company or a so-called 'White Knight'. The active search for a white knight, which comes to the aid of the target company, can, however, in regard to a neutrality obligation of the board of directors also be problematic. If a white knight is found, the takeover can be relieved for him through the issuance of new shares on the basis of capital approved earlier. Simultaneously through the issuance of new shares to a third party it will be made more difficult for the aggressor to gain control over the company because he now has to acquire more shares than before.

Issuance of New Shares

Through the issuance of registered shares instead of bearer shares the board of directors can obtain a better overview of the share structure and in this way possibly recognise a takeover attempt beforehand and implement countermeasures. If the registered shares are issued as transferable only with the issuing company's consent, in addition, the consent of the board of directors is needed for the sale of shares.

Buyback of Self-Owned Shares

The buyback of one's own shares leads to an increase in price of the shares and in this way makes the takeover of a company more difficult. In most countries, however, to defend against a hostile takeover only a certain part of the share capital may be acquired; furthermore, for that a resolution from a shareholders' meeting is required.

Additional Purchase of Other Companies

Short-term additional purchases of other companies through the target company can also make a takeover difficult in that as a result of the additional purchase, authorisations for the takeover are excluded under cartel law. However, it appears questionable whether this strategy complies with a neutrality obligation of the board of directors.

'Crown Jewels'

A particularly risky measure of defence is the sale of one or more of the most lucrative divisions of the company ('Crown Jewels') that the aggressor had possibly particularly coveted. This can work out as extraordinarily detrimental because the survivability of the company will possibly be endangered. In addition, this strategy cannot be tied to a neutrality obligation of the board of directors and in an individual case regularly requires the permission of the shareholders' meeting.

'Pac Man'

With 'Pac Man' the target company attempts to win over the aggressor. This is permissible in some countries, however, only if the share of the aggressor in the target company does not exceed a certain total because otherwise the implementation of the takeover is prohibited.

5 Mergers

With the preparation and implementation of M&A as well as with the merger of combined business units it is a matter under corporation law (above all, within the framework of the set business goal), to best configure, adapt or support on the one hand the existing realm of public political order (questions of legal form) and on the other the balanced interests of the shareholders (internal rules among the shareholders). The measures under corporate law thereby concern mostly questions of:

- The assumption of new shareholders
- The change of the capital with corporations (which can also lead to the assumption of new shareholders)

- The establishment of a partnership or corporation
- All forms of conversion, such as
  - merger
  - splitting
  - transfer of assets
  - change in form.

In practice, aside from the conversion possibilities the traditional instruments of restructuring a company (contribution of companies, capital increases as well as the change in the partnership structure by calling upon the principle of accrual) are significant.

Types of Conversion

As types of 'conversion' a number of national legal systems contain, in particular, rules for mergers, splitting, the transfer of assets and the change in legal form. The same applies to the determination as to whether the company is to be seen as capable of being converted.

Merger

During a merger, the business of one or more companies are transferred as a whole to a new or already existing legal entity for which shares in this legal entity are again granted to the owners of the transferred company. In the member countries of the EU the European guidelines are to be taken into account.

In some European countries direct cross-border mergers of companies are not allowed according to the so-called 'Theory of principal place of business' because currently only the companies existing in the legal form of the national law can be merged. In order to overcome these and other obstacles of national legal systems, European law has pushed for a harmonisation of the national company and corporation laws as well as for the creation of a supranational company form.

Since the establishment of the European Business Community (EBC) experts have been working on the creation of a European private company and a European corporation, with no success as of yet, if one disregards the 'European Business Interests Association' (EBIA), which is rather meaningless in terms of legal practicality. The main difficulty for the development of such European company forms exists above all in the fact that the participation rights of the employees in the member states of the EU are extremely non-uniform.

The recommendation has therefore been made to open the European private company, if necessary only for companies with fewer than 500 employees, in order to avoid co-determination problems. This starting point makes sense because more than 99 per cent of European companies employ fewer than 500 employees.

Practical experience therefore compels one to create own models, in order to permit mergers of global enterprises. Those national legal systems are thereby served that offer complex transactions the greatest possible freedom of formation.

An example is the 'Business Combination Agreement' of DaimlerChrysler that can serve as a model for further supranational company mergers. Although this core agreement of the merger in many aspects relies on German law for measures it takes under corporate law, the parties to the contract were put under the control of the more flexible law of the US state of Delaware.

Splitting

Splitting processes have always been possible through certain other legal constructions, in particular through the transfer of individual rights. The conversion laws of some national legal systems open up the additional possibility of splitting through universal succession. It is therefore important to distinguish between:

- Split-up
- Split-off
- Spin-off.

With a *split-up*, the legal entity liquidates without a settlement in that through a special succession, it divides its entire business to some other legal entities (at least two); for this, the shareholders of the transferring legal entity are granted shares in the acquiring (possibly new) company, as with a merger. A legal entity (transferring entity) can thus split up its business without a liquidation:

1. For the assumption, through simultaneous transfer of parts of the business, respectively, as an entirety, to other existing legal entities (assuming entities) or
2. For the new establishment, through simultaneous transfer of parts of the business, respectively, as an entirety, to other, newly established legal entities in exchange for the granting of shares or membership in these legal entities to the shareholders of the transferring entity.

With a *split-off*, a legal entity transfers only a part or parts of its business so that it remains existent. For the transfer of part of the business, generally one or more operations, the holders of the transferring entity are again granted shares in the assuming entity. With the split-up the company that transfers its assets is liquidated. With the split-off and the spin-off, in contrast, the company remains along with the receiving company. Correspondingly, a legal entity (transferring entity), upon the split-off of its assets, can split off one or more parts:

1. For the assumption, through the transfer of this part or these parts, respectively, as an entirety, to one or more existing shareholders (assuming entity) or
2. For the new establishment, through transfer of this part or these parts, respectively, as an entirety to one or more legal entities it has thereby newly established

in exchange for the granting of shares or memberships in this legal entity or these legal entities to the shareholders of the transferring entity.

The *spin-off* also sees to it that only a part or parts of the business are transferred to other legal entities. For this, the shares of the assuming or new company are transferred to the transferring company itself, not to its shareholders. Regarding the consideration for the transfer of a part or parts of the business the spin-off differs from the split-up and split-off in so far as with the spin-off the shares in the entity receiving the part or parts of the business are transferred to the transferring entity itself, in contrast to the split-off and split-up, in which the shares are transferred to the holders of the transferring entity. A legal entity (transferring entity) can, accordingly, spin-off one or more parts of its assets:

1. For the assumption, through transfer of this part or these parts of the business, respectively, as an entirety to one or more existing legal entities (assuming entities) or
2. For the new establishment, through transfer of this part or these parts of the business, respectively, as an entirety to one or more legal entities it has thereby newly established

in exchange for the granting of shares or memberships in this legal entity or legal entities to the transferring entity.

Splitting can also take place through the simultaneous transfer to existing and new legal entities.

The splitting and takeover agreement must, as a rule, contain the following information:

1. The *name* and the *headquarters* (seat) of the legal entity participating in the splitting
2. The *agreement* about the transfer of the part or parts of the business of the transferring entity respectively as an entirety in exchange for the granting of shares or memberships in the assuming entities
3. With the split-up or split-off, the *exchange relationship* of the shares and, if necessary, the amount of the (extra) cash payment or information about the membership at the assuming entities
4. With the split-up or split-off the details for the *transfer of the shares* of the assuming entities or about the acquisition of the membership at the assuming entities
5. The *point in time* from which these shares or the membership grants a right to a *share in the net income for the year* as well as all of the particulars in regards to this right
6. The *point in time* from which the activities of the transferring company are deemed to be undertaken on the account of each of the assuming company (*splitting date*)
7. The *rights* which the receiving companies grant to individual shareholders as well as to the holders of special rights, such as shares without voting rights, preferred shares, plural voting shares, bonds and profit-sharing rights, or the measures intended for these persons

8. Every *special advantage* that is granted to a member of a representative body or a supervisory body of the legal entities participating in the splitting, a managing shareholder, an auditor or a splitting examiner
9. The *exact description and division* of the *objects of the active and passive assets* that are transferred to each of the assuming companies, as well as the part or parts of the transferred business in relation to the receiving companies
10. With the split-up and split-off, the *division of the shares or memberships* of each of the participating legal entities to the shareholders of the transferring entity as well as the standard and parameters for the division
11. The consequences of the splitting for the *employees and their representatives* as well the measures laid out to this effect.

Transfer of Assets

The transfer of assets differs from the merger also through the type of consideration. With an asset transfer, assets as a whole are also transferred to another legal entity by way of a universal succession; however, usually the consideration does not exist in the granting of shares to this legal entity, but rather is provided in another form, in particular in cash.

According to special provisions of the respective legal systems a legal entity (transferring entity) can under liquidation without settlement split up by transferring its assets as an entirety to another existing legal entity (receiving company) or split off a part or parts of its business by transferring the assets as an entirety to another existing legal entity (receiving company) in exchange for a consideration to the shareholders of the transferring company that does not exist in shares or in memberships (complete transfer).

A legal entity (transferring entity) can, according to individual legal systems:

1. Under liquidation without settlement split up its assets by a simultaneous transfer of the parts of the assets respectively as an entirety to other existing legal entities
2. Split off one or more parts of its assets through the transfer of this part or parts, respectively, as an entirety to one or more existing legal entities
3. Spin off one or more parts from its assets through the transfer of this part or parts, respectively, as an entirety to one or more existing legal entities

against the granting of the consideration in cases 1 and 2 to the shareholders of the transferring entity, and in case 3 to the transferring entity (partial transfer).

A complete or partial transfer is, according to individual legal systems, possible to only a limited extent.

The Change in Form

A change in form – other than with the forms of conversion mentioned above – does not pertain to a transfer of assets *per se*; the respective company merely changes its legal form and legal structure but not its identity. In relation to the restructuring of companies after the purchase of a company the change in form from a corporation to a partnership is of particular interest in order to thereby create additional write-off potential through an increase in book value. The cash flow of the acquired company can thereby be raised and thus the financing of the purchase eased.

The change in form is also possible for liquidated legal entities if their continuation in their former legal form can be resolved.

Companies Capable of Conversion

The European Business Interest Association

The European Business Interest Association (EBIA) is a legal vehicle beyond the bounds of national laws that offers a certain (limited) attractiveness for international cooperation.

Some of the advantages of the EBIA are the relatively low costs for formation and administration, the limited registration requirements and the flexibility regarding the rules about the management and business of an EBIA, which can be tailor-made to each cooperative project. However, EBIAs are subject to considerable limitations:

- An EBIA must have members with headquarters in at least two member states of the EU or (now) within the further European Economic Zone (EEZ)
- The purpose of an EBIA must not be for profit
- The activities of an EBIA must be subordinate to the business activities of its members (this means that it may not be active in another area or itself conduct independent business)
- An EBIA cannot employ more than 500 employees
- An individual member of an EBIA cannot hold a voting majority in a company
- Existing members must unanimously approve the acceptance of new members
- The members of an EBIA are jointly and severally liable without limits for their debts and obligations
- A member of an EBIA is liable for debts that were incurred during its membership for a time period of five years following termination of its membership.

The European Stock Corporation

In the world of European economics many hope that a non-country-identified form of a company can develop in the shape of a European Stock Corporation that could serve as an appropriate vehicle for border-crossing European companies or, in relation to joint ventures, as a joint venture vehicle for joint venture partners with headquarters in different European legal systems. These ideas rest on a recommendation of the EU Commission. The goal should be to provide a company vehicle for the cooperation between companies from different member states and thereby contribute in clearing away the national barriers that deter the development of a common market. Moreover the regulatory strategy of the European Stock Corporation is to ease cross-border mergers, consolidation procedures and alliances within the EU. Through the creation of a company form to a great degree independent of the individual national company legal systems, the existing hindrances relating to corporation law, tax and psychological effects should be diminished. The plan aims at creating a new type of company independent of national law, a so-called 'Societas Europaea' or SE.

With the Societas Europaea first of all a legal entity independent from the company legal systems of the nation-states will be available. The European Stock Corporation, however, is often obligated to allow employee representatives onto their supervisory or administrative bodies. This can make the participation of companies with high (national) co-determination levels unattractive. According to a corresponding Resolution of Principle of the state and governmental leaders at the EU summit in Nice on 20 December 2000, the Ministers of Labour and Ministers of Social Welfare agreed on a compromise about the representation and co-determination of the employees in the Societas Europaea. Thus the path is now cleared for the long-discussed provision of a European joint stock corporation as company holder.

The underlying Ordinance Draft about the public law Statute of the European Stock Corporation (VO 14717/00 SOC 500 SE8), as well as the guidelines draft on the representation and joint management of the employees (RL 14791/00 SOC 501 SE9), passed the European legislative proceedings without substantial changes on 8 October, 2001 (Regulation EC 2157/2001). A three-year time limit is assigned for national legal systems to adapt the ordinance and apply the guidelines so that the new legal forms will be available as of 8 October, 2004.

A European Stock Corporation can be created by a merger as well as by the formation of a holding company or subsidiary. Moreover, the possibility of a form-changing conversion of existing companies into a European Stock Corporation is regulated. A condition for each situation is that the companies participating in the establishment or conversion either are subject to the law of different member states or have a branch office or location in another member state.

The Directive contains, along with the directives on the establishment of a European Stock Corporation regulations on its inner structure, its shareholders' meeting, the relocation of its headquarters as well as on the company's termination, liquidation and inability to pay, whereby the member states are given room in numerous places for precise definitions and modifications of the basic models. Incidentally (for example, in regard to the raising and receiving of capital as well as accounting), the European Stock Corporation is subject to the ordinances valid in the country of its headquarters about Stock Corporations within the meaning of the respective relevant national legal system – in Great Britain, for example, the ordinances about public companies limited by shares.

The Directive (2001/86/EC) about the representation and co-determination of the employees in the European Stock Corporation on the one hand contains the establishment of a particular employee representation ('representative body') with informational and consulting rights with regard to the company. Moreover, it regulates the long-disputed participation of employees in 'supervisory' or 'administrative bodies' (in the supervisory board or board of directors) of the company.

As a matter of priority a rule about the precise form of the rights of the representative body of employees as well as the participation of the employees in the supervisory body or the administrative body should – similar to the procedure of creating a European Works Council – be made through agreements. Responsible for the execution of such an agreement are the companies participating in the establishment of the European Stock Corporation as well as a 'special negotiations committee', comprising representatives of the employees of all the companies participating in the establishment. The member states can plan, in this regard, that members of the 'special negotiations committee' can also become external union representatives.

Regarding content, the companies participating in the establishment of the European Stock Corporation and the 'special negotiations committee' enjoy great freedom to design. In the case of the 'representative body' of the employees, the directive simply recognises that such a body is to be established and grants rights to information and hearings. The guidelines entrust negotiating partners with determining the make-up of the representative body, the process of its creation as well as the precise configuration of its rights and obligations. However, the directive clarifies that it is not possible by way of agreements to limit the use of the Employees Representation Acts of the individual countries. Along with the 'representative body' of the employees the European Stock Corporation must therefore allow the formation of further employee representation in member states that have Employees Representation Acts – thus in Germany and Austria, for example, the creation of a works council.

The directive grants a wide range of creative freedom to the 'special negotiations committee' and the companies participating in the formation of the company, and for the co-determination of the employees through representatives in the supervisory or administrative bodies of the European Stock Corporation. They can even agree that the European Stock Corporation does not have to allow any employee representatives into their supervisory or administrative bodies, although this would actually be provided for through the usual conditions of the directive.

The 'representative body' of the employees to the European Stock Corporation is made up of employees of the company, together with those of its subsidiaries. A membership of external union representatives – other than is the case for the special negotiations committee – is not envisaged. The appointment or voting of the members of the representative bodies of employees is incumbent upon the representative bodies of employees already formed under national law – in Germany and Austria, therefore, the works councils existing in the European Stock Corporation and its subsidiaries. In the case of the lack of such employee representation, the members of the employee representation of the European Stock Corporation are chosen from the entirety of employees of this company and its subsidiaries.

The responsibility of the 'representative body' of the employees is not limited to the European Stock Corporation, but extends also to its subsidiaries. Regarding content, the employee representation has the right to be regularly informed about certain subjects and to be heard on these topics. This concerns, in particular, the structure of the company, its economic and financial situation, the potential development of its business, production, and turnover, its employment activities, investments, fundamental changes in the organisation, the introduction of new work or manufacturing processes, relocation of production, mergers, downsizing or closing of companies, businesses or other important parts of these businesses and mass layoffs. The right to information and consultation of the employee representation of the European Stock Corporation thereby exceeds to a considerable degree that of the employee representation already existing under national laws.

According to the guidelines, the employee representation of the European Stock Corporation furthermore is specifically expected to inform the other employee representations in the company and its subsidiaries and operations about the results of the information and hearing proceedings. It thereby takes on a binding function toward the other employee representations.

If one of the companies participating in the establishment of a European Stock Corporation is subject to directives about employees' participation in company management, in particular co-determination according to national law, the European Stock Corporation must also allow employee representatives into their supervisory body or administrative body corresponding to the proportional percentage that was decisive for the company subject to the national law. If several founding companies are subject to directives about co-determination according to national law, the number of the employee representatives in the supervisory body or administrative body of the European Stock Corporation is determined according to national laws. In practice these regulations will probably turn out to be hurdles for the participation of companies that are subject to 'strict' national co-determination rules in the founding of European Stock Corporations.

The guidelines contain no necessary projections regarding the procedure of choosing the employee representative in the supervisory body or administrative body of the European Stock Corporation. In this respect the member states are exempted from determining within the framework of the implementation of the guidelines whether the employee representatives are elected by the employees or appointed from a third party or rather the employees are simply granted a right to propose or right to reject regarding their representative in the supervisory or administrative body. In each case, the employee representatives in the supervisory or administrative body must, however, be given or have imposed upon them the same rights (including voting rights) and obligations as the shareholder representatives.

In the case of a company's conversion into a European Stock Corporation all valid co-determination rules exist before the conversion apply without alteration after the conversion. If no company participating in the establishment of a

European Stock Corporation is subject to co-determination rules under national law, the European Stock Corporation is not obliged to allow employee representatives into their administrative or supervisory bodies.

Summarising, the key features are:

- An SE must have operations (for example, branch offices or subsidiaries) in more than one member state
- An SE will be registered in the member state in which it has its headquarters
- Each member state can decide whether an SE will have a single-tier or two-tiered board of directors
- An SE can be established through a merger as a new company or (which in relation to joint ventures is more probable) through the establishment of a holding company for subsidiaries in different member states or through the establishment of a joint subsidiary
- The SE will be similar to a stock corporation in the respective member states; provisions should thereby be used that apply to such stock corporations in the respective member state, in order to fill in possible holes in the general framework of the planned company law; in particular the national law will be further useable in such important areas as: tax treatment (including cross-border activities of the SE), auditing and accounting requirements, liability of the board of directors as well as raising, reducing and receiving capital.

On the whole the rules about co-determination in the supervisory and administrative bodies of the European Stock Corporation prove to be a hindrance for the inclusion of companies which, according to national law, are subject to the co-determination rules because their participation in the founding of the European Stock Corporation leads to the fact that these employee representatives must also be allowed into their supervisory or administrative body. It is also uncertain whether the European Stock Corporation represents the long-overdue company form freed of particular national characteristics because in many areas the company is subject to the respective national directives about stock corporations. The combination of laws creates considerable uncertainties. Without a genuine EU-wide harmonisation of company taxes, tax factors will also remain decisive for the establishment and location of international joint ventures.

The Procedure During Conversions

With all types of conversions a contract (merger or splitting contract) is to be regularly executed. The autonomy of the shareholders affected by the conversion processes and the protection of the employee interests are to be observed.

6 Joint Ventures and Alliances

Joint ventures and alliances have become an undeniable part of international economic life. They offer an important strategic option for companies that, within the framework of globalisation efforts or on the basis of other competitive pressure, do not themselves possess sufficient capital, knowledge or access to the market, which are necessary to reach their commercial goals in a certain sector.

Introduction and Conceptual Definition

It is thus hardly surprising that joint ventures have become common worldwide as a form of company organisation. Yet, in most countries there is neither a special form of company that is legally recognised as a joint venture nor a particular joint venture law.

Therefore, a clear definition of the concept joint venture does not exist. In general, it can be said that joint ventures cover a wide spectrum of agreements by which two or more existing companies agree to begin a mutual company or mutual business activities.

The differentiation between a *contractual joint venture* and an *equity joint venture* has been proven to make sense. Contractual joint ventures consist of purely contractual arrangements between the participating companies without the result of an organisational independence of the intended cooperation taking the form of a project company. Equity joint ventures, in contrast, are indicated by the existence of a joint venture company, be it in the form of a limited partnership or a corporation.

Central Regulatory Areas of Joint Ventures

During the planning and implementation of a joint venture certain key problems regularly arise, in particular in relation to international undertakings in which assets and/or parties from different legal systems are involved. For the arrangement of the joint venture the following aspects thus need to be considered.

Liability

The joint venture partners will as a rule be interested in limiting their liability. Liability can be limited for an equity joint venture through the choice of a limited liability company. The liability in the internal relationship between the joint venture partners should also be regulated.

Tax Burdens

The estimation of the tax burdens that ensue through a certain arrangement is of fundamental importance. In many cases the establishment of a partnership can achieve greater tax efficiency. On the basis of their tax transparency the initial payments can be directly ascribed to the joint venture partners and set off against their profits. This can be of particular importance if losses are expected in the initial years of the joint venture.

Treatment of the Balance Sheet

The treatment of the business of the joint venture in the balance sheets of the parent companies can be significant and will be arranged, among other things, according to the size and influence of the participation of each of the parent companies in the business of the joint venture. In this regard the question thus arises whether it is necessary or desired that the results of the joint venture can be consolidated with their balance sheets.

Foundation Formalities

In regards to the formalities of foundation it is determined that a partnership or a simple contractual agreement in general offers a structure for a joint venture that can be set up quickly and without unnecessary registration fees. This can be particularly advantageous in terms of timing. In comparison, the establishment of a corporation implies more formalities, establishment prerequisites and registration requirements to fulfill.

Direction and Decision-Making Responsibility

The direction of the joint venture and the distribution of its decision-making responsibilities (corporate governance) must be clearly regulated. For a contractual joint venture it is always possible to create a controlling authority to which questions of doubt or dispute can be addressed. For an equity joint venture the question of the appointment of management, boards of directors and supervisory boards and their responsibilities is of central importance. Different legal requirements have to be observed.

Financing

The financial burden between the partners needs to be determined. In order to secure the financing, precise rules about the budgets, payment requirements, payment time periods and the consequences of late or completely missing payments are also necessary.

Resignation of Members or End of the Joint Venture

A special rule is required to determine under which conditions the joint venture should cease as well as under which conditions a party to the contract should have the right to resign from the joint venture. The possibility of a compulsory expulsion of a joint venture partner must be regulated. In particular, the financial ramifications of the resignation of a partner from the joint venture require detailed regulations.

Dispute Settlement

In order to avoid the collapse of a joint venture in the case of differences of opinion, regulatory mechanisms must be available to solve internal disputes. Particularly well suited for this are the actions of looking to a higher authority as well as calling in a third party.

With the shift to a higher authority, higher-level decision-makers of the joint venture are brought in. As long as a fundamental consensus exists between them, in most cases they will find a solution. In addition, a certain psychological pressure is exerted on the persons directly participating in the joint venture, who as a rule seek to avoid their managers from being involved in every dispute.

When calling in a third party it is usually an expert, who makes a decision in place of the party to the contract, or a court of arbitration, which makes binding decisions. Governmental courts, in contrast, are unsuitable because of the surrounding publicity and the length of the process.

Contractual Joint Ventures

With a contractual joint venture – as already pointed out – no legally independent entity exists with respect to the joint venture partners. This is sufficient particularly if the parties cooperate regarding a one-time project.

A contractual joint venture can cover a wide spectrum of different conditions and agreements. The exact formation depends greatly on the characteristics of the actual contract.

Only a few general statements can be made about the formation of the agreement(s) with a contractual joint venture. However, the following should always be considered.

Liability Rules

With a contractual joint venture the liability of the participants to third parties and among each other is to be regulated.

In the external relationship the joint venture partners are usually jointly and severally liable. However, a project contract with the third party can also be executed only through one joint venture partner so that this partner is liable to the third party. The equalisation among the partners is then facilitated through the joint venture contract.

It is also possible that the joint venture partners are externally held jointly and severally liable, but internally are treated like independent third parties. Above all with large construction projects individual areas are assigned to the respective joint venture parties that take on sole responsibility. Given deficits in the respective area, compensation payments are then due in the internal relationship.

Resignation of Members

A typical case for a contractual joint venture concerns the application for a certain project. Until the application for the project is submitted, the resignation of a joint venture member for a particular reason is permitted. As soon as the joint venture partners have submitted their application – or, at the latest, if they are awarded the contract for the project for which they have joined – cancelling on a joint venture contract should fundamentally no longer be possible, except for an important reason or with adequate notice periods.

The important reasons for cancelling a joint venture should, as for as possible, be explicitly stated in the joint venture contract. Important reasons for cancellation should above all be threatening insolvency proceedings for one of the parties to the contract or repeated, serious violations of the contract. In addition, it should be agreed that the remaining party to the contract can continue to lead the project alone. Regulations regarding the financial consequences of any resignation must also be established.

The Strategic Alliance as a Special Form of Contractual Joint Venture

The strategic alliance can be seen as a special form of contractual joint venture that is a less definite form of cooperation. There is no exact definition of a strategic alliance. With some strategic alliances, it can simply be a 'friendly' framework for future cooperation from project to project. With others, more solid ties can come into play in the form of cooperative research, employee exchanges and/or a combining of resources. Some strategic alliances can cement the entire relationship in that each party assumes a small share in the share capital of the other, or that it *appears* as a pre-phase for an equity joint venture.

Equity Joint Ventures

The choice of the legal form of an equity joint venture is determined above all by tax considerations. In addition, important criteria for the decision are the flexibility and the sufficient steering possibilities through the joint venture partners.

The Legal Form of a Company in an Equity Joint Venture

Increasingly, right at the beginning the legal form of the independent joint company (equity joint venture) is chosen for the cooperation between companies.

A legal vehicle for international cooperation beyond the boundaries of national laws is the legal form of the European Business Interest Association (EBIA) and the European Stock Corporation.

An EBIA, however, is of little use if the first priority of the joint venture is to operate a profit-making business. It has, however, proven itself to be an appropriate vehicle for cross-border business alliances for auditors, attorneys and business associations. It can also be an appropriate vehicle for cross-border cooperation in the areas of research and development (R&D) between European companies or for other non-profit enterprises. Beyond that, however, it has shown itself to be, in practice, not very suitable.

The Principal Place of Business of the Company in an Equity Joint Venture

Another central question in establishing an international joint venture is the location of the company's headquarters. Usually the company's headquarters are situated in the country in which the joint venture is active. If the joint venture partners, however, wish to establish headquarters in a country in which the venture is not active, then questions of international corporation law come into play. Some legal systems unreservedly release the joint venture partners from such questions in that they enact the so-called 'Theory of principal place of business', according to which the company is subject to that legal system in which it actually has its administrative headquarters.

The Negotiation of the Joint Venture

Aside from the questions as to which rules must be effected in a joint venture contract and how the content of these rules is to be summarised, there are further issues that must always be addressed. This refers above all to the negotiation of the joint venture between the parties to the contract which, despite great differences between individual joint ventures, mostly proceeds according to the same fundamental pattern.

The Agreement on Principle

The decisive part of most negotiations of joint ventures is an Agreement on Principle, Agreement on a Term Sheet or Memorandum of Understanding (MoU), or at any rate a declaration of intent at a relatively early stage if the company management is to demonstrate the seriousness of its intentions and solidify the essentials of its planned relationship.

Often in such Agreements on Principle conditions about 'exclusivity' are agreed upon, meaning a prohibition on negotiations with third parties within a certain time period. In addition, in relation to the negotiations about a joint venture confidentiality agreements are reached that should also have a legally binding effect.

Approval of Third Parties

For joint ventures it is imperative to establish early on which special approvals for third parties are necessary for the establishment of the joint venture and what effects these could have on the timing of the course of the joint venture's establishment. The following points need to be considered:

1. *Approval of cartel office* Joint ventures and agreements on cooperation often need approval under cartel law. The details are treated comprehensively under Part 2, Chapter 7.
2. *Approval of the shareholders and supervisory boards* Depending on the shareholder configuration of the participating joint venture partners the approval of the shareholders and of the supervisory boards can be necessary on the basis of the shareholder agreement or the statutes.

   Actions of the board of directors that bring about a serious intervention into the membership and asset rights of the shareholders need the approval of the shareholders' meeting; shareholders outside of the consolidated companies have a right to compensation for any disadvantages they suffer through such agreements. The sale of a substantial part of the company also requires a resolution of the shareholders' meeting.
3. *Employees' rights* Obligations to consult with employee representatives over the timing of the plans of the joint venture can also be of great significance. With the implementation of the transfer of a business and the transfer of the corresponding employees to a joint venture as well as for the restructuring and reorganisation measures tied to the establishment of the joint venture company, protective directives on employees' rights must be observed. This is especially the case if the joint venture leads to substantial layoffs or a significant change in the working conditions of the employees in the joint venture.[3]

The Joint Venture Agreement

Following the Agreement on Principle the parties agree on the Joint Venture Agreement, the actual 'basic law' of the joint venture. Most of the regulation subjects of a joint venture noted above are addressed in this.

If consolidated companies are participating, subsidiaries will often hold shares in the joint venture. In spite of that, a participation of the parent company is imperative for the joint venture contract, because the important decisions are made with the parent company, and it usually offers the financial resources.

The contractual rules for the *contractual joint venture* should take into consideration in particular the following aspects:

- Parties to the contract
- Preamble
- Definitions
- Scope of the joint venture
- Responsibilities of the parties
- Timing plan
- Background/technology
- Project know-how
- Use of know-how
- Confidentiality
- Structure
- Project management
- Changes/restructuring/reorganisation
- Financing/investments
- Ownership/uses
- Liability/responsibility
- Force majeure
- Duration/Termination
- Exclusivity
- Arbitration rules
- Agreement on non-competition
- Miscellaneous.

The contractual rules for the *equity joint venture* should take into consideration in particular the following aspects:

- Parties to the contract
- Preamble
- Definitions
- Establishment of the joint venture.
  - Object
  - Company structure
  - Company's purpose:

  a Legal form, name, headquarters
  b Bylaws, order of business
- Business transfer date for establishment
- Administration:
  a Board of Directors/Business management
  b Staffing
  c Management
  d Administrative headquarters
  e Supervisory board
  f Shareholders' committee
- Contribution to the joint venture:
  a Participation of the parties to the contract
  b Principles of the mutual cooperative management of business activities
  c Assets/Items of property/Investments.
  d Know-how
  e Patents, protected privileges
  f Licence agreements, cooperation agreements, consultation agreements
  g Distribution agreement
  h Offers/Orders on hand
  i Ancillary agreements
  j Employees
  k Transition of contractual relationships
- Contribution of the business areas as well as of the participations inside and outside the country

- Balance sheets/Compensation:
  - Balance sheets
  - Compensation/Adjustments
- Conditions precedent/Closing
  - Conditions precedent
  - Closing
- Relations of the parties to the contract to each other and to the joint venture:
  - Principals:
    a Parity, agreeability
    b Arm's length
  - Financing of the joint venture/Cash management/Securities
  - Partner committee
  - Company contract
  - Reporting authority, Annual report and investor relations
  - Prohibition on competition
  - Licence agreement and services agreement:
    a Operational protective rights
    b Name and trademark licence agreement
    c Other services agreements
  - Integration concept and management appraisal
- Compensation payments:

  - Valuation
  - Balance sheet guarantee
  - Compensation
- Warranties, due diligence:
  - Warranties:
    - a Mutual warranties
    - b Time period of warranty
  - Legal consequences of warranties:
    - a Rectification of defects/Indemnity
    - b Exclusion of further rights
    - c Tax-free amount and upper limit of liability
    - d Statute of limitations
    - e Offset prohibition, right of retention
  - Due diligence
- Exemption:
  - Legal disputes before the transfer date
  - Revocation action/Recall action
  - Environmental disturbances
- Commencement of the joint venture:
  - Conditions precedent, reservations of consent
  - Release under cartel law
  - Closing
    - a Day of Closing
    - b Closing activities
    - c Continuation of the areas of business until closing
- Duration of the joint venture, Termination:
  - Duration
  - Change of control
  - Sale of assets:
    - a Obligation for tender/Put option/Call option
    - b Right of preemption
    - c Legal succession
- Miscellaneous:
  - Enforcement of the rights and obligations from the agreement
  - Liability
  - Costs
  - Confidentiality, communication
  - Choice of law, jurisdiction, arbitration clause
  - Further agreements, written form, headings
  - Severability clause
  - Statement addressees

Company Statutes

With an equity joint venture, along with the joint venture agreement there must also be the execution of company statutes or shareholders' agreements. Fundamentally it would even be possible with an equity joint venture to refrain from a joint venture contract and incorporate all rules in the company statutes or shareholders' agreements. The related publicity (the company statutes are publicly available), however, usually leads to the execution of a joint venture agreement separate from the company contract.

In addition, it is necessary to see to that the company statutes or shareholders' agreements are coordinated with the joint venture agreement. Therefore, in the joint venture agreement corresponding obligations to conform to the company statutes or shareholders' agreements should also be included in case contradictions appear. In addition, in the joint venture agreement the precedence of the joint venture contract over other contracts, in particular the company statutes or shareholders' agreements, should be specifically emphasised.

Warranty and Due Diligence

An important special problem, which continually develops during negotiations on a joint venture, is the question as to what extent warranties, releases and/or indemnifications from the other joint venture party can be requested. In particular, if a significant part of the assets or a business is contributed, on the side of the joint venture party legitimate interest exists about knowing whether the contributed assets actually correspond to the assumed value and do not reveal any deficits.

The same also applies for the requests of a joint venture party to reveal business affairs or matters regarding the assets which are contributed into the joint venture, within the framework of a due diligence at the onset of negotiations or at least before the execution and signing of the contracts.

In summary, it can be said that the warranty as well as the implementation of due diligence, along with the respective questions attached to them, make up a much-discussed problem. The negotiations of an extensive warranty package, in the cooperative and constructive atmosphere of the negotiations, can often be unhelpful. Similarly, the implementation of due diligence into all its details can often leave the impression of a lack of trust and be seen as a superfluous formality.

It is argued against warranties that upon their violation, realising them is often not possible. Once the joint venture company has been established, a complaint against the business partner is only in the rarest cases realistic business behaviour. Legal action against a joint venture partner is hardly consonant with upholding a cooperative relationship, as is necessary for the continuation of a joint venture.

Undoubtedly the choice of the joint venture partners is of significance. And given that a later fulfilment of warranty rights is hardly realistic, except under particular, extreme circumstances, it is helpful to implement due diligence or another inspection before execution of the contract on the basis of which the other party and the condition of its business or its assets can be judged.

In addition, warranties at least establish – even if their realisation is rather unrealistic – psychological pressure on the other side to disclose all important circumstances for the joint venture. It can be argued against a sceptical party that warranties for the most part are instituted not just one-sidedly but rather by both parties and in this way the need for security of both joint venture partners can be satisfied.

7 Corporate Succession

The corporate successions in particular of small to medium-sized companies opens up numerous questions in relation to corporation and inheritance as well as tax law. The complexity of the rules needed in this case is especially apparent with partnerships that have many shareholders.

If the (majority) shareholder of a small to medium-sized company dies, this regularly leads to the dissolution of the company. The company transforms into a so-called 'liquidation company', which means that the purpose of the company from then on consists only of its dissolution and settlement. This means the break-up of a living company which, because of the substantial loss in value, is most often not wanted by any of the remaining participants. The shareholders could, indeed, decide together to continue the company.

However, enormous problems could occur if the deceased shareholder leaves behind many heirs. The joint ownership of the co-heirs is to participate as a full shareholder in all decisions of the company, but experience shows that joint ownerships of coheirs are often able to act only to a limited degree. This can be the result of the incompatibility of the heirs concerned as well as of the approval requirements necessary according to inheritance law. The goal of a logical rule of succession must therefore be first of all to secure the continued existence of the company through a formation of the shareholders' agreement.

For such a formation, for example, a regulation under corporation law comes into consideration according to which the company will simply continue as is with the current shareholders. The deceased shareholder thus resigns from the company and the heirs are granted a claim against the company.

Depending on the level of the company shares and the value of the company, claims benefiting the heirs can substantially strain the company. It is therefore to be considered whether continuing the company with the heirs makes sense. If the shareholders' agreement contains a clause according to which the heirs can continue the company, the joint ownership of the co-heirs will not be split up but rather the share of the bequeather and the individual heirs join the company. However, where not every one of the heirs is willing or able to continue the company, the continuation is considered with an heir to be determined in the shareholders' agreement or the statutes.

With the formation of the shareholders' agreement, aspects of inheritance law cannot be left out of consideration. Should the company continue with only one heir, claims for compensation for respective co-heirs can develop if the value of the share is higher than that of the value of the share in the heir's estate. This can be avoided, for example, by transferring the share by way of an advance bequest.

Along with the clauses that regulate an automatic transfer of the share of the deceased shareholder, so-called entry 'clauses' can be used in the shareholders' agreement, which grant an heir or a third party the right to enter into the company. In this case, the heir noted in the clause receives an option right whether he would like to make use of the right to entry or not. This avoids the situation that the person entitled after the death of the bequeather is, without any further consideration, liable for the obligations of the company. This liability consequence applies fundamentally to the heir, who, on the basis of the successorship clause becomes a shareholder.

With entry clauses, the question of a right to compensation is relevant in two ways. Such a right of the heir in respect to the company can result if a third party is granted the right to entry and the deceased shareholder resigns from the company. Rights of the co-heirs to compensation under the laws of succession result if a right to entry into the company is granted to a third co-heir. As a simple resolution a contractual decision can accept, with certain limitations, completely excluding the right to compensation for resigning shareholders. This will, however, not often meet the need of the shareholders to leave their shares to their families and heirs.

The rights to compensation stemming from the law of succession make clear that it is important to interpret the rules of the succession as a unity, which encompasses the formation of the shareholders' agreements as well as the testamentary dispositions. Only an integral regulation in the shareholders' agreement and testament or contract of inheritance/succession can guarantee that desired effects under corporate law are not quashed again through laws of succession.

From the perspective of tax law there are naturally the aspects of succession duty, gift tax and income tax to consider in order to reach an optimal formation of the company succession.

There is no patented recipe for how legally to form the company succession. The number of variations under the law of succession and corporation law makes it much more necessary to determine in the individual case which individual features and needs of the company should be observed. In particular, this includes the question of whether individual shareholders for certain reasons are to be treated differently, whether there even are any co-heirs appropriate for continuing to manage the company and whether the liquidity of the company is enough to buy out potential heirs and those entitled to statutory shares. In each case it should be considered whether a transfer of shares during the shareholder's lifetime can offer advantages by way of a succession.

8 Management Buy-Out and Management Buy-In

The volume of management buy-outs (MBO) in which often long-term successful managers acquire the companies they manage using their knowledge of companies or the market and its value as well as the cash flow found in the object company has increased substantially in recent years; this is the same for management buy-ins (MBI) in which managers buy outside companies.

Such kinds of transactions are especially to be found among mid-level companies that face grave problems with succession. Frequently the seller also seeks a solution to various management problems, in particular to spin off or split off or to divest affiliated companies that no longer fit into the business concept of the consolidated companies.

On the manager's part, an MBO or an MBI mainly represents the desire for independence and entrepreneurial freedom. Because the group of managers as a rule independently does not have sufficient share capital resources, the MBO and MBI are mostly financed from the outside with help from investors or creditors within the framework of a so-called Leveraged Buy-Out (LBO) or Leveraged Buy-In (LBI). These concepts lead back to the leverage effect that results from the acquirers acquiring comparatively large companies with a relatively small capital input of their own whereas simultaneously the share capital return with a total capital yield that is above the interest of the outside capital rises disproportionately.

The increase in MBOs and MBIs can also be traced to an increasing trend that fund companies, affiliated companies or venture capital companies are looking for new investment possibilities for a wide circle of investors and are increasingly making use of this kind of transfer form (Figure 4.3 and 4.4).

The reason for the growing popularity of the MBO and MBI is evident in that a managing body that participates in the success of the company as a co-shareholder is regularly greatly motivated and interested with its insider knowledge of the strengths and weaknesses in bettering the company's success. With a company's own management the goals are most frequently reached of maximising the shareholder value, meaning the interest value or company value using the so-called 'value management' or 'appreciation management' with the goal of a further sale with the best possible profits or of reaching a share price as high as possible.

The features of the MBO and MBI should not blind one to the fact that these forms of company transfer bring up the same questions and problems as a normal purchase of a company, a letter of intent, due diligence by the acquirer or investors, warranties of the seller, etc. Along with the seller's warranties and guarantees, many independent statements of guarantee of the management take place with an MBO; given the background of their insider know-how, these are an important basis for financing with outside capital and the investment readiness of investors

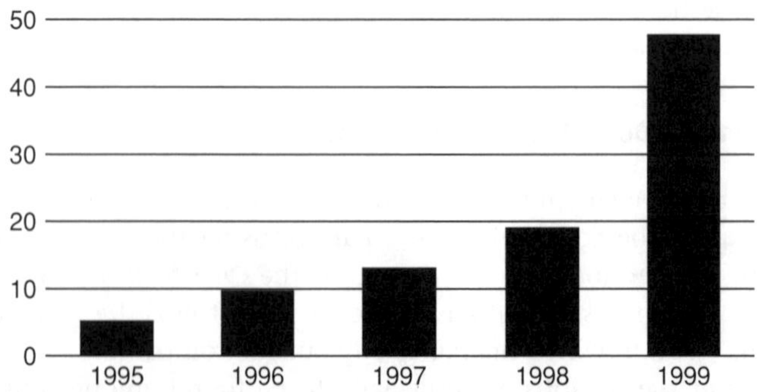

Figure 4.3 Investments in the USA, private equity gross investments, 1995–9, US$ billion
Source: Venture Economics and National Venture Capital Association.

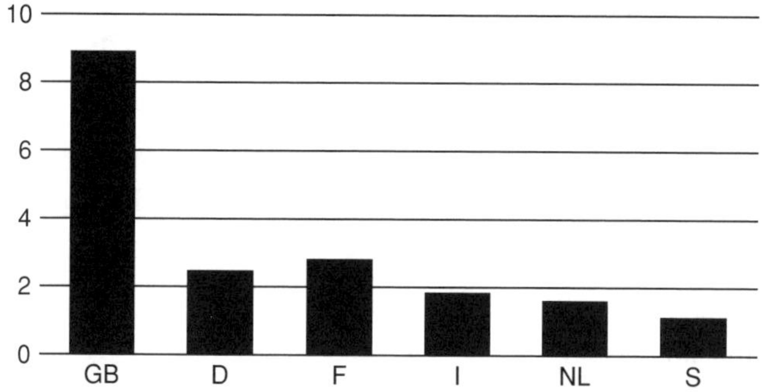

Figure 4.4 Investments in Europe, designated countries of European private equity investments, 1999, EURO billion
Source: Evca; PriceWaterhouseCoopers.

in those cases in which the transfer of a company is financed through fund companies and affiliated companies or other investors by way of a LBO or LBI. It must thereby be taken into consideration that the decisive goal with a MBO or MBI is attaining a stable cash flow. Only on the basis of a stable cash flow can the mostly high financing with outside capital be paid back in a reasonable period of time. For this reason, investors regularly request a five-year plan, which presents the future earning power of the company and is the basis of the cash flow calculation, the repayment plan and the return on investment.

It should also never be forgotten that with the establishment of this plan managers end up in a not inconsiderable conflict of interest. On the one hand they are obligated to protect the interests of the current shareholders or of the company; on the other hand they represent already as (co)-acquirers solid self-interests. The managers must therefore deliver as a basis of the negotiations numbers and prognoses that are objectively comprehensible and easily examined.

Business Prerequisites of the LBO or the LBI

Special economic features of the LBO or the LBI purchase of companies result from the high level of financing with outside capital, particularly as the target company must as a rule furnish the security for the financing as well as generate the resources for servicing the financing. A further result from this is that not every company is suitable for an LBO- or LBI-financing. Trade and services companies as a rule seldom come into consideration for such a financing: suitable transfer objects are primarily production companies. Considering that the financing volumes can be reduced only in the long term solely through access to the cash flow and the hidden reserves, the influx of liquidity often rises through additional measures. In particular, unnecessary assets, businesses or parts of businesses are often sold after the transfer and as far as is necessary, for example, further held by way of a lease-back.

Business prerequisites for an LBO or LBI are therefore:

- A favourable cash flow prognosis for the time following the MBO or MBI

- A sale of the assets not necessary for business
- A concept for measures that may increase productivity.

Financing Forms of the MBO or MBI

Assuming that the MBO and MBI financing takes place fundamentally through recourse to the value of the target company, in practice three financing models are used:

- The loan model
- The security model
- The seizure/pledge model.

With the *loan model* the target company being acquired grants a loan for the financing of the purchase price that the target company generally must refinance at a financial institution to the takeover company or holding company which is established by management and, if necessary, by investors for the acquisition of the target company; the loan is secured through a pledge of the assets of the target company (Figure 4.5).

With the *security model* the takeover or holding company itself takes out a loan at a financial institution for the financing of the purchase price that is secured through a pledge of the assets of the target company (Figure 4.6).

With the *seizure/pledge model* the takeover or holding company itself (as with the security model) takes out a loan at a financial institution for the financing of the purchase price that is secured through a pledge of the shares in the target company (Figure 4.7).

Legal Formation of the MBO or MBI

As already mentioned, the terminology of the MBO/MBI must not be misleading, so that this form of company transfer at first presents the same questions and problems as a normal company purchase. On the basis of acquiring managers' insider knowledge, however, numerous difficult questions – for example, the due

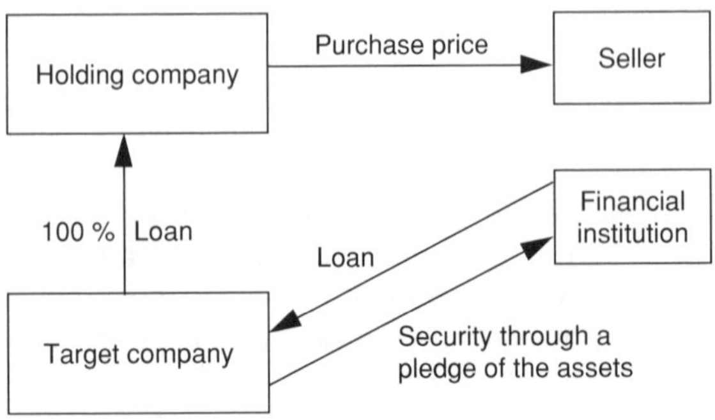

Figure 4.5 The loan model

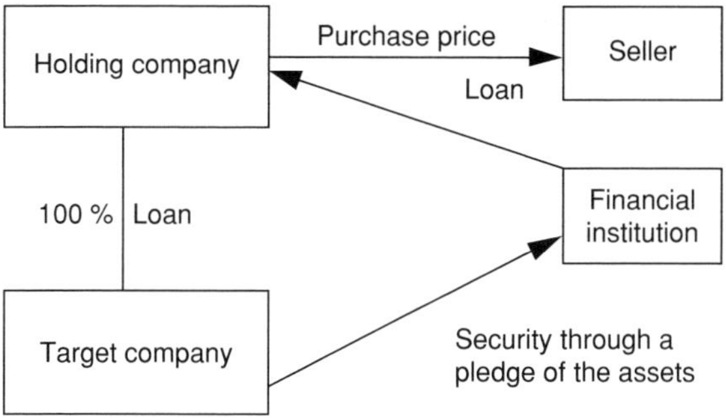

Figure 4.6 The security model

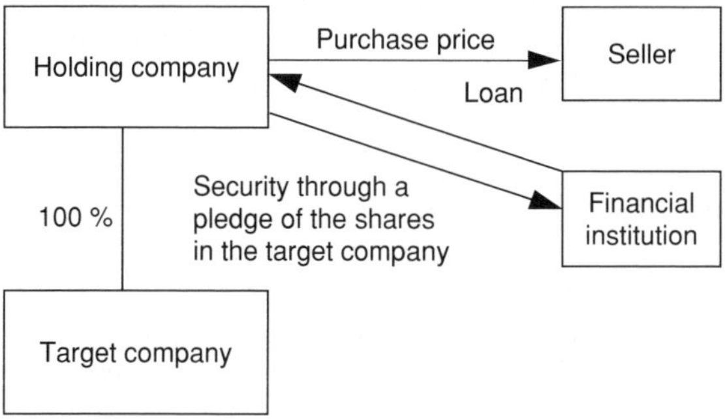

Figure 4.7 The seizure/pledge model

diligence examination or the warranty – lose their significance. Along with the warranties and guarantees of the seller in the purchase and sale agreement, numerous independent statements of guarantee materialise that in consideration of their insider knowledge are an important basis for the outside financing and the investors' readiness to invest.

MBOs are created according to corporation law in a single stage or – in particular for tax reasons – in two stages. With a single-stage MBO a direct acquisition of the target company takes place without involving a takeover company, which the target company buys. This kind of MBO comes into play only if the target company harbours no hidden reserves, which could be revealed following the acquisition during a restructuring effort to establish an additional tax-relevant write-off potential. A single-stage MBO is furthermore possible if a domestic corporation or an actual/individual person sells its shares. With the most frequently used, indirect, or two-stage MBO the takeover company, also designated as the holding or acquisition company, acquires the shares of the target company in the first stage. Because with a share deal it is fundamentally impossible to convert the company's hidden reserves paid along with the purchase price into a potential write-off, following the acquisition in the second stage:

- Either the target company's assets are transferred by way of a single transfer to the takeover company (asset deal model)
- Or the target company is converted into a tax-privileged form of company (conversion model).

It thereby becomes possible for the target company's hidden reserves – meaning the purchase price *minus* the book value of the assets of the target company – to be revealed in a fiscally neutral way, and a corresponding write-off potential to be created.

With an asset deal model a takeover company established as an intermediary holding company by the managers and possibly by the investors purchases all assets of the target company as a group of assets in the second stage. These assets are then transferred by way of a single transfer of rights to the takeover company. The assets of the target company then become assets of the takeover company so that the outside financing can be directly secured through the takeover company's assets. The acquisition according to this model takes place with the following steps:

- Establishment of the takeover company
- Acquisition of all shares in the target company; activation of the shares in the takeover company at acquisition costs
- Purchase of the assets of the target company through the takeover company at market value; activation of the assets in the takeover company at acquisition costs (book value increase)
- Distribution of the target company's designated profits gained from the sale of the individual assets to the takeover company
- Distribution-dependent write-down of the takeover company's value to the book value of its interest in the target company
- Suspension of the activity of the target company following the distribution of its profits to the takeover company.

9 Going Public/Initial Public Offering

Growing Significance of IPO

The Stock Exchange has developed into an excellent vehicle for improving companies' total amount of the equity and reserves.

Motives for an Initial Public Offering

The motives for an initial public offering (IPO) are many. The main motive for going public focuses on strengthening the equity base for the financing of further corporate growth, in particular through M&A. Furthermore, shareholders can aim for considerable profits through the sale of their assets either with or following the IPO.

Particularly on the international scene company founders experienced a true gold rush that has recently been substantially tempered. Driven by information and communications technology, enormous profits as well as the investment-seeking risk capital of investors and venture capital companies spurred on start-up companies. Under these conditions investors' money and the business plans of junior management for their funds were virtually imposed upon venture capital companies.

An IPO is in many ways an ideal escape for a company from the problems of securing a succession. Other motives include the rise in the level of the company's recognisability and degree of fame as well as the easy recruitment of qualified employees, not least by the creation of corporate value-oriented compensation models (see Part 3, Chapters 9 and 10). In most cases a sharper focus on 'share-holder value' evolved, and a remarkable number of new jobs were created.

Yet, increasingly IPOs result from successful corporate acquisitions or are even the motive for an acquisition. Most of all the spin-off of parts of businesses or of affiliated companies and their entry into the market following a corporate acquisition can offer the possibility of an increase in value or of a concentration on the core areas of the company and simultaneously of the financing of a transaction.

Steps of an IPO in Detail

An initial public offering should entail all the following steps:

- Strategic planning
- Selection of banks and consultants
- Presentation of equity story and examination of readiness of the company for the stock market
- Legal measures to be followed in preparation (e.g. conversion into a company form allowed on the stock market)
- Examination and valuation by issuing banks (due diligence)
- Resolutions of the shareholders regarding capital increase, etc.
- Execution of the underwriting agreement
- Production of the sale prospectus/corporate report
- Presentation before the admissions committee of the responsible institution of the stock exchange
- Application for approval of the sale prospectus/corporate report by the responsible institution of the Stock Exchange
- Application for becoming listed on the Stock Exchange by the responsible institution of the Stock Exchange
- Approval of the sale prospectus
- Press conference and publication of the sale offering with a given price range
- Determination of the issuing price in the 'bookbuilding' procedure
- Determination of the final subscription price (issuing price)
- Capital increase, subscription to shares/registration with the commercial register
- Allocation of shares and publication of subscription price
- Listing on the Stock Exchange (stock market price).

Strategic planning and the careful selection of banks and consultants that possess the necessary know-how and the practical experience begin the process for a successful IPO. Companies or current owners who have decided on an IPO will, on their own, with their management and with their own know-how, not be able to reach the necessary economic, legal, tax-related, and communicative requirements and attain the company's maturity for the stock market.

In conversations between the company's management as well as the banks and consultants, the goals and timing of the IPO are then determined, the company's current status assessed and possible hindrances identified. Checklists are used to analyse typical problematic points and the company's maturity for the stock market.

Presented below are the significant required measures; where necessary, the measures are explained more thoroughly. These tables concern a purely national IPO and do not reflect a simultaneous listing on a foreign Stock Exchange.

(1) Instructions to consultants

Measure	Explanation	Documents	Timing
• Instructions/ orders to consultants	• As necessary, IPO consultants • Bank leading the consortium (lead manager) • Auditors • Attorneys • Advertisement agency • Printer/translator	• Engagement letter(s)	• Selection before kick-off meeting; advertisement agency, printer and translator later • Engagement letter(s) should be signed, if possible, before kick-off meeting (in practice, however, mostly only afterwards)

(2) Kick-off meeting

Measure	Explanation	Documents	Timing
• Kick-off meeting	• Introduction of company to consultants through the management	• Documents similar to a 'Management presentation'	• Contact with attorneys and the bank leading the consortium (lead manager) if possible before kick-off meeting

(3) Start of due diligence/production of prospectus

Measure	Explanation	Documents	Timing
• Start of due diligence and production of prospectus	• The consultants of the company and – according to discussion with bank leading the consortium – the lead manager's consultants (in particular, attorneys and auditors) examine the significant company documents, files and data that are put together by means of the request lists and provided to the consultants in a 'data room'; the results of the due diligence are incorporated into the prospectus	• Due diligence lists for the 'data room' • If necessary, due diligence report (at least if no due diligence is conducted by the bank leading the consortium) (lead manager) • Recommended also for internal control	• Closely following kick-off meeting • Due diligence and production of prospectus can occur simultaneously • The attorneys' due diligence list and that of the bank leading the consortium (lead manager) should be in agreement • After approximately two weeks the significant results of the due diligence should be available • A total time period of approximately 10 weeks should be set for the due diligence process and production of the prospectus with several 'drafting sessions' for the prospectus

Central to the procedure of becoming listed on the Stock Exchange is always the prospectus, which is to be produced in the national language and generally in English and which simultaneously represents a critical marketing tool. National requirements regulate the details for the prospectus.

The prospectus provides information about the actual and legal situation of the company and the IPO that are necessary for the evaluation of the shares being offered. In the prospectus the company, along with its banks and consultants, presents its actual and legal relationships that investors need for the evaluation of the shares being offered. The prospectus must be complete and accurate.

Information is necessary about the shares, the issuer, the issuer's capital and business activities as well as the persons and companies taking over the responsibility for the content of the prospectus. Furthermore, the prospectus contains information about the issuer's assets, financial status and earnings status, its accounting, management, the source and use of funds, respective participating companies, yield and dividends per share, the most recent course of business as well as information about the issuer's business prospects and risks.

Within the framework of the so-called 'prospectus liability' the company, the banks and other signatories of the prospectus are liable to the investors for the prospectus' comprehensiveness and accuracy.

(4) (First) shareholders' meeting (if applicable)

Measure	Explanation	Documents	Timing
• (First) shareholders' meeting (if applicable)	• If no company is ready to be listed on the exchange: conversion of the company into one ready for an IPO as well as appointment of management and supervisory committees • If necessary, first (cash) capital increase in order to achieve a balanced relationship between shares being placed and those remaining with the current shareholders	• Application to the Registration Court for the appointment of an auditor concerning the foundation/ formation • Resolution for a conversion with bylaws as well as selection of the initial management and supervisory committees • Report on formation and auditor's report • Resolution for capital increase with certificates of subscription and payment • Respective registration (at the Commercial Registry)	• Application for the appointment of an auditor • Resolution for conversion as soon as possible (if a works council: delivery of the draft of the conversion resolution before the final drafting of the resolution) • Registration at the Commercial Registry after the announcement

The conversion into a company ready to be listed on the Stock Exchange should as a rule occur as soon as possible. With young companies, according to national legal systems, in cases of expansion efforts in the first years following their formation so-called 'post-formation formalities' are to be observed for acquisitions, including an authorising resolution from the shareholders' meeting.

For the board of directors of the corporation that is planning the company's IPO, the question arises, above all, as to which measures require the approval of the shareholders' meeting/general assembly.

The agreements (in particular the underwriting agreement) to be executed by the board of directors during the process of the IPO and the application for admission to trade on the exchange are common measures of management for which no resolution of the shareholders' meeting is needed. Nevertheless, an authorising resolution of the shareholders' meeting can be necessary if the IPO contains significant structural measures. Factually speaking, an IPO commonly leads to a substantial restructuring of the company. It is therefore recommended that an authorising resolution of the shareholders' meeting be obtained. This will generally be the case if the IPO is tied to a capital increase – as, for example, prescribed in Germany for an initial listing on the 'New Market'. As a rule a three-quarters majority is necessary for the share capital present upon the resolution, as long as, on the basis of particular provisions in the bylaws, a simple majority does not suffice. The same applies if other structural measures are necessary for the listing on the stock exchange.

(5) Introduction to the Stock Exchange (if applicable)

Measure	Explanation	Documents	Timing
• Introduction/ presentation to the Stock Exchange (if applicable – for example, in Germany for the 'New Market')	• Introduction of the company to the Admissions Committee of the responsible institution of the Stock Exchange	• Presentation documents (on the basis of the documents for kick-off meeting)	• Should occur shortly after kick-off meeting (about four weeks)

The presentation to the Admissions Committee of the responsible institution of the national Stock Exchange and the beginning of the marketing campaign end the preparatory phase of the IPO.

Shares can be issued directly to the public (direct issue) or to a consortium of banks (global depositary receipts). As a rule the shares are issued by way of global depositary receipts through a consortium of banks that underwrite the shares at their own cost and then themselves sell the shares to the public. The legal relationships between the issuer, the selling shareholders and the bank consortium are regulated in the Underwriting Agreement, which takes the place of the former usual multi-sided offer of the banks. In scope and style this agreement resembles the Anglo-American purchase and sale agreements concerning companies.

(6) Negotiation of the significant agreements and the underwriting agreement

Measure	Explanation	Documents	Timing
• Negotiation of the significant agreements, in particular the takeover agreement ('Underwriting Agreement') with the bank leading the issuance (lead manager/ book runner)	• The significant agreements are standardised and, are proposed by the bank leading the consortium (lead manager); only limited negotiating room exists	• Underwriting Agreement with attachments (in particular 'legal opinions' of the attorneys representing the company and the bank leading the consortium (lead manager) as well as the auditor's 'Comfort letter'; agreement determining the price) • Sponsors' agreements with the 'designated sponsors' • Number and depository agreement • Consortium Agreement ('Agreement among Underwriters') • Stock lending for 'Greenshoe', if necessary	• Underwriting Agreement should be negotiated before the submission of the prospectus – but is mostly negotiated only shortly before the beginning of the 'bookbuilding' • If the sponsors' agreements are not negotiated on time, the sponsors often demand somewhat absurd fees • The company influence has only over the choice of the consortium banks; the Consortium Agreement (Agreement among Underwriters) itself does not concern the company and will not always be provided to the company

An Underwriting Agreement contains, above all, the obligation of the issuing bank to the issuer or the selling current shareholders to subscribe (underwrite) a certain number of shares. In practice, the actual allocated quotas of shares are differently and flexibly regulated between the issuing banks. Newly obtained shares are thereby first underwritten by the lead manager, the 'global coordinator,' and then distributed to the other banks in the consortium. This avoids the difficult procurement for the interests of foreign banks of proof of representation, in particular to the Commercial Registry. With this underwriting obligation the issuing bank is further obligated to place the shares with the public. New shares are thereby underwritten within the framework of a capital increase.

As a rule this occurs by way of an exclusion of subscription rights of the current shareholders. It can be agreed in the Underwriting Agreement that before the public placement the shares shall be first offered for subscription to the existing shareholders. In this situation, no exclusion of subscription rights occurs.

The obligation to underwrite the shares being placed is, as a rule, under the condition precedent that the representations and warranties of the issuer and/or current shareholders granted in this agreement are not incorrect in substantial points and will not be incorrect up to the actual underwriting of the shares.

Furthermore, legal opinions of the consulting attorneys of the issuer, an Officers' Certificate signed by the board of directors of the issuer in the name of the company about the correctness of the representations and warranties of the company as well as a 'comfort letter' of the issuer's auditor regarding the financial data contained in the prospectus must all be supplied.

A further condition precedent for the obligation to underwrite the shares is an agreement about the issuing price.

It should be observed that the distribution of the shares to the investors and the assumption of trade on the Stock Exchange with the placed shares often follows a number of days before the transfer of the issue proceeds. A resettlement, reversed transaction and/or return of performances of the already executed share purchase agreements is therefore technically no longer able to be effected.

In order to guarantee the conditions of the underwriting, legal opinions of the consulting attorneys, an officers' certificate signed by the issuer's board of directors in the company's name as well as a 'Comfort letter' of the auditor must be provided. In these documents the correctness and properness of the data and the procedure, respectively, is confirmed at different points in time. The Underwriting Agreements thereby give the banks the possibility to stop and resettle or reverse the IPO until the subscription price has been determined.

With the placement of new shares these shares develop and arise originally in the hand of the issuing banks at the point in time of the subscription, and in many legal systems the registration of the corresponding capital increase in the Commercial Registry. In many legal systems the listing on the Stock Exchange is possible only after the registration of the capital increase in the Commercial Registry. Furthermore, with the onset, introduction and initiation of trading a deadline of approximately three days is regularly to be observed. In addition, for technical reasons the issuing banks require a time period of approximately two days between the entry and distribution of shares on the one hand and the transfer of the issue proceeds to the issuer on the other.

Underwriting Agreements therefore regularly contain conditions whereby the aforementioned conditions precedent must be fulfilled at the date of the transfer of the subscription certificate or the submission of the registration at the Commercial Registry for the registration of the capital increase (first closure).

Moreover, directly before the transfer of the issue proceeds a legal opinion, an officers' certificate and a 'Comfort letter' are again to be provided, stating that since the underwriting of the shares no circumstances have developed which have substantial negative effects on the business activities or the financial situation of the issuer (second closure).

It is thereby problematic that the shares to be placed have already been created at the hands of the bank consortium after the successful registration of the capital increase; and therefore a resettlement, reversed transaction and/or return of the agreement comes into consideration only if one of the conditions for underwriting the shares no longer exists.

Far-reaching *force majeure* clauses are also often the subject of negotiation. On the basis of such clauses the banks can, under certain circumstances, avoid underwriting the shares if the placement appears endangered owing to an unforeseen occurrence.

The consortium of banks subscribes to newly issued shares as a rule at the nominal amount. The consortium of banks transfers the difference between the nominal amount and the subscription price (issuing price) of the placed shares to the issuer on the basis of a contractual obligation in the Underwriting Agreement (two-stage procedure).

The subscription at the nominal amount takes place above all because the difference between the nominal amount and an issuing price above the nominal amount would regularly be payable in full according to the national legal systems before the registration of the capital increase. A reason given for the subscription at nominal value is in part that this makes possible the flexibility in time required by the determination of the issuing price through 'bookbuilding' proceedings. Registrations at the Commercial Registry, however, occur quickly, so that the subscription of the shares and the registration of the capital increase often takes place only after the close of the 'bookbuilding' period, so that a subscription at nominal value would not be necessary for timing reasons.

The consortium of banks, upon the subscription at the issuing price, would therefore have to temporarily finance the difference between the time period of the registration of the capital increase and the time period of the credit entry of the issue proceeds. This would in particular hardly be explicable to American banks because with American issuances the banks normally purchase the shares from the company step by step with payment of the issue proceeds. Furthermore, subscription occurs at nominal value in order to allow a reaction following the registration of the capital increase to any negative influences on the capital market. An otherwise necessary mark-down of the share price owing to possible price fluctuations can thus be avoided.

Before the beginning of the bookbuilding process, during which an order book is produced on the basis of the submitted purchase orders, and the price determination and the distribution of shares remains open until the execution of the submitted purchase order, it may be necessary to incur a mark-down of the share price at 15 to 25 per cent of the expected market price; this should in any case be avoided, in the interest of the existing shareholders to avoid a rate dilution, if their right to subscription is excluded.

The resettlement of the agreement, reversed transaction and/or return of performances often foreseen in Underwriting Agreements following registration of the capital increase creates substantial problems under many national legal systems because the banks fulfil their obligation to underwrite the shares with the transfer of the subscription certificate.

In any case as a rule contractual regulations that obligate the company to the implementation of a corresponding capital decrease for the possibility of a retreat or resignation of the consortium of banks should be avoided. Such a capital decrease, which does not serve to abate the negative net worth, adverse balance or capital impairment, is possible only according to the rules of an ordinary capital decrease.

Also legally ineffective are as a rule clauses whereby the company, within a time period of two to three months following the failure of a placement of shares, has the right to name a third party to the consortium of banks to which the shares are to be sold at a certain price, whereby following the fruitless close of this time period the consortium of banks is entitled to sell the shares on the market at a certain price they determine themselves.

The representations and warranties of the issuer contained in Underwriting Agreements as a rule correspond to the representations and warranties contained in the purchase and sale agreements of mergers and acquisitions. In addition, the issuer or the current shareholder regularly guarantees that all information in the prospectus that is significant for investors' decisions is substantially correct. Regulations are legally dubious that plan on all damages resulting from the breach of a guarantee being rectified for the issuing banks, especially as a possible prospectus liability of the issuing banks to investors also falls under this.

If it concerns shares of existing shareholders being sold, a violation can exist against national directives on maintenance of capital regarding unjustifiable allocation to the shareholders who are selling, if the corporation has no interest in the sale of the shares. Of course, with an IPO it is truly the case owing to the representative advantages for the corporation – in particular a high recognisability and an easing of raising capital – that upon the sale of the shareholders' shares an interest also exists for the corporation and thereby no violation occurs against national directives on maintenance of capital.

According to national legal systems clauses in Underwriting Agreements whereby the issuer commits to carry out no further capital increases within a time period of six to twelve months after the placement of shares are commonly problematic. As long as this does not concern the use of authorised capital, such a statement of obligation by the board of directors as signatory of the underwriting agreement can be made only upon the agreement of the general assembly, which bears the responsibility of declaring capital increases.

(7) (Second) shareholders' meeting (if applicable)

Measure	Explanation	Documents	Timing
• (Second) shareholders' meeting/ general assembly (if applicable)	• Capital increase for the IPO (in the official trade the exclusive placement of existing shares is possible: necessary, for example, for the 'New Market' in Germany) • To be subscribed by the leader of the consortium of banks (lead manager) • If necessary, other changes to the bylaws, in particular authorised capital for, among others, the 'greenshoe' (i.e. surplus allocation option for the leader of the consortium of banks (lead manager) in case of an oversubscription • The 'greenshoe' shares are mostly lent from the existing shareholders and either bought from them following the exercise of the 'greenshoe' or returned to them following the implementation of a capital increase from authorised capital), and contingent capital for employee participation ('stock option plan')	• Resolution for a capital increase and resolution for other changes to the bylaws • Registration at the Commercial Registry	• Can occur up to just before the application for listing • Documents, however, must be completed beforehand and given to the judge at the Commercial Registry; this is unquestionably the one with whom the registration (which should be just before listing) should be negotiated

In contrast, according to national legal systems, clauses whereby the company merely commits within a defined period of time not to offer publicly shares obtained by capital increases and not to enter shares onto the market by broadly spreading them are effective. Such clauses serve the justified interest of the company without disturbing the legally assigned responsibilities of the company's management.

If only shares from existing shareholders are sold during an IPO, the company gains no capital from it. IPOs where exclusively existing shares are offered therefore occur rarely. In Germany's 'New Market', one of the prerequisites for listing is that at least half of the shares offered come from a capital increase so that the company receives fresh capital. But also, with a new listing in official trade, the offering of new shares betters the chance for the exchange price. A 'story of growth' develops only with difficulty without such fresh capital.

The new shares for the IPO can fundamentally be obtained either from authorised capital or through a regular capital increase. With authorised capital, the shareholders' meeting gives the board of directors the power to itself make a resolution for a capital increase, upon agreement with the supervisory board. The nominal value of the authorised capital can normally be up to half of the company's share capital. The capital increase from authorised capital is somewhat easier to implement with corporations with diversified holdings than the usual capital increase; on the other hand, this opens up the possibility of using the authorised capital for later acquisitions following the IPO without new resolutions of the shareholders' meeting.

Within the framework of the (second) shareholder's meeting that decides on the capital increase for the IPO, resolutions on further capital measures are often made, in particular to obtain contingent capital for stock option plans and for authorised capital, in particular for later acquisitions.

(8) Analyst presentation

Measure	Explanation	Documents	Timing
• Analyst presentation	• Introduction of the company or the shares by company management to the analysts of the bank consortium • The Analyst Reports are the significant marketing instrument of an IPO • The Analyst Reports are distributed by the leader of the consortium of banks (lead manager) to chosen institutional investors	• Documents for the analyst presentation	• The Analyst Reports are sent to potential investors usually three to four days following the presentation; they should be sent not too long before the listing, but in an appropriate period of time before the 'black out period' • The analyst presentation is terminated

(9) Application for approval of the prospectus/submission of the prospectus

Measure	Explanation	Documents	Timing
• Application for approval of the prospectus • Submission of the prospectus	• In its function as a sale prospectus, the document is regularly approved by the responsible institution of the Stock Exchange; at this point still without notice of the price for the shares ('Incomplete prospectus')	• Application for approval of the prospectus to the responsible institution of the Stock Exchange through the leading bank of the consortium (lead manager) • Incomplete sale prospectus	• Approximately three weeks before the onset of 'bookbuilding'

(10) Application for listing on the Stock Exchange

Measure	Explanation	Documents	Timing
• Application for listing on the Stock Exchange	• The shares are to be listed by the responsible institution of the Stock Exchange for official trade or for the regulated market	• Application for listing • Prospectus for listing on the Stock Exchange (the Sale prospectus is simultaneously the prospectus for listing on the Stock Exchange) • If necessary, 'lock-up' declarations of the existing shareholders – i.e. obligation to refrain from selling the existing shares for a period of (about) six months	• Usually and sensibly submitted together with the application for approval of the Prospectus, but can also occur later (up to four days before the intended listing)

(11) 'Black out period'

Measure	Explanation	Documents	Timing
• 'Black out period'	• Before 'bookbuilding', a period of time is usually upheld by the leader of the consortium of banks (lead manager) in which no more analyst reports are distributed		• Usually two weeks before 'bookbuilding'

(12) Submission of the 'comfort letter' and legal opinions

Measure	Explanation	Documents	Timing
• Submission of the 'Comfort letter' and legal opinions	• Auditor's (Comfort letter) and attorney's (Legal Opinions) confirm for their respective area of responsibility to the leading bank of the consortium (lead manager) that the information in the prospectus is correct and not misleading	• Comfort letter • Legal opinion	• Leading banks in some nations (lead managers) demand submission of a 'Comfort letter' and legal opinions multiple times, first before the approval of the Incomplete Prospectus • Leading banks of an American consortium (lead managers) mostly submit the information with the signing of the Underwriting Agreement

(13) Approval of the (incomplete) prospectus

Measure	Explanation	Documents	Timing
• Approval of the (Incomplete) Prospectus	• Through the responsible institution or the listing committee of the Stock Exchange	• Approval statement	• 15 trading days after submission of the application • Normally the application is submitted two days beforehand • The date should be in sync with the Stock Exchange

(14) Public announcement of a reference to the prospectus for the Stock Exchange and the listing procedure

Measure	Explanation	Documents	Timing
• Public announcement of a reference to the Prospectus for the Stock Exchange and the listing procedure	• In national journal for statutory Stock Market advertisements	• Public notice • Incomplete prospectus (must already be available at the appropriate locations)	• The day after approval

(15) 'Roadshow'/'bookbuilding' / 'auction proceedings'

Measure	Explanation	Documents	Timing
• 'Roadshow' • 'Bookbuilding' • 'Auction proceedings'	• 'Roadshow' – i.e. visit by company management to the potential institutional investors to introduce the company or the shares with the support of the leading bank of the consortium (lead manager); simultaneously serves the purpose of 'bookbuilding' – i.e. collection of the (binding) sales offers in the 'Order Book'	• 'Roadshow' documents	• At the earliest on the day after publication; therefore often: approval of the Prospectus on Friday, announcement of the notice on Saturday, beginning of 'bookbuilding' on Monday • At the latest two days before the beginning of 'bookbuilding' the Underwriting Agreement must be fully negotiated; otherwise the leading bank of the consortium (lead manager) will not begin 'bookbuilding' • Length of time: normally up to 20 days

Only with the publication of the (Incomplete) Prospectus are a public offer of shares and thus the beginning of the actual sales activities possible.

The Incomplete Prospectus does not yet contain an offer price (issuing price) for the shares. With almost all IPOs the determination of the issuing price occurs through a so-called 'bookbuilding' process. This is particularly the case if the subscription right of the existing shareholders is partially or completely excluded.

'Bookbuilding' entails drawing up the order book on the basis of submitted purchase orders for which the price determination and the distribution of shares remains open until the close of the collection of orders. Bookbuilding, which as a rule last about 14 days, is prepared through a pre-marketing phase and 'roadshows' – i.e. through presentations of representatives of the issuer and the leading bank of the consortium directly to the investors. In the actual bookbuilding phase the shares are offered for sale. At this time investors can submit purchase orders. These orders by investors take place on the basis of the previously published company valuation information conducted by the lead manager in agreement with the issuer. The entirety of the applications submitted to the lead manager and the other banks in the consortium make up the order book, which develops through the evaluation of individual orders (bookbuilding). Directly following the last day of bookbuilding the lead manager, the issuer and, if necessary, the existing shareholders determine the price. Next, the shares are allocated. Delivery of the shares against payment of the purchase price to the investors follows approximately five–seven days later.

It should be noted that in some national legal systems the board of directors of the issuer may not leave the determination of the subscription price entirely up to the banks. The subscription price is on the one hand a condition of the issue of shares so that in some national legal systems a determination requires the agreement of the supervisory committees. On the other hand, the board of directors is responsible in the case of an exclusion of a subscription in the interest of the existing shareholders for a determination of a subscription price oriented toward the market price. As far as the subscription price is determined through a bookbuilding process the supervisory committee can give the board of directors a certain range of fluctuation within which the board of directors is to determine the subscription price. The issuing price goal on the market is estimated on the basis of previously established abstract criteria so that the administrative committees may meet their monitoring duties.

Often an enormous gap opens up between the issue/offering price of a share and its first quotation and stock price. The high subscription profits, of course, please investors; however not the candidates for the Stock Exchange themselves, especially as the IPO could have brought in considerable more money for the company at a higher asking price. But the normal bookbuilding procedure also has disadvantages for the private investor; they often come up short with the allotment. With a considerable oversubscription, the decision is made by casting lots.

One way out is to determine the issuing price by auction. During an auction a price spread is often renounced and a price margin is often waived with the issuance. Each interested party should intensively analyse the business and subscribe within limits. After the close of the subscription deadline the interested parties receive an allotment, beginning with the highest bid, until the allotment is 'met' by the volume of the issuance. The lowest bid that receives an allotment determines the allotment price. In this way the auction proceedings, from the start of the Stock Exchange on, lead to a valuation on the basis of the market and to similar chances for the subscribers and bind such investors who are interested in a long-term investment.

It should be critically noted with this procedure that it is difficult even for analysts correctly to analyse companies. Only a small number of private investors will be able to determine an appropriate price for the share. In each case the information in the Prospectus must be substantially more detailed than is usually the case and contain, among others, comprehensive estimates of the development in profits and earnings as well as detailed comparative data with other companies in the industry. This causes the concern that hopes for the market price with new issuances can be lost during the auction. The intended advantages of the auction can be balanced out through an adaptation of the price range during the subscription time period. Moreover, the candidate for the issuance loses the possibility of determining the structure of investors himself and thus seeing to a balanced mix between private and institutional investors.

If only for this reason, certain modifications of the auction procedure are necessary. In the case of enormous oversubscription it could in the future lead to an increase in the span of the price; this situation concerns a process that has long been used in the USA.

(16) Publication of the application for listing

Measure	Explanation	Documents	Timing
• Publication of the application for listing • Through the Stock Exchange	• Publication of the application for listing in a national journal for statutory stock market advertisements		• Three days before listing • Date can be determined in conjunction with the Stock Exchange

(17) Signing of the underwriting agreement

Measure	Explanation	Documents	Timing
• Signing of the Underwriting Agreement	• With the signing of the Underwriting Agreement the leading bank (lead manager) commits to underwrite and place the shares • The Underwriting Agreement is the central agreement of an IPO that, in particular, contains also the significant obligations of the selling shareholders and the company, including comprehensive representations and often with voluntary 'lock up'	• Underwriting Agreement with all attachments, in particular the Legal Opinions and the Comfort letter	• Occurs at the earliest shortly before beginning of 'bookbuilding' (after determination of the price span) • Mostly only with the close of 'bookbuilding' process (because the lead manager knows only as of this time whether the placement will be successful)

(18) Possible signing of the subscription certificate/payment of the capital increase/registration at the commercial registry (if applicable)

Measure	Explanation	Documents	Timing
• Possible signing of the Subscription Certificate • Payment of the capital increase • Registration at the Commercial Registry (if applicable) • 'First Closure' The conditions precedent regularly contained in the Underwriting Agreement must be fulfilled at the time of the transfer of the subscription certificate or notification at the Commercial Registry about registration of the capital increase	• The lead manager itself subscribes to the new shares and must then make available the nominal capital amount of the company shares to the company • The notification at the Commercial Registry is complete only upon the submission of the subscription certificate	• Subscription Certificate • Notification at the Commercial Registry	• Should occur if possible only directly before the stock listing in order to keep the time period short, if possible, between the payment of the capital increase and the receipt of the placement profit by the lead manager

(19) Possible notification of the capital increase at the commercial registry (if applicable)

Measure	Explanation	Documents	Timing
• Notification of the capital increase at the Commercial Registry (if applicable)	• The new shares materialise only with the registration of the capital increase at the Commercial Registry • The notification of the registration is a condition for the listing of the shares	• Notification of the registration	• Critical moment in time • Only when the judge at the Registration Court permits a registration specified for a particular day is the time period between the subscription of shares and the listing to be kept short (day before or even of the listing)

The point in time of the registration of the capital increase (if applicable) for the IPO is a critical moment when not just existing shares are sold.

The bank that exclusively subscribes to the new shares in order then to place them with the public must pay the nominal value of the capital increase in full. Proof of the payment is a condition for the registration of the capital increase. The new shares regularly develop only with the registration of the capital increase and can only then be listed on the Stock Exchange.

The entire time plan of the IPO thus relies in any case of the placement of new shares corresponding to the conditions of the national legal systems on the timely registration of the capital increase. The point in time of the registration, however, is not at the discretion of the participants, but rather only at that of the responsible Registration Court judge. It is therefore necessary that in particular the attorneys advising the issuers work closely in agreement with the Registration Court judge. Regarding IPOs, most Registration Court judges are ready to allow registration for a specific day, as long as complete documentation is provided. Nevertheless, no right exists to this process. An uncooperative Registration Court judge can cause overwhelming problems for a successful IPO.

(20) End of 'bookbuilding'/price determination/allotment

Measure	Explanation	Documents	Timing
• End of 'Bookbuilding' • Price determination • Allotment	• The Order Book is evaluated, the sales price determined and the allotment of shares for the acquirers established • Signing of the Price Determination Agreement	• Price Determination Agreement	• Day before listing

(21) 'Bring down call'/'blood Letter'/submission of the prospectus for listing on the Stock Exchange

Measure	Explanation	Documents	Timing
• 'Bring down call' • 'Blood letter' • Submission of the Prospectus for listing on the Stock Exchange	• 'Bring down call': consultants question company management about new developments that have yet to be mentioned in the Prospectus • 'Blood letter': letter of the lead manager to the company with listing of the Prospectus data that originate with the lead manager (and the correctness for which the lead manager is liable within the internal relationship) • Determination and transmission of the final Prospectus (with the purchase price of the shares) to the Stock Exchange	• 'Blood letter' • Prospectus for listing on the Stock Exchange (as a rule in the national language and in English translation)	• Day before listing

The 'Bring down call' and 'Blood letter' serve to cover the changes that are still to be included in the final draft of the Prospectus. The final version of the Prospectus that also contains the issuing price after the end of the 'bookbuilding' process is then newly submitted for approval to the responsible institution of the Stock Exchange.

(22) Listing of the shares for trade

Measure	Explanation	Documents	Timing
• Listing of the shares for trade	• Listing for official trade or regulated market	• Listing notification of the responsible institution of the Stock Exchange	• Day after the end of 'bookbuilding' process

(23) Announcement of reference

Measure	Explanation	Documents	Timing
• Public announcement of a reference to the Prospectus for listing on the Stock Exchange and the listing	• Reference to the publication of the Prospectus and the listing	• Announcement of the reference to the Prospectus for listing on the Stock Exchange and the listing	• Day following the listing • At least two weeks before quotation

(24) Start of quotation

Measure	Explanation	Documents	Timing
• Start of quotation	• Start of shares being quoted		• At least three days after announcement of the reference to the publication of the Prospectus and the listing • At the latest six months after listing • Often: listing on Friday, announcement of reference on Saturday, start of shares being quoted on Monday

With the beginning of the quotation the IPO is completed. With the onset of quotation the issuer faces new and different obligations corresponding to the provisons of the respective national legal systems. Thus, following listing on the Stock Exchange, the issuer must regularly publish a report that contains financial information about its business operations and results, in particular profits and losses, yearly surpluses or deficits as well as a capital funds statement. Furthermore, reports should clarify turnover, order book, cost and price development, R&D activities as well as the number of employees and the level of investments. The calling of a shareholders' meeting as well as information on the distribution of dividends, on the issuance of new shares and the exercise of swap, stock or subscription rights are all to be published.

The annual report is to be drawn up regularly according to International Accounting Standards (IAS), according to the American Generally Accepted Accounting Principles (GAAP) or according to national accounting procedures must contain a calculation of the transition and is to be published with the status report. In addition, the issuer must recognise the Takeover Code of the commission of experts on the Stock Exchange or similar regulations.

At the beginning of each fiscal year a business calendar is to be created in the national language and in English that contains information about important dates – such as, for example, place and time of the shareholders' meeting, press conference on accounting information and meetings of analysts.

As a rule within a period of six months following listing significant changes in the information contained in the prospectus about the company must be published by way of a supplement. Furthermore, company management is subject to further obligations about publicity following the IPO; for example, within the framework of their so-called 'obligation for ad hoc publicity', management must immediately publish conditions that have a substantial influence on the company's market price.

(25) 'Closing'

Measure	Explanation	Documents	Timing
• 'Second closing'	• Calculation and transfer of placement earnings • The issuance earnings (difference between nominal value and subscription price and after deduction of provisions and costs) are transferred to the company and the selling shareholders	• Legal Opinion, Officers' Certificate and 'Comfort letter', according to which the underwriting of the shares does not fall into any circumstances that have a disadvantageous outcome for business operations or the financial situation of the issuer	• Usually two days following IPO

As already explained above, Underwriting Agreements regularly contain provisons according to which the conditions precedent must be fulfilled at the point in time of the transfer of the subscription certificate and (if applicable) the registration at the Commercial Registry of the capital increase (First Closing).

Moreover, directly before the transfer of the issuance earnings a Legal Opinion, an Officers' Certificate and a 'Comfort letter' are to be provided again, according to which no circumstances have arisen since the underwriting of the shares that have a disadvantageous outcome for business operations or the financial situation of the issuer (Second Closing).

Only following this will the earnings of the issuance (difference between nominal value and subscription price and after deduction of provisions and costs) be transferred to the company and the selling shareholders.

(26) 'Greenshoe' exercise

Measure	Explanation	Documents	Timing
• Possible exercise of a 'greenshoe' option	• A 'greenshoe' option is exercised to influence the market – i.e. only if the price of the listing has risen • The shares lent by the lead manager are almost always allotted	• Following the exercise of a 'greenshoe' option: – either the existing shareholders conclude with the banks corresponding security loan agreements for use – or institutional investors refuse the delivery of a certain number of shares until the close of the 'greenshoe' period • Capital increase by authorised capital • Resolution of the board of directors and (if applicable) the supervisory board and (if applicable) the registration at the Commercial Registry	• Within about 30 days following the IPO

Issuing banks are regularly granted a 'greenshoe' option on an IPO.

The concept of a 'greenshoe' option goes back to the issuance of the Greenshoe Manufacturing Company for which this instrument for influencing the market was first used. The group of issuing banks receives the allocation option to underwrite and to allocate further shares beyond the initial issue volume at a total nominal value of 10 per cent to 15 per cent of the original underwritten shares at the same price that was determined during bookbuilding within a time period usually of about 20 to 45 days following placement of the shares ('greenshoe' period).

Although these new shares are not yet underwritten they are already allocated with the other shares shortly before listing occurs in that either the existing shareholders conclude with the banks corresponding security loan agreements of stocks for use or institutional investors refuse the delivery of a certain number of shares until the close of the 'greenshoe' period. In this way the banks can influence the market price and, in the case of the market price of the shares placed falling under the subscription price, take shares from the market through support buying in order to restabilise the market price. As long as support buying is not at all or only partially necessary the issuing banks exercise their option at the end of the 'greenshoe' period and can thus transfer back the borrowed shares or effectively deliver the further allocated shares.

The mere possibility of such support buying as well as the exercise of a 'greenshoe' option at the end of the 'greenshoe' period is seen by the capital market as a positive sign and leads in all cases to a positive price valuation.

The ability to implement a 'greenshoe' option can be secured through a capital increase already established and approved at an earlier point in time, within the framework of which the board of directors receives the power to increase the capital at the exclusion of the shareholders' subscription rights. With an IPO the exclusion of subscription rights is, in principle allowed if the necessary number of shares can be made available only in this way and the company can show objective reasons, overwhelming the interest of the existing shareholders. It suffices to rewrite in general and in the abstract to the shareholders' meeting the measure that supports the exclusion of subscription rights at the point in time of the drafting of the resolution about the empowerment of the board of directors.

When the 'greenshoe' option is exercised the market price of the shares placed normally lies above the original subscription price; if the market price falls namely below the subscription price during the 'greenshoe' period, it results in support buying with the consequence that the 'greenshoe' option is later not exercised at all, or only in part.

(27) 'Greenshoe' closing

Measure	Explanation	Documents	Timing
• 'Greenshoe' closing (if applicable)	• Settlement and transfer of the profits from placing the 'greenshoe' shares	• The Underwriting Agreement often provides again for the submission of a 'Comfort letter' and Legal Opinions	• Directly following registration of the capital increase

(28) End of the 'black out period'/requirements for post-formation acquisition

Measure	Explanation	Documents	Timing
• End of the 'black out period'	• Analyst reports can be distributed again		• Regularly 40 days after the listing

(29) Post-formation requirements

If a company is converted into a stock corporation, provisions of so-called post-formation requirements must be observed in the period following conversion, in particular after stock exchange listing.

With agreements according to which the company acquires investments and assets for payment that is partially (e.g. one-tenth) above the share capital and which are executed in the first two years following the registration of the new company in the Commercial Registry, according to some national legal systems not only is a resolution of the shareholders' meeting necessary, but also a post-formation acquisition examination, a post-formation acquisition report of the supervisory committees and registration in the Commercial Registry. In newly established or converted corporations many conditions of the bylaws exist that explain comprehensively the acquisition of companies and other assets for the object of the company.

10 International (Cross-Border) M&A

The internationalisation of the economy, and not least the increasing influence of investment banks, corporate finance departments of the large auditing companies and the international law firms, contribute to the fact that, increasingly, Anglo-American law determines the content and style of international (cross-border) mergers and acquisitions.

This is true also for the formation of purchase and sale agreements that according to the principles of Anglo-American law are much more influenced by comprehensive and detailed regulations than agreements under other national legal systems.

According to the so-called 'parole evidence rule' of Anglo-American contract law, neither the preliminary correspondence nor the negotiations of the parties to the contract as extending evidence ('parole evidence') are allowed as proof or interpretation of the content of the agreement. In the interest of legal clarity and their own security, the parties to the contract are therefore recommended to uphold thoroughly and comprehensively all regulations in the agreement. Furthermore, agreement clauses, which enumerate certain facts, extend only to those facts that belong to the type listed. This pertains in particular to questions of liability, so that from the perspective of common law practice it is highly recommended that all facts regarding representations and warranties are to be included in detail in the text of the agreement.

The considerable scope of international purchase and sale agreements resulting from this creates the impression that all agreements and conditions pertaining to the transactions are conclusively included in the agreement. Furthermore, in many ways the impression exists that all legal questions of the transaction can be put under the control of a desired legal system with a choice of law clause.

Such an idea, however, does not recognise that cross-border transactions pertain to numerous areas of law to which the parties to the contract do not have access by way of a choice of law. This is particularly the case for questions of international property law, corporation law and employment law. Despite a corresponding choice of law clause it can be questionable which national law pertains in a share deal to the transfer of shares and in an asset deal to the transfer of assets, to the transition of employment contracts, to the financing and last but not least to the form requirements that are to be observed. This is also the case with the submission of a corresponding Letter of Intent.

This makes it necessary to take into consideration the aspects under international and civil law that may come up during international company acquisitions, such as:

- Contract law:
  - Principles of the choice of law
  - Scope of the choice of law
  - Law to be applied given the lack of a choice of law
- Dispositions:
  - Principles
  - Moveable goods
  - Intangible assets
  - Other (*rights in rem*)
- Representation of a company within the framework of a transaction
- Form requirements:
  - Undertakings
  - Dispositions
  - Authentication by a notary
  - Side letter with confidential side arrangements for the purchase and sale agreement
- Liability from asset acquisition and continuation of a company/business
- Employment and co-determination law
- Financing
- Corporate law:
  - Company statute
  - Relocation of headquarters
  - International corporation law relating to groups
  - Cross-border conversions.

Notes

1 See M&A in 30 legal systems worldwide, in Law Business Research (2000) *Getting the Deal Through*. Details of M&A in Germany, Eastern Europe (Russia, Poland, Hungary, Czech Republic), Asia (China, Hong Kong/China, India, Singapore, Indonesia and Japan) and South Africa are described by Picot (1998). See also Picot, (2000a), and (2000b).
For further information see <www.mergers-and-acquisitions.de>

2 Council Directive 98/50/EC of the European Union of 29 June 1998 amending Directive 77/187/EEC on the approximation of the laws of the Member States relating to the safeguarding of employees' rights in the event of transfers of undertakings, businesses or parts of businesses.

3 See Chapter 9, and in particular the Council Directive 98/50/EC of the European Union of 29 June 1998 amending Directive 77/187/EEC on the approximation of the laws of the Member States relating to the safeguarding of employees' rights in the event of transfers of undertakings, businesses or parts of businesses.

Bibliography

Ellison, J. and Kling, E. (1997) *Joint Ventures in Europe*, 2nd edn (London).
Global Competition Review (2000) *Getting the Deal Through* (London).
Hewitt, I. (2002) [1887] *Joint Ventures*, 2nd edn (London).
Micheler, E. and Prentice, D. D. (2000) *Joint Ventures in English and German Law* (London).
Law Business Research (2000) *Getting the Deal Through* (London).
Picot, G. (1998) *Unternehmenskauf und Restrukturierung* (Company Purchasing and Restructuring), 2nd edn (München).
Picot, G. (2000a) *Mergers & Acquisitions in Germany – Handbook*, 2nd edn (New York).
Picot, G. (2000b) *Handbuch Mergers & Acquisitions*, 2nd edn (Stuttgart).
For further information see <http://www.mergers-and-acquisitions.de>

5
Due Diligence

Heinrich Pack

1 Introduction

The euphoria surrounding M&A contrasts somewhat with the high risk that is still associated with such transactions. Empirical surveys reveal failure rates of between 30 and 70 per cent, with the term 'failure' not necessarily being limited to a formal breakdown, but rather meaning that the results achieved fall well short of the objectives set (essentially the harnessing of synergy effects). The main reasons cited for the high disappointment quota are as follows:

(a) Insufficient knowledge of the candidate company and its suitability for, or adaptability to, the planned strategy
(b) Overvaluation of the synergy potential and, as a result, agreement of an inflated purchase price for the acquisition target
(c) Difficulties with the integration of the target company within the corporate organisation of the acquiring company.

The problems indicated under (a) and largely also those indicated under (b) can, however, be minimised by an objective, systematic analysis of the acquisition target. The process applied in this respect is generally known as *due diligence*.

2 The Pre-Contractual Phase in the Acquisition of a Target Company

Owing to the complexity of the problems that occur when purchasing/taking over a company, it is essential to systematise the acquisition process.

Within this framework, the *pre-contractual negotiation phase* should ideally be utilised in order to explore the objectives of purchaser and seller, and to align these to one another to the maximum extent possible.

This phase is characterised by a high degree of uncertainty on the one hand, and pronounced mistrust on the other.

Consequently it is understandable that, at this juncture, there appears to be an abundance of conflicting interests between purchaser and seller that need to be reconciled.

In order to render the acquisition process simpler and more controllable, various practical instruments have been developed that impart some structure to the procedure (Table 5.1).

3 Philosophy, Origin and Content of the Due Diligence Exercise

The likelihood of joining the high failure rate statistics mentioned above, and thus the risk associated with the purchase of a company, depends in no small degree on the extent to which the perception that the acquiring company has of the target company actually coincides with reality.

The purchaser tends to lack a wide range of information required in order to determine, for example, an appropriate purchase price, to ascertain synergies, or to minimise risk. The seller, on the other hand, either has all such information readily to hand, or has the ability to obtain such information without undue difficulty.

Agreement to the performance of a 'due diligence' exercise signals the willingness of the seller to transfer his knowledge to the purchaser, and thus to eliminate the 'information asymmetry' (Figure 5.1).

'In this sense, the performance of a due diligence exercise can be regarded as the process of knowledge transfer on the part of the seller and knowledge acquisition on the part of the purchaser.'[1]

Origin of the Term 'due diligence'

The term 'due diligence' or the 'due diligence concept' has its origins in Anglo-American law, and particularly in the statutory regulations governing the capital market in the USA.

History

Looking after the interests, and the protection, of investors is the responsibility in the USA of the SEC (Securities Exchange Commission). Of particular importance for the M&A sector within the compass of the Securities Laws are the following:

- the Securities Act (1933), and
- the Securities Exchange Act (1934).

Table 5.1 Main steps in the acquisition procedure

• Confidentiality Agreement/Statement of Non-Disclosure • Letter of Intent (LOI) • Due diligence • Memorandum of Understanding (MoU)	**Pre-contractual phase**
• **Contract** • **Classification of outstanding problems (subject to...)** • **Closing**	

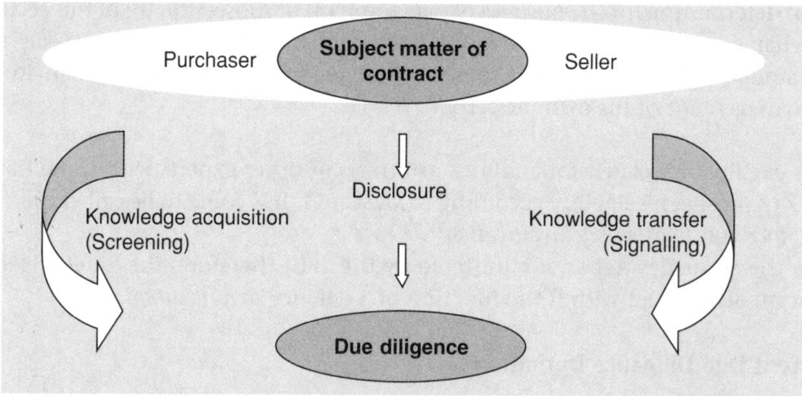

Figure 5.1 Due diligence exercise geared to overcoming information asymmetries prior to contract

While the Securities Act (SA) is concerned with the initial public offer (IPO) of stocks and bonds, the Securities Exchange Act (SEA) deals with the trading (and thus also the sale) of securities that have already been registered.

The SA controls the 'form, content and requirements of financial statements' within the framework of new issues.

The prospectus *liability* according to the Securities Act jointly affects not only the issuer and the transferee but also the auditors, consultants and all other experts involved, without the need for any direct contractual relationship (privity of contract) to exist between these and the purchaser of the security.

This third-party liability is made all the more onerous by the fact that the burden of proof lies almost entirely with the accused. For the plaintiff it is sufficient to prove that the 'Registration Statement' contains:

- An untrue statement
- A misleading fact, or
- An omission.

If the accused is unable to provide counter-evidence, exculpation can be achieved if he is able to prove that

> *he had, after reasonable investigation, reasonable ground to believe and did believe*, at the time such part of the registration statement became effective, that the statements therein were true and that there was no omission to state a material fact required to be stated therein or necessary to make the statements therein not misleading.

The terms *reasonable investigation* and *reasonable ground to believe* are closely defined in SA sec. 11c:

> In determining for the purpose of paragraph (3) of subsection (b) of this section, what constitutes *reasonable investigation* and *reasonable ground for belief*, the standard of reasonableness shall be that required of a prudent man in the management of his own property.

This exculpatory clause for auditors, attorneys or other experts within the framework of prospectus liability according to SA sec. 11 'has come to be called the *"Due Diligence"* or *"reasonable investigation" defence*'.[2]

In the Securities Act as administered by the SEC, therefore, the 'due diligence' concept also carries with it the function of a defence *in a litigation*.

Current Due Diligence Definition

With the further extension of the securities laws through the advent of the Securities Exchange Act 1934, the concept of 'due diligence' has been transformed into a preventive exercise aimed at the identification, disclosure and limitation of risks.

This further development already comes very close to the definition of the term 'due diligence' as currently applied in today's M&A sector.

Evolving from its literal definition of 'acting with proper prudence or reasonableness', the due diligence concept has crystallised into a purposeful, systematic, professional investigation of business opportunity and risk during on-going sale negotiations.

Through the application of as precise a set of analyses as possible – performed from the perspectives of the acquiring company's strategic objectives and the likely cost-reducing synergies – such an investigation enables an assessment to be made as to whether and to what extent the value of the company being acquired might be increased or should be discounted.

A more far-reaching approach is offered by Rockholtz[3] who allocates to the due diligence process the role of both early-warning system geared to flagging up acquisition risks, and of elementary information provider. Through the identification and assessment of the value increase potential of the target company, the due diligence exercise is thus expected to generate the basis not only for the subsequent valuation of the company but also for the realisation of this potential.

4 Planning and Performance of the Due Diligence

Sources of Information

The feasibility and the quality of a due diligence audit depends essentially on the information which is or can be made available.

Information concerning a company, particularly if it relates to sensitive areas or activities, is, however, normally not publicly available. Access to such knowledge can therefore be obtained only with the consent and assistance of the selling party.

The – in legal terms – weak position of the seller emanating from a Confidentiality Agreement or a Letter of Intent *can be an obstacle to the acquisition of information.*

Consequently, it is recommended in this regard to agree in the Letter of Intent a formulation relating to the due diligence exercise that allows sufficient room for manoeuvre so that the seller is ultimately obliged to provide the relevant information. Confidence-building measures on the side of the purchaser can be extremely helpful in this regard.

On the other hand, it should also be clear to the seller's team that the withholding of (valuation-relevant) information will lead to mistrust among the purchaser's team, with the consequence that the purchase price offered may be reduced or a demand for indemnities may be submitted.

External data relating to the target company can be obtained without recourse to the seller. It is thus a matter of the purchaser's skill to unearth data relevant to the decision-making and thus to the evaluation process, and to analyse this appropriately. There is no doubt, however, that the internal data of the target company will be of decisive importance for the overall assessment.

The Due Diligence Team

The performance of the due diligence exercise will, in most cases, be carried out by a project organisation. This means that, aside from a detailed time schedule, a clear definition of the scope of the investigation, the areas of activity and the spheres of responsibility is required from the outset. It is often advisable to form a team comprising not only purchasing company personnel but also, in most cases, external consultants. Whether employees from the target company are also involved, or whether the seller merely makes 'information material' available will depend on the type of purchase involved and the level of mutual trust that prevails.

The literature contains the following possible approaches to constituting and organising such a team:[4]

- Experts' approach
- Team approach
- Departmental approach.

The differences between the individual approaches appear to be minor, but in their practical implementation (i.e. in terms of the procedural organisation) there are significant differences.

In the *experts' approach*, the acquisition itself is driven by the purchaser's management. A team of experts from various disciplines is then constituted solely for the purpose of the due diligence exercise (and for valuation issues). External consultants may also be opted in as and when required.

The *team approach* entails the constitution of a team (specifically assembled for each acquisition), which then accompanies the acquisition throughout the entire process. Here, too, the team consists of experts from the acquiring company and, possibly, external specialists. The team leader assumes a major proportion of the responsibility, with the management intervening only in the event of disputes or other difficulties, and then subsequently in the final negotiating phase.

Adopting the *departmental approach* assumes that the acquiring company has its own M&A unit (department) that then supports the management throughout the process.

It is almost impossible to compare the relative merits of these various approaches, although in practice it can be safely said that the team approach dominates the scene.

Müller-Stewens[5] cites two interesting observations that have come to light as a result of specific investigations.

In terms of the *acquisition frequency*, those companies which, to date, have undertaken few acquisitions tend to adopt the experts' approach; companies with a significantly higher acquisition frequency prefer the team approach; and companies that are involved in a great many transactions (i.e. for which acquisitions are an important, integral and systematically pursued means of growing a business), prefer the departmental approach.

In *acquisition policy* terms, the experts' approach is frequently adopted for horizontal acquisitions. In the case of the team approach, too, the horizontal direction predominates; vertical transactions are also pursued on a secondary level. Corporate policy here is likely to be focused on expansion or supplementation of the company's product portfolio or market coverage. With the departmental approach, not only horizontal and vertical but also concentric/conglomerate acquisitions are pursued.

For the purchasing company, the team approach has the advantage that the contacts remain the same throughout the entire acquisition process. Organisational incorporation of the due diligence team might, therefore, take the form in Figure 5.2.

As a rule, the team is assembled from employees from the accounting, personnel, tax, law and sales functions. The external consultants incorporated into the

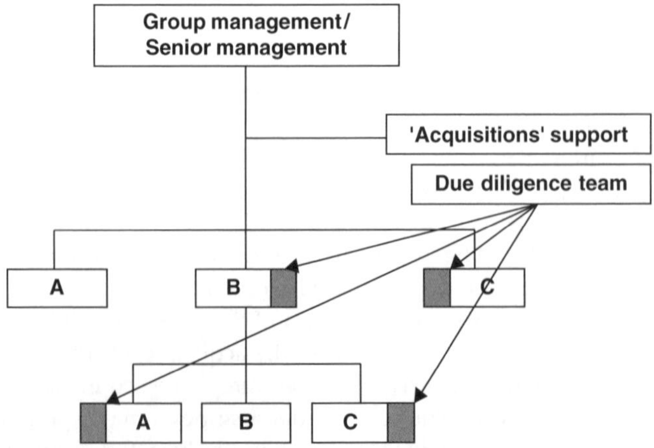

Figure 5.2 Organisational integration of the due diligence team

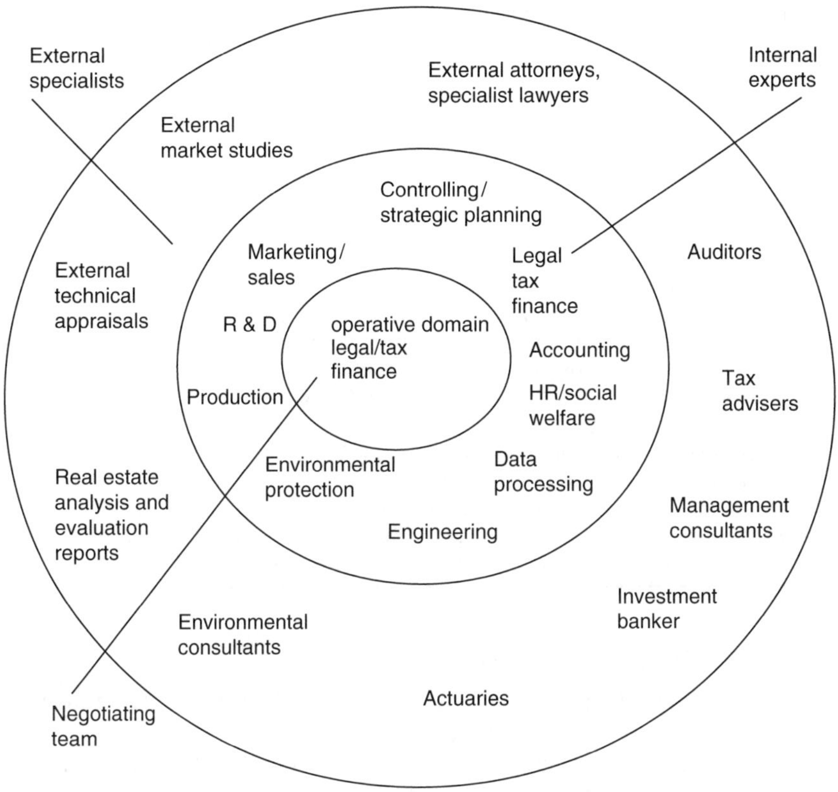

Figure 5.3 Simplified replication of the experts' system as applied by BASF in relation to acquisitions

team take the form, in the first instance, of attorneys, tax auditors or investment bankers.

Procedural Organisation of the Due Diligence Exercise

The organisational structure of the due diligence audit can essentially be divided into three main categories of activity:

- Information *gathering*
- Information *processing*
- Information *analysis*.

In many cases, the scheduling and content aspects of the due diligence exercise will be extensively stipulated in the Letter of Intent.

The typical sequence of events of a due diligence audit tends to follow the pattern indicated in Table 5.2.[6]

Table 5.2 Sequence of a due diligence audit

1. **Audit preparation**
   - Selection of site
   - Definition of audit objectives
   - Constitution of the audit team
   - Preparation of the audit plan (scope, priorities, processes, schedule)
   - Evaluation of documents already in hand
   - Possible distribution of questionnaires and checklists
2. **Audit performance**
   - Management presentation and meetings with employees
   - Facility inspection and analyses in the 'data room'
   - Examination of the defined investigation elements
   - Provisional evaluation of the audit results
   - Discussion of the provisional results with the seller's management
3. **Audit post-processing**
   - Detailed analysis and summary evaluation
   - Forecast of cash flow in financial plans
   - Coordination and authorship of the due diligence memorandum
   - Proposal of strategies for solving problems in relation to the acquisition target
   - Development, where appropriate, of a prioritised action plan.

Individual Due Diligence activities

The remit of the due diligence audit means that it is necessary to view and analyse the target company in all its functions.

Figure 5.4 shows a systematic structure of the individual functions and activities, although not all these areas need to be taken into consideration in every acquisition project. It must also be remembered that the individual areas exhibit significant degrees of interdependence, and these have to be taken into consideration in relation to specific investigations.

5 Functions of the Due Diligence Exercise

Basic and External Due Diligence

The basic and the external due diligence are only loosely related to the due diligence audit proper. The special status afforded to these two areas derives from the fact that certain information concerning the target company can be obtained *before* the detailed due diligence exercise (and thus without involving the seller). This information tends to be cross-functional in nature and can thus not be readily allocated for analysis to individual areas of the due diligence audit (Table 5.3).

Thus the gathering of the basic data concentrates mainly on information that will already have been assembled and collated, e.g. when selecting possible candidates for purchase, *prior to performance of the main due diligence audit.*

In the case of the other documents that belong to the basic due diligence, a distinction is made between company-internal and public-domain data (Table 5.4).

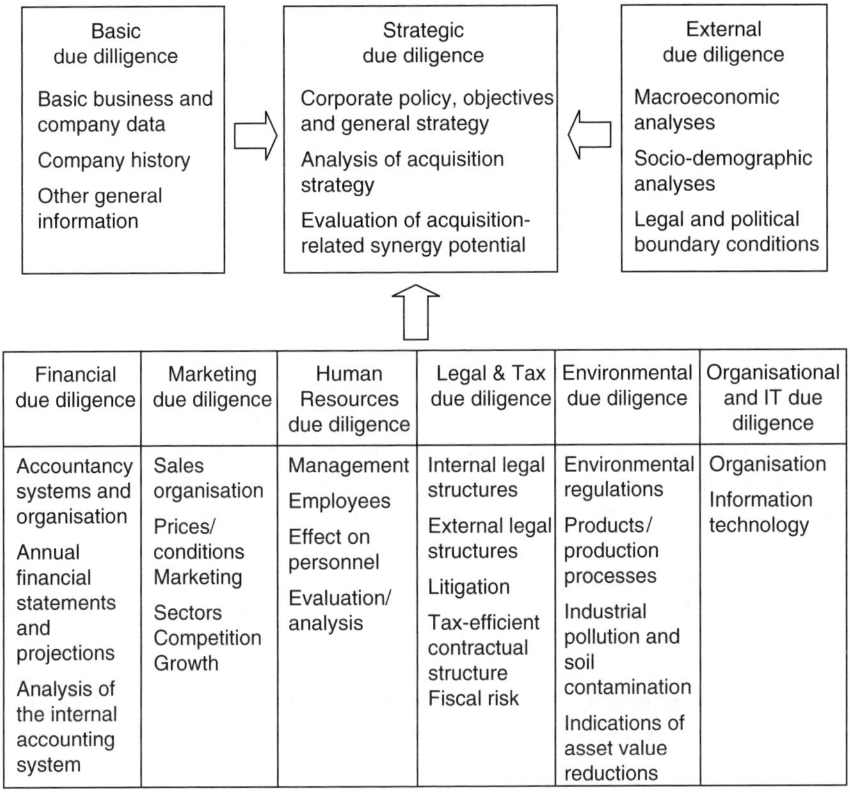

Figure 5.4 Individual due diligence activities
Source: Berens and Brauner (1999, p. 364).

Table 5.3 Basic data gathered during the basic due diligence exercise

- Name and legal form of company
- Domicile of company
- Addresses, telephone and fax numbers
- E-mail addresses, Internet homepage/website of company
- Contact names for selling price negotiations and the individual audits
- Names of directors, senior managers and M&A officers
- Date and place of establishment, entry in Commercial Register
- Founders and previous proprietors of company
- Brief history of company
- Brief description of business activities

The public domain data have, in principle, the same status as the basic data: their collection and collation can be organised in advance (i.e. without a due diligence approach).

Table 5.4 Other data collated for the basic due diligence exercise

- *Company–internal*
  - Minutes of board/management meetings
  - Minutes of AGMs/General Meetings of Members (shareholders' meetings)
  - Articles of incorporation and bylaws/Company statutes
  - Company reports and value appraisals
  - Reasons for selling the company
- *Public domain corporate data*
  - Press releases
  - Image/reputation of the company
  - Ratings assigned by information services

The company–internal data, on the other hand, can be obtained only via the due diligence audit, but are not assignable to any one particular area. Owing to the high sensitivity which attaches, for example, to minutes of board and managerial meetings, it is in any case questionable whether the seller would be prepared to disclose their content at this stage of negotiations.

The external due diligence exercise is concerned with the analysis of the factors that lie outside the area of influence of the target and purchasing companies. Not included are the analyses of the market or the sector in which the acquisition target is active or will be active. These items of information are a constituent part of the marketing due diligence. The essential contents of the external due diligence consequently lie in the developmental trends exhibited by the relevant general economic and outline business data.

The type of research necessary for acquiring such information is indicated in the list in Table 5.5 (cf. also the external due diligence checklist cited in Berens and Brauner (1999, p. 368).

Financial Due Diligence

The financial due diligence – frequently described as the 'focus' of the entire due diligence process – serves the purpose of acquiring and analysing information relating to the economic and financial situation of the acquisition target.

Although the database of the financial due diligence is predominantly oriented to the past and present, the conclusions drawn from the due diligence process do not remain within this framework. The current-data analysis has to be geared toward providing a decisive platform for preparing and examining projections and planning data. Through interaction with other activities of the due diligence process – particularly the market due diligence – existing plans can be examined for their plausibility, and initial budgets drafted.

The financial due diligence audit essentially relies on the data of the external accounting system, i.e. on:

- The *balance sheet* and
- The *statement of income* (aka earnings statement, profit and loss account)

Table 5.5 External due diligence research

- Analysis of the macroeconomic situation of countries in which the company is active or intends to be active:
  - Development of gross domestic product (GDP) and purchasing power
  - Balance of payments and exchange rate developments
  - State expenditures, state deficits, inflation
  - Taxes, subsidies
  - Capital market developments
  - Compensatory or exacerbating effect of business cycles in relation to those of parent company's country
- Analysis of demographic structure and education level prevailing in the relevant countries, and especially in regions in which the target company is active
- Analysis of infrastructure and its future development, particularly in the transport and telecommunications sectors
- Identification of extent of corruption and repression in relevant countries
- Examination of underlying conditions emanating from corporate, fiscal and labour law
- Developmental trends in relation to laws and legal provisions
- Identification of:
  - Dangers owing to political influence
  - Existing or expected protectionist measures
  - Repatriation problems or the possible threat of these
- Evaluation to determine what effects these factors are likely to have on the business activity of the target company

and also, where available, the management report/business review and the notes to the financial statements.

As a matter of primary importance, however, the audit should concentrate on the *organisation* of the accounting system. Statements and notes from the auditors (auditors' report, management letter, etc.) may be of decisive significance in this respect. Data from the internal accounting system can constitute an especially important source of information (also in regard to the preparation of budgets and projections).

As the balance sheet/statement of income are, generally speaking, prepared at the aggregation level of the 'corporate entity', the externally published accounting data often lack information relating to individual products. If in existence and available, therefore, product results, contribution costs (direct costings), cost budgets and similar data should be obtained from the internal accounting corpus and incorporated in the due diligence analysis.

The financial due diligence audit is usually performed with the aid of *structured checklists*. This approach has become generally accepted because the starting materials (balance sheet, statement of income) are also heavily pre-structured in line with legal requirements.[7]

Consequently, this present treatment of the subject can concentrate on just a few aspects that appear to be particularly important.

As already mentioned, the data tends to be subordinate to the organisation of the accounting system. Consequently, at the beginning of the financial due diligence exercise, the first step is to produce a description of the bookkeeping, balance sheet preparation and reporting systems.

The questions that arise relate to:

- The applied balance sheet preparation and valuation/accounting principles
- The consistency with which the balance sheet preparation and valuation/accounting principles are applied
- Possible infringements within the framework of the balance sheet preparation and valuation/accounting methods.

In the case of annual financial statements covered by an auditors' report, the comments and remarks of the auditors (e.g. as detailed in the management letter) may also be used in the analysis. However, discretion is advised where acquiring companies abroad.

Where internationally valid accounting standards such as IAS or GAAP are applied, the accounting principles are a known factor, while the application of national accounting and valuation rules that deviate from these international standards can occasionally impede an effective assessment and translation according to Germany's GOB (Principles of Orderly Accounting).

The analysis of the annual financial statements encompasses:

- The *balance sheet* and
- The *statement of income.*

For the analysis of the balance sheet, it is important to include in the overall appraisal the annual financial statements of the last three to five years and also an up-to-date interim financial statement. Essentially, the object is:

- to examine the *external assets* for hidden reserves/undisclosed encumbrances and for items not necessary for the business, and
- to examine the *equity capital/stockholders' equity* and the *liabilities* of the company for full and complete disclosure.

In the case of the fixed assets, it is bound to be difficult to determine a market value from original or historical cost. Owing to the conservative approach of Germany's GOB, there are frequently hidden reserves in:

- Property and buildings, and
- Machinery, plant and equipment

in which case an investigation is advisable to determine whether a higher current/fair market value may actually be realisable for property/buildings if a sale of such assets were to be seriously pursued.

In the case of machinery, plant and equipment, the cause for a market value exceeding a book value often lies in the fact that the useful service lifetime can extend well beyond the depreciation period.

Special caution is advised in relation to intangible fixed assets. The options available concerning the valuation principles that may be applied (market or cost) render an estimate of the real worth of these items complicated.

Considerable care is also advised with respect to current assets, i.e. when valuing stocks and inventories. In the case of raw materials and supplies, and also semi-finished products, it must be ensured that sufficiently high corrections (in practice this usually means deductions) are applied to take into account non-currency, technical obsolescence or surpluses. Cases of appreciation, upward revaluation and write-ups occur rather more rarely.

Contract-related stocks are indiscernible in the balance sheet. Only in conjunction with the corresponding information from the internal accounting system (preliminary costing data/concurrent costing data) can an investigation be carried out to determine whether there is appropriate provision for loss-making orders. The requisite allocations to liability reserves stand in direct relationship to such risks.

Of a similarly high importance as the valuation of the inventories is the analysis of the accounts receivable. The adequacy of specific and general allowances for bad debts can be examined on the basis of analyses of past adequacy (general allowances) and also an ABC analysis of the most important debtors (specific allowances).

On the liabilities side, the critical variable affecting the due diligence audit is that of the provisions item (aka accruals, accrued liabilities). The loss provisions already mentioned, and also provisions for warranties, pensions and other personnel-related items are all of major significance. Here, too, the valuation in the balance sheet should be examined on the basis of information obtained from the internal accounting system and/or through externally performed appraisals. In the event that, in spite of corresponding research, there is still uncertainty, it is advisable at this point to consider the possibility of demanding relevant balance sheet guarantees, i.e. seller indemnities.

In analysing the profit or loss on the basis of the statement of income, the continuity of earnings constitutes an important criterion. In addition, the *types* of earnings need to be separated, and it is particularly important to identify special influences or one-off effects – the so-called extraordinary and exceptional (non-operating) items.

Whether and to what extent earnings figures relating to certain products or regions are available will depend on the existence and accessibility of information from the internal accounting system.

The projections and forecasts drafted for planning control purposes also need to be examined for quality, plausibility and thus planning reliability. Owing to the high influence exerted by projected earnings on the assessment of strategic objective feasibility, and thus on the purchase price, considerable attention will have to be given to an analysis of the planning fundamentals and the degree of coordination applied to the individual subplans (sales, costs, capital expenditures, etc.). The market-related assumptions made for the projections must also be compared with/aligned to the results of the marketing due diligence audit.

The results of the financial due diligence are certainly indispensable. However, it should also be mentioned that sometimes criticisms are made where a due diligence may have been excessively biased toward the accountancy side.

Huemer[8] and also Bühner[9] show considerable mistrust when it comes to accountancy data – and especially data emanating from the external financial statements. The reasons for this can be summarised as follows:

- The balance sheet and statement of income are inevitably aligned to the past
- The earnings/loss disclosure can be influenced by the accounting principles selected
- The lack of yield data that are relevant to the real worth appraisal but cannot be derived from the financial data (business risk, financing risk, investment requirements).

Marketing Due Diligence

The marketing (commercial) due diligence intermeshes seamlessly with the financial due diligence. Its task is to provide a bridge between the rather historically oriented financial due diligence audit and the business strategy that is aligned to future potential for success.

One of the quite specific objectives in the marketing due diligence appraisal is therefore to determine whether the premises and assumptions taken as the basis for corporate planning are plausible and cogent. The marketing due diligence audit thus makes a significant contribution to underpinning the *validity of the selling price,* because the value of a target company (irrespective of the valuation method applied) is significantly influenced by the prospect of future earnings.

The general objective of the marketing due diligence exercise can thus be defined as to reveal the *corporate and market-related opportunities and risks* that will determine the future development of the company and thus the success of the acquisition transaction.

Aside from the time dimension (historical/future-oriented), there is also another difference between the marketing due diligence and the financial due diligence: while the financial due diligence is predominantly introverted and consequently almost exclusively involved with internal company data, the marketing due diligence includes an analysis of the external (market) environment. In this way, the marketing due diligence exercise interlinks the customer/market aspects with those relating solely to the company.

The specific objectives of the marketing due diligence audit are as follows:[10]

1. Ascertainment of the *competitive position* of the acquisition target
2. Analysis of the *future viability* of the sector or market
3. Appraisal of the *synergy potential* and *verification of the strategic planning.*

Internal Company Analysis

The internal analysis encompasses all the activities of the target company that are relevant to the marketing function. The fields of activity that come into play are shown in Figure 5.5.

One of the more important analyses relates to the product range of the company. Questions relating to the structure and weighting of the individual products within the overall portfolio need to be answered:

- Likely *growth* in respect of the main products
- The *market shares* of the various products
- The *age* of the products.
- The *lifecycle* of individual products
- The proportion of *new products* (younger than 5 years) in the portfolio
- *Volume sales* structure.

However, so-called 'soft factors' are also important, such as:

- The product *image*
- *Substitution* risks
- *Functions and properties* of specific products
- *Seasonal* fluctuations/business cycles.

On the sales side, questions of interest include:

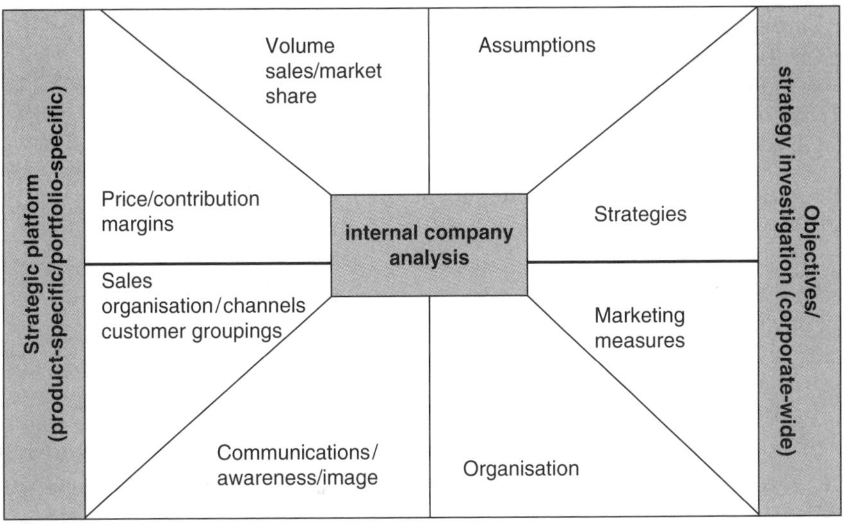

Figure 5.5 Fields of internal company analysis
Source: Internal company analysis MDD; compare Sebastian, Niederdrenk and Tesch (1999, p. 297).

- The *customer structure*
- The *number* of customers
- *Dependency* of customers (more than 10 per cent of the sales of a product)
- *Regional distribution* of sales.

The basic strategies applied in the sales domain also need analysing:

- Description of the *sales organisation*
- Methods of *distribution/sales channels*
- *Supply* obligations
- *Own sales force/dealerships*
- *Sales personnel.*

As do questions relating to marketing measures:

- Level and distribution of the *advertising budget*
- *Market research*
- Participation in *fairs, exhibitions, catalogues*
- Contributions to *trade journals*, etc.

Of importance in the field of prices and conditions are aspects such as:

- *Price developments* in relation to *individual products*
- *Price developments* in relation to *certain markets*
- *Own price* policy
- *Bulk purchase/key account discounts*
- *Terms of payment*
- *Credits, annual quantity rebates*, cash *discounts*, etc.
- *Warranty obligations.*

External Company Analysis

The purpose of the external company analysis within the framework of the due diligence is:

- To assess the *market or sector*, and
- To determine the *competitive position*

of the target company.

The information relating to the sector or relevant market can be obtained relatively easily because, as a rule, there are statistical data available both within the company and in freely available documents. The main research activities required relate to:

- The *structure* of the business sector (number of companies, size of companies, level of concentration in the sector)

- *Growth* of the sector, and
- *Sector attractiveness* (growth forecast, growth markets, concepts for utilising growth potential).

In order to determine the strengths and weaknesses of the company under consideration in relation to its market environment the factors characterising the competition must thus be identified and appraised. According to Porter,[11] the competitive environment can be characterised as follows:

- The threat represented by (new) competitors
- The negotiating power on the purchaser/customer/demand side
- The negotiating strength on the seller/supply side
- The possible threat of product substitution (Figure 5.6).

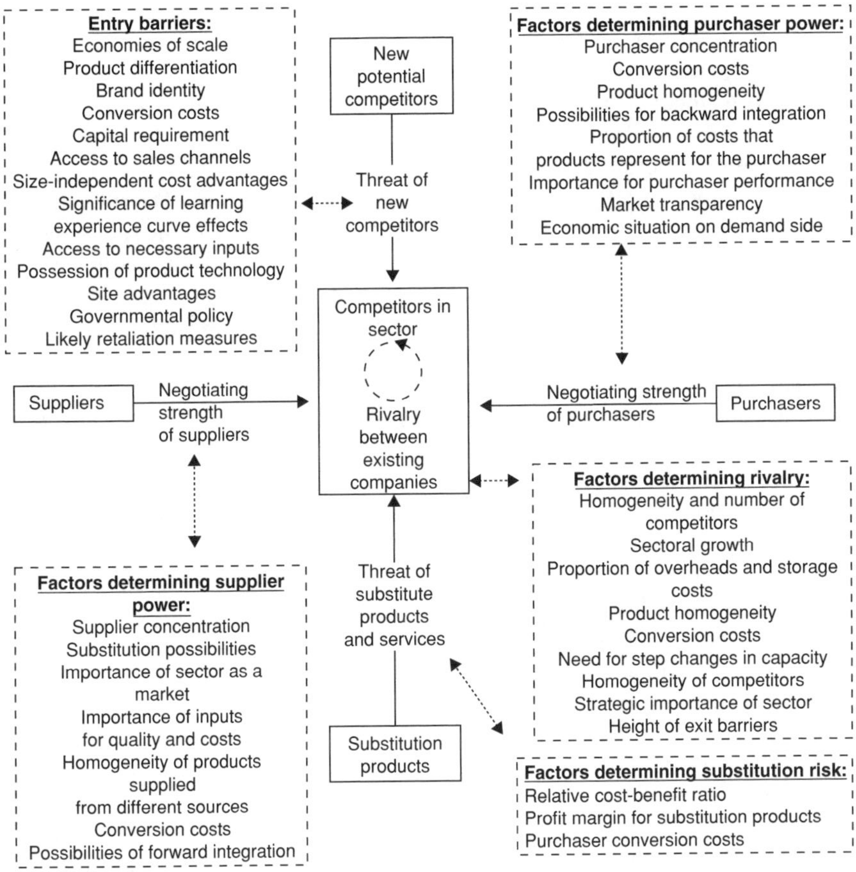

Figure 5.6 Factors determining competitive intensity
Source: After Porter (1992).

Human Resources[12]

> The leadership qualities of the management and the qualifications of the employees, the corporate culture, the loyalty and, associated with this, the rate of management and employee turnover, and particularly the attitude of staff/workers to the acquisition and the merger or integration process are, in the final analysis, important factors that can have a decisive effect on the success or lack thereof of a corporate fusion.[13]

The significance attached in this statement to human resources (HR) in relation to the purchase of a target company has yet to be properly recognised in practice. Human resources analyses incorporating the above-described 'soft factors' do not yet take on the level of importance that they deserve within the overall framework of the due diligence. On the other hand, research has recently been more and more occupied with an isolated evaluation of human capital.

Initial aspects of a 'value accounting model for human resource accounting' can be found in Flamholtz and Coff.[14] The advantage of this approach lies in the fact that the value of human resources is defined as the present discounted value of their future benefit. 'This enables the future performance potential and the job-related replacement costs of the employees to be effectively quantified.'[15]

Parallels with the discounted cash flow (DCF) method applied in normal company valuations are unmistakable. However, the problems of the DCF method become even more pronounced when this approach is transferred to HR valuation (e.g. value-related assessment of the contributions made by individual employees in the future). Consequently, it is not surprising that methods of quantifying the value of human resources have not yet been adopted in practice.

The common and usual HR checklists applied in the due diligence process indicate that personnel as a factor is still regarded more as a liability than an asset (see Table 5.6).

The cause of this negative approach can doubtlessly be found in the M&A activities of the past in which the focus has been on the synergies derived from cost reductions. As a rule, the mergers concerned have tended to be of the horizontal kind, associated with the redundancy of a large number of employees. Problem areas such as periods of notice, termination modalities, social and socio-political obligations (understandably) play an important role in this respect. The issues described are synonymous with the stringent provisions contained in § 613a BGB (German Civil Code).[16] Consequently, in Germany, HR tends in many cases to be a subordinate aspect of the legal due diligence. Many a deal has failed in the past because of the significance of § 613a (aka the 'deal breaker' clause).

A fundamentally different situation arises where the employees of an acquired company constitute its main 'capital'. This applies particularly to M&A transactions in the service sector (telecommunications, new media, etc.). Here the success or failure of a transaction may depend on whether the existing personnel can be retained. Unlike in the previously described scenario, the retention of all (or at least a very large majority) of employees may, in such cases, constitute the '*conditio sine qua non*' for the deal taking place.

Table 5.6 Checklist for the HR due diligence

Human resource checklist

- Personnel structure (number, qualification, function, age, employee turnover)
- Collective-bargaining arrangements (e.g. collective wage and salary agreements; internal wage and salary agreements; promissory commitments/general agreements)
- Individual contractual arrangements
- Wage and salary regulations; development of personnel expenditure structure in the last five years; business and work-time arrangements; overtime; short-time working overviews
- Arrangements covering company pensions and other company welfare facilities and payments; absenteeism data over the last five years, broken down according to illness, accidents and other reasons; accident statistics
- Corporate culture; company atmosphere; participation in improvement processes (e.g. idea management, company suggestions scheme)
- Personnel planning taking into account the labour market situation (e.g. acquisition, disposal; training and qualification measures)
- Membership in employers' associations; trade union membership; degree of trade union organisation amongst the employees
- Labour-management relations and joint consultation bodies; representative committees
- Assessment of procedures relating to labour law with which seller compliance is required.
- For acquisitions abroad: underlying conditions as defined by national/local labour and social welfare laws.

Potential synergies/risks

- Attitude of management and other know-how sources to the acquisition and their remaining in the company
- Necessity for personnel adjustments (accommodation of conflicting interests; social/redundancy plan)
- Dual occupancy of functions
- Need to adjust collective and individual contractual arrangements
- Different corporate structures, demotivation, resistance.

Source: Acquisition Controlling Mannesmann AG.

HR in the Due Diligence Phase

If, from the resource-based view,[17] an enduring competitive advantage is apparent owing to resource advantages accruing to a company, then increasing importance must be allocated to the human resources because all the other resources such as the machinery, financial resources and information are likely to be available to all the participants in the market at comparable conditions. The personnel of a company thus receives a higher priority rating as a result and may possibly become a decisive strategic factor. This means that the HR aspect needs to be given greater attention even (or particularly) during the early phase of project appraisal.

The main problem associated with an HR analysis during the due diligence phase is that of the necessary secrecy as defined, for example, in the Confidentiality Agreement. In the pre-contractual phase, in which only a quite limited circle of people have knowledge of the acquisition proposal, it is difficult to perform the type of investigation necessary in order to identify HR potential. 'Competency-based assessments' such as those proposed by Aldering and von Hutten (1999, p. 322), are not possible, or only possible to a limited extent. (They should, however, be implemented as a matter of urgency in the PMI – post-merger integration – phase).

In spite of these restrictions, there still remain a number of good possibilities for identifying 'value increase potential' in the due diligence process.

As an initial precaution, it is usually advisable to ensure that there is 'personnel expertise' in the due diligence team so that HR aspects receive the attention they merit. Whether this is provided by a line manager of the acquiring company, an external consultant or both depends essentially on the character of the acquisition.

The remit for the HR audit within the overall due diligence process can thus be summarised as follows:

(a) To determine the effects of a takeover on employees
(b) To analyse and assess existing HR assets.

Employee response to an acquisition, and the effects this can have, have long been known under the heading of *merger syndrome*. The merger syndrome relates to the collective mood of the employees and therefore the atmosphere that reigns in the company before, during and after the acquisition. The term thus covers the psychological impact of acquisition transactions on staff, and the consequences that ensue.[18]

From empirical investigations it is known that approximately 30 per cent of employees tend to regard the acquisition as positive, while a slightly smaller proportion (20 per cent) is likely to be decidedly against such a change (Figure 5.7).

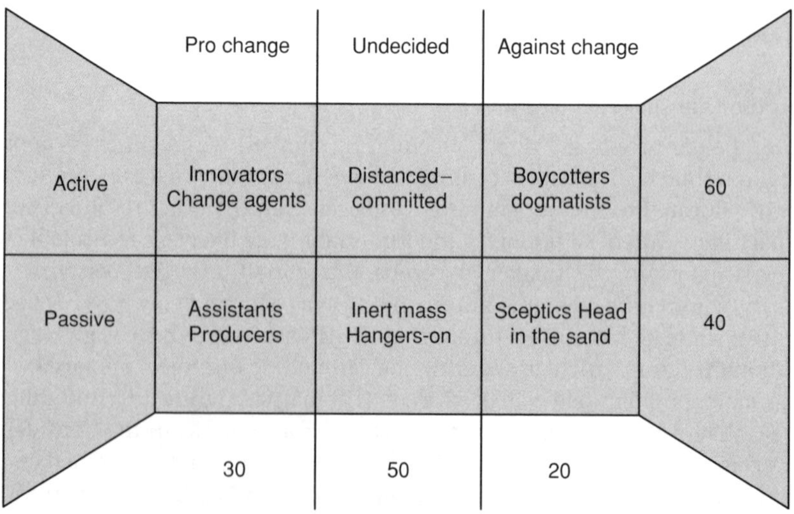

Figure 5.7 Attitudes of employees to the change process, per cent
Source: Diagram after Kienbaum Management Consultants GmbH, as cited in Aldering and von Hutten (1999, p. 318).

By far the greatest proportion of the employees can be assigned to the neutral, undecided group. Decisive for the 'general atmosphere' is the group that contains the *opinion-formers* of the company.

Knowledge of this merger syndrome and thus its divulgence in the due diligence is of crucial importance because of the likely personnel-related consequences:

- Changes in *performance and productivity*
- Changes in *absenteeism* patterns
- Increase in the staff *turnover rate*
- Decrease in *work satisfaction and loyalty.*

An appraisal of the current HR assets constitutes a core aspect of the HR due diligence. As already mentioned, the high degree of confidentiality that prevails during the pre-contractual stage of the audit has a substantial inhibitive effect. Nevertheless, there are various instruments with which, in spite of the limitations indicated, more scope for implementing the HR due diligence can be created.

Instruments for Analysis of the So-Called 'Hard Factors'

The due diligence exercise can provide protection from problems emanating from so-called 'hard factors' and enable the effective control of formal uncertainties through the application of an appropriately prepared checklist. The main aspects of such a checklist are indicated in Table 5.6).[19]

Instruments for Analysis of the So-Called 'Soft Factors'

Important indications of functional feasibility can be derived from the organisation of the personnel management system. Although a reliable breakdown of the strengths and weaknesses of individual employees is unlikely to ensue, major items of information can nevertheless be derived from a study of the relevant structural and procedural details.

Such an investigation should include a corresponding *document analysis* covering:

- Annual reports (personnel expenditures, labour costs, etc.)
- Training/further education and qualification statistics
- Analysis reports relating to personnel turnover, illness/absenteeism levels, loyalty, employee satisfaction
- Personnel development programmes
- Improvement suggestions schemes

and similar exhibitory information available from within the company.

Indications of the individual strengths and weaknesses of the personnel are particularly difficult to acquire within the due diligence process. Opportunities for getting to know representatives of the target company's management are available in the form of the management presentation that is frequently integrated as a constituent part of the pre-contractual phase. If this is the case, then the acquiring company has the possibility of becoming acquainted with the management team and can venture an initial appraisal of the capabilities it embodies.

In addition, the management presentation can provide an overview of the focal points and strategic alignment of the existing management team.

> The professionalism of the presentation, the structure and also the type and number of management instruments applied (for example: product-oriented contribution costings or portfolio analyses) can provide the acquiring company with further indications as to where there is potential for improvement on the management side in the acquisition target.[20]

Further sources of information for assessing the HR assets include:

- Employee questionnaires/surveys
- Management audit
- Individual assessments.

Whether and to what extent these quite useful instruments can be effectively deployed depends on the level of confidentiality that applies.

Legal and Tax Due Diligence

Legal Due Diligence[21]

The legal classification of the target company, the examination of its corporate legal structures and the legal relationships it maintains with third parties characterise the remit of the legal due diligence exercise. Another approach divides the legal due diligence exercise into an investigation of the internal and external legal structures.

In the case of the *company–internal* legal structures, the areas of interest are:

- *Company law* issues
- *Proprietary/property* law issues
- *Contractual* issues (with the limitations that here only company–internal contracts and agreements are to be considered).

As regards the aspects under company law,[22] the investigation needs to determine the legal form of the company, its Articles of Incorporation and bylaws, current certificates of registration, participation/shareholding ratios and internal powers of attorney. The information acquired is frequently of a descriptive character, and overlaps with the basic due diligence are possible.

An analysis of the real estate assets provides a counter-check to the balance sheet values. Inspections of land register abstracts and certificates, land charge certificates and deeds, land development plans and building schemes all count among the individual tasks that have to be carried out. Interactions with the balance sheet analysis within the financial due diligence exercise are possible.

Investigations into company–internal contractual agreements relate essentially to contracts of employment. Within this context, particular attention should be given to the contracts of the management personnel and members of the board and other executive/supervisory bodies. Detailed procedures in this regard are described in the HR due diligence.

Investigations into the *external legal structures* will relate to the contracts and agreements that the company has concluded with the outside world. These include:

- Contracts with customers, suppliers, competitors
- Rent and lease agreements
- Joint ventures/alliances
- Warranty and guarantee agreements
- Litigation risks.

Special attention should be given to the level of customer orders on hand, as these can be a source for future losses.

Aside from these internal/external legal structures, the legal due diligence also includes within its remit a search for numerous specialty items. These may include some or all of the following:

- Official permits/approvals (encumbrances, threats of revocation)
- Clauses requiring repayment of subsidies/grants/allowances, etc.
- Contentious matters and litigious proceedings
- Insufficient insurance cover
- Risks arising from the assumption of liabilities (guarantees, warranties, letters of comfort/intent/awareness/responsibility)
- Risks arising from joint ventures/consortia (deferral of payment, joint and several liability)
- Competition agreements, agreements and undertakings affected by antitrust laws
- Risks arising from continuation of business up to effective takeover.

Tax Due Diligence

The tax due diligence exercise is primarily concerned with two completely independent tasks:

(a) Ensuring fiscally optimised acquisition arrangements for purchaser and seller
(b) Protection of the purchaser against tax-related financial risks arising from the past.

Maximising the tax efficiency of the company takeover is essentially of prime interest to the seller. However, the purchaser may also gain certain benefits from finding an optimum arrangement. Aspects which could be included in such a solution are:

- The fiscal utilisation of *losses carried forward*
- A fiscally neutral means of *disclosing hidden reserves*
- Tax-reducing treatment of the *financing costs* (interest)
- Special earnings-reducing measures (e.g. *special depreciation allowances*)
- Special earnings-boosting measures (e.g. *grants, subsidies*).

In addition, it is also in the interests of the purchaser to support the seller in reducing his or her tax liability as this creates a better negotiating position for the purchaser.

However, a more important activity incorporated in the tax due diligence exercise from the point of view of the purchaser relates to avoiding risks which have arisen from the non-compliant tax treatment of certain matters in the past, and which can consequently lead to back tax having to be paid.

The associated investigations will initially concentrate on the tax declarations of the last few years and the last company tax audit. Tax declarations *after* the last tax audit likewise require examination for financial irregularities (e.g. relating to the formation of and addition to reserves). Where there is significant cause for disquiet, possible risks should be covered by the appropriate indemnity clauses in the contract of sale.

The audit will need to establish the relevant tax liabilities emanating from:

- Corporation tax
- Trade tax
- Value added/turnover tax.

In the event that the assets of the acquired company include real estate, an arrangement will have to be made in relation to the land transfer duty payable.

In the tax due diligence report, therefore, the following should be stipulated:

- An agreement as to who is responsible for the business-related closing tax amounts expected to arise as at the hand-over date
- An agreement indicating who is responsible for unexpected back tax payments or tax refunds not taken into account in the sale price (so-called tax audit clause)
- An agreement on who bears liability for additional tax payments arising from constructive dividends/disguised profit distribution/previously non-deductible dividends

It may be necessary to include these items in the contract of sale.

Environmental Due Diligence[23]

The task of the environmental due diligence audit is to identify and evaluate environmental risks. Originally limited to the problem area of 'soil contamination', the environmental due diligence has developed into a complex analysis which, aside from a large number of environmentally relevant issues, also includes in its terms of reference the legal provisions that form the basis of legislative environmental protection. The purposes of the environmental due diligence in detail are:

- To provide the acquirer with an overview of the environmental situation regarding the target company, and to identify potential environmental *risks*
- To cost-in environmental factors likely to reduce a company's value and modifications needed for *environmental protection facilities*.

The first part of the remit essentially involves a global approach, while the second part presupposes a case-by-case study.

The purpose of the analysis of the environmental situation (which should include an inspection of the facilities of the businesses concerned) is to identify the risk potential of the target company. Such risks can arise from:

- The *location* of the site
- The *building morphology* (possibly as an indication of former landfill sites or similar)
- The *historic utilisation* of the site (previous owners, sectors)
- The method of *land development*
- The *machinery* and *equipment* installed.

In its subsequent development, however, the analysis needs to go far beyond the physical examination of the site. It should include the organisational and hierarchical structure of the target company (environmental managers, environmental reports) and also the environmental compatibility of its products and production processes.

Another focal point of the environmental analysis comes under the heading of 'Legal Compliance'. The Legal Compliance audit is performed to determine whether, and to what extent, environmental regulations are being or have been properly met. The remit covers, in particular, legal obligations, approvals, permits and licences, official rules, bylaws, orders and provisions, regulatory ordinances and administrative directives.[24] In Germany, there are at the time of writing approximately 800 environmental laws, 3000 ordinances and approximately 500 administrative directives.

Owing to the general volatility of the legal framework, it is also advisable to carry out an appraisal of expected developments and intended changes in law.

With the case-by-case examination, the object is to identify specific risks, and to evaluate these accordingly. Aside from the costs for the rehabilitation of contaminated soil, the following also have to be determined within this framework:

- Costs for *replacement investments* (if facilities are likely not to meet official requirements)
- Costs of *demolition* and *removal*
- Costs of *rehabilitation* work.

An important question within this context is whether, and to what extent at this stage of the due diligence audit, in-depth analyses such as test drillings need to be performed.

As company acquisitions are invariably conducted under significant scheduling duress, time-consuming investigations frequently have to be left to one side. On the other hand, the knowledge gained during this phase of the environmental due diligence audit must be reliable if it is to provide a cogent basis for risk evaluation. Because of the wide scope for interpretation in evaluating suspicions that cannot be confirmed or discounted, the approach adopted in ascertaining the likely cost will usually be that of assessing the best-case and worst-case scenarios.

Owing to the large number and current relevance of the regulations and laws that have to be considered, the environmental due diligence exercise can be conducted only by experienced specialists. The composition of the *audit team* is therefore of particular importance. It will need to assembled in accordance with requirements – and usually on an interdisciplinary basis. The inclusion of external advisers appears to be both advisable and necessary, given the wide terms of reference involved.

Organisational and IT Due Diligence

The main questions that have to be answered in the organisational and IT due diligence exercise are whether the organisation of the acquisition target is appropriate and cost-efficient, and whether the information technology that it has at its disposal is fit for its future purpose.

Within the framework of the organisational due diligence, the structures of the company are examined in terms of both their procedural and hierarchical efficiency. On the hierarchical side, the main issue of interest is whether the size of the organisation is appropriate to the volume of its operative business.

The object of the procedural analysis is to ascertain the time-related, location-related and task-related pattern of work processes, and the correlation of the individual tasks to working procedures.[25] The object is thus to determine whether the organisation is balanced, and whether there are clearly defined responsibilities for specific activities.

Closely related to the Organisational due diligence is the IT audit. Problems can arise in the course of subsequent integration within the IT environment of the acquiring company, and there the eradication can constitute a heavy burden on resources.

The IT checklist developed by Berens and Brauner (1999) and reproduced in Table 5.7 forms a good basis for providing more certainty in this area.

6 Due Diligence and Company Valuation

The object of the due diligence exercise is to create a picture of the target company per se, its structure, the capabilities of its employees, and its market opportunities and risks. Initially, the audit is less concerned with the probability distribution of projected withdrawals.[26]

Table 5.7 The IT due diligence checklist

- List of *hardware* and *software* used in the various sections
- *Contract expiry dates* and costs of contracts to date with suppliers of hardware and software
- Assessment of the quality of the *IT* in individual functional units
- Examination to determine whether there is an adequate *contingency plan* in place for the event of a system failure
- Appraisal of the overall situation regarding the information technology installed, particularly *compatibility* and *networking* in the individual functional units
- Identification of *major burdens* in relation to hardware and software that could impede integration of the information systems of the target company and the purchasing company
- Scope of *software* specially developed for the target company, as this usually gives rise to greater integration problems than standard software
- Quality of existing *management information systems* (MIS)
- Compatibility with the *systems* of the purchasing company
- Estimation of the *integration* costs
- Identification of major *potential improvements* and scope of the inputs necessary for these
- Estimation of the *total investment requirement* in information technology in the next three years.

This statement appears to confirm the existence of a clear distinction between the tasks of the due diligence on the one hand and a company valuation on the other. This is not to say, however, that the results of the due diligence are irrelevant to determining future income expectations. The importance of the due diligence for the valuation of a going concern also, of course, depends on the valuation method applied. Essentially, three different approaches (valuation categories) can be applied for determining the value of a company:

1. The *net asset value or intrinsic valuation method* as a comparison with the costs that arise, or that have arisen, in the creation or establishment of a company
2. The *capitalised earnings method,* i.e. a comparison with the essential attributes, particularly the benefits, that companies offer
3. The *market value method,* i.e. a comparison with prices that other acquiring companies have paid for similar businesses (Figure 5.8).

The value of the due diligence for a company valuation depends heavily on the method selected.

The relationship between the due diligence and the value of the company (shareholder value) is most apparent where the net asset method is used. Within the financial due diligence, the book values applied are based on the replacement or market values of the assets concerned, while asset items not necessary for the business are ignored. Consequently, the result of a financial due diligence conducted in this way is tantamount to determining the intrinsic or net asset value of the company.

The due diligence exercise can also be of significant assistance when determining the capitalised earnings value, irrespective of whether (for example, for

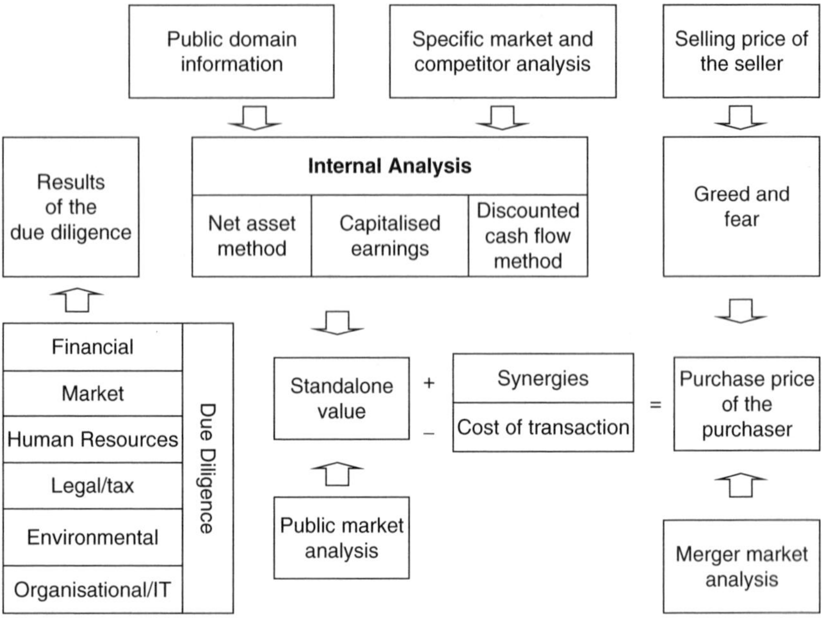

Figure 5.8 Process of company valuation and selling price calculation

simplification purposes) EBIT or a cash flow parameter is applied. The prime instruments here are, first the financial due diligence with its projections element (performance measurement and matching of subplans in specified planning periods), and secondly the market due diligence with the valuation of future potential from the point of view of the market and competitive situation.

It is then a relatively simple matter to apply a standardised valuation model to the data material that has been acquired and examined within the framework of the financial and market due diligence audits, in order to determine the capitalized earnings value or the DCF.

The capitalised earnings method is, so to speak, the instrument for calculating the value, while the due diligence is the process which largely determines the inputs to be applied within the instrument.[27]

It is somewhat more difficult to discern the relationship between the due diligence and the company valuation when applying the market value approach (merger market or public market method), i.e. where the company is valued on the basis of the current stock market list price or with EBIT multipliers that have been derived from similar transactions of the past.

In these cases, the due diligence process can provide only limited assistance. For example, the information gained during the due diligence audit can enable the application of cogent deductions, allowances or multipliers.

To summarise, it can be said that the due diligence process can provide significant assistance in value determination (particularly in the case of the capitalised earnings method), and beyond that, it constitutes an aid to argumentation during the subsequent price negotiations.

7 Summary

With the exception of the hostile takeover, in which a due diligence is not possible, the instrument of the due diligence audit should be incorporated as a fixed component of M&A projects. A systematic analysis properly integrated within the overall acquisition process can greatly reduce risk and the danger of failure by:

- Providing essential inputs for determining the *contractual structure*, particularly in relation to the incorporation and formulation of warranties/guarantees/ indemnities;
- Providing *decisive information and assistance* relating to the valuation of the company and in the price negotiations.

In addition, the results emanating from the due diligence process can be used to pave the way for successful integration management.

The subdivision of the due diligence exercise into individual activities is advisable, although the weighting of individual audits will vary from case to case:

- The *financial due diligence* is indispensable to obtaining an overview of the acquisition target; it is important when considering the net asset value of the candidate company and also the effects of any possible integration of its accounting system (equity, goodwill).
- The strategic analysis of the opportunities and risks involved in the acquisition is significantly aided by both the *market due diligence* and the *HR due diligence,* with the latter gaining more and more importance within the context of mergers transacted in the service sector. Expansion of the concept to incorporate a due diligence exercise geared toward the identification, assessment and realisation of acquisition-related synergy potential (as proposed by Rockholtz[28]) fits very nicely into this framework.
- The *legal, tax and environmental due diligence* audits essentially serve to eliminate any losses likely to arise from entering into a contract of sale.

The checklists common to all the individual due diligence audits constitute a handy aid but their value should not be overestimated. The due diligence approach should be adopted as a necessary instrument in all M&A projects, and while its application is no guarantee for success, its omission increases the risk of the project turning sour.

Notes

1 Berens and Strauch (1999), p. 5. A detailed historical derivation of the due diligence concept can be found on pp. 6–10.

2 Cf. Berens and Brauner (1999), p. 8.
3 Cf. Rockholtz (1999, p. 179).
4 Cf. Müller-Stewens and Schreiber (1993, pp. 277–80).
5 Müller-Stewens and Schreiber (1993, p. 290).
6 Cf. Rockholtz (1990, p. 87).
7 Detailed checklists can be found, *inter alia*, in Jansen (1998, pp. 215–216) or Berens and Brauwer (eds) (1999, p. 369).
8 Huemer (1991, p. 44).
9 Bühner (1990, pp. 14–29).
10 Cf. Sebastian Niederdrenk and Tesch (1999, p. 295).
11 Porter (1992, p. 26).
12 See Chapter 10.
13 Aldering and von Hutten (1999, p. 316).
14 Flamholtz and Coff (1989, p. 43).
15 Gut-Villa *et al.*, (1997, p. 187).
16 See Chapter 4 and Chapter 9.
17 For details of the resource-based view, cf. Schaper and Rinkel (1998, pp. 32–43).
18 Gut-Villa *et al.* (1997, p. 121).
19 For a detailed checklist, see Berens and Brauner (1999, p. 378).
20 Funk (1995, p. 501).
21 See Chapter 4 as well as Picot (1998, Part 1, Vertragsrecht, IV.6. RN 41 ff).
22 Cf. Koch and Wegmann (1998, pp. 93.ff).
23 See Kummer, in Picot (1998, Part VII Umweltrecht).
24 Cf. Pföhler (1997, p. 629).
25 Cf. Berens, Hoffjan and Strauch (1999, p. 144).
26 See Berens, and Strauch (1999, p. 18).
27 Berens and Strauch (1999, p. 18).
28 Rockholtz (1990, pp. 245ff).

Bibliography

The contributions marked with *have been taken from Berens and Brauner (eds) (1999).

Aldering, C. and Freiin von Hutten, Y. (1999) *Due Diligence u. Human Resources.

Berens, W. and Brauner, H. U. *Die Due Diligence bei Unternehmensakquisitionen* (Stuttgart).

Berens, W., Hoffjan, A. and Strauch, J. (1999) *Planung und Durchführung der Due Diligence.

Berens, W. and Strauch, J. (1999) *Herkunft und Inhalt des Begriffes Due Diligence.

Born, K. (1995) *Unternehmensanalyse und Unternehmensbewertung* (Stuttgart).

Brauner, H. U. and Grillo, U. (1999) *Die Due Diligence aus strategischer Sicht.

Bühner, R. (1990) *Das Management-Wert-Konzept* (Stuttgart).

Dabui, M. (1998) *Postmerger-Management* (Wiesbaden).

Dielmann, K. (1997) Unternehmenskauf und Human Resourcen Due Diligence-Prüfung, *Personal*, 9.

Flamholtz, E. C. and Coff, R. (1989) Valuing human resources in buying service companies, *Mergers & Acquisitions*, 4.

Funk, J. (1995) Aspekte der Unternehmensbewertung in der Praxis, *Zfbf 47*, 5.

Gut-Villa, C. (1997) *Human Resource Management bei Mergers & Acquisitions* (Bern, Stuttgart, Vienna).

Huemer, F. (1991) *Mergers & Acquisitions, Strategische und Finanzielle Analyse von Unternehmensübernahmen* (Frankfurt am Main).

Jansen, A. (1998) *Mergers & Acquisitions* (Wiesbaden).

Kittner, M. (1997) Human Resources in der Unternehmensbewertung, *Der Betrieb*, 4.

Koch, T. and Wegmann, W. (1998) *Praktiker-Handbuch Due Diligence*, (Stuttgart).

Lehnert, I. (1997) *Unternehmensübernahmen in den USA in den 80er Jahren* (Wiesbaden).

Müller-Stewens, G. and Schreiber, K. (1993) Zur organisatorischen Anbindung des Akquisitionsprozesses im Käuferunternehmen, *Die Unternehmung*, 4.

Picot, G. (ed.) (1998) *Unternehmenskauf und Restrukturierung* (Munich).

Pföhler, M. and Hermann, M. (1997) Grundsätze zur Durchführung von Unwelt – Due Diligence, *Die Wirtshaftsprufüng*, 18.

Porter, M. E. (1992) *Wettbewerbsstrategie* (Frankfurt am Main).

Rockholtz, C. (1990) *Marktwertorientiertes Akquisitionsmanagement* (Frankfort am Main).

Rockholtz, C. (1999) *Due Diligence – Konzeption zum synergieorientierten Akquisitionsmanagement.

Schaper-Rinker, W. (1998) *Akquisitionen und strategische Allianzen* (Wiesbaden).

Schulte, C. (ed.) (1994) *Beteiligungscontrolling* (Wiesbaden).

Sebastian, K. H., Niederdrenk, R. and Tesch, R. (1999) *Market Due Diligence – Die Sorgfältigkeitsprufüng aus der Sicht des Marktes.

6
Corporate Valuation

Frank Richter

1 Introduction

The analysis of the economics of corporate acquisitions, divestitures and mergers (i.e. M&A transactions) is based primarily on a comparison of the value of a firm that is to be acquired or sold and the potential transaction price. From this comparison, information on changes in the value of the firms participating in the transaction as well as potential share price reactions can be derived. Consequently, economic analysis is equivalent to a *value-enhancement analysis*. It requires methods to determine firm values as well as to estimate potential transaction prices.

If changes in the total market value of acquiring firms and target companies are considered, the majority of M&A transactions in the second half of the 1990s resulted in value increases that were substantial. However, this economic success was divided up unequally – the selling parties captured the bigger part of the pie by far. Therefore, the systematic implementation of value-enhancement analysis is key to ensuring M&A success.

This chapter does not primarily deal with the presentation of technical details of valuation but concentrates on introducing the basic principles, not overlooking the fact that the details of correct application in practice are certainly important. There are numerous valuable publications dealing with this subject in detail. An overview of sources covering this as well as related topics can be found on p. 213.

The economic objectives of M&A transactions outlined above will be addressed and applied to different types of transactions (corporate acquisitions; initial public offerings; joint ventures) in the second section. The third and fourth sections deal with the determination of firm value and the estimation of potential transaction prices, respectively. On the basis of this information, changes in value that are induced by the realisation of specific values and prices during and subsequent to the transaction process can be analysed.

2 Economic Objectives of M&A: Realisation of Value and Stock Price Increases

In this section, the evaluation of transactions will be based on an economic perspective. This implies the assumption that transactions are executed only if they increase the wealth of the owners of the company that carries out the transaction.

Introductory Example

We consider the sale of a wholly-owned subsidiary of VICTORY Group that, from the perspective of the owners of VICTORY, has a value of $2.5 billion. For the VICTORY Group we assume a market value of $12 billion (including the subsidiary). The announcement of the sale of the subsidiary to the HOPE Group for $3.5 billion would result in an abnormal return of 8.3 per cent to the owners of VICTORY. HOPE has a market value of $8 billion prior to the transaction and expects the creation of additional value amounting to approximately $700 million owing to operating improvements and other synergies resulting from the acquisition, which is not yet included in the value of $2.5 billion of the target firm. On the basis of these numbers, the share price of HOPE will most likely decline by approximately 3.8 per cent. In sum, HOPE pays a premium of $1 billion (40 per cent) that accrues to the owners of VICTORY. However, the additional value created by the transaction for HOPE amounts to only $700 million, resulting in a loss of $300 million for the shareholders of HOPE. Despite this uncertainty, in sum the transaction is beneficial to the shareholders of both VICTORY and HOPE as total economic performance of both companies will improve due to synergies (Table 6.1).

Success and Failure Rates of M&A Transactions

The situation described in the example above quite frequently applies to M&A transactions. McKinsey & Co., Inc. concluded from an empirical study that almost three out of four transactions with a volume of more than US$ 500 millions executed among listed corporations in Europe and the USA in the years 1996 to 1998 were value-enhancing when assessed from a combined perspective of the buying and the selling side. The acquirers experienced a positive stock price reaction in half of the cases and declining stock prices in the other. On the seller's side, stock prices rose in 92 per cent of the cases and declined in only 8 per cent of the cases (see Figure 6.1).

In absolute amounts, successful acquirers created a total value of US$ 88 billion, whereas unsuccessful acquirers destroyed value in the amount of US$ 101 billion.

Table 6.1 VICTORY and HOPE: company data, US$ billion

Item	VICTORY	HOPE	Total
Market value prior to transaction	12	8	20
Transaction price	+3.5	−3.5	
Value of subsidiary	– 2.5	+ 2.5	
Potential synergies		+ 0.7	+ 0.7
Value change	+ 1.0	– 0.3	+ 0.7
Stock price reaction	+ 8.4%	– 3.8%	+ 3.5%

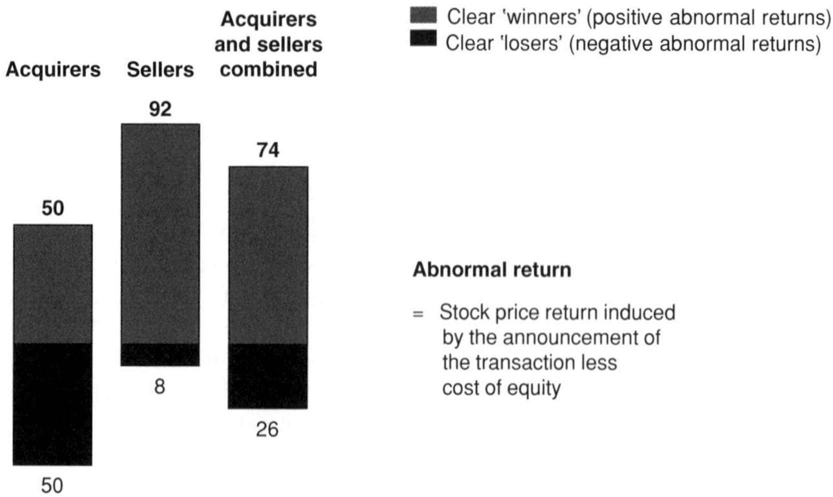

Figure 6.1 Abnormal returns following M&A transactions, per cent
Source: McKinsey.

Successful sellers of companies realised an additional value amounting to US$ 102 billion, whereas unsuccessful sellers destroyed value in the amount of US$ 21 billion. In sum, US$ 68 billion of net value were created through M&A transactions.[1]

Basic Principles of the Analysis of the Economics of M&A Transactions from a Capital Market Perspective

Conducting an analysis of the economics of M&A transactions means quantifying the additional value that is created by the transaction and anticipating potential stock price reactions before the announcement, given that the participating companies are listed on a stock market. The basic approach is presented on the basis of the introductory example.

The Seller's Perspective

What is the reason for the rise in the stock price of VICTORY after the announcement of the sale of the subsidiary? Prior to the announcement of the transaction on 1 January 2000, market participants expected cash flows per share of $2.30, $2.50 and $2.75 for the years 2001, 2002 and 2003, respectively. Expected long-term growth rates beyond the year 2003 were 3 per cent p.a. These expectations were based on the consensus estimates of the financial analysts covering the company. Assuming that the cost of equity is 10 per cent, the observed market price of the stock is calculated as:

$$\frac{2.30}{1.1}+\frac{2.50}{1.1^2}+\frac{2.75}{1.1^3}+\frac{2.75\cdot 1.03}{(0.1-0.03)\cdot 1.1^3}=36.62$$

The formula for calculation is:

$$p = \frac{cf_1}{1+k} + \frac{cf_2}{(1+k)^2} + \frac{cf_3}{(1+k)^3} + \frac{cf_3 \cdot (1+g)}{(k-g) \cdot (1+k)^3}$$

with:

p share price
cf_t cash flow to shareholders (per share) in period t
k cost of equity
g long-term growth rate of cash flows

Multiplication with the number of shares outstanding of 327 467 012 yields a market capitalisation of approximately \$12 billion for VICTORY. The above numbers include the expected cash flows of the wholly owned subsidiary of \$0.50, \$0.54 and \$0.57 per share. The cost of equity and the expected long-term growth rates of the subsidiary do not differ from the numbers of the parent company. Hence, the portion of the stock price of VICTORY attributable to the subsidiary equals \$7.63, from which a value of \$2.5 billion results. After the sale of the subsidiary, the cash flows per share of VICTORY are reduced by the subsidiary's cash flows and the stock price declines to \$28.99, which in turn has to be increased by the sales price per share:

$$\frac{1.80}{1.1} + \frac{1.96}{1.1^2} + \frac{2.18}{1.1^3} + \frac{2.18 \cdot 1.03}{(0.1 - 0.03) \cdot 1.1^3} = 28.99$$

As the number of shares outstanding remains unchanged after the transaction, the market value is \$9.5 billion and is increased by the sales price of \$3.5 billion or \$10.69 per share outstanding to \$13 billion. As a consequence, the stock price rises by 8.3 per cent from \$36.62 to \$39.68 after the announcement.

From this example, an important conclusion can be drawn for the seller: market expectations have to be analysed beforehand to anticipate the market's reaction to the announcement of corporate transactions. From the anticipated market reaction, the market value of the corporate unit to be sold as well as its share of the total market value of the parent company can be assessed. Comparing this value with the potential transaction price yields the value change resulting from the transaction for the owners of the selling company.

Not surprisingly, these calculations are far more complex in practice, as the following factors have to be taken into account in addition to the highly simplified calculations outlined above: differences in cash flows and earnings per share (only the latter are easily available), taxes resulting from the transaction, potential synergies between the business unit to be sold and the parent company as well as transaction costs and the capital market environment at the time of the transaction.

Nevertheless, the basic proceeding remains unchanged. If the companies involved in the transaction are not listed on a Stock Exchange, market expectations are replaced by forecasts of the owners.

The Buyer's Perspective

The basic approach presented from the seller's point of view also applies to the buy side since the main objective of the analysis is the alignment of the value and price of the target company from an overall perspective (see Table 6.2). First of all, the market value of the acquiring company has to be determined. As a first step, the target – in our example the subsidiary of VICTORY – is valued without considering potential improvements and synergies achievable together with the buyer. For this purpose, the acquirer creates his own forecasts or uses observable market expectations. Frequently, a substantial part of the value increase results from operating improvements, which could basically also be achieved without a change in the ownership structure. However, often an exogenous impulse that induces structural changes is necessary for a company to exploit its potential for improvement.

The synergies that cannot be realised by either company stand-alone can be classified into three categories:

- *Universal synergies* that could be realised with any potential acquirer who has a high-quality management and adequate resources. These synergies include economies of scale, e.g. in the field of administration.
- *Endemic synergies* that can be achieved only with a small number of acquirers who are typically operating in the same industrial sector as the target firm. These include economies of scope such as, for example, an extended geographical area of operations as well as a certain potential for rationalisation, e.g. in sales and marketing.

Table 6.2 Value changes caused by the acquisition

	Item	**Example US$ billion**
	Value of the acquiring firm	8000
+	Value of the target firm (stand-alone)	2500
+	Value increase from operating improvements that could also be achieved without change in ownership structure	600
+	Value of synergies	
	A – universal synergies	150
	B – endemic synergies	0
	C – specific synergies	0
–	Integration costs	50
+/–	Miscellaneous value effects (taxes, financing, etc.)	(to be quantified)
=	**Value of combined business**	**11 200**
–	Market value of the acquirer	8000
–	Purchase price of the target	3500
=	**Value change as a result of the acquisition**	**–300**
→	Potential stock price reaction after announcement	–3.75%

– *Specific synergies* that can be realised only with certain acquirers such as growth opportunities that can be seized only by using a specific patent-protected technology.

In addition to such value increases from improvements and synergies, integration costs as well as potential value effects from taxes and financing of the transaction have to be considered. The expected change in value is finally obtained from the value of the combined business less the market value of the acquirer as a stand-alone entity and the transaction price.

Approach to Mergers and Joint Ventures

The analysis presented above is also applicable to mergers and joint ventures. In this context, the determination of the exchange ratio that is fundamental to the value changes resulting from the transaction is a crucial aspect. If, for example, the VICTORY Group and HOPE Group decide to merge and the exchange ratio is calculated on the basis of the respective market values, the following results are obtained:

Value change for VICTORY shareholders:

$$\frac{\frac{12}{20}\cdot(12\,000+8\,000+700)}{12\,000}-1=3.5\,\%$$

Value change for HOPE shareholders:

$$\frac{\frac{8}{20}\cdot 20\,700}{8\,000}-1=3.5\,\%$$

The formula for calculation is:

$$\Delta r=\frac{a\cdot V_{total}}{V_0}-1$$

with:

Δr	additional return on stock price induced by transaction
a	share in the new combined business (derived from share in the sum of values of separate businesses)
V_{total}	total value of the combined business
V_0	value (price) of the own firm prior to transaction

If HOPE is merged with VICTORY and their share prices are \$36.62 and \$11, respectively, which is assumed here, the exchange ratio will be 3.33 to 1, i.e. HOPE shareholders will receive three new VICTORY shares for 10 (old) HOPE shares.

For practical application of this concept, the following aspects must be taken into consideration:

- In some countries, exchange ratios are determined on the basis of values that have been calculated by means of *discounted cash flow* (DCF) analysis, not on the basis of observed market values. The procedure is basically the same, but the value changes that are to be expected depend on the contractually agreed exchange ratio.
- In many cases, at least one of the parties *owns shares in the other involved firm* prior to the transaction. This has to be considered in the calculation of the exchange ratios.
- Fairly often, a *premium* is offered to motivate shareholders to tender their shares, as for the HOPE shareholders in our merger example. This also has an impact on the change in value resulting from the transaction.

In general, these aspects are not negligible and have to be taken into account when conducting a value-enhancement analysis.

Causes for Differences Between Value and Price

In perfect markets, there is no difference between value and price. The market anticipates activities of the management, the results of these activities are translated properly into market prices and trading on the market is unrestricted and free of transaction cost. However, it is common knowledge that markets are imperfect for a number of reasons. These reasons include information asymmetries (e.g. in IPOs), unanticipated strategy changes and the legal framework (including taxes).

Asymmetric Information

The possibility of asymmetrically distributed information cannot be ruled out, e.g. in IPOs. The existing owners of the company have access to detailed information about the company that is to be made available to the primary capital market, which outsiders do not have to the same extent. If potential buyers of the new shares suspect that there are better informed insiders, this will have an impact on the share price the former are willing to pay in the IPO.

Let us assume that in the IPO of HOPE, which is scheduled to take place shortly before its acquisition of the subsidiary of the VICTORY Group, 80 per cent of all investors rely on the information provided in the IPO prospectus. This group of investors does not know the exact firm value. They assume a firm value of either $4 billion or $8 billion or $12 billion with a probability of one-third each.[2] The remaining 20 per cent of the investors know the precise firm value of $8 billion, which is expected to be realised immediately after the listing of the company. If the issue price is fixed at a level below the firm value of $8 billion, all investors subscribe for the new shares and the resulting wealth increase accrues to all of them in equal terms. If the issue price is fixed above the firm value, only the imperfectly informed investors will, at least in part, be willing to subscribe for the shares and, hence, fully bear the wealth reduction from the discrepancy between the company's value and price. Rational investors anticipate this risk of losses resulting from uncertainty and, according to Rock's model, will only accept issue prices up to the following limit :

$$\frac{0.8 \cdot 12\,000 \cdot \frac{1}{3} + 8\,000 \cdot \frac{1}{3} + 4\,000 \cdot \frac{1}{3}}{0.8 \cdot \frac{1}{3} + \frac{2}{3}} = 7\,714$$

The formula for calculation is:

$$P_{max} = \frac{x \cdot P_1 \cdot q_1 + P_2 \cdot q_2 + P_3 \cdot q_3}{x \cdot q_1 + q_2 + q_3}$$

with:

P_{max} Maximum issue price accepted by incompletely informed investors
x Proportion of the incompletely informed investors in the total number of investors
P_1 Issue price that induces subscription by all investors
P_2, P_3 Issue prices that induce fully informed investors not to subscribe
$q_{1,2,3}$ Probabilities

Owing to the uncertainty that results from the asymmetric distribution of information on the side of the investors, the issue price must not exceed $7714 million, if all investors including those with incomplete information are to be motivated to subscribe. On the market, the firm value of $8 billion will be realised immediately after this uncertainty has been resolved. As a result, underpricing amounts to 3.6 per cent.[3]

Unanticipated Strategy Changes and Operating Improvements

Before the IPO, the management and the existing owners of HOPE had announced that they would use part of the IPO proceeds to implement a growth strategy already outlined. Smaller acquisitions, which could not yet be identified at that time, were part of this strategy. Larger transactions, such as the subsequent acquisition of the subsidiary of the VICTORY Group, were not deemed feasible. This strategy which had been communicated to the market and the expectations regarding its operational implementation were reflected in the estimated earnings per share.

The management of the VICTORY Group was under a growing compulsion to dispose of activities not associated with its core businesses for which the company could not make use of its specific competencies. Institutional investors caused the VICTORY Group to revise its strategy. The sale of its subsidiary mentioned above was part of this change in strategy. Up to this point in time, the market assumed the value of the subsidiary within the group to be $2.5 billion. Not surprisingly, potential operational improvements worth $600 million had also been identified by the analysts covering the company. However, the market estimated the probability of realising this potential within the VICTORY Group to be close to zero. In other words, the conglomerate discount of the group amounted to up to 5 per cent (=600/12 000).

The stock prices of both HOPE and the VICTORY Group reflected market expectations based on the strategies communicated. Demand for and supply of the shares of both companies resulted in market prices corresponding to the expected fundamental performance. Only the revision of market expectations induced the adjustment of share prices. The strategic refocusing of the VICTORY Group and the imminent opportunity for divestitures raised the probability that the existing value potential of $600 million could be realised to above zero for the first time. In addition, synergies amounting to $100 million net of transaction costs, which had not been seen prior to the transaction, were identified to be realisable. As a consequence, the change in market expectations resulted in the creation of an additional (market) value of $700 million.

Market Imperfections

Market imperfections such as tax barriers may also result in differences between value and price. The VICTORY Group might have had good reasons not to sell its subsidiary, because in many cases the high taxation of capital gains is an obstacle to such transactions.[4]

To give an example, if the tax rate is fixed at 50 per cent and the equity of the subsidiary has a book value of $1.9 billion, a bid of at least $3.1 billion is required to make a sale of the subsidiary preferable to keeping it, assuming the latter yields a net value of the subsidiary of $2.5 billion. The taxes on the sales price amount to 0.5 (3.1 –1.9) = 0.6 $billion, resulting in a sales price after taxes of 3.1 – 0.6 = 2.5 $billion.

Although goodwill implies increased tax-reducing amortisation for HOPE, provided that HOPE generates sufficient profits, the net present value of this tax advantage from amortisation is typically smaller than the tax payment of the seller. As a consequence, tax effects potentially make the transaction more expensive, or might even prevent it.

Illiquidity is another important source of market imperfection. At the beginning of an economic downturn, an excess supply of production factors in the sectors hit by recession can often be observed. In such a situation, many of the firms in these sectors attempt to reduce overcapacities. If overcapacities exist in sectors using highly specific technologies that cannot be employed in other industrial sectors not affected by recession, it will be difficult to find buyers for these technologies. In this case, either no transaction will take place or the transaction price will be far below the value of the production factors if employed optimally.

The above examples of imperfections of the market for corporations and corporate stakes and others more do not render accurate company valuations useless.

The opposite is true: imperfections can only be identified, and in some cases even made use of, by means of fundamental analysis.

Value-Enhancement vs. Earnings per Share: Challenges for Investor Communication

Within a capital market-oriented approach to the economics of corporate transactions, the analysis of potential value changes is a first substantial step. The second step deals with the perception of the transaction by third parties, i.e. shareholders, financial analysts and institutional investors. This external view of a transaction is of vital importance for the translation of value-enhancement potential into actual market price reactions. The calculated value changes resulting from the transaction are derived from corporate valuations, which are based on long-term estimates of future earnings. Details of the valuation cannot be communicated to the market. Many of the underlying facts are complex – as is the case, for instance, with joint ventures in the field of research and development (R&D). Sometimes even the benefits from corporate transactions cannot be communicated explicitly, if this might delay or impede antitrust permit procedures. Even if the companies involved in the transaction succeeded in communicating all details relevant for pricing to the market, this would not necessarily lead to appropriate share prices because the management of a company does not always have sufficient credibility, especially if market expectations have been missed in the past.

Given this uncertainty and incompleteness of information, financial analysts often base their quantitative assessment of a transaction on the dynamics of earnings per share in the two or three years subsequent to the transaction. If earnings per share are increased, the transaction is called 'accretive'. If earnings per share decrease, it is called 'dilutive'. Though earnings per share are not a generally suitable indicator for the value change since they are impacted, among others, by the choice of accounting methods, such as the treatment of amortisation and the form of financing, it is regularly used as a 'stick in the fog' to deal with uncertainty. If the transaction results in a significant dilution of earnings within the three years following the transaction, a value increase can be regarded as unlikely.

In the example of the acquisition of the VICTORY subsidiary by HOPE, a goodwill of $1.6 billion results from the book value of the target's equity of $1.9 billion and the purchase price of $3.5 billion. This goodwill has to be written off from the tax base over a period of 15 years and results in annual amortisation charges of $106.7 million before taxes and $53.35 million after taxes (under the assumption of a tax rate of 50 per cent), respectively. One part of the purchase price ($1.5 billion) is paid in cash; the other part is paid with shares of HOPE, which increases its capital by $2 billion[5] for this purpose. The share price of $11 requires the issuance of 181 818 182 new shares which will raise the number of shares outstanding of HOPE to 909 090 909. Synergies are expected to increase earnings by $70 million per year (i.e. a NPV of $700 million), interest expenses for the cash component of the purchase price amount to $45 million after taxes. These numbers result in the changes in earnings per share shown in Table 6.3.

Table 6.3 Calculation of accretion/dilution, 2001–3, US$ million

	2001	2002	2003
EBIT HOPE	800	800	800
EBIT VICTORY subsidiary	164	177	187
Total	964	977	987
Synergies/Improvements	70	70	70
Interest expenses	45	45	45
Goodwill amortisation	53	53	53
EBIT new	**936**	**949**	**959**
EPS[1] new (incl. goodwill)	**1.03**	**1.04**	**1.05**
EPS new (excl. goodwill)	1.09	1.10	1.11
EPS before	1.10	1.10	1.10
Dilution (incl. goodwill)	**−6.4%**	**−5.1%**	**−4.1%**
Dilution/Accretion (excl. goodwill)	−1.1%	0.2%	1.2%

Note:[1] EPS values are rounded.

If goodwill amortisation is included, the transaction results in a dilution of earnings per share of 4 to 6 per cent in the three years following the transaction. If amortisation is not considered in this calculation, dilution is reversed to an accretion of EPS from 2002 onwards.

Hence, our example deals with a transaction that results in reduced earnings per share and, at the same time, wealth losses for the shareholders of HOPE. However, as calculations of accretion/dilution and value changes do not generally lead to the same conclusions with respect to the economic success of a transaction, the classification in Table 6.4 is useful.

The advantages of a transaction have to be communicated in detail if the transaction induces an increase in corporate value which, however, will become evident in income statements only after a couple of years. In the examination of the success prospects of M&A transactions cited above, the proportion of value-increasing transactions from the acquirers' point of view was measured as 50 per cent. However, the majority of these transactions resulted in a dilution of earnings per share. Therefore, the development of an appropriate communication strategy is typically of vital importance for the parties involved in the transaction, especially for the acquiring side.

Table 6.4 Classification of transactions

Accretive	Warning should be considered	'Easy win'
Dilutive	Beyond remedy by communication	Specific communication of value creation potentials
	Value-reducing	***Value-enhancing***

3 DCF Valuation

Within the analysis of the economics of M&A transactions, the valuation of the companies plays a central role. In the following, we present the WACC or entity version of the discounted cash flow (DCF) valuation method, which has a sound theoretical foundation and is commonly applied in business practice. As a first step, the cash flow relevant for valuation has to be defined and forecasted for a period of 5 to 10 years. Following that, these cash flows are discounted with the weighted average cost of capital (WACC) in the second step. In the third step, the continuing value that includes the cash flow after the period of explicit forecasting is determined. The fourth step comprises the calculation of the valuation results as well as a sensitivity analysis.

Definition and Forecast of the Relevant Cash Flow

The key issue of the valuation of companies is the creation of a business plan from which the cash flow generated by the company can be derived. This business plan should facilitate a complete cash flow statement for the purpose of valuation. Therefore, simplified but complete and consistent balance sheets and income statements are needed. However, standard planning of financial data is not sufficient. Sector- and company-specific planning models that interrelate expectations concerning revenues and cost structures to the development of competition in the sector are required.

Definition of Cash Flow

Basically, cash flows can be defined in several ways. A consistent structure of the valuation calculation is therefore of vital importance. The choice of cash flow definition at the same time determines both the calculation of the discount rate and the derivation of the equity value. The discounted cash flow method that is primarily considered here is based on the definition of cash flow in Table 6.5.

Total free cash flow after corporate taxes is always equivalent to the cash flow available to the investors of the company. Therefore, free cash flow can also be calculated from a financial view as in Table 6.6.

Both methods of calculation (Tables 6.5 and 6.6) must yield the same result and should always be conducted to ensure consistency of the cash flow definition.

Table 6.5 Definition of free cash flow: operating view

	Earnings before interest and taxes (EBIT)
–	Corporate taxes on EBIT
+	Depreciation and amortisation
+/–	Change in provisions
=	**Gross operating cash flow**
–	Investments
+/–	Change in working capital
=	**Operating free cash flow**
+	Cash flow from non-operating investments
=	**Total free cash flow**

Table 6.6 Definition of free cash flow: financial view

	Interest payments
–	Corporate taxes on interest payments
+	Repayment of debt
–	New credits raised
=	**Net payments to creditors**
	Dividends
+	Chargeable corporate tax/tax credits (if applicable)[1]
+	Share repurchases and other payments to owners
–	Issues of new capital and other payments from owners
=	**Net payments to owners**
	Net payments to creditors
+	Net payments to owners
=	**Total free cash flow**

Note:[1] Chargeability of corporate taxes for shareholders exists in only some countries.

Development of Industry-Specific Forecasting Models

Forecasting cash flows is the central problem of the valuation of businesses and, hence, of value-enhancement analysis as a whole. All considerations should focus on such forecasts which, however, are difficult to generalise. In the following, we describe the basic approach using an example from the pharmaceutical industry.

The development of future revenues has a substantial impact on the value of a company, which requires a sound forecast of the relevant factors. In our example from the pharmaceutical industry shown in Figure 6.2, the development of the population is the basis of all further considerations. As a next step, the spread of an exemplary disease is analysed. This determines both the number of potential patients and the medical needs. Subsequently, the rate of appointments with physicians, the rate of successful diagnosis as well as the rate of pharmaceutical medication are examined. This eventually results in the number of patients which will potentially be treated with the pharmaceutical product.

Another central assumption has to be formulated with respect to the market share of the product. In this context, the broad concept of strategic planning can be applied. The expected market share can be derived from the relation between the comparative product characteristics from the customers' perspective and the relative price of the product. In a last step, the duration of medication as well as the price per unit of the pharmaceutical product needs to be determined to calculate the revenues for the respective year.

Without doubt, the example presented here is a specific one. Nevertheless, the basic principle of the analysis of underlying economic factors should generally be used and it should also be applied to the most important items of cost structure. This improves quality of planning, makes implicit assumptions more transparent and provides a fact base from which to derive value enhancing options.

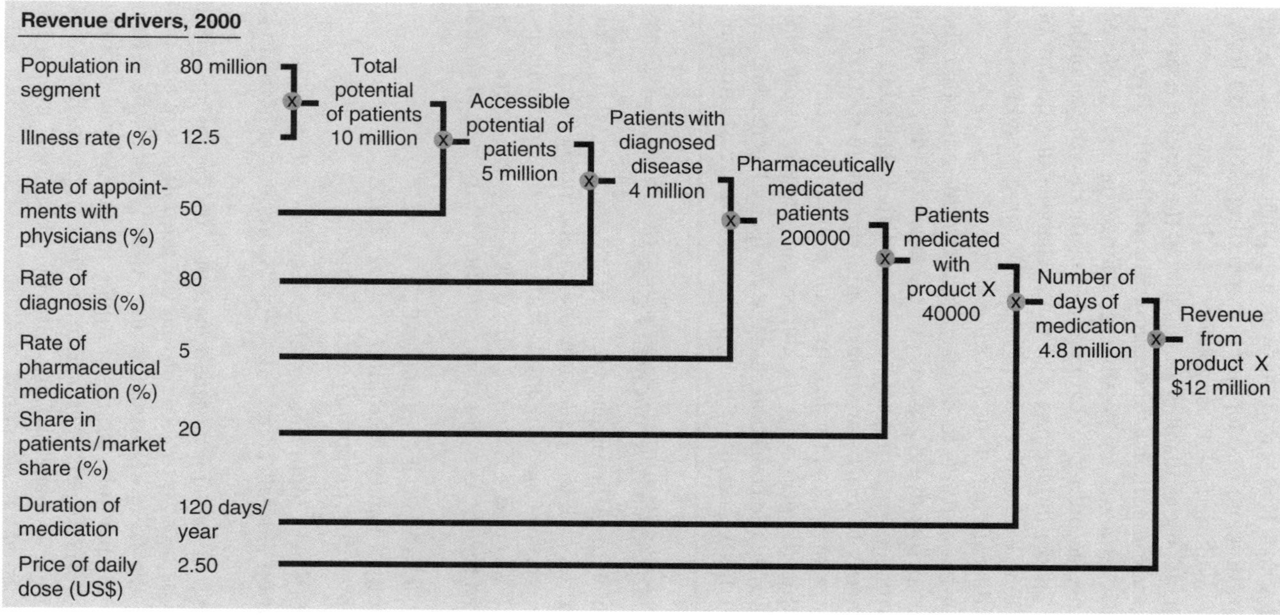

Figure 6.2 Revenue forecast for a pharmaceutical product, using Germany as an example

Determination of the Explicit Forecast Period

The period of explicit and detailed forecasting of future proceeds is called the *explicit forecast period.* This period, for which explicit assumptions are made concerning composition and development of operating gross cash flow, investment and changes in working capital, is typically 5 to 10 years.

On the one hand, the availability and quality of the data necessary to model free cash flow is of vital importance for determining the length of the explicit forecast period. If robust estimates are possible for a longer period, the forecast horizon should be defined according to that period to facilitate a deeper understanding of value and the factors influencing it. If the availability and quality of the data is insufficient, a long explicit forecast period results in a pseudo-accuracy that adds little to the understanding of the resulting value.

On the other hand, it has to be taken into consideration that the end of the explicit forecast period marks a point in time at which the environment and the economic situation of the company to be valued are balanced in an equilibrium. Therefore, it needs to reach far enough into the future so that unanticipated changes in competition and the institutional environment can be assumed to be completed within the period. At the same time, the end of the explicit forecast period has to satisfy the condition that the company has reached an equilibrium in economic terms, especially with respect to growth, cost structure and investment activities.

Definition and Determination of Cost of Capital

The returns which investors demand on their invested capital are derived from the prices of securities that are traded on the capital market and are similar with respect to risk structure and duration. If the cash flow definitions from Tables 6.4 and 6.5 are taken as a reference, the weighted average return as claimed by owners and creditors are used for the calculation of the cost of capital:

$$\begin{aligned}&\text{Weighted Average Cost of Capital (WACC)}\\&= \text{cost of equity} \times \text{equity proportion of total capital}\\&+ \text{cost of debt} \times \text{debt proportion of total capital}\end{aligned}$$

$$\begin{aligned}&\text{equity proportion of total value} = \text{value of equity} \div \text{total value}\\&\text{debt proportion of total capital} = 1 - \text{equity proportion of total value}\end{aligned}$$

In the following, we explain the determination of the cost of equity and the cost of debt. It has to be taken into account that the proportions of equity and debt are calculated on the basis of market values, which reflect the returns currently demanded by the investors. Empirical studies for the German capital market that were conducted on the basis of quoted industrial companies for the years 1987–98 have resulted in an average cost of capital of between 8.7 per cent and 11.6 per cent, with a mean of 9.8 per cent.[6]

According to this study, the average cost of capital with respect to total value of the entity is 9.8 per cent. This is a nominal rate after corporate taxes and before individual investor taxes. Despite the decrease in interest rates in the years 1996 and 1997, the average cost of capital increased in this period owing to shifts in capital structures of the companies.

Cost of Equity

Investors expect an appropriate return on the money they invest which has to be at least equal to the risk-free rate of return. This basic rate of return can be derived from the yields on long-term government bonds. However, as returns from a stake in a company are uncertain, the owners claim a compensation for the risk they take, i.e. a risk premium. Under the assumption that investors do not only hold shares in a single company but diversify their portfolio widely in order to minimise risk, the well-known and Nobel Prize-winning Capital Asset Pricing Model (CAPM) can be applied under the idealised conditions of perfect markets. Within the CAPM, only the so-called 'systematic risk' that cannot be eliminated by portfolio diversification is relevant for the determination of the returns demanded. This risk can be derived from the correlation between the return on the stocks of a company and the return on the market portfolio. On the basis of the CAPM, the return claimed by the owners for their firm-specific investment can be calculated as follows:

Cost of equity ('expected return of the owners')
= Risk-free rate of return
+ Correlation coefficient × Standard deviation of stock return
× (market risk premium on equity ÷ standard deviation of the return on the market portfolio)

The correlation coefficient measures the standardised covariance between the stock return of a company and the return on the market portfolio. It is limited to values between −1 and 1. A correlation coefficient of 1 indicates that both variables move perfectly in line with one another, a correlation coefficient of −1 indicates movements in strictly opposite directions and a coefficient of 0 means that there is no systematic linear relationship. The correlation coefficient is to be multiplied by the standard deviation as a measure of stock price volatility. Finally, the market price per unit risk has to be taken into account to calculate the risk premium.

Risk-free investments are characterised by zero variance by definition and, therefore, by an expected return equal to the risk-free rate. The same applies to investments that have a correlation coefficient of 0 as explained above. The return on these investments is not known with certainty but risk can be eliminated almost completely by portfolio diversification.

The product of the correlation coefficient and the ratio of standard deviations is often summarised by the so-called 'Beta'[7], so that the cost of equity can also be expressed as follows:

Cost of equity = Risk-free rate of return + Beta × Market risk premium

The weighted average of the Beta factors of all shares included in the market portfolio is equal to 1 by definition. Companies with a Beta exceeding 1 feature above-average risk, whereas a Beta of less than 1 indicates below-average risk.

There are a number of research papers in which industry-specific Betas were calculated for different countries that, after some modification, can also be used for the valuation of non-listed companies and business units. Beside these empirically observed Betas, more recent approaches have been developed that serve to determine future-oriented Betas that are not critically dependent on the existence of historical returns of comparable quoted companies.

Across industrialised countries, the observed market risk premium was between 5 and 8 per cent p.a. Table 6.7 shows the results of several empirical studies which support these numbers.

The market risk premiums regularly used in practice range from 3 to 5 per cent and are thus slightly below the range given above. The cost of capital calculation in the study on German industrial companies cited in note 6 was based on a risk premium of 5 per cent. The reason for the resulting deviation from empirical data can be found in statistical estimation errors. The indices used as a basis for the calculations do not include the complete portfolio of stocks with uncertain returns. Stocks that are excluded from the index owing to bankruptcy of the issuing companies or for other reasons are replaced by the stocks of other companies. Through this procedure an index of successful firms is created in the long run with the consequence of an upward-biased return of the market portfolio. A

Table 6.7 Country-specific market risk premiums

Study	Country	Observation Period	Nominal Returns (%)	Risk Premium (%)
Stehle (1998)	Germany	1948–97	stocks: 14.5 bonds: 6.7	7.8
Bimberg (1993)	Germany	1954–92	stocks: 14.1 bonds: 6.8	7.3
Uhlir and Steiner (1991)	Germany	1953–84	stocks: 14.4 bonds: 7.9	6.5
Siegel (1994)	USA	1926–92	stocks: 12.0 bonds: 5.2	6.8
Siegel (1994)	USA	1946–92	stocks: 12.7 bonds: 5.3	7.4
Dimson, Marsh and Staunton (2000)	USA	1900–2000	stocks: 12.2 bonds: 5.0	7.2
Dimson, Marsh and Staunton (2000)	UK	1900–2000	stocks: 12.1 bonds: 6.1	6.0
Dimson and Marsh (1999)	UK	1919–98	stocks: 12.1 bonds: 6.5	5.6
Gallais-Hamonno and Arbulu (1995)	France	1950–92	stocks: 15.5 bonds: 10.5	5.0

small number of analyses covering this phenomenon have found that this 'survival bias' may amount to approximately 2 percentage points per year, thus explaining the observed difference.

It must also be taken into account that the cost of equity resulting from this calculation represents demands for returns by the equity holders that are determined after corporate taxes but before individual income taxes of the equity holders. Consistency in the determination of cash flow and discount rates must also be ensured in this regard.

Cost of Debt

The cost of debt can generally be derived from publicly available statistics prepared by national central banks. The statistics provided by Germany's Bundesbank include current market yields of corporate bonds. Between 1987 and 1997, the average yield of corporate bonds was 7.2 per cent. Thus they exceeded the yield of government bonds, which is used as basic risk-free rate of return, by 0.4 percentage points. These yields are given as nominal rates of return before taxes. To determine the effective cost of debt that is compatible with the cost of equity, the corporate taxes have to be taken into account. The cost of debt after taxes is calculated as follows:

Cost of debt
= Risk-free rate of return
+ Risk premium
− Corporate tax rate × (Risk-free rate of return + Risk premium)

It is assumed that the risk premium is already included in the market yield of corporate bonds. Table 6.8 displays the risk premiums for different corporate ratings from August 1999, which can be used for a differentiated analysis.

Determination of Target Capital Structure

In this article, the assumption is made that the management of the company has specified its financial policy. The question of how to determine a potentially optimal capital structure is a complex financial problem which will not be discussed

Table 6.8 EURO corporate spreads in basis points

	Rating			
Maturity	**AAA**	**AA**	**A**	**BBB**
all	33	45	68	92
1–5 years	27	37	61	88
5–10 years	38	52	73	97
>10 years	36	47	88	n.a.

Source: *Handelsblatt.*

here. Instead, it is important to state that the capital structure of the firm is a target parameter defined by management. If the financial policy of a company or a group of companies is aimed at achieving an AAA rating, certain requirements laid down by the rating agencies with respect to a number of financial and economic figures and ratios have to be met also at the level of the business units and subsidiaries.

The 'Circularity Problem' and the Time-Dependent Cost of Capital

The level of the cost of capital that serves as discount rate for the free cash flows has a substantial impact on the result of the valuation. As a consequence, this parameter is the subject of frequent discussions, which regularly focus on the following two main problems:

- To calculate the average cost of capital correctly an iterative procedure is necessary since the WACC depends on the leverage ratio of the value of company's debt to its total value. However, the value of the company results from the valuation, which seems to create a *circularity problem.*
- Variations in the capital structure that result from changes in the level of debt as shown in the projected balance sheet relative to the value of the company require an adjustment of the average cost of capital. As a consequence, the cost of capital has to be specified for *each period within the explicit forecast horizon.*

Both arguments are at least in part based on unrealistic assumptions and are often not relevant in practice. This can be explained as follows:

- The *target capital structure* is a planning assumption made by management, like the expected growth rates of revenues, the cost structure, the required replacement investment and other parameters. Of course, the payout policy of the company has to be determined so that it facilitates the investment and financing policy as planned. The debt to equity ratio observed at the time of valuation on the basis of the market value may differ from the targeted capital structure. However, for the purpose of valuation the future rather than the present financing is relevant. Therefore, there is no circularity problem.
- Changes in the debt to equity ratio basically have to be considered in the calculation of the average cost of capital. Therefore they are *time-dependent.* For this purpose, the relationship between the average cost of capital and the debt to equity ratio needs to be determined at first. In this context, the well-known theorems of Modigliani and Miller are frequently applied. They imply that the average cost of capital is continuously decreasing in the leverage if taxation is taken into consideration. The reason for this inverse correlation are the tax-related advantages of debt to equity financing that were taken into account. However, this approach does not consider the fact that the probability that companies will actually be able to benefit from these tax advantages decreases with the level of debt because of the increasing risk of losses. If the risks of losses and insolvency are taken into account, the average cost of capital shows only low sensitivity with respect to small changes in the debt to equity

ratio. Thus, given the general uncertainty, an adjustment of WACC to changes in the capital structure is required only in exceptional cases.

Finally, a more general approach to including value effects from financing in valuation should be mentioned. The so-called 'adjusted present value' method quantifies, among other things, the tax shield of debt financing by calculating its net present value (NPV) separately. With this method, changes in financing policy can be included explicitly in the valuation in a simpler and more transparent way.

Estimation of the Continuing Value

Basically, the firm value to be calculated can be subdivided into the NPV of cash flows during the explicit forecast period and the NPV of cash flows after this period, which is referred to as *continuing value.*

To determine the continuing value, three methods with different underlying assumptions can be recommended: (1) long explicit forecast period, (2) constant growth rates in free cash flow in perpetuity and (3) constant growth rates in free cash flow in perpetuity with explicit consideration of net new investment. Of these three methods, the latter has proved to be the most suitable.

Long Explicit Forecast Period

One of the alternatives of including the continuing value in the valuation calculation is explicitly to model free cash flows on a very long-term basis. In doing so, cash flows that are generated in the distant future contribute little to total value because of the discounting effect (at least if the growth rate in cash flow is smaller than the discount rate). This explicit forecast has the advantage that it avoids structural interruptions in the transition from the explicit forecast period to the subsequent period of implicit modelling. To decrease complexity, the level of detail in forecasting cash flows can be reduced over time. To give an example, cash flows in the first five years can be obtained from complete balance sheets and the corresponding income statements, which are also based on an explicit forecast of individual items. After this period, the forecasting can be restricted to key parameters such as the growth rate in sales (g), the capital turnover (CTO) and the return on sales (ROS). These three parameters are based on the following definitions:

$$CTO = \frac{Sales}{IC}$$

$$ROS = \frac{\text{EBIT after adjusted taxes}}{Sales} = \frac{NOPLAT}{Sales}$$

$$IC_t = \frac{(1 + g_t) \cdot Sales_{t-1}}{CTO_t}$$

Invested capital IC = tangible assets + working capital
NOPLAT = Net operating profit less adjusted taxes.

With the three parameters g, ROS and CTO, the free cash flow (FCF) can be determined:

$$FCF_t = ROS_t \cdot Sales_{t-1} \cdot (1 + g_t) - g_t \cdot IC_{t-1}$$

On the basis of these definitions, the total firm value V can be calculated as follows:

$$V = \overbrace{\frac{FCF_1}{1+WACC} + \frac{FCF_2}{(1+WACC)^2} + \frac{FCF_3}{(1+WACC)^3} + \frac{FCF_4}{(1+WACC)^4} + \frac{FCF_5}{(1+WACC)^5}}^{\text{Basis: planned balance sheets with income statements}}$$
$$\underbrace{+ \frac{FCF_6}{(1+WACC)^6} + \ldots + \frac{FCF_{150}}{(1+WACC)^{150}}}_{\text{Basis: assumptions regarding } g, CTO, ROS}$$

With this procedure, an explicit estimate of the continuing value is not necessary.

Constant Perpetual Growth in Free Cash Flow

If the parameters sales growth (g), capital turnover (CTO) and return on sales (ROS) are assumed to be constant after the explicit forecast period, the corresponding cash flows can be aggregated within one formula. With $T = 5$ being the end of the explicit forecast period, the following holds:

$$V = \overbrace{\frac{FCF_1}{1+WACC} + \frac{FCF_2}{(1+WACC)^2} + \frac{FCF_3}{(1+WACC)^3} + \frac{FCF_4}{(1+WACC)^4} + \frac{FCF_5}{(1+WACC)^5}}^{\text{Basis: planned balance sheets with income statements}}$$
$$\underbrace{+ \frac{FCF_5 \cdot (1+g)}{WACC - g} \cdot \frac{1}{(1+WACC)^5}}_{\text{Continuing value}}$$

The second line of the above equation displays the calculation of the continuing value. The free cash flow forecasted for the period 5 increases continuously at its expected constant growth rate g. The cash flows generated after period 5 are discounted by the difference between the average cost of capital and the growth rate.[8] From this results the continuing value by the end of period 5, which has to be discounted by $(1 + WACC)^5$ to obtain the net present value at the beginning of period 1.

The virtue of this approach is given by its simplicity. However, the fact that the continuing value – and, hence, the resulting total value of the firm – substantially depends on the assumed long-term growth rate, is a potential disadvantage. In practice, g is often set equal to the inflation rate expected on a long-term basis. But this frequently results in a significant underestimation of the continuing value – and, consequently, in an undervaluation of the company as a whole.

This problem becomes evident if one considers long-term growth perspectives that are included implicitly in share prices: on the basis of the share prices observable in July 1998, long-term growth rates of 9 per cent could be derived for companies in the computer networks sector, 7 per cent for the pharmaceutical sector and 5 per cent for the retail and trade sectors. As can be seen from these numbers, analysing implicit capital market expectations regarding comparable companies is one possible way to substantiate the assumptions regarding long-term growth rates.

Constant Growth in Free Cash Flow with Explicit Consideration of Returns on Net New Investment

Another approach to substantiating expectations regarding long-term growth rates can be based on the assumption of unconstrained competition in product markets. The assumption is made that companies operating in highly competitive markets are unable to make net new investments that yield returns exceeding the cost of capital in the long run. In this scenario, strong competition leads to an equilibrium in which the marginal revenues are equal to the marginal cost and where marginal returns are equal to the marginal cost of capital.

To understand the effects of the assumptions underlying this scenario it is assumed that operating earnings after taxes remain constant after the end of the explicit forecast period, if depreciation is equal to reinvestment. Growth can be achieved only if investments exceed depreciation, i.e. through net new investment. Hence, the growth of free cash flows depends on the amount of net new investment and the returns thereon. If, for example, net operating profit less adjusted taxes (*NOPLAT*) is \$100 million and the average cost of capital is 10 per cent, then the firm value is calculated without considering growth as \$1 billion. If the assumption is made that net new investment is fixed at 20 per cent of NOPLAT, then the free cash flow in the first period is \$80 million instead of \$100 million. Given a rate of return of 10 per cent on net new investment and the resulting growth rate of cash flow of 2 per cent, the following period yields a cash flow of \$102 million (20 per cent of which is again invested) and a firm value of \$1 billion is again obtained:

$$CV = \frac{80}{10\% - 2\%} = \frac{100}{10\%} = 1000$$

The growth in the free cash flow of 2 per cent resulting from net new investment obviously does not create additional firm value. This is due to the fact that the rate of return on net new investment exactly equals the cost of capital. As a consequence, the NPV of the investment is zero.

This result can be generalised as follows:

$$CV = \frac{NOPLAT \cdot \left(1 - \frac{g}{r}\right)}{WACC - g}$$

with:

g	growth rate of NOPLAT, free cash flow and invested capital
r	rate of return on net new investment
$WACC$	weighted average cost of capital

Here, g denotes the growth rate in perpetuity of NOPLAT and, hence, of the free cash flow which is always a fixed proportion of NOPLAT, under the assumption that NOPLAT remains constant if depreciation is reinvested and that net new investment has a constant rate of return of r. The expression g/r represents the proportion of NOPLAT invested in additional capital (= net new investment) or the investment rate. So the overall expression in the numerator represents NOPLAT *minus* the proportion of NOPLAT spent on net new investment, or free cash flow. To obtain the firm value, the free cash flow is again discounted by $WACC-g$.

In the competition scenario described in the introduction to this section, $r = WACC$, i.e. the marginal rate of return converges with the cost of capital in the long run. Therefore, the calculation of the continuing value is reduced to dividing NOPLAT in $T = 6$ by the cost of capital. Thus, the valuation formula is given as follows:

$$V = \overbrace{\frac{FCF_1}{1+WACC} + \frac{FCF_2}{(1+WACC)^2} + \frac{FCF_3}{(1+WACC)^3} + \frac{FCF_4}{(1+WACC)^4} + \frac{FCF_5}{(1+WACC)^5}}^{\text{Basis: planned balance sheets with income statements}} + \underbrace{\frac{NOPLAT_5 \cdot (1+g)}{WACC} \frac{1}{(1+WACC)^5}}_{\text{Continuing value given } r = WACC}$$

It should be noted that this calculation of the continuing value does not imply zero growth but assumes that long-term growth does not result in additional firm value.

The choice of either of the methods presented above should be made dependent on the possibility to make plausible and realistic assumptions with respect to the relevant parameters. However, no generally valid propositions can be made concerning such assumptions. For companies to which the assumption that marginal rates of return will converge with the cost of capital applies, an explicit formulation of growth expectation is not needed. This is most likely the case with companies operating in mature markets (e.g. steel, chemical products). By contrast, the point in time of convergence is presumably in the very distant future for companies in high technology industries, requiring a longer explicit forecast period. Furthermore, it is important, especially for the formula-based approaches, that the initial cash flow is defined consistently. In cyclical industries, parameter values should be adjusted to business cycles to avoid inconsistencies.

Summary of the Valuation Results

Finally, two further steps are necessary to obtain the valuation result:

- First, the *equity value* has to be derived. The NPV of the free cash flow during the explicit forecast period and the continuing value that is discounted to the time of valuation add up to the NPV of (operating) free cash flow. Total firm value is obtained by adding the value of non-operating assets and excess cash. In a final step, the value of a company's equity is determined by subtracting from the total firm value the market value of its entire interest-bearing debt, hybrid securities, minority interests and similar liabilities. In this context, it has to be considered that the definition of the free cash flow and the cost of capital imply unequivocally which components of the total firm value have to be eliminated to obtain the value of equity. Table 6.9 summarises the interrelation between cash flow, cost of capital and calculation of the valuation result.
- Secondly, the formally completed valuation needs to be subjected to a comprehensive plausibility check. For companies that are listed on a stock exchange, the market capitalisation represents a first benchmark. If the calculated value deviates too much from the market value, the reasons for this deviation should be investigated.

The finalised valuation provides a set of *performance figures* (e.g. rate of return on invested capital, market to book ratio, prospective earnings margins, capital turnover, etc.). These key figures can be used as a basis for comparisons and cross-checks (e.g. cross-sectional comparisons, time series comparisons), which are indispensable for a profound understanding of the valuation result as well as for a thorough plausibility check. Finally, a sensitivity analysis that quantifies the impact on the firm value of all assumptions regarding relevant parameters helps to deepen the understanding of the composition of firm value. Only if the formal calculation of the value components has been supplemented by a comprehensive plausibility check, the valuation can be regarded as finally completed.

4 Estimation of Potential Transaction Prices with Multiples

In the context of a value-enhancement analysis of M&A transactions, multiples are used to estimate potential transaction prices which, in turn, are compared to firm value as calculated. Multiples are based on realised prices that are related to a pre-defined reference figure such as revenues, cash flows, earnings or book values of capital. The underlying prices are derived from past transactions or market values. The latter are to be increased by a transaction premium if necessary.

On the one hand, multiples that are based on the price of equity and multiples based on the price or the value of the entity can be distinguished. According to this distinction, the multiples are denoted either as equity multiples or as entity/enterprise multiples.

Table 6.9 Valuation with a WACC approach

EBIT – corporate taxes + depreciation and amortization + increase in provisions – reduction of provisions – investment in tangible assets – increase in working capital + reduction of working capital	=	Interest payments (less associated tax benefits) + repayment of debt – raise of new debt	÷	Interest on bebt less relative tax benefit	=	Value of debt
		Dividends + share repurchase – capital increase	÷	Cost of equity according to CAPM	=	Value of equity
Free cash flow		*Cash flow to investors*		*Cost of capital*		*Enterprise (entity) value*

On the other hand, the distinction can be drawn according to the variable used as reference, i.e. as denominator of the multiple term. If flows with the dimension monetary unit per unit of time are used, multiples can be interpreted as paybacks. By contrast, multiples based on end-of-year variables are absolute measures without a dimension. Table 6.10 exhibits a number of exemplary multiples.

Before multiples can be applied a sample of comparable companies, the so-called 'peer group', needs to be put together. Following that, multiples are calculated for the companies of this sample and the median of these multiples is determined.

Table 6.11 presents the enterprise/sales multiples for a sample of German corporations as of December 1997 on the basis of market values. These public market multiples do not include any premiums which need to be considered and calculated separately for the company to be priced in the context of a transaction.

It is certainly not easy to identify actually comparable companies. One way of solving this problem is to include in the sample only companies that are operating in the same industry as the target company. Thus, comparability is considered as equivalent to belonging to the same industry.

A more sophisticated selection of comparable companies can be obtained by considering additional criteria such as profitability, growth and risk. It could even be argued that industry is irrelevant, if the companies of the peer group are sufficiently homogeneous with respect to the factors determining value. These value – and, hence, price-determining – factors can be easily isolated by means of simple valuation models. On the basis of the continuing value model applied on p.206, the following relationship can be derived for the enterprise/sales multiple:

$$\frac{V}{S}=\frac{1}{S}\frac{NOPLAT\cdot(1+g)\cdot\left(1-\frac{g}{r}\right)}{(WACC-g)}=\frac{ROS\cdot(1+g)\cdot\left(1-\frac{g}{r}\right)}{(WACC-g)}$$

Table 6.10 Categories and examples of multiples

Reference base	**Equity**	Price-earnings ratio	Market to book ratio
	Entity/Enterprise	Enterprise/sales Enterprise/EBIT Enterprise/EBITDA[1]	Enterprise/book value of invested capital
		Based on flows	**Based on end-of-year variables**

Note:[1] EBITDA = Earnings before interest, taxes, depreciation and amortisation.

Table 6.11 Enterprise/sales multiples, 1993–7

	1993	1994	1995	1996	1997
Mean	0.5368	0.5541	0.6046	0.6141	0.7830
Median	0.3850	0.3644	0.3083	0.3865	0.5030
Standard deviation	0.5350	0.8653	1.3072	0.9430	1.5247
Correlation	0.7915	0.8018	0.7012	0.6847	0.6476

with:

V	Market value of equity and debt (Enterprise)
S	Sales
ROS	Return on sales after taxes
g	Long-term growth rate
r	Rate of return on net new investment
$WACC$	Weighted average cost of capital

According to the definitions given by this equation, companies should exhibit comparable enterprise/sales multiples if they have similar returns on sales, growth rates, rates of return on net new investment and average cost of capital.

The close correlation between the enterprise/sales multiples and the return on sales of companies can be shown empirically as well, as can be seen from Figure 6.3. Figure 6.3 also indicates that current profitability alone is not sufficient to explain the valuation of firms by the market.

The application of the so-called 'fundamental multiples' can be presented as follows: first of all, the data of all available listed firms are examined. As a next step, returns on sales, growth rates, rates of return on net new investment and cost of capital are calculated for each of the peer companies. Ideally, these calculations should be based on analysts' forecasts. As far as return on net new investment is concerned, the current rate of return of the company could be used as an approximation where there is no data forecast available. When all value-relevant parameters are determined, the same procedure is applied to the company to be analysed, which may not be listed. In the next step, a tolerance factor is defined that determines the maximum percentage rate of deviation of the company-specific values estimated for the identified value-relevant factors from each other.

If, for example, the return on sales of the company to be valued is 12 per cent and the tolerance factor is set to 20 per cent, all companies that generate returns on sales of between 9.6 and 14.4 per cent are filtered out of the totality of companies listed on the stock exchange. Subsequently, all firms that are not within the tolerance range with respect to growth rates, rates of return on net new investment and cost of capital are removed from the sample. Through this procedure, one obtains a sample of companies that are indeed comparable with regard to all relevant parameters influencing their values. Only these companies are actually used for the determination of the multiples. First experiences in practical application of this new multiple approach indicate that the results obtained with these multiples are by far more exact than results obtained with industry multiples.

In conclusion, it can be stated that the discounted cash flow methods available today as well as the refined multiple approaches are instruments that facilitate the implementation of a comparatively reliable value enhancement analysis and, thus, potentially improve the prospects of success of M&A transactions.

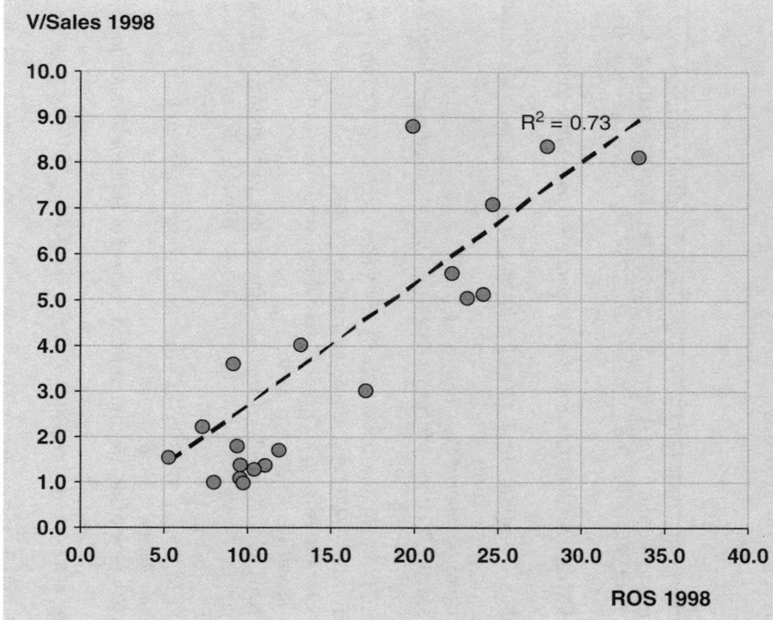

Company	ROS 1998	V/Sales 1998
PFIZER INC	26.6	11.0
ASTRAZENECA PLC	19.9	8.8
BRISTOL-MYERS SQUIBB CO	28.0	8.4
GLAXO WELLCOME PLC	33.4	8.1
MERCK & CO., INC.	24.7	7.1
SMITHKLINE BEECHAM PLC	22.3	5.6
AMERICAN HOME PRODUCTS	24.3	5.1
NOVARTIS AG-REG SHS	23.2	5.1
PHARMACIA & UPJOHN INC	13.2	4.1
MONSANTO CO	9.1	3.6
DU PONT (E.I.) DE NEMOURS	17.1	3.0
RHÔNE-POULENC	7.3	2.2
UNION CARBIDE CORP	9.3	1.8
DOW CHEMICAL	11.9	1.7
HOECHST AG	5.3	1.5
CLARIANT AG-REG	11.1	1.4
EASTMAN CHEMICAL COMP	9.7	1.0
BAYER AG	10.4	1.3
AKZO NOBEL	9.6	1.4
BASF AG	9.6	1.1
SOLVAY SA	8.0	1.0

Figure 6.3 Correlation between enterprise/sales multiples and returns on sales, chemical and pharmaceutical industries
Source: Bloomberg.

Notes

1 Note that these value changes were measured over a period starting five days before and ending five days after the announcement of the transaction. Technically spoken, cumulative abnormal returns (CARs) relative to the cost of equity on the basis of the Capital Asset Pricing Model (CAPM) were measured for this period.
2 From this follows that the expected firm value is equal to $8 billion, which induces risk-neutral rational investors to subscribe for the shares with certainty up to this limit price.
3 Although this model is strongly simplified, it shows the effects of information asymmetries.
4 In Germany, the government announced plans to exempt profits from the sale of companies as well as stakes in companies from taxation as a part of the pending tax reform for the first time in December 1999. The capital market reaction to this announcement was extremely positive. The tax reform became effective in January 2002.
5 This denotes the market value of the new issue, not the nominal value.
6 The sample comprised the industrial companies included in the German stock index CDAX, for which complete data was available. In total, 295 companies were included in the sample. The capital market and annual report data were taken from DATASTREAM, the necessary information on interest rates was obtained from the Deutsche Bundesbank.
7 Beta = Correlation coefficient × standard deviation of stock return ÷ standard deviation of the return on the market portfolio.
8 This formula is applicable if $WACC > g$.

Bibliography

Bimberg, L. H. (1993) *Langfristige Renditenberechnung zur Ermittlung von Risikoprämien: empirische Untersuchung der Renditen von Aktien, festverzinslichen Wertpapieren und Tagesgeld in der Bundesrepublik Deutschland für den Zeitraum von 1954 bis 1988*, 2nd edn (Frankfurt am Main).

Brealey, R. A. and Myers, S. (2000) *Principles of Corporate Finance*, 6th edn (Boston: McGraw-Hill).

Copeland, T., Koller, T. and Murrin, J. (2000) *Valuation, Measuring and Managing the Value of Companies*, 3rd edn (New York).

Damodaran, A. (1996) *Investment Valuation* (New York).

Dimson, E. and Marsh, P. (1999) Murphy's Law and Market Anomalies, *Journal of Portfolio Management*, 25 (2), pp. 53–69.

Dimson, E., Marsh, P. and Staunton, M. (2000) *The Millennium Book: A Century of Investment Returns* (London: ABN AMRO and London Business School).

Gallais-Hamonno, G. and Arbulu, P. (1995) La rentabilité réelle des actifs boursiers de 1950 à 1992, *Économie et Statistique*, 280, pp. 3–30.

Inselbag, I. and Kaufhold, H. (1997) Two DCF Approaches for Valuing Companies under Alternative Financing Strategies (and How to Choose Between Them), *Journal of Applied Corporate Finance*, 10, pp. 114–22.

Modigliani, F. and Miller, M. H. (1963) Corporate Income, Taxes and the Cost of Capital, *American Economic Review*, 53, pp. 433–43.

Rock, K. (1984) Why new issues are underpriced, *Journal of Financial Economics*, 15, pp. 187–212.

Siegel, J. J. (1994) *Stock for the Long Run: A Guide to Selecting Markets for Long-term Growth* (Chicago).

Stehle, R. (1998) Aktien versus Renten, in: Cramer, J.-E., Förster, W. and Ruland, F. (eds.) *Handbuch zur Altersversorgung* (Frankfurt am Main), pp. 815–31.

Uhlir, H. and Steiner, P. (1991) *Wertpapieranalyse*, 2nd edn (Heidelberg).

7
Merger Control

Helmut Bergmann

1 Preliminary Remarks

Competition law and in particular the law relating to merger control is of primary importance in the planning and implementation of mergers and acquisitions (M&A). An increasing number of transactions need to be notified with the relevant competition authorities prior to completion and their implementation is often dependent on the approval of a number of competition authorities around the world. It is therefore essential to raise and consider competition issues early on in the planning phase of an acquisition, a merger or the creation of a joint venture.

The first issue for consideration is whether the planned transaction needs to be notified (and if so with which competition authorities), and whether the investigation into the merger is likely to raise any competition problems. If a merger leads to the creation or strengthening of a market-dominant position in one or a number of affected markets, the parties should consider early on whether the sale of parts of the target company or of certain critical business sectors of the acquirer is necessary and possible in order to obtain approval to the implementation of the rest of the transaction.

In evaluating the company or business to be acquired and determining its purchase price offer the purchaser should also have a clear understanding of whether there will be parts of the target it will not be able to acquire for competition reasons, or whether it will be required to divest them following the acquisition. This is particularly so when there is some concern that the approval of the competition authority will be denied precisely because of a business of the target which is of particular interest to the purchaser ('crown jewels').

Conversely, the seller of an undertaking will often seek a purchaser on competition law criteria. If, as a result of high combined market shares with one particular purchaser, problems and delays in the merger control procedure are to be expected, or the granting of approval is doubtful, then – all other things being equal – the seller will often favour a purchaser who raises no or little competition concerns, even though the seller will in any case try and shift the merger control risks as much as possible onto the purchaser.

Since the introduction of merger control in 1990, mergers of 'Community dimension' must be notified exclusively to the European Commission in Brussels. The national competition authorities of the EU member states essentially have no jurisdiction over such mergers. Where mergers do not fall under the jurisdiction of EC merger control but impact on one or more EU member states, they will usually have to be notified with a number of national competition authorities. In addition, a number of East European countries have now also introduced merger control rules based on the Western model. In transatlantic transactions a close cooperation between the competition lawyers in the USA and in Europe will often be advisable and necessary, in particular where global markets are affected. Currently over 90 countries worldwide have merger control laws.

Merger control has gained significant importance over the last 10 years. The ever-increasing number of notifications to the European Commission and to the German Federal Cartel Office, for example, reflects the continuing increase in M&A activity in Europe. The number of formal merger decisions by the European Commission increased from 60 in 1991 to 345 in 2000. Since the introduction of European merger control, the Commission has only prohibited 15 mergers, although it has made its approval subject to commitments in over 100 cases. Since the introduction of merger control in Germany in 1973 until 2000, the Federal Cartel Office has investigated around 26 000 cases, of which only 131 have been prohibited. However, the relatively low prohibition rate should not obscure the fact that the existence of merger control alone often results in the parties refraining from going ahead with their plans. This is particularly so where, following a thorough review by the competition lawyers and informal preliminary discussions with the relevant competition authorities, it becomes apparent that the planned transaction cannot be approved and that the sale of parts of the business is not possible for legal, practical or economic reasons. To this extent, merger control has a substantial preventive effect. This is demonstrated by the fact that, from 1973 to 2000, 345 proposed transactions were abandoned or modified in the course of the proceedings with the Federal Cartel Office.

The following account describes the most important provisions of EC and German merger control law for the planning and implementation of mergers and acquisitions. The main focus is on the conditions under which transactions must be notified to the Commission in Brussels or the German competition authority in Bonn, as well as on the essential substantive and procedural provisions. This section also provides a short overview over notification requirements and procedural rules in all EU member states and selected other countries worldwide.

2 EC Merger Control

Scope of Application

M&A which impact on the territory of the EU and/or the European Economic Area (EEA) are subject to the review of the Merger Task Force of the European Commission to the extent that the EC Merger Regulation (ECMR)[1] is applicable. If so, the ECMR takes precedence over the respective national merger control laws. Transactions come within the scope of the ECMR, and may therefore be implemented only following approval by the European Commission, if they qualify as a merger within the meaning of Article 3 ECMR and if the undertakings participating in the merger attain the revenue thresholds of Article 1 ECMR.

Merger Criteria

General remarks. The function of EC merger control is to monitor structural and long-term changes in the competitive situation on the affected markets and, if necessary to preserve competitive market structures. Agreements, arrangements and other types of conduct which do not lead to a change in the external structures of the companies concerned are, from a merger control perspective, as insignificant as purely internal growth.

Article 3 ECMR lists the types of transaction which involve structural changes. Contrary to, for example, German law, EC merger control recognises only two types of concentration: the 'merger' and the 'acquisition of control over another undertaking'. The Commission has summarised its practice on the interpretation of a concentration in a particular notice.[2]

Merger. A concentration shall be deemed to arise where two or more previously independent undertakings merge to form a new undertaking. Such a merger can occur through the creation of a new entity or through the takeover of one by the other undertaking. In addition, it is sufficient according to the Commission for previously independent undertakings to pool their activities and to become subject to a joint economic management. The Commission considers the following to be indications of a merger in substance: internal profit and loss agreements between the participating undertakings, joint liability to third parties and capital interrelations between the undertakings.

Acquisition of control. By far the most common type of concentration is the acquisition of control over another undertaking. The acquisition of control usually occurs through one or more undertakings or persons, who already control at least one undertaking, through the acquisition of shares ('share deal') or assets ('asset deal'). Control may also be acquired in other ways, as long as the right of direct or indirect influence is obtained.

The determining factor for the assumption of the acquisition of control includes rights, contracts or other means, which alone or together, considering all factual and legal circumstances, accord the possibility to exercise a decisive influence over the activities of an undertaking. This includes in particular property or usage rights in the whole or parts of the assets of the undertaking, as well as rights or contracts which enable a decisive influence to be exercised over the composition, consultation or resolutions of the bodies of the undertaking.

A distinction needs to be made between the acquisition of *sole control* (including the transition from joint to sole control) on the one hand and the acquisition of *joint control* by several undertakings (including the transition from sole to joint control) on the other. What is decisive for the acquisition of control is the transfer of a single or of several undertakings to one or several other undertakings. An internal reorganisation within a group of undertakings is therefore not a concentration and is not subject to EC merger control. A typical example of the acquisition of *sole control* is the creation of a majority participation in another undertaking, that is the acquisition of a majority of the voting rights in the shareholders' meeting of another undertaking.

On the other hand, and contrary to (for example) German law, a simple minority participation will not generally be seen as amounting to a concentration, since the acquirer is not granted the possibility of acquiring a decisive influence over the other undertaking. A decisive influence in the case of an acquisition of a minority holding is possible only in exceptional cases in which, for specific legal or practical reasons, the possibility of influence exists. Typical examples of this would be qualified rights of a minority shareholder or a small presence of other shareholders in the shareholders' meeting where the remaining shares are largely dispersed so as to give the minority shareholder a *de facto* majority. The Commission judges whether the acquirer will have a *de facto* majority in shareholders' meetings in the future on the basis of the circumstances over the last three to five years.

Even the transition from joint to sole control alters the possibilities of influence in a substantial way and so satisfies the concept of a concentration under EC merger control. Typical examples of such a concentration are the acquisition of shares by other current shareholders whereby the acquirer obtains sole control over the undertaking, or the breaking up or dissolution of a joint venture.

Joint control exists where several shareholders must cooperate and reach agreement on major management decisions of the company. The pressure to reach an agreement, which itself can be evidence of joint control, exists in the event of deadlock. Pressure will, however, also exist where one shareholder has a veto right over decisions which not only concern everyday business but also the strategic commercial behaviour of the undertaking. Crucially, the veto right holder's rights of influence must go beyond the rights normally accorded to minority shareholders. Joint control therefore exists where a shareholder is in a position, as a result of their veto right, to influence decisions on the business plan, investments and the appointment of the management. In addition, veto rights may also give a controlling influence in relation to the development of new products or the positioning of the company. Whether such an influence exists must be assessed by considering the overall picture having regard to the actual decision-making processes. In addition, joint control may also exist through voting right obligations of several shareholders. These can be the result of legally binding agreements (vote pooling) or the substantive result of existing possibilities of influence.

A subcategory of acquisition of joint control is the creation of a joint venture which performs on a lasting basis all the functions of an autonomous economic entity. These joint ventures are known as 'full-function joint ventures' and are subject to merger control because of the lasting changes in the structure of the participating undertakings which they bring about.

Whether the joint venture also results in the coordination of the competitive behaviour of the parent companies is, since the revised version of the ECMR came into effect, irrelevant. Prior to the revised version, which came into force in March 1998, the ECMR was not applicable to cooperative joint ventures. Today, both cooperative and concentrative joint ventures are subject to the ECMR. Only the substantive investigation now differs, in that cooperative joint ventures must also be appraised in accordance with the prohibition of anti-competitive agreements under Article 81 EC Treaty.[3]

The Commission has summarised the criteria for the assessment of whether the creation of a joint venture falls within the applicability of the EC merger control rules in its notice on the concept of full-function joint ventures.[4] According to this notice, the essential criterion is whether the joint venture operates on the market on a lasting basis and in an autonomous way. This will not be the case where the joint venture takes over only certain functions within the parent companies' business activities. A full-function joint venture company will have its own management and sufficient resources, such as finance, staff, and tangible and intangible assets.

The strong presence of one or several parent companies in upstream or downstream markets of the joint venture and a voluminous exchange of goods or services between the joint venture and its parents does not in itself, according to the Commission, affect the full-function character of the joint venture if these relationships are limited to a start-up period. The joint venture may also use the distribution facilities of its parent companies without losing its full-function character so long as the parents operate as the independent joint venture's sales representative.

Exceptions to the concept of concentration. The ECMR provides for a number of exceptions to the concept of a concentration. Where credit institutions, financial institutions or insurance companies acquire shares in another undertaking with a view to reselling them to third parties, this does not constitute a concentration if the disposal of the shares takes place within one year of the date of acquisition and the voting rights connected with the shares are not exercised. In addition, no concentration shall be deemed to arise where, for example, control is acquired by an official receiver in the event of insolvency of an undertaking ('insolvency clause'). Similarly, no concentration is deemed to arise where financial holding companies acquire control over other undertakings and the voting rights are exercised simply to maintain the full value of the investments without thereby affecting the competitive conduct of those undertakings.

Purely internal transactions within a group of companies do not usually amount to a concentration within the meaning of the ECMR since these do not involve a change in competitive structures. The merger, or the acquisition of control, between undertakings which are controlled by the same parent company or companies is therefore not subject to merger control.

Revenue thresholds for filing. Concentrations are subject to EC merger control only if they have a Community dimension within the meaning of Article 1 (2) or (3) ECMR. The determining criterion for this is the size of the undertakings concerned in the concentration, which is measured in terms of revenue. The concentration will become subject to EC merger control only on the attaining of certain revenue thresholds. If these revenue thresholds are not met, filing requirements under the national merger control laws of EU member states need to be reviewed.

According to Article 1 (2) ECMR, a concentration has a Community dimension where:

- The combined aggregate worldwide revenues of all the undertakings concerned exceed EUR 5 billion, and
- The aggregate Community-wide revenues of at least two of the undertakings concerned exceed EUR 250 million.

Under Article 1 (3) ECMR, concentrations also have a Community dimension where, although the above-mentioned revenue thresholds are not met, the undertakings concerned are active in several member states of the EU and achieve certain minimum revenues in those countries. Accordingly, a concentration will be subject to EC merger control where:

- The combined aggregate worldwide revenues of all the undertakings concerned exceed EUR 2.5 billion
- in each of at least three member states the combined aggregate revenues of all the undertakings concerned exceed EUR 100 million
- in each of at least three of the above-mentioned member states, the aggregate revenues of each of at least two of the undertakings concerned exceed EUR 25 million, and
- the aggregate Community-wide revenues of each of at least two of the undertakings concerned exceed EUR 100 million.

This additional 'three-country rule' was introduced with the reform of the ECMR in 1998 in order to reduce the number of multijurisdictional filings within the EU. EC merger control was thereby extended to concentrations having substantial effects on competition in several member states without reducing the general revenue thresholds.

Where the revenue thresholds referred to in Article 1 (2) or (3) ECMR are met, concentrations of a predominantly national character will exceptionally not be subject to EC merger control if the undertakings concerned achieve more than two-thirds of their aggregate Community-wide revenues within one and the same member state ('two-thirds rule'). In such a case, the relevant national merger control rules must be applied.

The calculation of the revenue thresholds is based on the revenues of the undertakings participating in the merger. This concept is explained in more detail in the Commission's notice on the concept of undertakings concerned.[5] Which of the undertakings participating in the transaction are considered to be 'undertakings concerned' depends on the type of concentration. For straightforward mergers the parties concerned are the merging parties. In the case of the acquisition of sole control the undertakings concerned are the undertaking acquiring control and the undertaking or part of the undertaking being taken over. The seller is not an undertaking concerned so that the seller's revenues are not taken into account. Where, as a result of the concentration, joint control by a number of undertakings is established, the undertakings concerned are the undertakings or parts of undertakings acquired and all of the undertakings acquiring control. Therefore, in the case of the creation of a joint venture all controlling parent companies as well as the joint venture itself will usually be undertakings concerned.

For the calculation of the revenue thresholds, the aggregate revenues of all undertakings concerned must be added together under Article 5 (1) ECMR. The revenues relate to the amounts derived by the undertakings concerned in the preceding financial year from the sale of products and the provision of services falling within the undertakings' ordinary activities. Sales rebates, value added tax (VAT) and other taxes directly related to revenue must be deducted. The Commission has set out details on the calculation of revenues in its notice on the calculation of turnover.[6]

As in the case of the substantive assessment, the undertakings concerned are not viewed in isolation in the calculation of the revenues. Rather, it is the revenues of the respective groups to which the undertakings concerned belong which are taken into account. This means that the revenues of subsidiaries, parents and sister companies and of any joint venture entities are added to the revenues of the respective participating undertaking.

In calculating the Community-wide revenues and the revenues in individual member states, a geographical allocation of the revenues is necessary. The calculation is based on the revenues achieved by the sale of products and services to undertakings or consumers in a particular territory. The determining factor is therefore not the seat of the undertaking which achieves the revenues but rather the territory in which the customers are located through whom the revenues are achieved.[7]

Special provisions apply to credit and other financial institutions, as well as to insurance companies. For these types of undertaking the income items (and for insurance undertakings, the growth premiums) defined in Directive 86/635/EEC[8] are taken into account.

Where the revenue thresholds set out in Article 1 (2) or (3) ECMR are met and the concentration is therefore of a Community dimension, the rules of EC merger control shall apply also to non-European concentrations. Accordingly, undertakings which are not based within the EU are nevertheless subject to EC merger control where the merger has appreciable effects within the EU ('effects doctrine'). Where the revenue thresholds of the ECMR are met, the Commission usually concludes that the concentration has appreciable effects within the EU.

Substantive Assessment of Mergers

If the ECMR is applicable, the Merger Task Force of the Directorate-General for Competition of the European Commission examines the transaction's compatibility with the Common Market. The main assessment criterion is whether the transaction creates or strengthens a dominant position as a result of which effective competition would be significantly impeded in the Common Market or in a substantial part of it.[9]

This test is of essential importance in the planning, and also the implementation, of mergers and acquisitions. Indeed, the result of this assessment will determine whether a particular planned transaction is possible from an EC competition law point of view. The criterion of the creation or strengthening of a market dominant position limits the possibilities of external company growth. Should there be a danger that an existing market dominant position will be strengthened, or will for the first time be created, as a result of the transaction, the parties should give intensive thought during the planning phase as to how the competition concerns can be addressed. It is therefore advisable to carry out a substantive review of the planned merger at an early stage in order to identify problem areas and to consider them during the planning and implementation stages.

Market Definition

General remarks. The concept of 'market dominance' is of primary importance in the assessment of proposed mergers. In carrying out its investigation as to whether a market-dominant position will be created or strengthened by the proposed transaction, the Commission first of all determines what the relevant product and geographical market is, before proceeding to the second stage of examining the conditions of competition within the defined relevant market(s).

The market definition plays an extremely important role in the assessment of a proposed merger since it sets the course for the permissibility of the proposed merger from an EC competition point of view. Generally, the narrower the product and geographic market definition, the higher will be the market shares of the undertakings concerned. However, a narrow market definition may also mean that there are no market share additions because the participating undertakings are active in different markets.

The relevant product market. According to the Commission's notice on the definition of relevant market for the purposes of the Community competition law,[10] the relevant product market comprises all those products and/or services which, by reason of their characteristics, prices and intended use, are regarded as *interchangeable* or *substitutable* by the consumer. As is the case under many national merger control regimes, EC law therefore focuses primarily on demand-side substitutability. In addition, supply-side substitutability can also be relevant in defining the relevant product market. This is particularly so where suppliers are able to switch production to the relevant products in the short term without incurring significant additional costs. In the case of such flexibility in the switching of products by suppliers, the relevant market may include products which the consumer would not normally regard as substitutable.

Besides the above-mentioned demand-side substitutability and supply-side flexibility, decisive criteria in the definition of the relevant product market also include the general conditions of competition, prices and the cross-price elasticity of demand. Here, for procedural and practical reasons the Commission's practice has been to concentrate on price movements in its defining of the relevant market. The determining question to be answered is whether customers of the parties would react to a hypothetical small and permanent increase in price (between 5 per cent and 10 per cent) for the products concerned by switching to other easily available products. If substitution is strong enough to make the price increase of the original product unprofitable owing to the resulting loss of sales, then substitutes and areas will be continue to be added to the definition of the relevant market until a small permanent increase in price would result in a profit being made.

The Commission applies an equivalent analysis to the examination of buying power (dominance on the demand side of a market). The starting point here is the supply-side substitutability. The application of the price test serves to identify the alternative distribution channels or outlets for the supplier's products.[11]

Examples of relevant product markets found by the Commission are: markets for mineral water,[12] pharmaceuticals with the same indications according to the third level of the Anatomical Therapeutic Classification (ATC) of the World Health Organisation,[13] aircraft according to seating capacity,[14] city buses, intercity buses and touring coaches,[15] passenger cars according to the category of car,[16] catalogue mail order services,[17] pay-TV,[18] electricity[19] and different types of insurance.[20]

The relevant geographic market. According to Article 9 (7) ECMR, the relevant geographic market consists of the area in which the undertakings concerned are involved in the supply or demand of products or services, in which the conditions of competition are sufficiently homogeneous and which can be distinguished from neighbouring areas. The Commission takes particular account in the determination of the relevant geographical market of the nature and characteristics of the products or services concerned and of the existence of entry barriers and consumer preferences. In addition, it considers appreciable differences in the market shares of the parties and substantial price differences in different areas, in particular in different EU member states.

The Commission has defined the geographic market as the EU or Western Europe in, for example, the following cases: car parts,[21] PVC,[22] ethyleneamines and polyethylene resins,[23] electronics[24] and metals.[25]

Differences in price and market shares between different member states are a decisive factor indicating that, despite growing integration within the Common Market, the starting point is still national markets. The Commission has, for example, found in favour of national geographic markets for the following products: pharmaceutical products,[26] mineral water,[27] replacement batteries[28] and mail order business.[29]

In addition, local or regional markets will be of importance only to the extent that certain market barriers, such as transport costs, prevent the integration of the Common Market. Regional or local geographic markets were, for example, found in the following cases: food retail shops,[30] state retail for agricultural products[31] and bricks.[32]

In individual cases the Commission has also found in favour of a global geographic market, for example for aircrafts,[33] platinum,[34] crude oil[35] and reinsurance,[36] for personal computers and medium sized computers[37] and for polyethylene technology licensing.[38]

Market Dominance

Contrary to, for example, German competition law, there exists in EC competition law no statutory definition of market dominance or any circumstances the existence of which lead to the presumption of a market-dominant position. According to the case law of the European Court of Justice (ECJ) and of the Court of First Instance, the term 'market dominance' must be understood as an economic position of strength which enables the parties to behave to an appreciable extent independently of their competitors, customers and consumers. A dominant position exists where the undertakings concerned benefit from a margin of conduct which is not sufficiently controlled through competition.

Article 2 (1) (a) and (b) ECMR sets out the criteria to be taken account of in assessing whether a concentration creates or strengthens a dominant position:

- The need to maintain and develop effective competition within the Common Market in particular in view of the structure of all the markets concerned and the actual or potential competition from undertakings located either within or without the Community
- The market position and the economic and financial power of the undertakings concerned, the alternatives available to suppliers and users, their access to suppliers or markets, any legal or practical barriers to entry, supply and demand trends for the relevant goods and services, the interests of the intermediate and ultimate consumers and the development of technical and economic progress provided that it is to the advantage of consumers and does not form an obstacle to competition.

The starting point for the assessment of a market-dominant position is the market share on the relevant product and geographic market as defined. In calculating the relevant market shares, the market shares of not only the undertakings directly concerned are taken into account, but rather those of the entire group.

The Commission presumes concentrations where the parties have a market share not exceeding 25 per cent to be compatible with the Common Market.[39] Where the market shares are below 15 per cent there is no affected market within the meaning of the form necessary for the notification, which has the consequence that no detailed data need to be provided in relation to these markets.

Even market shares of over 25 per cent are frequently categorised by the Commission as unproblematic according to its general case law. Usually, things start to get critical from around 40 per cent. Should a merger lead to market shares of this order, then the competition issues need to be considered as soon as possible in the planning phase.

In some cases, the Commission was, however, willing to accept much higher market shares since, owing to particular circumstances, significant competition on the affected markets was expected to continue: Mercedes Benz/Kässbohrer,[40] Tetra Pak/Alfa-Laval,[41] Mannesmann/Hoesch[42] and Alcatel/Telettra.[43] Particularly strong buying power of the customers or strong potential competition may prevent high market shares leading to a dominant position. Conversely, split demand and high entry barriers will favour a finding of a market dominant position.

In analysing a potential dominant position, future developments in competitive structures need to be considered. The existence of high market shares in the past may be put into context by the expected opening up of the market and related entry of new competitors. Of significance is not only the level of the market shares of the parties in absolute terms, but also the margin to the next largest competitors.

Creation or Strengthening of a Market-Dominant Position

The assessment as to whether a proposed concentration leads to the creation or the strengthening of a dominant position is made on the basis of an analysis of existing competitive conditions and a prognosis of the future development of the competitive situation. This prognosis involves above all a consideration of developments which are already starting to happen or which can at least be expected with reasonable certainty in the foreseeable future, i.e. within the next few years. This means that an overall assessment of all effects on competition connected to the proposed concentration is carried out.

The Commission proceeds on the assumption that a concentration will result in the creation of a dominant position where, through the concentration, the parties will have a margin of conduct which is no longer sufficiently subject to competition. Of decisive importance is the independence of the parties in setting their prices. Further factors include the margin of play in quality and innovation competition.

According to the Commission, where a participating undertaking already holds a dominant position before the merger, an increase in percentage, however small, may lead to a strengthening of this dominant position. In addition, portfolio and assortment effects (i.e., the ability of the participating undertakings to win additional customers with the offer of a more complete range of products) may strengthen the market position. A mere strengthening in the financial power of an undertaking can also theoretically strengthen its market position.

In the assessment of the creation or strengthening of a dominant position a distinction needs to be made between *horizontal*, *vertical* and *conglomerate* concentrations. For the assessment of horizontal concentrations, market share additions will be the determining factor. As already mentioned, existing barriers to entry and the buying power of the business partners will also play an important role in the assessment. For vertical concentrations – that is, concentrations between manufacturers, suppliers or distributors at different levels of the production or distribution chain – market exclusion effects will be the most important. Particularly decisive will be the effects of the concentration on the supply or customer markets at the expense of actual or potential competitors. By comparison, conglomerate concentrations, which in the Commission's practice have been of little or no significance so far, will lead only to the creation or strengthening of a market-dominant position if they involve a significant strengthening in resources which is implemented in order to deter or discourage actual or potential competitors. A strengthening in resources alone will be sufficient only for the finding of a creation or strengthening of a dominant position in exceptional circumstances. It can therefore usually contribute to the dominant position of the participating undertakings only in connection with other factors.

The Commission will consider prohibiting a proposed concentration which leads to the creation or strengthening of a dominant position only if the proposed merger would significantly impede effective competition within the Community or a substantial part of it. Therefore, the creation or strengthening of a dominant position will not *per se* be prohibited, but rather only in the event of detrimental effects on the market. This qualification, however, has been of little practical significance so far. The Commission has only once (in Aérospatiale-Allenia/de Havilland[44]) questioned the relevance of the effects on competition when confronted with a case of only temporary market dominance.

Oligopolies

Contrary to, for example, German law, there is in the ECMR no specific oligopoly provision according to which a concentration will be prohibited where it leads to the creation or strengthening of a dominant position by two or more undertakings together. Nevertheless, according to the Commission's practice,[45] which has now also been confirmed by the ECJ and the Court of First Instance, EC merger control will also apply to cases of oligopolistic market dominance. A dominant oligopoly exists where there is no active competition between the members of the oligopoly and where the oligopoly is not subject to effective competition from third parties. Pursuant to the judgment of the Court of First Instance in Gencor/Lonrho[46] the following criteria indicate in particular that a dominant oligopoly exists:

- High market concentration
- Stable and symmetrical market shares of the members of the oligopoly
- Homogeneous products and high market transparency
- Similar cost structures
- Stagnant and inelastic demand
- Low technological development
- High market entry barriers.

Of particular significance is the coordinated market behaviour of the members of the oligopoly which may result in a margin of conduct *vis-à-vis* competitors and customers which is not sufficiently controlled.

Ancillary Restraints

Until June 2001, the Commission's analysis of a transaction used to extend to restrictions directly related and necessary to its implementation ('ancillary restraints').[47] Such restrictions cover ancillary agreements, such as non-compete clauses, which theoretically fall within the scope of application of the prohibition against anti-competitive agreements in Article 81 EC Treaty. In order to avoid a complicated double review, such ancillary agreements used to be assessed within the context of the merger control procedure and, where applicable, used to be cleared with the concentration. The pre-requisite for such a restriction on competition to be treated as an ancillary agreement was that the restriction should have a direct connection with, and be necessary for, the implementation of the concentration. However, with the introduction of its new notice regarding restrictions ancillary to concentrations on 27 June 2001,[48] the Commission has changed its policy and will now no longer assess ancillary restrictions in its merger decisions. Restrictions entered into by parties in the context of a concentration will therefore no longer benefit from the effect of a clearance decision. Instead, the parties will have to assess on their own whether any such restraints are in compliance with European competition law.

The most important ancillary restraints are non-compete clauses according to which the seller of an undertaking is restricted from competing with the purchaser for a certain period of time after the closing. Non-compete clauses aim at ensuring that the purchaser has the possibility to obtain the full value of the business transferred. According to the Commission's new notice on ancillary restraints, non-compete clauses are accepted as ancillary for a period of up to three years if goodwill and know-how are included and the non-compete is directly related to the transfer of the undertaking. Where only the good will but no know-how is transferred, the new notice provides that a period of two years will be sufficient. The scope of the non-compete clause must, from a geographic and subject-matter point of view, be limited to the areas in which the target undertaking was active.[49]

The transfer of a business often includes intellectual property rights and know-how. To the extent that the seller wishes to remain the owner of these rights, the parties will have to enter into licence agreements. Such licence agreements can be limited to particular areas of application. The licences can be granted for the full lifetime of the patents or connected rights, and for the normal commercial lifetime of the know-how. Geographic restrictions on manufacturing are not normally accepted and should therefore not be included in the licence. Supply obligations between the seller and the purchaser of a business can also constitute ancillary agreements, if they are entered into for a transitional period. However, exclusive supply obligations are not generally justifiable as ancillary restraints.

Procedure

Pre-Merger Notification Requirement

Concentrations with a Community dimension must be notified to the European Commission in Brussels within one week after the conclusion of a binding agreement, or the announcement of a purchase or exchange offer, or the acquisition of a controlling interest. A notification at such short notice is generally possible only where the parties start preparing the notification during the planning stages of the transaction. In those cases where the participating undertakings are particularly interested in obtaining a clearance decision of the Commission in the first phase of the procedure, it is essential that the parties contact the Commission at a very early stage. Such early contact with the Commission is advisable in any event in order to agree the content of the notification with the Commission ('informal guidance procedure').

Particulars relating to the notification, time limits and hearings are set out in Commission Regulation 477/98 of 1 March 1998.[50] Under Article 2 (1) of the Implementing Regulation, notifications must be made on 'Form CO' and one original and 23 copies of it submitted to the Commission in Brussels. Form CO comprises a lengthy questionnaire which includes details of the notifying parties and the proposed concentration, information regarding ownership and control, supporting documentation, detailed information on affected markets including revenue, market share and competitor information as well as details regarding suppliers and customers, information on cooperative effects of joint ventures, as well as a declaration on the correctness and completeness of the information submitted. During the informal guidance procedure, the questionnaire can be adapted to the concentration in question and some of the questions which the Commission does not require responses to can be excluded. In addition, certain joint ventures with minor activities in the Community can be notified using a short-form notification.

The parties to the merger – or, in the event of the acquisition of joint control, those acquiring joint control – must notify the planned transaction jointly. The seller is not subject to a notification obligation. In principle, it is possible for individual or all participants to submit a joint notification through a jointly appointed representative. The fact of notification is published in the *Official Journal* and third parties are given the opportunity to make comments within 10 days. Breaches of the notification obligation, and the submission of incorrect or misleading information, can be penalised by the Commission with a fine of up to EUR 50 000.

Prohibition to Complete Before Clearance

Concentrations of Community dimension may not be implemented prior to their notification and clearance. There is an exception to this for public bids and exchange offers to the extent that these have been properly notified and the acquirer does not exercise the voting rights attached to the securities in question or does so only to maintain the full value of those investments on the basis of a derogation granted by the Commission. In addition, for all other transactions the Commission may, on request, grant a derogation from the suspension of the concentration. In deciding on the request, the Commission will consider the effects of the suspension on the parties and on third parties, as well as the potential threat posed by the concentration on competition. However, the Commission is reluctant to grant such derogations. In principle, the request for the derogation can be made and granted prior to the notification. The derogation can also be made subject to conditions and undertakings in order to safeguard effective competition.

A breach of the principal obligation not to complete a transaction before clearance will result in the transaction being legally invalid. The transaction will become valid only once the Commission has adopted a clearance decision. As an exception to this, transactions in securities remain valid to the extent that these securities are recognised for trading on the market of one or more member states. However, only a *bona fide* purchaser is protected against a breach of the prohibition against implementation. The Commission may also punish breaches of the prohibition against implementation with fines of up to 10 per cent of the total revenues of the participating undertakings.

Proceedings

M&A which amount to concentrations of Community dimension must be notified to the Merger Task Force of the Directorate General for Competition at the European Commission. The Commission's review process is divided into two phases. During the first phase, which usually lasts one month, the Merger Task Force assesses whether the concentration notified may be cleared or whether, because the proposed concentration raises serious doubts as to its compatibility with the Common Market, the second phase of the investigation procedure needs to be opened. Following the start of the second phase, the Commission has an additional four months within which to come to a final decision on the proposed merger.

The majority of cases are decided within the first phase. Even in more problematic cases, the parties often try to eliminate the Commission's concerns by offering commitments, thereby avoiding a detailed second-phase review of the concentration, with its related delays. The chances of clearance within the first phase can be improved through early contact with the Merger Task Force. To this end, it is advisable to send the Commission a draft of the notification early on so that the Commission can already start working on the file before receipt of the final notification.

Should the parties not be able to convince the Commission within the deadline of one month that the concentration will not lead to the creation or strengthening of a dominant position, the Commission issues a formal decision in which it sets out its concerns with regard to the compatibility of the merger with the Common Market and by which it initiates the main proceedings. In the absence of any such decision, the concentration shall be deemed to be compatible with the Common Market.[51]

The period of one month for the first phase is exceptionally prolonged to six weeks if the undertakings concerned submit commitments with the intention of eliminating the Commission's competition concerns.[52] Such commitments must, if they are to be considered during the first phase, be submitted to the Commission within three weeks of the notification. The one-month time period will also be extended to six weeks in the event that a national competition authority requests a referral of the case. Such a referral is possible where it is feared that a dominant position will be created or strengthened in a particular market in this member state. If the referral is granted, the relevant national competition authority will review the proposed concentration according to its applicable national law.

Where the case stays with the Commission and the Commission initiates a second-phase investigation, the fact of the initiation of the main proceedings is published in the *Official Journal* and third parties are given the opportunity to make comments within 15 days. Should the Commission's concerns be confirmed during the main proceedings, then the Commission issues a Statement of Objections and invites the parties to comment on it in writing. The Commission is entitled to rely in its later decision only on the objections expressed at this stage in the proceedings. During the main proceedings, the parties have the right to access the Commission's file.[53] In addition, the parties are afforded the opportunity to put forward their arguments in an oral hearing. Third parties, such as competitors and customers of the parties, may be invited to take part in the oral hearing.

In appraising the planned concentration, the Commission has wide investigative powers. The Commission may, for example, send formal and informal information requests to companies, to the competent authorities of the member states or to governments. The Commission makes extensive use of these powers, particularly by sending detailed questionnaires with short deadlines to the parties' most important customers, suppliers and competitors in all affected markets. The Commission can also carry out on-site inspections, either itself or through the competition authorities of the member states. To this end, the Commission is entitled to enter all offices, premises and means of transport, to check all books and other business records, to make or ask for copies and to request oral explanations on the spot.

Towards the end of the second phase, the Directorate General for Competition prepares a draft decision and presents it to an advisory committee made up of representatives of the member states' competition authorities for its opinion. The Commission then decides as a collegiate body by majority voting of the 20 Commissioners whether the planned concentration will be cleared or prohibited.

Remedies

In a number of problematic cases in the past the parties were able to avoid a prohibition of the proposed concentration by offering *commitments*. In March 2001, the Commission published a notice on remedies acceptable in merger cases which summarises the Commission's views on substantial and procedural aspects of commitments.[54] Commitments must be submitted, if during the first phase, at the latest three weeks following notification, and, if during the second phase, within three months from the initiation of the main proceedings. They are intended to eliminate any concerns of the Commission as to the compatibility of the merger with the Common Market and to induce the Commission to clear the merger. It is generally advisable to discuss the content of and agree commitments with the Commission at an earlier stage in order to increase the probability that the commitments submitted will from the Commission's point of view be sufficient to eliminate any competition problem.

It should be stressed once again that it makes sense, in transactions which are problematic from a competition point of view, to think about possible amendments to the transaction during the planning stages. Indeed, fall-back positions can prevent the collapse of the transaction where competition problems do arise. The early consideration of such fall-back positions will enable the parties to react appropriately to the Commission's concerns within the short time frames given.

Commitments which may prevent the issuing of a prohibition decision include in particular sale and divestiture commitments by which subsidiaries or parts of undertakings in critical markets are sold to third parties. The parties may choose to either sell the affected parts of the undertakings prior to the clearance of the Commission or to do so after such clearance within the deadline set by the Commission, which is about six months on average. In addition to 'structural commitments', in exceptional cases 'behavioural commitments' may also be considered, by which the parties undertake to behave in a certain way aimed at maintaining effective competition on the affected markets. Occasionally, the Commission has also accepted an obligation of the participating undertakings to license certain key technology to interested third parties at market conditions.[55]

In order to ensure that the commitments submitted are actually adhered to, the Commission may include conditions and obligations in its clearance decision. This is now possible in both phases of the proceeding. Should the parties not comply with their commitments, the Commission can enforce compliance by imposing fines, and if necessary revoke the approval of the concentration.[56]

Appeals and Rights of Third Parties

The parties can appeal against prohibition decisions of the Commission, or against decisions subject to commitments and undertakings, within two months of the decision by lodging an action for nullity with the Court of First Instance. In addition, the parties have a right of appeal against formal decisions requesting information, verification orders and fines and financial penalties.

To the extent that third parties can prove a sufficient interest in the outcome of the proceedings – such as, for example, competitors, suppliers or customers, but also members of management bodies or employee representatives – they will have the right to certain information and the right to be heard during the proceedings. Economically affected competitors, customers or suppliers can also challenge a clearance decision of the Commission before the Court of First Instance.

Dissolution of Implemented Mergers

Where a merger is implemented without it having been notified to, and cleared by the Commission, the Commission may, where the conditions for a prohibition decision are met, order the dissolution of the merger. Such an order is subject to the general principle of *proportionality*. The Commission may take only such measures as are appropriate and necessary to restore effective competition. The Commission may impose penalty payments and fines to compel compliance with these orders.[57]

Article 81 and Article 82 EC Treaty and National Merger Control

Mergers and acquisitions which amount to concentrations within the meaning of Article 3 ECMR and with a Community dimension within the meaning of Article 1 ECMR are subject solely to the ECMR. To the extent that the creation of the joint venture subject to merger control results in a coordination of the competitive conduct of the parent companies, the applicability of Article 81 EC Treaty governing the prohibition against anti-competitive agreements will also be examined within the context of the merger control procedure. This does not, however, have any impact on the procedure. It simply widens the scope of the substantive analysis.

Since the ECMR is applicable only to full-function joint ventures, joint ventures which do not perform on a lasting basis all the functions of an autonomous economic entity will be subject to Article 81 and 82 EC Treaty exclusively. This is, for example, the case for joint ventures which are limited to research and development (R&D) or for production joint ventures. The same applies to cooperative joint ventures which, because they are not of Community dimension, are not subject to the ECMR.

In addition, mergers and acquisitions which fall outside the scope of application of the ECMR are subject to merger control provisions of the individual EU member states. Certain mergers and acquisitions which either do not constitute a concentration within the meaning of the ECMR (e.g. certain minority participations), or which have no Community dimension, may also be subject to national merger control provisions. The competition rules of the member states are inapplicable only to the extent that the ECMR applies.[58]

A member state will have jurisdiction over a concentration with Community dimension that falls under the ECMR only when the Commission refers the case to it on request of the competition authority of such member state.[59] Such a referral might be considered when a concentration threatens to create or strengthen a dominant position which will hinder effective competition on a market in that member state. In the event of such a referral the proposed concentration (or the part of it which is referred) is decided upon by the respective national authorities.

3 German Merger Control

Scope of Application

Mergers which are outside the scope of EC merger control must be notified to the Federal Cartel Office in Bonn prior to their completion if the criteria of German merger control law are met. Merger control in Germany was introduced as early as 1973; its history is thus about 20 years longer than that of EC merger control. Since 1973, the German merger control rules have been tightened up a number of times and loopholes in the law have been closed. The 6th Amendment to the Act against Restrictions of Competition (ARC), which came into effect on 1 January 1999, fundamentally revised German merger control and partly brought it into line with EU law. Moreover, its scope was extended by the lowering of the revenue thresholds which trigger a mandatory prior notification. At the same time, the post-completion announcement of a merger was abolished in favour of a general, preventive advance notification obligation.

M&A, the creation of joint ventures and other business transactions need to be notified to the Federal Cartel Office only where they fall within one of the statutory merger definitions and the undertakings participating in the merger achieve specified revenue thresholds.

Merger Criteria

General remarks. Under the ARC, only structural changes in competition conditions are caught by the merger control provisions. As part of the 6th Amendment to the ARC, the merger criteria as defined in section 37 ARC have been reworded and now reflect EU law insofar as the acquisition of control over another undertaking is also included among the circumstances which may constitute a merger. The other merger definitions, which in some cases are wider than those under EC law, have been retained. More specifically, the following forms of mergers may be distinguished:

- Acquisition of *assets*
- Acquisition of *control*
- Acquisition of *shares or voting rights*
- Acquisition of a substantial *competitive influence*.

German merger control applies only to undertakings. 'Undertakings' include all natural or legal persons which produce or supply goods or commercial services where these activities are not exclusively for private purposes, undertaken in the course of employment or fall within the jurisdiction of the public sector. Trading and non-trading companies, associations and societies generally all satisfy the definition of an undertaking if they are involved in the exchange of services within the market economy. Former public sector activities within the railways, post office and telecommunications industries have now all been privatised and are therefore clearly subject to merger control. Further, public sector bodies will also be regarded as undertakings within the meaning of the ARC if they carry out commercial functions, i.e., if they are engaged in the market. Natural persons, too, will qualify as undertakings if they are commercially active, either personally or through the holding of an interest in an undertaking, or if they are self-employed.

Acquisition of assets. Transactions in which an undertaking acquires the assets, or some of the assets, of another undertaking ('asset deal') fall within the merger definition of the ARC. For the purpose of this definition, assets include not only all tangible assets used in the business, such as production facilities, property rights and claims, but also rights in intangible property such as the goodwill of a business, customer lists, trade secrets, intellectual property rights (e.g., trade marks) or know-how.

German merger control applies not only where the entire assets of an undertaking are transferred, but also where – as is often the case – a purchaser acquires a substantial part of the assets of a business. According to case law, 'substantial' means any part of a business which has a certain element of independence and to which revenues can be attributed. This clearly applies to entire business divisions, but may also apply to the transfer of trademarks and other assets in isolation, if this will influence the acquirer's position in the relevant market.

Acquisition of control. In order to harmonise German and EU merger control rules, the *acquisition of control* was introduced in 1999 as one of the definitions of a merger. According to the Federal Government's commentary on this legislative provision, this definition is to be interpreted in accordance with the decisions of the European Commission and of the European Courts. As explained, 'control' is defined as the power to exercise a controlling influence over the activities of another undertaking. Such control may arise out of rights, agreements or other means. Section 37 (1) no. 2 ARC mentions property and usage rights in all or some of the assets of an undertaking, and rights and agreements which grant a controlling influence on the composition, consultation and resolutions of an undertaking's decision-making bodies. Regardless of the type of the transaction, any transfer of business resources from one or more undertakings to one or more other undertakings will be caught, if the purchaser or purchasers thereby acquire *new means of exercising influence*.

This means that an acquisition of control can be achieved through both an asset and a share deal. In practical terms, the most important form of an acquisition of control is the acquisition of a shareholding of over 50 per cent in another undertaking. An acquisition of less than 50 per cent may also amount to an acquisition of control where the acquirer has a *de facto* majority in shareholders' meetings on a lasting basis.

An acquisition of control regardless of the size of the shareholding is also possible where property or usage rights in all or some parts of an undertaking are acquired, e.g., through company leases or leases of operating facilities. In addition, group agreements or cross-relationships in terms of personnel may give rise to the type of controlling influence required to satisfy the definition of an acquisition of control.

Control may be acquired either by a single undertaking, or jointly by two or more undertakings. Joint control requires a joint interest on a lasting basis from which it can in all probability be expected that the joint influence will be exercised consistently and where the interest goes beyond a simple common interest in general terms. The exercise of influence by the jointly controlling parent companies may be governed by contract or be exercised on a *de facto* basis. The possibility of the majorities changing might seem to indicate that there is no joint control. However, this assumption may be displaced if the controlling influence in fact continues to be exercised in a consistent way.

Acquisition of shares or voting rights. A merger within the meaning of the ARC will exist where an undertaking acquires an interest in another undertaking and thereby acquires a 25 per cent or 50 per cent of that undertaking's capital or voting rights in total. Every acquisition in which these thresholds are achieved qualifies as a new merger which must be notified to the Federal Cartel Office if the relevant revenue threshold are met. In cases where the interest acquired exceeds 50 per cent, there will generally also be an acquisition of control.

An acquisition of a 25 per cent or 50 per cent interest constitutes a *merger* between the acquiring and the acquired undertaking(s). In addition, German law also construes such an acquisition as a merger between all of the undertakings holding interests of 25 per cent or more in the relevant undertakings. Accordingly, if several undertakings acquire interests of 25 per cent or more, either at the same time or one after the other, this will also be deemed to be a merger between all such undertakings holding interests of more than 25 per cent (at least on the market(s) on which the target company operates). This recognises the effect which such transactions can have on competition between the parent companies of joint ventures ('group effects' or 'spill-over effects').

In calculating the shareholding thresholds, an acquirer's existing shares are aggregated with its newly acquired shares. In addition, any shares held by other companies within the acquiring company's group will be counted as shares of the acquiring undertaking. Finally, any shares held by another undertaking for the acquirer on a trust basis will be also be included.

Acquisition of a substantial competitive influence. The acquisition of a *substantial competitive influence* constitutes a merger, too. This provision catches above all minority shareholdings below 25 per cent which, in the light of pre-existing relationships between the undertakings involved or together with other factors, can be expected to restrict competition between the participating undertakings to such a degree that they cease to act independently of each other in the market. This catch-all provision applies to transactions aimed at circumventing the legal provisions and to transactions in which a party acquiring an interest of less than 25 per cent achieves a legal position which would normally be enjoyed by a qualified minority shareholder. According to the Federal Cartel Office's practice, this will be the case, for example, where a shareholder is granted a right to be represented at certain board meetings, to be consulted on important business policy decisions, or where the management of certain parts of the undertaking is transferred to it.

Exceptions to the concept of merger. As under EU law, purely internal company or group restructurings or transactions do not constitute a merger under German law. Moreover, there is no obligation to notify a merger if the undertakings involved were already previously members of the same group of companies and the merger does not strengthen the existing relationship between the undertakings in any material way. This is in particular the case where a negligible number of further shares is acquired which does not alter the acquiring undertaking's ability to exercise influence in any significant way, or where an undertaking which already holds a majority acquires further shares. In many cases, however, attaining the statutory thresholds (25 per cent or 50 per cent) will boost the ability to exercise influence and will therefore qualify as a merger.

Another exception to the merger concept is the purchase of shares by credit institutions, financial institutions and insurance companies. Where such institutions purchase shares with a view to their re-sale, this will not constitute a merger so long as the voting rights attached to the shares are not exercised and the shares are re-sold within one year. An application for an extension of this one-year period may be made to the Federal Cartel Office.

Revenue Thresholds for Filing

As under EU law, the German merger control provisions apply only if the participating undertakings achieve certain specified revenue thresholds. The Federal Cartel Office must be notified of all mergers where the aggregate world-wide revenues of the undertakings concerned exceeded EUR 500 million in the financial year preceding the merger and at least one of the undertakings generated revenues in excess of EUR 25 million within Germany. The intention of the 'de *minimis*' threshold of EUR 25 million, introduced by the 6th Amendment to the ARC, is to take foreign mergers out of the scope of German merger control if their effect in Germany is only minimal.

If the above revenue thresholds are exceeded, foreign mergers will generally also be subject to German merger control. Whilst section 130 (2) ARC provides that the merger control provisions only apply if a transaction has an appreciable effect in Germany ('effects doctrine'), the Federal Cartel Office considers an appreciable domestic effect in Germany to exist whenever one of the undertakings involved conducts business in Germany which generates at least EUR 25 million in revenues.

The only situation in which this does not apply is where there is no connection between the merger and the German domestic activities of the undertakings involved, so that there is no direct effect on competition in Germany. In all cases where there is any doubt, it is sensible – given the potential fines and the risk that the transaction agreements could be held void under German law – to take the precaution of notifying any proposed transaction to the Federal Cartel Office – or, if the parties decide not to notify, to do so only after having consulted first with the Federal Cartel Office.

Section 35 (2) ARC exempts both 'de *minimis*' and 'bagatelle market' transactions from German merger control. In order to make it easier for small and medium-sized undertakings to exploit the value of their assets, mergers between independent undertakings which do not belong to a group of companies and whose sales revenues are below EUR 10 million are not subject to German merger control. However, this exemption does not apply to mergers affecting competition between publishers and the production or distribution of newspapers and magazines, or parts of them.

Also exempted from merger control are mergers affecting markets in which products or commercial services have been supplied for a minimum period of five years and for which the total market revenues were less than EUR 15 million in the last calendar year. Whether the conditions for the application of this 'bagatelle market' provision are met will depend above all on the definition of the relevant product and geographic markets. In many cases, therefore, there will be uncertainty as to whether this exception applies. Moreover, any effects on any markets other than the 'bagatelle market' will bring the merger within the scope of merger control. If it is not possible to define the relevant market with sufficient certainty, it is advisable to take the precaution of notifying the transaction in order to avoid potential fines and the risk of the transaction being declared void for failure to notify. Alternatively, the parties should dispense from a notification only after prior consultation with the Federal Cartel Office.

The relevant date for the calculation of the revenues is the date of notification, so that the sales revenues for the most recent completed financial year will normally be used, adjusted by recent acquisitions or divestitures. Revenues in foreign currencies must be converted using the official published exchange rate for the relevant year set by the Deutsche Bundesbank. As under EU merger control, the relevant revenues are the group revenues of the participating undertakings, i.e. the revenues of the participating undertakings' parents and subsidiaries, and their subsidiaries in turn, must all be included in the calculation. However, revenues from sales between associated undertakings, and VAT and excise duties, are not taken into account.

There are special provisions for the calculation of revenues from trade in goods, where only three-quarters of the revenues is taken into account in deciding whether the thresholds are met. Similarly, in the case of publishers, the production and distribution of newspapers, magazines, and any parts of them, the production, distribution and organisation of broadcasting programmes and the sale of advertising time, the actual revenue figure is multiplied by 20 in determining whether the revenue thresholds have been reached.[60] The aim is to protect the freedom of the press, which is enshrined as a constitutional right, by making smaller mergers in this market also potentially subject to German merger control.

Substantive Assessment of Mergers

The Federal Cartel Office prohibits a merger where it is likely to create or strengthen a dominant market position, unless the undertakings involved are able to show that the merger will also result in an improvement in the conditions of competition and that these improvements outweigh the disadvantages of market dominance.

As described above in respect of EU merger control, the parties should carry out a substantive analysis of the proposed merger well in advance of the notification, so that any potential competition law problems which may affect the subsequent implementation of the transaction may be identified and considered during the planning phase. This makes it possible to address potential problems early on and to structure the proposed transaction in a competition law-compliant way.

Market Definition

General remarks. As a starting point in assessing market dominance, the relevant *product and geographic markets* must be defined. The definition of the market influences to a large extent the answer to the question whether an undertaking holds a dominant position in the relevant market. In many cases, the definition of the market is crucial to obtaining clearance from the Federal Cartel Office.

The relevant product market. The definition of the relevant product market is based on the substitutability of the products or services from a demand point of view. The Court of Appeal in Berlin ('Kammergericht') has held in a leading judgement that the relevant product market comprises 'all products' which, 'by reason of their characteristics, intended commercial use and price, are so similar that a reasonable consumer will regard them as equally suitable for a particular requirement and therefore as being interchangeable'.[61]

However, the determining criterion of functional substitutability for a specific requirement or use should not be misunderstood to mean that only products with identical characteristics are interchangeable. Rather, it is the particular requirement which can be satisfied by a whole range of products or services which is important. A too narrow interpretation of the concept of demand substitutability would lead to markets being restricted to individual products or services in which individual undertakings would be the sole suppliers and therefore dominate the market. Both the intended use and the particular characteristics of the product are equally decisive factors. In addition, price often plays an important role in practice, because substantial price differences may fundamentally limit the substitutability of the relevant products/services.

In addition, in accordance with the policy of the European Commission, the Federal Cartel Office increasingly takes into account the flexibility of supply. Accordingly, products which are not directly substitutable from the point of view of the purchaser may nevertheless be included in the relevant product market if the suppliers are able to switch their production to other products at short notice and without great cost. Similarly, product ranges which are generally offered by all manufacturers and purchased as entire ranges by the buyers will also commonly be defined as a single market. The decisive factor here is not so much the individual product with its particular characteristics and specific use, but rather the range of products typified by its *typical characteristics*.

Practical examples of relevant product markets in German merger control practice include: tin-foil, cling film and freezer bags,[62] car radios,[63] chemical substances with particular characteristics,[64] stainless steel cutlery,[65] liquid tinned food,[66] raw, roasted and instant coffee,[67] carburettor fuel[68] and newspaper printing paper.[69]

The process of assessment of the market power on the demand side is similar to that on the supply side. In defining the relevant demand-side markets in the area of retail sales, the Federal Cartel Office looks at a typical range in retail sales.[70] The Court of Appeal in Berlin, by contrast, is of the view that this market should be defined more narrowly, i.e. on the basis of specific product groups.[71] In practice, many questions of detail relating to the definition of demand markets still remain unclear.

The relevant geographic market. The relevant geographic market, too, is defined in accordance with the principle of functional substitutability from the point of view of the purchaser. All those supplies which are accessible to a particular purchaser will, from that purchaser's point of view, be substitutable. Accordingly, from a practical point of view, the starting point in many cases is the area in which the undertaking concerned operates.

In a large number of cases, the relevant geographic market is the whole of Germany. In the 'oven market case',[72] the Federal Supreme Court ('Bundesgerichtshof') held that the territory of the German Federal Republic constitutes the outer boundary for the purposes of defining the geographic market. Accordingly, territories outside of Germany may not be included in the relevant geographic market, and competitors not active in Germany may therefore, in the assessment of market dominance, be considered only as potential but not as actual competitors.

Smaller regional or local markets may arise as a consequence of legal provisions or factual circumstances. Examples in this area include the TÜV Act (Act on the Technical Supervisory Associations), which sets particular geographic areas of activity, or the limited transportation radiuses for cement.[73] In addition, limited possibilities and habits of purchasers may result in narrower markets, e.g. as is the case for example for supermarket areas[74] and the local subscription of newspapers.[75]

Market Dominance

The ARC contains an express legal definition of market dominance. An undertaking is dominant in the relevant market if:

- It has no competitors or is not subject to any significant competition and thus benefits from a *de facto* monopoly position.
- It holds a superior position on the market *vis-à-vis* its competitors. The following criteria in particular will be considered in this respect: market share, financial strength, access to supply or sales markets, relationships with other undertakings, legal or factual barriers to market entry, actual or potential competition by undertakings based in or outside the territory of applicability of the ARC, the ability to switch supply or demand to other products or services, as well as the ability of the customer to switch to other supplies.
- There is no significant competition between two or more undertakings in relation to a particular type of product or service and those undertakings taken together are either not exposed to any significant competition or hold a dominant market position compared with the other competitors.

Market dominance is assessed in accordance with the criteria laid down in the statutory definition. All relevant circumstances, taking particular account of the conditions of competition in the relevant market, must be considered as part of an overall assessment. In addition to the important structural aspects of the market, it may also be possible to draw conclusions from the actual behaviour of the undertakings operating on the relevant market. Market dominance exists whenever, from an overall market perspective, margins of conduct are no longer adequately controlled by the forces of competition.

Of particular importance in this context is the *market share* of the undertaking concerned. This market share is all the more important because of the presumptions of market dominance laid down in section 19 (3) ARC which refer to specific market shares. An undertaking will be presumed to have a dominant position in the market if it has a market share of one-third or more. Several undertakings will be regarded as being jointly dominant in the market, if three or fewer undertakings together have an aggregate market share of 50 per cent or if five or fewer undertakings together have an aggregate market share of two-thirds (oligopoly).

Those legal presumptions allow a preliminary assessment as to what market share levels may be problematic under German competition law. The practical significance of these presumptions is limited, however, insofar as they do not allow the Federal Cartel Office or the courts to forgo a full assessment of the competitive situation in the relevant markets. Even where the preconditions for those presumptions are satisfied, it is possible to rebut them by showing that the competitive conditions are such that significant competition may nevertheless be expected and that the parties do not enjoy a dominant market position. Only where the existence of a dominant position cannot be excluded with certainty and where there is no evidence of significant competition would it be possible for the Federal Cartel Office to prohibit a merger on the basis of the presumption of market dominance. Factors which may be used to rebut a presumption of market dominance include: low barriers to market entry, significant potential competition, permanent overcapacities, technological changes and strong buying power of customers countervailing the suppliers' market power.

Creation or Strengthening of a Market-Dominant Position

The assessment as to whether a merger leads to the creation or strengthening of a market-dominant position is made on the basis of a prediction as to the future. This prognosis involves a comparison between the competitive structures existing before the merger and the changes in the competitive conditions which the merger will bring about. Prospective changes in market conditions must be considered where they are concrete enough and there is a sufficient likelihood that they will occur. Prospective market entries and technological developments can therefore significantly impact on the assessment of a proposed merger.

The strengthening of a dominant position will occur in particular through an appreciable increase in *market shares*. Even in the absence of an increase in market shares, however, a dominant position may be strengthened where the growth in resources, or aggressive competitive practices, of the dominant undertaking intimidate existing competitors and deter potential competitors from entering the market. According to the practice of the Federal Cartel Office, the existence of substantial market shares means that even small effects on the remaining market will generally be sufficient to justify prohibiting a proposed merger. In addition, particular know-how, new technological developments and the acquisition of brands and trademarks may all help to further strengthen the position of a company which is already dominant on the market, irrespective of market share changes. Since each case needs to be decided on its own facts, any general or formalistic assessment would be inappropriate.

Balancing Provision

A merger which leads to the creation or strengthening of a dominant position must not be prohibited by the Federal Cartel Office if it can be shown that the merger also results in improvements in the conditions of competition and that these improvements outweigh the disadvantages associated with market dominance. Given that merger control is concerned only with structural changes in the competitive situation, any negative effects on competition resulting from the creation or strengthening of a dominant market position may be compensated only by structural improvements associated with the merger. Any rationalisation, therefore, may be taken into account only where there are related structural repercussions on the market.

This balancing provision is of particular relevance in those cases where a merger, which has an overall beneficial effect on competition, leads to the creation or strengthening of a dominant market position in individual insignificant markets. Positive effects on other markets may therefore also compensate the negative effects of the creation or strengthening of a dominant position. However, any such positive effects on competition in other markets must also be attributable to the merger.

Beneficial effects on the economy as a whole, e.g. improvements on the employment market or regional development, are not within the scope of merger control. The consideration of such factors is reserved to the Minister of Economy in the context of the ministerial approval procedure.

Procedural Rules

Pre-Merger Notification Requirement

Since the coming into force of the 6th ARC Amendment of 1999, all concentrations which are subject to German merger control must be notified to the Federal Cartel Office prior to their completion. The filing obligation lies on all participating undertakings in the merger, i.e. in the case of real mergers the merging undertakings, and for the acquisition of assets and shares, the acquirer and the company or business being acquired. In practice, notifications are often filed by the acquiring firm for itself as well as on behalf of all other participating undertakings, in particular for the seller. The notification can be submitted as soon as the merger proposal is sufficiently concrete to enable the Federal Cartel Office to assess it, i.e. *even prior to the conclusion of the relevant contracts*, which is an important difference to EU merger control law.

The ARC, contrary to EU merger control, does not provide for a form which lists the information necessary for a notification. The minimum content requirements of the notification are set out in section 39 (3) ARC. In addition to a description of the type of proposed concentration, the minimum information to be provided is the following:

- Description of the participating undertakings
- Place of establishment or seat of company
- Type of business

- Revenues within Germany, the EU and worldwide
- Market shares of the parties including the basis for their calculation or estimate to the extent that the market shares exceed 20 per cent.

In addition, where a party has its registered office outside of Germany, a person authorised to accept service within Germany must be named. Any incorrect, incomplete or late notifications can be fined with up to EUR 25 000.

A notification is not necessary where the concentration was notified to the European Commission under the ECMR and the European Commission has referred it back to the Federal Cartel Office on the office's application. The only exception to this is where the notification to the European Commission was not made in the German language. In such a case, an additional notification in German must be submitted along with the information required under German merger control.

Proceedings

The submission of the complete notification with the Federal Cartel Office triggers the 'pre-procedure' (first phase), in which the Federal Cartel Office decides whether a further investigation of the merger in main review proceedings (second phase) is necessary. To the extent that there are no indications that the merger will create or strengthen a market dominant position, the Federal Cartel Office clears the proposed transaction by simple notice to the notifying parties. Since this is not a formal administrative decision, it cannot be made subject to commitments or conditions and it is given without reasons.

The main review proceedings involve a detailed investigation of the merger. This review must be closed by a formal decision within four months from submission of the complete notification. Should the Federal Cartel Office not be in a position within the four-month deadline to come to a conclusive assessment, the deadline for a final decision may be extended, provided that the parties agree.

In the context of the investigation, the Federal Cartel Office has wide powers of investigation. Among other things, the Federal Cartel Office may request from each party information regarding market shares, including the basis for the calculation or estimation, as well as information regarding revenues. In addition, to the extent that this is necessary for the assessment of the merger, the Federal Cartel Office may request information from third parties and may review documents and business records and require these to be handed over. The Federal Cartel Office has the right to collect evidence through inspection, witnesses or experts, on-site searches and seizures.

Mergers may not be implemented so long as they have not been cleared by the Federal Cartel Office or the deadlines for prohibition have not expired. Implementation includes all acts through which the merger is effected and the acquiring firm is given the possibility to influence the target company or parts thereof. Acts of implementation will include in particular the actual transfer of the assets or shares concerned, the exercising of voting rights (e.g. in respect of the removal and new appointment of directors) or any type of influence over the conduct of the target undertaking. Preparatory measures, such as in particular the conclusion of the necessary agreements, do not amount to implementation. It is usual to address the prohibition to complete the transaction in the relevant agreements by including conditions which make the implementation of the merger dependent on approval from the relevant competition authorities or on the expiry of the time limits for prohibition.

The Federal Cartel Office may exempt the parties from the prohibition to complete a transaction before clearance where the parties can show important reasons, in particular in order to avoid serious damage to a party or to a third party. The current practice of the Federal Cartel Office regarding such exemptions is rather restrictive. The Federal Cartel Office needs to weigh the public interest in the enforcement of a prohibition to complete the merger against the potential damage to the parties or to third parties.

The contracts relating to a transaction which requires notification will be legally valid under German law only once the merger control proceedings are completed and have been closed, either by a clearance decision or as a result of the expiry of the deadline with no prohibition order issued. Transactions which are completed in breach of the prohibition to complete are invalid under German law. There is an exception to this consequence of invalidity for contracts for a real merger ('fusion') (by way of transformation, integration or creation of a new company) or contracts between undertakings which become valid on their registration in the Commercial Register.

A breach against the prohibition to implement the merger before clearance and any participation in such implementation can be penalised by a fine of up to EUR 500 000. In addition, the fine can amount to three times the level of the additional receipts obtained through the offence.

The main review proceedings are closed by decision of the Federal Cartel Office, which either clears or prohibits the merger. The clearance can be made subject to conditions and obligations. A decision issued at the conclusion of the main review proceedings, irrespective of whether it is a prohibition or a clearance decision, constitutes an administrative act which is subject to appeal. The final decision must be reasoned, served upon the participating undertakings and published in the *Federal Bulletin*. The obligation to give reasons and to publish the act are intended to increase the transparency of administrative decisions of the Federal Cartel Office. Second-phase decisions of the Federal Cartel Office may also be viewed on its homepage.[76]

If the proposed merger is cleared by the Federal Cartel Office, the parties are free to proceed with its completion. The completion of the merger must immediately be notified to the Federal Cartel Office. In this completion notice, reference can be made to the documentation submitted with the original notification. The completion is subsequently published in the *Federal Bulletin*.

Remedies

In order to remove competition concerns, the parties may offer undertakings to the Federal Cartel Office with the aim of preventing the creation or strengthening of a market-dominant position or to contribute to an improvement in the competition conditions, which outweigh the downsides of market dominance. The German legislator has, with the 6th ARC Amendment of 1999, regulated the practice of the Federal Cartel Office of accepting undertakings which up until then had no statutory basis. Concentrations may now no longer be prohibited or cleared only in their totality, but clearance decisions may also be granted subject to undertakings and commitments. Only structural measures may be considered, since the participating undertakings should not be made subject to an ongoing control on behaviour. Measures which may be imposed include divestiture undertakings through which the parties undertake to sell to third parties particular shareholdings, companies or parts of companies (such as, for example, individual plants), commitments to open up the market by granting to third parties certain participations or licences, or commitments restricting the parties' influence, such as for example voting right restrictions which limit the possibilities of influence on the competitive behaviour of other undertakings.

The Federal Cartel Office has the possibility, in the event of non-fulfilment of a commitment, to withdraw the clearance or to amend it by ordering certain conditions or renewed undertakings. The same applies to clearance decisions which are based on incorrect or incomplete information of the participating undertakings. In such a case, the Federal Cartel Office will have the option of withdrawing the clearance decision and re-opening the procedure and then, if need be, prohibiting the transaction.

Appeals and Rights of Third Parties

Appeals to the Court of Appeals in Düsseldorf can be made against prohibition orders within one month of service. Such an appeal does not have suspensory effect, meaning that the participating undertakings remain unable on the basis of the prohibition to complete the concentration concerned. However, the implementation of the proposed concentration may be granted by interim order. The Düsseldorf Court of Appeals may, during the appeal procedure, review questions of both fact and law.

A further appeal against the decision of the Düsseldorf Court of Appeals can be made to the Federal Supreme Court. Leave to further appeal must be granted by the Düsseldorf Court of Appeals in all cases other than for procedural irregularities. Review by the Federal Supreme Court is limited to questions of law so that the Federal Supreme Court is bound by the findings of fact of the Düsseldorf Court of Appeals. Leave to further appeal must be applied for within the one-month time limit set out in section 66 (1) sentences 1 and 2 ARC.

Third parties who are affected by the clearance decision of the Federal Cartel Office also have the right to file a complaint under section 63 (1) ARC. According to the 1999 revision of the ARC this is at least so for formal clearance decisions made in the main review proceedings. The possibilities of filing a complaint are in particular open to participants in the proceedings, i.e., interested competitors, suppliers, customers or other persons or associations of persons whose interests have been substantially affected by the decision. Whether other participants who were not summoned in the main review proceedings also have the right to make a complaint is still not clear.

In principle, any undertaking whose interests are substantially affected by a decision in merger control proceedings may apply to be summoned in the proceedings. The Federal Cartel Office decides on such application after a due assessment of the circumstances and considers, in addition to legal interests, also the economic interests of the applicant. If summoned, the third party has the same rights as the other participants in the proceedings. Third parties, such as competitors or customers of the participating undertakings often intervene informally against the proposed merger and attempt to convince the Federal Cartel Office of the inadmissibility of the proposal. Such an informal intervention has the advantage that the undertakings concerned in the merger are not told the identity of the complainant.

Ministerial Approval

Where a proposed merger is prohibited by the Federal Cartel Office because it creates or strengthens a dominant market position, the merger can nevertheless be allowed to proceed by the Federal Minister for Economic Affairs. Such an approval is possible where in an individual case the restrictions on competition are outweighed by the overall economic advantages of the merger or where the merger is justified by an overwhelming general public interest. Owing to these stringent requirements, ministerial approval has up until now only had very little practical significance. The Federal Minister for Economic Affairs has a wide margin of discretion in making its decision. The application for ministerial approval must be made in writing to the Federal Ministry for Economic Affairs within one month of service of the prohibition order. The decision concerning the approval must then be made within four months. Prior to a decision, an opinion must be sought from the Monopolies Commission, and the relevant state (Land) authorities in whose region the parties have their seat must be given the opportunity to put forward their views.

Dissolution of Implemented Mergers

Where a merger on which the Federal Cartel Office has jurisdiction is implemented without a clearance decision, and the Federal Cartel Office then prohibits the merger, the merger may have to be dissolved. The measures necessary for the dissolution of a merger are laid down by the Federal Cartel Office. Nevertheless, such a break-up is according to case law admissible only for as long as the substantive and formal conditions for a prohibition apply.

The aim of a dissolution is the removal of the restrictions of competition created by the merger. These may be removed in a way other than a reconstruction of the previous circumstances. According to the principle of proportionality, measures are admissible only where they affect the participating undertakings to an extent which is absolutely necessary for the removal of the restriction on competition. The competition concerns resulting from a merger can often be addressed through partial divestitures rather than through a full dissolution.

The separation order of the Federal Cartel Office can be enforced through the imposition of fines in an amount of between EUR 5 000 and EUR 50 000, through the prohibition or restriction of the exercise of voting rights, or through the appointment of trustees to carry out the dissolution of the concentration.

In the event of foreign concentrations, the power of the Federal Cartel Office to prohibit a merger and to order its dissolution is limited to the effects within Germany. Addressees of orders for dissolution can therefore be only the German subsidiary companies of the participating undertakings in the merger.

Merger Control and Section 1 ARC

Joint Ventures

In addition to merger control, joint ventures may under German law (as under EU law) be subject to the prohibition against anti-competitive agreements contained in section 1 ARC to the extent that their creation entails a coordination of the competitive behaviour of the parent companies ('group effect'). Cooperative joint ventures in particular are subject to a 'double review' under merger control rules on the one hand and the prohibition against anti-competitive agreements on the other. Therefore, within the merger control procedure, the Federal Cartel Office will also review whether, under section 1 ARC, the parent companies are susceptible to coordinate their competitive behaviour in a prohibited manner. *Sales joint ventures* in particular may violate section 1 ARC, even in the absence of an express obligation of delivery, since they result in the coordination of the selling activities of the parent companies. According to the practice of the Federal Cartel Office, purchasing joint ventures with high purchasing volumes or legal and/or substantive purchasing pressure on the members may also be subject to the prohibition against anti-competitive agreements, even though purchasing cooperations between independent small and medium-sized trading companies are generally viewed positively from a competition point of view.

Joint ventures which are created as a tool to coordinate market behaviour of the parent companies are subject exclusively to section 1 ARC. Such joint ventures are viewed as pure cartels which must be assessed under section 1 ARC just as any other anti-competitive agreement.

Concentrative joint ventures, on the other hand, are subject exclusively to merger control rules. According to the Federal Cartel Office, a joint venture is of purely concentrative nature, if:

- It possesses the most important functions of an undertaking and is able to function independently
- It has activities in the marketplace and is not exclusively active on a downstream or upstream market of the parent companies
- The parent companies themselves are no longer active in the substantive market of the joint venture.

If these conditions are satisfied, the creation of or participation in a joint venture is no longer reviewed under section 1 ARC. Solely excessive restrictions on competition, i.e. restrictions which are not necessary for the functioning of the joint venture, will fall under section 1 ARC.

'Non-Compete' Clauses[77]

Although 'non-compete' clauses in principle fall within the prohibition against anti-competitive agreements contained in section 1 ARC, 'non-compete' clauses in purchase agreements between the parties to a merger are not generally inadmissible. Their validity is dependent on whether they are necessary from a substantive, geographic and duration point of view in order to secure the transfer of the full value of the undertaking to the purchaser, including any related *intangible values*, particularly goodwill. The necessity and proportionality of such a 'non-compete' clause will vary from case to case. Case law generally views 'non-compete' clauses of up to three to five years as necessary for the transfer of the undertaking. 'Non-compete' clauses of a longer duration will be upheld only in exceptional circumstances.

4 Multijurisdictional Merger Control

Introduction

The importance of multijurisdictional merger control for international mergers and acquisition projects is constantly increasing. Presently, more than 90 countries have competition laws in place and some 60 jurisdictions have pre-merger notification and review requirements. In an environment of multinational firms and global markets, an increasing number of mergers and acquisitions are reviewed by multiple national authorities. Although discussions in respect of some standardisation of the various reporting thresholds and procedures are under way,[78] national authorities still apply different laws which vary in many important respects, including their procedural features, substantive review standards and approaches to enforcement.

This situation requires the involvement of specialised competition counsel with expertise in international merger control very early on in transaction projects. Involving specialised competition counsel only late in the proceedings can result in the risk of severe fines, if deadlines for the submission of notifications are missed or the transaction is closed without having obtained all required clearances. In order to conduct multijurisdictional merger filings it is necessary to have (1) regularly updated information on merger control laws in all relevant jurisdictions and the application of such laws by local competition authorities around the world; (2) contacts and good working relationships with competition counsel in the various jurisdictions with merger control around the world; and (3) experience in the coordination of the filings and in establishing a detailed schedule for filings which accommodates all relevant filing deadlines and waiting periods. The more countries are involved, the more important it becomes to have a central coordination of the multinational filings in place, not only when making the decision as to where to notify, but even more so when it comes to the actual preparation of the various notifications and the handling of the national proceedings.

Where to Notify?

As a first step, one needs to examine carefully in which countries a transaction project must be notified. Most countries make use of *revenue tests*, i.e. a filing is required, if the acquirer's and/or the target's worldwide and/or domestic revenues exceed certain thresholds. In addition to these revenue tests, a number of countries use (alternative or cumulative) market share tests[79] and/or asset tests,[80] i.e. a filing is required if the parties' aggregate market shares and/or the value of the parties' assets in the respective jurisdiction exceed certain thresholds. Calculation of revenues is usually done on the basis of the companies' revenues in their last business year. Currency conversions within the EU have to be done on the basis of the official conversion rates of the European Central Bank (ECB)[81] and the fixed conversion rates among the EU member states participating in the euro.[82]

These various threshold tests result in a significant amount of information being required for the assessment of merger filing requirements. While revenue data is in most instances readily available and revenue thresholds are relatively easy to check, market share tests are more difficult to assess, since they not only depend on the appropriate definition of the relevant product and geographic markets, but also require detailed sales information broken down by the affected product and geographic markets and information as to the total size of these markets. Especially where the product markets have to be defined on a very narrow basis,[83] the workload in respect of collecting the necessary information can be quite high. Also, market share tests are likely to result in legal uncertainty since the product market definition is often not entirely clear.

Once the jurisdictions in which the relevant thresholds are exceeded have been determined, the parties must identify, in a second stage, in which of these jurisdictions the transaction will lead to an appreciable effect on the domestic markets. Generally speaking, this will be the case in all countries where the target *generates revenues*. Only in those countries where the target does not generate any revenues at all or the target's revenues are insignificant, a filing may not be necessary owing to the fact that there is no appreciable effect. However, a filing may be advisable nevertheless if the country is of specific importance to the purchaser's operations. In each case, the parties should carefully assess the risks associated with not filing, and should carefully check the actual filing requirements with local counsel, since merger control is an area of law which is under constant development.[84] Also, the advice of local counsel and detailed knowledge on the standard practice of the relevant national competition authority can be required in assessing whether a transaction has appreciable effects on a national market. When in doubt as to whether a transaction is notifiable in a given jurisdiction, companies can in many instances achieve legal certainty by requesting an opinion from the national competition authority on the filing requirement. Especially in countries which are important for the operations of the companies concerned, it may be advisable to submit such a 'no-jurisdiction-letter', if this is possible under the merger control law of the jurisdiction concerned.[85] A request for an opinion of the relevant competition authority appears to be particularly advisable where the filing requirement is dependent on market share tests and the product market definition is not entirely clear.

Finally, it must be considered that in some jurisdictions,[86] the submission of a notification is only voluntary. Since the competition authorities in these cases may require information and have the competence to block transactions if competition problems occur, the parties may decide to voluntarily notify the transaction in order to avoid the risk of the authority investigating the deal at a later stage.

Preparation and Submission of Notifications

As soon as the parties have decided to notify a transaction in a particular jurisdiction, local counsel should be contacted quickly (if not already done for determining the filing requirement) to start the process of collecting the required information. Although there are certain pieces of information which are required in almost every jurisdiction, the extent of information required varies significantly between the various countries. While some countries require only a minimum amount of information on the parties, the transaction and the affected markets, others have followed the approach of the European Commission and require very detailed information.[87] Also, it should be noted that in some jurisdictions not only is the acquiring company under a filing obligation, but also the seller.

It is crucial to establish a detailed schedule for the notifications which accommodates all relevant filing deadlines and waiting periods. Some countries have very short filing deadlines[88] and impose severe fines for late filing, although the authorities may have considerable time to examine the transaction.[89] Timing is also of the essence in respect of the waiting periods: quite a number of countries[90] provide for a suspensory effect, i.e. the transaction may not be closed before either regulatory approval has been granted or the relevant waiting period has expired. Only few countries which require a pre-merger notification allow a transaction to be implemented before clearance has been granted.[91] In countries with such suspensory effect, notifications have to be submitted in such a way as to ensure that all clearances will have been granted by the intended closing date.[92] If a required clearance cannot be obtained by the intended closing date, international transactions may in most instances be closed globally, if the closing documents provide for a 'carve-out' of those jurisdictions where the clearance has not yet been granted. In such a case, local assets of the target may not be transferred to the purchaser.[93] Again, before the implementation of any local carve-outs, local counsel should be contacted in order to ensure compliance with local laws.

Finally, it is advisable to take a number of formal and practical issues into consideration when establishing the filing schedule. In some jurisdictions, waiting periods do not run if the national competition authority issues formal information requests. Also, national holidays can have some impact on notification schedules. Therefore, the schedule should allow for sufficient extra time. Also, appropriate time should be allowed for the preparation of translations: often, the process of drafting the notifications by local counsel will be done in English for review and coordination purposes. However, since only few competition authorities accept notifications in the English language, a translation into the local language will have to be prepared. Also, local counsel will require powers of attorney from the merging parties (in some instances also from the seller) and in some countries, notifications are not signed by local counsel but must be signed by representatives of the parties. In some cases, the parties' signatures (both on the power of attorney and on the notification) will have to be notarised and the notarisation must be accompanied by an *apostille* pursuant to the Hague Convention. Finally, it should be noted that many countries have introduced filing fees which must be submitted along with the notification.

Specific Country Information

We now set forth specific information relating to merger control laws and their application in selected countries in which filings typically may be required. However, there are numerous other countries which have merger control and in which a filing may be required, depending on the particular circumstances of each individual case.[94] It should also be noted again that national merger control rules of the EU member states[95] are not applicable if the concentration falls within the scope of the ECMR.

Argentina

In Argentina, a pre-merger filing is required if the parties' combined revenues in Argentina exceed US$ 200 million. Acquisitions of companies in which the acquirer already owns more than 50 per cent of the shares are not subject to control and neither are intra-group transactions. Also, the acquisition of a company in Argentina by a foreign investor is excluded from the scope of merger control, if the acquirer did not previously own shares or assets in Argentina. A further exception to the filing requirement exists, if the value of assets to be transferred in Argentina or the value of the transaction in Argentina does not exceed US$ 20 million, provided that the acquiring party has not previously acquired assets in Argentina which pertain to the same market and the aggregate value of such previous assets or transactions in Argentina did not exceed US$ 20 million within the last year, or US$ 60 million within the last three years.

In terms of procedure, the filing has to be made prior to or within seven days from the date of the conclusion of the agreement, or the publication of the purchase or exchange offer for the acquisition of a controlling interest, whichever occurs first.

Foreign-to-foreign mergers or acquisitions would generally require filing in Argentina if (1) the parties (the acquirer and target in a stock acquisition or the merging companies in a merger) both have a physical presence (i.e. a subsidiary or branch) in Argentina; *or* (2) the target has a physical presence in Argentina; *or* (3) both parties only conduct sales in Argentina (or if the acquirer has a physical presence and the target only conducts sales) where those sales are substantial and habitual. The Argentine Commission has not yet clarified the meaning of the terms 'substantial' and 'habitual', although it seems to require that the parties have sold products in Argentina which horizontally or vertically overlap, and those sales have been made on a regular basis for the last three years. With regard to substantial sales in Argentina, the Commission's opinions differ on what the sales should be compared against (i.e. total amount and volume of imports of the products into Argentina, vs. total size of the market for those products) and the percentage they must represent. For example, sales representing 15 per cent and 20 per cent of the total market have been considered to be substantial, while sales of 14 per cent of the same market have not. Until this test is defined more clearly, it seems advisable to approach the Commission in all cases where sales are not clearly unsubstantial.

Argentinean merger control provides for a suspensory effect, so that the transaction does not have any legal effects *vis-à-vis* the contracting parties or third parties until the concentration has been approved. The Argentinean authorities have 45 working days following the submission of a complete notification to clear the transaction (if necessary, subject to conditions) or to deny approval. It should be noted that the Argentinean authorities may suspend the 45-working-day waiting period for good cause. Also, the authority may initiate a phase II in-depth investigation. Special rules apply to business activities in telecommunications, insurance, and banking.

Austria

In Austria, a pre-merger notification has to be submitted to the Cartel Court in Vienna if (1) the combined worldwide sales of both parties are at least EUR 300 million, *and* (2) the combined domestic revenues of both parties in Austria exceed EUR 15 million, *and* (3) the worldwide revenues of each of at least two parties exceed EUR 2 million. Foreign-to-foreign mergers are also caught by the pre-merger notification requirement if the revenue thresholds are exceeded.

There is no deadline for filing. However, approval must be obtained from the Cartel Court before the transaction can be closed. Owing to this suspensory effect, any implementing measures prior to clearance are void. Where the Cartel Court deems that no investigation is necessary, clearance should in practice be given after about six to seven weeks after the notification (phase I). In cases where further investigations appear necessary (phase II), a decision will be issued within five months following the submission of the notification.

Failure to notify a transaction or implementation of a transaction before clearance will lead to fines amounting up to EUR 116 000. In certain cases, additional penalties up to EUR 725 000 may be imposed on the companies involved. Special rules apply to media businesses, banks and insurance companies.

Belgium

In Belgium, a pre-merger filing is required if (1) the combined revenues of both parties in Belgium exceed EUR 40 million *and* (2) both parties individually generate sales in Belgium of at least EUR 15 million. Foreign-to-foreign mergers are caught if the thresholds are met.

A pre-merger notification has to be submitted within one month following the date of the conclusion of the relevant agreements, the announcement of a public bid or the acquisition of a controlling interest. Since Belgian law provides for a suspensory effect, approval must be obtained from the Belgian competition authority before the transaction can be closed. Implementing measures before closing may not be enforceable, although exceptions to this rule exist in respect of acquisitions of shares.

Phase I of the investigations takes 45 days following the submission of the notification. The authority may open in-depth investigations which take 60 additional days. Transactions are cleared automatically where the parties' market shares in Belgium do not exceed 25 per cent.

Failure to notify will be sanctioned with fines reaching from BEF 20 000 (about EUR 500) to BEF 1 million (about EUR 25 000). Should the transaction be implemented before clearance the Belgian authority may impose fines of up to 10 per cent of the parties' revenues and/or daily penalties of up to BEF 250 000 (about EUR 6200).

Special rules apply to foreign investments in the banking, insurance and media sectors.

Brazil

In Brazil, a pre-merger notification is required if (1) the resulting market share equals to or is higher than 20 per cent of a relevant market, *or* (2) one of the parties had worldwide revenues exceeding R$ 400 million (about EUR 202 million) in the last business year. Foreign-to-foreign mergers are caught if they have or may have effects on the domestic market in Brazil.

Notifications have to be submitted prior to or within 15 working days following the date when the transaction becomes effective in the relevant market or starting from the first binding document signed by the parties. Missing this very short filing deadline will result in the imposition of severe fines for late submission of the notification. Along with the notification, the parties must pay a filing fee of R$ 45 000 (about EUR 23 000).

In Brazil, notified transactions are reviewed by three authorities, i.e. SAEA (Economic Policy Secretariat), SDE (Economic Law Office) and CADE (Administration Council for Economic Defence). The review periods are for SEAE 30–45 days, for SDE 30–34 days, and for CADE up to 120 days. On average, a clearance may require up to four months in less complex cases and up to six months in more complex cases. However, the transaction can be implemented after the submission of a notification since Brazil merger control law does not provide for a prohibition to complete.

Czech Republic

The Czech Republic introduced a new merger control law as of 1 July 2001. Pursuant to the new rules, Czech merger control requires a merger filing if (1) the parties' combined worldwide revenues for the last fiscal year exceeded CZK 5 billion (about EUR 145 million) *or* (2) the parties' combined revenues in the last fiscal year on the market in the Czech Republic exceeded CZK 550 million (about EUR 16 million), *and* at least two of the companies involved each achieved net revenues in excess of CZK 200 million (about EUR 6 million). A horizontal or vertical overlap between the parties' business activities is not required. Foreign-to-foreign mergers are caught if the revenue thresholds are met and the transaction results, or may result, in a distortion of competition on the Czech market, the latter being subject to a divergence of opinion within the Czech authority.

Notifications have to be filed within seven days following the conclusion of the relevant agreements. In the case of a public offer, the notification must be filed before the offer has been published. Until the decision of the Office on the grant of approval has become final, the parties may not implement the concentration. The Czech authority can decide to grant an exemption from this prohibition following a written application supported by reasons. Should the Office discover that companies have implemented a merger without filing a notification, the Office may order the parties to dispose of shares or a business, or parts thereof, acquired as a result of the merger, cancel a contract or adopt other measures necessary to restore effective competition on the relevant market.

The Competition Office decides whether a notified merger shall be approved within 30 days of the commencement of the proceedings. In cases where the merger requires the approval of the Office and where the merger will not result in a significant distortion of competition, the Office will, within the same time period, deliver a decision granting approval of the merger. Where a decision has not been delivered within the above time period or where the parties to the proceedings have not been notified that the Office intends to continue the proceedings, the merger shall be deemed to have been approved at the expiry of the above period. If the proceedings are continued, the Office must deliver a decision within five months from the commencement of the proceedings (in the case of public takeovers, within two months). Otherwise the merger shall be deemed to have been approved.

Breaches of the law (including failure to file, late filing or effecting the merger before the Office has granted its approval thereto) will be fined up to CZK 10 million (about EUR 300 000) or up to 10 per cent of the parties' net revenues in the previous calendar year. In cases of failure to provide the Office with correct and complete information, fines of up to CZK 300 000 (about EUR 9000) can be imposed and the non-fulfilment of Office decisions may lead to fines of up to CZK 1 million (about EUR 30 000).

Denmark

Merger control in Denmark applies to concentrations where (1) the parties have combined revenues in Denmark of at least DKR 3.8 billion (about EUR 510 million) *and* at least two of the parties individually have total revenues in Denmark of DKR 300 million (about EUR 40 million) or more, *or* (2) one of the parties has revenues in Denmark of at least DKR 3.8 billion (about EUR 510 million) *and* at least one of the other participating parties has annual world-wide revenues of at least DKR 3.8 billion (about EUR 510 million). The conditions mentioned under (2) have been included because a merger between a dominant Danish company and a foreign competitor can significantly distort competition in Denmark.

Parties are obliged to notify the Competition Authority no later than one week after the signing of the agreement, the publication of an acquisition or public offer, or the acquisition of control. Phase I of the procedure takes four weeks, while phase II may take up to three months and mergers cannot be put into effect until the Council has approved them.

Fines may be imposed on undertakings for failure to comply with their obligations under the Competition Act. In particular, failure to suspend the implementation of a concentration pending examination or putting into effect a concentration prohibited by the Competition Council exposes the companies concerned to fines. In addition, periodic penalty payments may also be imposed under certain circumstances. The Competition Council may also revoke its clearance decision in the event of a breach of the undertakings or where the decision is based on incorrect information.

Finland

In Finland, a pre-merger filing has to be submitted if (1) the combined worldwide revenues of both parties exceed EUR 336.4 million, *and* (2) the worldwide revenues of each of both parties is in excess of EUR 25.2 million. Foreign-to-foreign transactions are caught by the Finnish Competition Act only if the target company holds a physical presence in Finland such as a subsidiary, a sales office, or an appointed agent. The filing needs to be made within one week from the signing of a binding agreement, the acquisition of control, the announcement of a public bid, the decision to merge, or the holding of a constitutive meeting of the joint venture. A pre-notification to the Finnish Competition Authority (FCA) is recommended.

Generally, the transaction must be suspended until clearance. However, in the case of a Competition Council investigation, the suspension is limited to the period of one month from the FCA's request for investigation, unless the Competition Council orders an extension. Phase I and II of the proceedings are handled by the FCA and take one or three to five months, respectively. The latter can be extended by a maximum of three additional months in exceptional cases and is then handled by the Competition Council.

A failure to file or an implementation before clearance will result in fines ranging between EUR 840–670 000 or, in exceptional cases, up to 10 per cent of the parties' revenues. Also, a dissolution may be ordered by the Competition Council. Special rules apply to the electricity sector.

France

France has adopted new merger control rules which came into force in May 2002. Pursuant to the new rules, a mandatory pre-merger merger filing is required if (1) the parties have combined worldwide revenues of more than EUR 150 million, *and* (2) two or more of the undertakings which are parties to the concentration have each achieved revenues in France of at least EUR 15 million. Foreign-to-foreign transactions are caught if they are likely to affect competition within France.

The new French law provides for a suspensory effect, so that the transaction cannot be enforced prior to approval. A failure to notify or the implementation of the transaction before clearance will lead to penalties of up to 5 per cent of the parties' pre-tax revenues in France in the same way as a non-filing.

The new French merger control law will grant the competition authority a five-week time limit to clear the transaction (phase I). During this time period, the relevant parties may be able to remedy competition issues by proposing commitments to the transaction or by accepting commitments proposed by the authority. If the commitments are proposed two weeks after receiving the filing, the first decision of the authority shall be given three weeks after receipt of these commitments (which would bring phase I of the review to a maximum of eight weeks). In case of serious doubts on competition issues, the authority may still refer the matter to the Competition Council for an advisory opinion (phase II). The Council will have a three-month time limit for assessment. The competition authority will then have a four-week time limit from the receipt of the Council opinion to issue its final decision.

Special rules apply to the press and audio-visual sectors as well as to banks and insurance companies.

Greece

In Greece, a pre-merger filing has to be submitted to the competition authority if (1) both parties generate combined revenues of at least EUR 150 million in Greece, *and* each of both parties have revenues in Greece of at least EUR 15 million, *or* (2) if the participating undertakings have a combined market share of at least 35 per cent in the relevant Greek market. It seems unclear at present whether the Greek competition authority considers this test to also be fulfilled in circumstances where only one party to the transaction holds a market share of more than 35 per cent. Special provisions exist for the calculation of the relevant thresholds for banks and insurance companies. Foreign-to-foreign mergers are caught if the thresholds set out above are met and the transaction has actual or potential effects in Greece.

A notification must be submitted within 10 working days from the signing of a binding agreement, the announcement of public bid or the acquisition of control. The Competition Commission may impose fines for late notifications of at least EUR 15 000 and possibly of up to 7 per cent of the parties' combined revenues in Greece. The filing fee currently amounts to approximately EUR 1000. Concentrations cannot be implemented until the Competition Commission has issued a clearance decision. However, exceptions to this waiting obligation exist for public bids and for the acquisition of securities, provided that the acquisition has been duly notified and the acquirer does not exercise the voting rights. The Commission may also grant exemptions from the prohibition to complete.

The proceedings take three months until adoption of a final decision. The Greek competition authority will examine whether the concentration falls within the scope of Greek merger control and whether the notification is complete. Within one month following the submission of a complete notification, the authority will refer the notification to the Competition Commission for further investigation as to the substance which will take an additional two months.

An implementation of the transaction before clearance can lead to fines of at least GRD 10 million (about EUR 30 000) and possibly of up to 15 per cent of the parties' combined revenues in Greece. The Commission may require divestitures and the implementation of a merger before clearance or without exemption can also be treated as a criminal offence.

Hungary

In Hungary, a pre-merger filing is required if (1) the parties' combined net revenues in Hungary exceed HUF 10 billion (about EUR 39 million), *and* (2) the net revenues in Hungary of at least two of the parties including the target exceed HUF 500 million (about EUR 2 million). As an exception to this rule, these thresholds are not applicable to the creation of a joint venture. Non-Hungarian transactions are caught by the Hungarian Competition Act if they have an appreciable impact on the local market.

A pre-merger filing has to be submitted within 30 days from the earliest of the following events: publication of the invitation to tender, conclusion of the contract or acquisition of the right of control. A filing fee of HUF 2 million (about EUR 8000) must be submitted with the notification. The Hungarian Competition Office's decision deadline is 90 days from the receipt of application. This period may be extended by a maximum period of 60 days but is usually shorter if there are no overlaps in the parties' business activities in Hungary. Hungarian law does not provide for a prohibition to complete. The parties may close the transaction following the submission of the notification. However, exercising voting rights is suspended until clearance.

Special foreign investment rules apply to the financial, media, telecommunication, energy and gas sectors. There are also special rules for public takeovers.

Ireland

In Ireland, a pre-merger filing is required if (1) the value of the gross assets of each of the two parties is not less than IR£ 10 million (about EUR 12 million), *or* (2) if the revenues of each of the two parties exceeds IR£ 20 million (about EUR 25 million). In the case of the acquisition of assets, the same thresholds apply to the assets acquired. However, it is still unclear under the Irish Competition Act whether these figures relate to the parties' worldwide activities or to Ireland only. In practice, if the parties meet the gross assets or the sales test only on a worldwide basis but not with regard to the Republic of Ireland, the Irish competition authority will require only a short notification which is a brief summary of the merger. Normally, in such a case the Irish competition authority will swiftly issue a letter to the effect that it does not assert jurisdiction over the case.

Notifications have to be submitted within one month of an offer capable of acceptance and will then lead to a phase I investigation that takes one month from notification (but may be extended by information request) or a phase II which will take three months from notification. A transaction may be closed outside of Ireland before clearance, but under Irish law title to shares and assets do not pass until approval has been granted. A failure to notify is treated as a criminal offence and fines will be imposed (and may also be imposed on the companies' officers). Furthermore, a breach of the obligation to notify will lead to the invalidity of the transfer of assets or shares.

There are special notification requirements for transactions involving, among others, a newspaper printer or publisher, banks or insurance companies.

Israel

Under the laws of Israel, a merger is defined as the acquisition of the principal assets of another company, or of shares which give the acquirer more than a quarter of the capital or voting rights, the right to select more than a quarter of the directors or the right to participate in more than a quarter of the earnings.

A pre-merger notification is required if (1) the parties' combined revenues in Israel exceed NIS 150 million (about EUR 43 million) *and* either each of at least two of the parties has revenues in Israel of at least NIS 10 million (about EUR 3 million), *or* (2) the parties will together control more than 50 per cent of the local relevant market (whether or not it results in an increase in market share). Furthermore, a transaction has to be notified if one of the companies is a 'monopolist' (based on the presumption of a monopoly at over 50 per cent market share), notwithstanding the fact that the concentration may relate to a completely different product market. However, merger control applies only if both companies are registered, or directly/indirectly conduct business in Israel. This has to be interpreted extensively, and may also be satisfied in cases where there are permanent employees or subsidiaries in Israel or where the parties have an interest in Israeli companies of more than 25 per cent. It is important to note that a foreign corporation's *first acquisition* in Israel is not covered.

There is no specified filing deadline but clearance is required before the concentration can be implemented. The procedure takes 30 days from notification; this period can be extended and has a suspensory effect. Imprisonment of up to two years, fines of up to NIS 1.5 million, divestiture and civil actions are the consequences of a failure to file or of an implementation before clearance. Special provisions apply to mergers in the telecommunications, media, banking, cable and insurance sectors.

Italy

In Italy, a pre-merger filing is required if (1) the combined revenues of both parties in Italy exceed ITL 730 billion (about EUR 377 million) *or* (2) if the target achieved revenues of more than ITL 73 billion (about EUR 37.7 million) in Italy. This also applies to foreign-to-foreign mergers.

The notification may be filed at any time before completion and the subsequent procedure will either take 30 days (15 days for public bids) from notification for phase I and 45 additional days (can be extended to 75 days in case of insufficient information) for phase II. There are no suspensory effects during this period, so that transactions may be implemented following the notification before a clearance decision is rendered. However, the parties involved are then running the risk of a possible divestiture if the Italian authority issues a blocking decision after completion of the review process. Fines for failure to notify may amount to 1 per cent of the parties' revenues in Italy in the year preceding the statement of objections. If parties implement the transaction notwithstanding a prohibition decision, the authority may impose fines of between 1 per cent and 10 per cent of the revenues of the businesses concerned in the transaction.

Special provisions apply to the following sectors: electricity, gas, broadcasting, film distribution, banks and insurance companies.

Japan

Japanese merger control law requires the notification of a merger of Japanese companies (including subsidiaries) involving (1) an acquiring company with gross assets in Japan of more than Yen 10 billion (about EUR 110 million) *and* (2) a Japanese target company with gross assets or revenues from those assets in Japan of more than Yen 1 billion (about EUR 11 million) *or* a non-Japanese target company whose revenues in Japan (including revenue of its subsidiaries in Japan) exceed Yen 1 billion (about EUR 11 million). A filing must also be submitted in the case of foreign-to-foreign mergers where the domestic revenues of one company exceed Yen 10 billion and the domestic revenues of the other company exceed Yen 1 billion (excluding mergers of parent-and majority-owned subsidiaries and mergers between sister companies).

If these thresholds are exceeded, a transaction needs to be notified 30 days before the closing of the merger or within 30 days of the closing for a share acquisition of a Japanese company. The procedure will then take 30 days from notification (but can be extended by 60 additional days or shortened in exceptional cases). During this period, the transaction may not be completed. However, a decision to open a formal procedure may be taken within 120 days of notification (or 90 days from submission of the requested information). For foreign-to-foreign mergers the 30-day waiting period starts when the authority formally accepts the notification.

A failure to notify, or the implementation of the concentration before clearance, may result in fines of up to Yen 2 million (about EUR 19 000), divestiture and proceedings to nullify the merger. Special filings may also be required under the Foreign Exchange and Foreign Trade Law.

Mexico

In Mexico, a pre-merger notification is required if (1) the target's value in Mexico exceeds 12 million times the minimum wages (currently about US$ 49 million), *or* (2) 35 per cent or more of the assets or shares of a corporation with sales/assets of more than US$ 49 million are being acquired, *or* (3) where two or more firms with combined sales of about US$ 194 million or more are involved and the value of additional assets acquired exceeds US$ 19 million. Foreign-to-foreign mergers are caught if they affect the assets or operations of economic agents doing business in Mexico. No filing is required if the transaction does not involve a direct or indirect acquisition of additional assets in Mexico.

In case of a filing requirement, a notification must be submitted before the closing of the merger. Closing before clearance is possible, however, as long as the parties do not integrate their Mexican operations. The authorities have 20 days to request additional information (the period may be extended) and the parties have 15 days to respond. Subsequently, the authorities have 45 days from the submission of the additional information (or from notification if no additional information was requested) for their final decision. In complex cases, this period may be extended to 145 days but in practice it takes the authorities about 40 days to reach their decision if the submission is complete and there are no substantial antitrust issues.

The fines for failure to file can currently go up to about US$ 350 000 and in addition divestiture can be ordered. As regards the agreement itself, it can be declared null and void. In cases of particularly serious infringements, the authorities are entitled to impose fines of up to 10 per cent of the value of the parties' assets or revenues.

Special rules apply to the bank and telecommunication sectors. Furthermore, in some sectors the percentage of foreign investment is limited to less than 49 per cent unless the Mexican authorities grant an authorisation to exceed the mandatory limitations, and in other industries, no foreign investment is permitted at all.

Netherlands

Under Dutch law, a pre-merger filing is required if (1) the parties' combined worldwide revenues exceed EUR 113.45 million *and* (2) the revenues of at least two companies in the Netherlands individually exceed EUR 30 million. Foreign-to-foreign transactions are caught if the thresholds are met. A physical presence of the parties in the Netherlands is not required.

Subject to limited exceptions, the transaction must be suspended until clearance. In phase I of the proceedings, the Director General decides whether an investigation is required within four weeks from notification. If so, the Director General decides in phase II within 13 weeks following the submission of the notification. A failure to notify or an implementation before clearance will lead to fines of up to EUR 23 000. Also, the transaction will be void and does not produce legal effects.

Since 1 January 2000, Dutch merger control also applies to banks and insurance companies.

Norway

Under the present rules, there is no mandatory pre-merger filing requirement in Norway and there are no jurisdictional thresholds. The parties may submit a voluntary notification if they foresee significant competition problems as a result of the merger. As a rule of thumb, only those cases where the combined market share of the parties exceeds 40 per cent or the market shares of the three largest market players, including the parties, exceeds 60 per cent are investigated by the Norwegian competition authority (NCA). However, there is a mandatory notification requirement under the Norwegian Business Acquisition Act for the acquisition of a Norwegian company if it has (1) more than 50 employees, *or* (2) annual revenues of more than NOK 50 million (about EUR 6 million) *or* (3) received state research and development (R&D) grants. The NCA seldom takes an interest in foreign-to-foreign mergers and has never intervened against such a transaction.

As there is generally no mandatory filing requirement,[96] there is no filing deadline and no sanction for not filing. Nevertheless, it is recommended to submit a notification as soon as a final binding agreement is concluded in order to obtain certain benefits which come with a voluntary filing. Once a notification has been voluntarily submitted, the NCA is obliged to inform the applicant within three months as to whether an intervention may take place (phase I). Phase II will trigger an additional three-month period.

If an intervention is made on the authority's initiative, then it has to take place within six months after the final agreement has been concluded. If special circumstances exist, this period may be extended to one year. The NCA has the power to suspend the implementation of a transaction prior to its clearance. Unless it does so, an implementation before clearance is not prohibited and therefore not penalised. If the NCA suspends the implementation, non-compliance with this decision constitutes a criminal offence under Norwegian law and can lead to fines, imprisonment, periodic penalties and/or the relinquishment of all resulting gains.

Special rules apply to certain sectors (such as power, telecoms, media, insurance, banking, oil and gas, agriculture, shipping and mining) and some involve a mandatory pre-filing and clearance before the implementation.

Poland

According to the Polish Act on Protection of Competition and Consumers of December 2000 which came into force on 1 April 2001, a notification is required if the parties' combined worldwide revenues exceed EUR 50 million. However, according to *de minimis* exemptions, no notification is required if (1) the target undertaking's and the seller's combined revenues in Poland did not exceed EUR 10 million in any of the two years preceding the notification, or if (2) the parties' aggregate market share does not exceed 20 per cent in any of the product markets in which the parties are active. If the parties are unclear about the notification requirement, legal certainty may be achieved by requesting a formal written opinion from the authority on the obligation to notify prior to notification. Such opinion can usually be obtained in approximately two to three weeks' time.

It should be noted that a pre-merger notification must be submitted within seven days following the execution of the relevant agreements and that the Antimonopoly Commission will impose fines for late notifications in the range of EUR 1000 to EUR 50 000. A failure to notify can also lead to fines of up to 1 per cent of the undertakings' average monthly revenues (in the year prior to the decision on the penalty) for each month the notification has not been made. There are also individual fines for the responsible managers of the undertakings, which may amount to up to 10 times the average monthly salary for each month/part month of delay.

The general decision deadline is two months, but in practice most decisions are taken within five to six weeks. For banks and publicly listed companies the deadline is only two weeks. It should be noted that these deadlines exclude periods when supplementary information required by the authority is still outstanding. The new

Polish merger control law provides for a suspensory effect. An implementation before clearance may result in fines of up to 15 per cent of the parties' average monthly revenues in the year prior to the decision on the penalty.

Foreign investment permits may be required and special rules apply to banks, public companies, investment and pension funds. Finally, it should be considered that, according to Polish law, interlocking directorships may already constitute a merger.

Portugal

In Portugal, a pre-merger filing is required if (1) the combined revenues of both parties in Portugal exceed PTE 30 billion (about EUR 150 million), *or* (2) the combined market share of both parties in Portugal exceeds 30 per cent. This also applies to foreign-to-foreign mergers which have an effect in Portugal.

The merger control law of Portugal provides for a prohibition to complete the transaction before clearance. Implementing measures will not produce any legal effects until clearance is granted. Phase I of the procedure takes up to 40 days from notification and may be extended by an information request or even 90 days if it is an *ex officio* procedure. Phase II lasts between 50 and 95 days from notification depending on the positive or negative assessment of the operation. There are fines of between PTE 100 000 (about EUR 500) and PTE 100 million (about EUR 500 000) in case of a failure to file. In addition, the transaction has no legal effects until it is cleared.

Portuguese merger control provisions do not apply to the banking, financial and insurance sectors, which are subject to special provisions of a prudential nature. Neither do they apply to public service concessions. Among other regulations, the Commercial Companies Code, financial and securities legislation and foreign investment rules may be relevant, too.

South Africa

Pursuant to the Competition Act 89 of 1998 (2nd amendment in force since 1 February 2001), South African merger control law differentiates between small, medium-size and large mergers.

Small mergers do not have to be notified unless the Competition Commission expressly requires the parties to do so. A 'small merger' is a concentration where (1) the combined revenues in, into or from South Africa *or* (2) the combined assets in South Africa *or* (3) the revenues of the acquiring firms *plus* the value of target's assets in South Africa *or* (4) the target's revenues *plus* assets in South Africa of the acquiring firms is below R 200 million (about EUR 28 million), *or* (5) the target's revenues or assets in South Africa are below R 30 million (about EUR 4 million).

Large mergers have to be notified. A 'large' merger is a concentration where (1) the combined revenues in, into or from South Africa, *or* (2) the combined assets in South Africa, *or* (3) the revenues of the acquiring firms *plus* the target's assets in South Africa, *or* (4) the target's revenues *plus* the assets in South Africa of the acquiring firms, *or* (5) the target's revenues or assets in South Africa equal or exceed R 3.5 billion (about EUR 500 million).

Medium-size mergers have to be notified. A 'medium-size' merger is a concentration which falls between the lower and the higher thresholds. Although both large and medium-size mergers have to be notified, there are different regimes for the investigations. For both types of merger, a notification must be submitted within seven days from the conclusion of the merger, the announcement of the bid, or the acquisition of a controlling interest, depending on which occurs first.

As regards the procedure for medium-size mergers, phase I takes 30 days and phase II 60 days. For large mergers, the 60 days of phase II may be extended by a 20-day period for the Commission to refer the concentration to the Tribunal which then has 15 days (which may be extended by 10-day periods) to schedule a hearing. Apparently, there is no prescribed time limit for a final decision and the transaction has to be suspended until approval has been obtained. For a medium-size merger, a filing fee of R 75 000 (about EUR 11 000) will be charged which is R 250 000 (about EUR 36 000) for large mergers. Foreign-to-foreign mergers are caught by this legislation if they have an impact in South Africa.

The sanctions for a failure to file or for an implementation before clearance range from fines of up to 10 per cent of the parties' revenues in South Africa together with the exports from South Africa to orders to reverse the merger or divestiture (which is considered the remedy of last resort). Sector-specific rules apply to banking and broadcasting activities.

Spain

Spain applies an alternative market share and revenue test. A pre-merger filing is required if (1) the parties' combined revenues in Spain were more than ESP 40 billion (roughly EUR 240 million) during the last financial year, provided that the revenues in Spain of each of at least two parties were in excess of ESP 10 billion (roughly EUR 60 million), *or* (2) if a market share of 25 per cent or more in Spain is acquired or increased. Foreign-to-foreign mergers are caught if the thresholds are met. National presence in Spain is not required.

Filing is required prior to the completion of the transaction and filing fees were introduced in March 2000 with the Competition Act Amendment. Phase I of the procedure takes one month from the date of notification. Subsequently, phase II – if deemed necessary by the authority – may take two months from its initiation. After this, the government itself may have to decide the matter in phase III within one further month.

The new rules which left the thresholds untouched introduced a suspensory effect in respect of all transactions subject to the Spanish merger control regime. Therefore, transactions caught by the Spanish merger control rules may not be put into effect until clearance from the Spanish competition authorities has been obtained. An exemption may be sought and decided upon at the end of phase I. The obligation to suspend the transaction and the possibility to submit a request for exemption is also applicable to public takeover bids. A breach of the waiting obligation will be subject to fines of up to 10 per cent of the Spanish revenues of the undertakings concerned. A failure to file will be penalised by fines of up to ESP 5 million (about EUR 30 000) and penalties of ESP 2 million (about EUR 12 000) per day will be applied in case of a failure to notify after a request by the Spanish competition authorities. If the parties do not comply with the government's decision, they may be fined 10 per cent of their revenues and/or be subject to divestiture. In addition to the already existing sanctions for breach of the obligation to notify, a Royal Decree introduced the possibility for the authority to initiate a merger procedure on its own motion (which may result in a final prohibition of the transaction).

Separate foreign investment rules and special provisions apply to the electricity, banking, insurance and telecoms sectors.

Sweden

A concentration must be notified to the Swedish competition authority if (1) the undertakings concerned have combined aggregate worldwide revenues of more than SEK 4 billion (about EUR 467 million), *and* (2) at least two of the undertakings concerned have individual revenues in Sweden of more than SEK 100 million (about EUR 11 million). If the threshold of SEK 4 billion is fulfilled but the undertakings concerned do not reach the second threshold of SEK 100 million, the competition authority may in a particular case require a party to a concentration to notify the concentration where particular grounds exist for doing so. A party to a concentration always has the right to voluntarily notify such a concentration. The undertakings concerned are the merging undertakings or the undertaking or undertakings acquiring control and the undertaking over which control is being acquired.

From the date of receipt of a complete notification, the competition authority has 25 working days to render a decision either that there are no grounds for action or that it shall initiate a special investigation. During this time no action may be taken to put the concentration into effect. The competition authority may in a particular case make an exception to this prohibition. After a decision to carry out a special investigation, the competition authority has further three months in which to take legal action against the concentration before the Stockholm City Court. The three-month period may be extended by the Stockholm City Court provided that the notifying parties agree to it or there are special reasons for doing so.

A concentration that must be notified or has been voluntarily notified can be prohibited if the concentration creates or strengthens a dominant position which may significantly impede effective competition in Sweden or a substantial part of Sweden. A prohibition must not threaten essential national security interests or national resources. Less extensive intervention may also be appropriate. A party to a concentration may be obliged to sell an undertaking or parts thereof or to perform some other pro-competitive measures. The parties may also voluntarily make commitments to the competition authority and the commitment may be made subject to a penalty of a fine. Such a fine shall be imposed by the Stockholm City Court at the request of the competition authority.

A decision by the competition authority not to take action against the concentration shall also cover restrictions directly related and necessary to the implementation of the concentration. The competition authority has published guidelines on the concept of a concentration, on joint ventures, on the concept of undertakings concerned and on calculation of revenues which correspond to the European Commission's notices.

Switzerland

In Switzerland, a pre-merger filing has to be submitted if (1) the combined worldwide revenues of both parties in the previous business year were at least SFR 2 billion (about EUR 1.25 billion) *or* if the combined revenues of both parties in Switzerland were at least SFR 500 million (roughly EUR 312 million), *and* (2) the revenues of each of two parties in Switzerland were at least SFR 100 million (about EUR 62 million). A notification is also required (irrespective of the revenue thresholds) where an undertaking has been found to have a dominant position in the relevant Swiss market or in a neighbouring, upstream or downstream market in previous proceedings.

There are no deadlines for filing but Swiss merger control law provides for a suspensory effect. Unless specifically authorised, there is an obligation to suspend the transaction until clearance and a breach of this obligation may be a reason for fines of up to SFR 20 000, for a penalty of up to SFR 1 million as an administrative sanction and/or for divestiture. The transaction may not be closed for a period of one month or until the Competition Commission has issued its clearance decision, whichever is earlier. If deemed necessary by the Swiss authority, a phase II investigation of four additional months can be initiated.

Special rules apply for media companies, insurance companies, banks, Swiss real estate companies and companies holding special concessions and licences.

Turkey

Turkey applies an alternative market share and revenue test. A pre-merger filing is required if (1) the parties' combined market share in Turkey exceeds 25 per cent, *or* (2) the parties' combined revenues in Turkey exceed TRL 25 trillion. Due to the high inflation in Turkey, care should be taken when converting the TRL amount into EUR. In March 2002, the EUR equivalent of the TRL filing threshold was about EUR 21 million. Foreign-to-foreign mergers are caught if they have any significant, direct or indirect effects on the Turkish market. This will be the case if the market share of the target in Turkey exceeds 25 per cent.

Turkish law provides for a prohibition to complete and the implementation of the transaction must be suspended until clearance. The Competition Board must take a preliminary decision within 15 days from receipt of the notification. If there is no reaction within 30 days, the transaction may be considered as tacitly approved and will be deemed effective as of the 30th day. Otherwise a six-month phase II investigation will follow.

Fines of up to TRL 3100 million (in March 2002 about EUR 2600) may be imposed for a failure to file and, in addition, fines of up to 10 per cent of the above-stated amount may also be imposed on individuals. If a merger which was not notified but implemented creates or strengthens a dominant position, a substantive fine of up to 10 per cent of the revenues in the preceding year with a minimum of TRL 12 400 million (in March 2002 around EUR 10 000)) will be imposed on the parties. Furthermore, prohibition and other measures to restore competition are possible. The Turkish authority is also entitled to impose periodic penalty payments and fines for failure to provide correct information during the proceedings.

UK

The UK does not have mandatory pre-merger control. A voluntary filing may be submitted if (1) the target's worldwide gross assets are valued at more than UK£ 70 million (about EUR 115 million), *or* (2) the merger results in a combined market share in the UK of more than 25 per cent. There is neither a formal time limit for the filing nor a formal timetable for the proceedings. However, phase I usually takes four to seven weeks and phase II three to six additional months. The procedure has no suspensory effects, and thus there are no penalties for a failure to file or for an implementation before clearance. Special provisions exist for media, water companies and banks.

USA

A merger has to be notified pursuant to the Hart–Scott–Rodino 'HSR' Act if the following conditions are met: (1) the acquirer or the target is engaged in US commerce or an activity affecting US commerce ('commerce test'), *and* (2) for transactions with a value between US$ 50 and 200 million, the transaction involves a US$ 100 million- and a US$ 10 million-size party, valued either in worldwide revenues or in assets ('size of parties test'). Transactions with a value below US$ 50 million do not need to be notified whereas transactions of over US$ 200 million have to be notified, regardless of the size of the parties ('size of transaction test'). A number of exceptions to the filing requirement exist for US-to-foreign transactions and entirely foreign-to-foreign transactions. Foreign-to-US transactions may be caught by the filing requirement but are exempted below certain thresholds.

The HSR does not provide for a filing deadline. Therefore, filing can be made any time after the signing of a definitive agreement, a letter of intent, or a notice of tender offer. The initial waiting period is 30 days (only 15 days for cash tender offers). If the government issues a 'second request' for additional information, the waiting period is extended to 30 days (10 days for cash tender offers) following full compliance with the request. The transaction may not be consummated until clearance. A breach of the waiting obligation or the obligation to notify may result in fines of US$ 11 000 per day. Also, the authorities may require equitable relief (e.g. a divesture).

Fees of between US$ 45 000 and US$ 280 000 will be charged for the filing, depending on the value of the transaction.

Notes

1 Regulation 4064/89 of 21 December 1989 on the control of concentrations between undertakings, *OJ* 1990, L 257/14, amended by Regulation 1310/97 of 30 June 1997, *OJ*

1997, L 180, correction in *OJ* 1998, L 40/17, consolidated version as working paper available under <http://www.europa.eu.int/comm/competition/mergers/legislation/regulation_en.html>
2 Notice on the concept of concentration, *OJ* 1998, C 66/5.
3 Article 2 (4) ECMR.
4 *OJ* 1998, C 66/1 (see also the Commission Information on the assessment of full-function joint ventures pursuant to the competition rules of the EC, *OJ* 1998 C 66/38).
5 *OJ* 1998, C 66/14.
6 *OJ* 1998, C 66/25.
7 Article 5 (1) and (2) ECMR.
8 *OJ* 1986, L 372/1.
9 Article 2 ECMR.
10 *OJ* 1997 C 372/5.
11 Commission notice on the definition of relevant market, paragraph 17.
12 *Nestlé/Perrier, OJ* 1992 L 356/1.
13 E.g. *Ciba-Geigy/Sandoz, OJ* 1997 L 201/1; *Glaxo/Wellcome, OJ* 1995 C 65/3.
14 *Aérospatiale-Alenia/de Havilland, OJ* 1991 L 334/42.
15 *Mercedes Benz/Kässbohrer, OJ* 1995 L 211/1.
16 *BMW/Rover, OJ* 1994 C 93.
17 *Otto/Grattan, OJ* 1991 C 93.
18 *Nordic Satellite Distribution, OJ* 1996 L 53/20.
19 *VIAG/Bayernwerk, OJ* 1994 C 168/0.
20 *Winterthur/DBV, OJ* 1994 C 168/0; *AAG/AMEV, OJ* 1990 C 304/0.
21 *BTR/Pirelli, OJ* 1992 C 265; *Bosch/Allied Signal, OJ* 1996 C 155; *Torrington/NSK, OJ* 1995, C 104; *Mannesmann/Boge, OJ* 1991 C 265.
22 *Hoechst/Wacker, OJ* 1993 C 171.
23 *Dow Chemical/Union Carbide,* <http://www.europa.eu.int/comm/competition/mergers/cases/ decisions/m1671_en.pdf>
24 *Enderly/SBE, OJ* 1996 C 266.
25 *St Gobain/Wacker-Chemie*/NOM, *OJ* 1997 L 247.
26 *Ciba-Geigy/Sandoz, OJ* 1997 L 201/1; Glaxo/Wellcome, *OJ* 1995 C 65/3.
27 *Nestlé/Perrier, OJ* 1992 L 356/1.
28 *Magneti Marelli, OJ* 1991 L 222/CEAC; Varta/Bosch, *OJ* 1991 L 320.
29 *Otto/Grattan, OJ* 1991 C 93.
30 *Rewe/Billa, OJ* 1996 C 306.
31 *Cargill/Unilever, OJ* 1990 C 327.
32 *Steetley/Tarmac, OJ* 1992 C 50.
33 *Aérospatiale-Alenia/de Havilland, OJ* 1991 L 334/42.
34 *Gencor/Lonrho, OJ* 1997 L 11/30.
35 *Elf/Occidental, OJ* 1991 C 160.
36 *Schweizer Rück/Elvia, OJ* 1992 C 027.
37 *AT + T/NCR, OJ* 1991 C 016.
38 *Dow Chemical/Union Carbide,* <http://www.europa.eu.int/comm/competition/mergers/cases/ decisions/m1671_en.pdf>
39 Recital 15 ECMR.
40 *OJ* 1995 L 211/1, para 61.
41 *OJ* 1991 L 290.
42 *OJ* 1993 L 114/34.
43 *OJ* 1991 L 122.
44 See n. 33.
45 E.g. *Nestlé/Perrier.*
46 Judgment of 25.03.1999 in *Case* T-102/96.
47 See *OJ* 1990, C 203/5.
48 *OJ* 2001, C 188/5.

49 See paragraphs 16 and 17 of the notice.
50 *OJ* 1998, L 61/1, hereinafter 'Implementing Regulation'.
51 Article 10 (6) ECMR.
52 Article 10 (1), (2) ECMR.
53 Article 18 (3) sentence 3 ECMR.
54 *OJ* 2001 C 68/3.
55 See, e.g. *Dow Chemical/Union Carbide* <http://www.europa.eu.int/comm/competition/mergers/ cases/decisions/m1671_en.pdf>
56 Article 6 (3) (b) and Article 8 (5) (b) ECMR.
57 Article 14 (2) (c) and Article 15 (2) (b) ECMR.
58 Article 21 (2) ECMR.
59 Article 9 ECMR.
60 There are other special provisions for the calculating of revenues in special cases, e.g. for financial institutions.
61 Court of Appeal (Kammergericht) Berlin, 'Handpreisauszeichner-Entscheidung' (manual price tagging decision), WuW/E (*Wirtschaft und Wettbewerb*) (Journal of German and European Competition Law), OLG 995, 996.
62 *'Melitta-Kraft'*, WuW/E BKartA 2370.
63 *'Blaupunkt'*, WuW/E, OLG 4047.
64 *'Chemische Grundstoffe II'*, WuW/E OLG 1507.
65 *'Edelstahlbestecke'*, WuW/E OLG 3137.
66 *'Pillsbury-Sonnen-Bassermann'*, WuW/E OLG 3759.
67 Activity Report of the Federal Cartel Office 1985/86, p. 74.
68 *'Agip'*, WuW/E BKartA 1494.
69 *'Haindl-Holzmann'*, WuW/E BKartA 1475.
70 *'Metro-Kaufhof'*, WuW/E BKartA 2060.
71 *'Coop-Wandmaker'*, WuW/E OLG 3917.
72 WuW/E BGH 3026, 3029.
73 *'Zementmahlanlage II'*, WuW/E BGH 1655.
74 *'Tengelmann-Gottlieb'*, WuW/E BKartA 2441.
75 *'Sarstedter Kurier-Kreisanzeiger'*, WuW BKartA 2641.
76 <www.bundeskartellamt.de/fusion.htm>
77 See pp. 94–5, 225.
78 See, for example, the Initiative for a Global Competition Forum (CGI), hosted by the International Bar Association.
79 Market share tests exist for example under the merger control laws of Brazil, Greece, Israel, Norway, Poland, Portugal and Spain.
80 Asset tests exist for example under the merger control laws of Finland, Ireland, Japan, Mexico and South Africa.
81 Available in the ECB's *Monthly Bulletins* and its *Annual Reports* (Available online at the ECB's Website under <www.ecb.int>).
82 For ease of reference, all national revenue thresholds given below have been converted into Euro amounts (only the laws of Belgium and Greece give revenue thresholds in Euro). However, please note that the decision whether to notify must be based in each case on an accurate currency conversion using the correct conversion rates for the relevant currencies and time periods.
83 E.g. in the pharmaceutical or in the pesticides industry.
84 This is evidenced for example by the following changes: Denmark introduced new rules as of 1 October 2000, Argentina amended its Defence of Competition Law in February 2001, South Africa amended its 1998 Competition Act as of 1 February 2001, the USA amended the Hart–Scott–Rodino (HSR) Act as of 1 February 2001, Poland significantly modified its merger control law as of 1 April 2001, and the Czech Republic introduced new merger control as of 1 July 2001. The introduction of mandatory merger control in France came into force in May 2002.

85 This is the case, e.g. in Argentina, the Czech Republic, Germany and Poland.
86 This used to be the case in France (under the old merger control law) and currently is the case for example in Norway, the UK and for small mergers within the meaning of South African merger control law.
87 Such as Greece, Hungary, Italy and Romania. See also the European Commission's Form CO (available in the EU's *Official Journal* L61 of 2 March 1998 and at the European Commission's Website under <www.europa.eu.int/comm/competition/mergers/legislation/mergir98.html>)
88 E.g. Argentina (7 days), Brazil (15 working days), Czech Republic (7 days), Denmark (7 days), Finland (7 days), Greece (10 working days), Poland (7 days) and South Africa (7 days).
89 For example in Brazil, where a transaction must be notified no later than 15 working days after the execution of the relevant agreements, the competition authorities may take up to half a year for approval of the transaction.
90 E.g. Austria, Belgium, Germany, Netherlands, Poland, Portugal, Sweden and Turkey to name but a few.
91 E.g. Brazil, the Czech Republic, France, Hungary, Italy and Romania.
92 If for example a transaction must be notified in Austria, Italy, and Germany, the Austrian filing should be submitted at least 6 – 7 weeks prior to the intended closing date and the German notification should be submitted at least one month before the intended closing date. Italian merger control, on the other hand, does not provide for a suspensory effect. Therefore, the concentration may be implemented as soon as the notification has been submitted.
93 It is evident that such a carve-out is easier to perform in asset transactions. Share transactions require more sophisticated carve-out provisions which may employ trustees or other customised solutions.
94 Most competition authorities around the world make information available on their respective websites. They are in most instances accessible through the European Commission's website at <www.europa.eu.int/comm / competition/other_sites>.
95 I.e. Austria, Belgium, Denmark, Finland, France, Germany, Greece, Ireland, Italy, Luxemburg, Netherlands, Portugal, Spain, Sweden and the UK.
96 Unless a Norwegian company is involved.

Bibliography

Ahlborn, C. and Turnver, V. (1998) Expanding Success? Reform of the E C Merger Regulation, *ECLR* 1998, p. 249.

Alonso, J. F. B. (1994) Market Definition in the Community's Merger Control Policy, *ECLR* 1994, p. 195.

Baker, S. and Wu, L. Applying the Market Definition Guidelines of the European Commission, *ECLR* 1998, p. 273.

Bergmann, H. (1993) Settlements in EC Merger Control Proceedings, *Antitrust Law Journal*, 62, p. 47.

Bellamy, C. and Child, G. D. (1996) *Common Market Law of Competition* (London).

Bos, P., Stuyck, J. and Wytinck, P. (1992) *Concentration Control in the European Economic Community*, (London).

Campbell, C. and Davies, J. (2001) *Getting the Deal Through* (London).

Canenbley, C., Wiedemann, G. and Turner, V. (1999) *EC Merger Control Monitor* (Cologne).

Cook, C. J. and Kerse, C. S. (2000) *EC Merger Law* (London).

Drauz, G. (1997) Remedies under the Merger Regulation, in Hawk, B. E. (ed.) *International Antitrust Law and Policy, Annual Proceedings of the Fordham Corporate Law Institute*, 1996 (New York).

Faull, J. and Nikpay, A. (1999) *The EC Law of Competition* (Oxford).

Fiebig, A. R. (1998) International Law Limits on the Extraterritorial Application of the European Merger Control Regulation and Suggestions for Reform, *ECLR* 1998, p. 323.
Goyder, D. G. (1998) *EC Competition Law* (Oxford).
Griffin, J. P. (1998) Antitrust Aspects of Cross-Border Mergers and Acquisitions, *ECLR* 1998, p. 12.
Jones, C. and Gonzáles-Díaz, E. (1992) *The EEC Merger Regulation* (London).
Kerse, S. (1998) *EC Antitrust Procedure* (London).
Levitt, M. (1997) Commission Notice on Internal Rules of Procedure for Access to the File, *ECLR* 1997, p. 187.
Robinson, V. (2000) *Essential Merger Control Quarterly,* A regularly updated description of the merger control laws of the EU and its Member States (London).
Rowley, J. and Baker, D. I. (2001) *International Mergers – The Antitrust Process* (London)
Singleton, E. S. (1992) *Introduction to Competition Law* (London)
Waelbroeck, M. and Frignani, A. (1999) *European Competition Law* (Ardsley)
Zonnekeyn, G. A. (1998) The Treatment of Joint Ventures under the Amended EC Merger Control Regulation, *ECLR* 1998, p. 414.

Part 3

Integration and Implementation of Mergers and Acquisitions

8
Post-Merger Integration

Tomas Koch

1 Introduction

Mergers and acquisitions currently form part of the standard strategic toolkit of many growth-hungry companies. Hardly a month goes by without a mega-merger being negotiated or completed. However, the rewards to the acquirers often prove dubious, with the strategic premiums paid exceeding the expected synergy potentials.

To realise the synergy potentials identified at the outset, and also to identify new opportunities over the long term, effective *post-merger integration* (PMI) is essential. The background to the integration is a decisive factor here. Are the managers' hands tied, for example, by political agreements on plant location or job protection commitments? What is the scope of integration? Is the acquisition target merely being 'annexed' to its buyer, or are the two companies to be completely merged? Both extremes have advantages and disadvantages, which have to be weighed up for every individual integration process (see Table 8.1).

This chapter will deal only with the case of the complete merger. Several of the elements considered can, however, be applied directly to annexation. Depending on the scope and complexity of the merger, an integration project can take

Table 8.1 Pros and cons, by type of integration

	Pros	Cons
Annexation	• Preserves company-specific strengths • Fast integration • Preserves momentum of business	• Preserves company-specific weaknesses • Limited cost synergies • No shared corporate/ performance culture
Merger	• Creates new, shared corporate/ performance culture • Improves operational excellence through intensive exchange of know-how	• Integration is time-intensive • Danger of slow decision-making paralysing organisation

anything from one to two years. A multitude of individual projects will be needed. Clearly structured project management has therefore to be put in place, consisting of two phases fundamentally differing in nature: the *integration design* phase, in which all the principal elements relating to the aspiration level and the implementation of the project are defined by the top people involved, and the *practical implementation* phase, where a large number of project teams will address a wide variety of topics.

2 The 'Duty' Towards the Owners

The financial markets react immediately to news of mergers or acquisitions; the short-term reaction can be observed in the first few days after the announcement. However, it is also illuminating to track the long-term development of stock prices, i.e. two to three years after the integration. The former indicates what shareholders expect of the new company, while the latter is an evaluation of the extent to which these expectations have been fulfilled in the post-merger period.

Short-Term Stock Market Reaction as Feedback from the Owners

The shareholders and 'owners' of the new company have most interest in a successful merger. They have paid part of the expected value creation potential from the merger directly to the seller in the form of a premium, and have to realise the expected remaining synergies reflected in its share price by a well-managed integration process.

In the case of the example of an acquisition presented in Figure 8.1 in simplified terms, the premium paid came to EUR 675 million and the expected value for the acquirer to EUR 250 million. In order to realise the total synergy assumed by the owners, amounting to an increase in market value of EUR 925 million, synergy potentials in the order of EUR 90–100 million per annum have to be realised.

From this estimate, it is possible to derive the minimum target an acquisition by a listed company has to meet in order to justify its stock price. While management has to take up this challenge at least, it should also define a target of its own which lies above that of the financial market, and is based on best practice or on an 'ideal' company.

Long-Term Value Creation as a Challenge for Management

The stock price increase in the first few days after the announcement of the merger simply reflects market expectations. However, it is the long-term development of the stock prices (or the profit and growth trends[1] in smaller acquisitions) which shows how far the companies have been able to live up to these expectations. Extensive studies have shown that the majority of integration projects create value on balance, but are not successful from the acquirers' point of view. As long ago as 1983 a survey demonstrated that only 36 per cent of mergers in Germany were successful.[2] This result has been confirmed in studies by a large number of management consultancies and institutes. The success rates from the acquirers' point

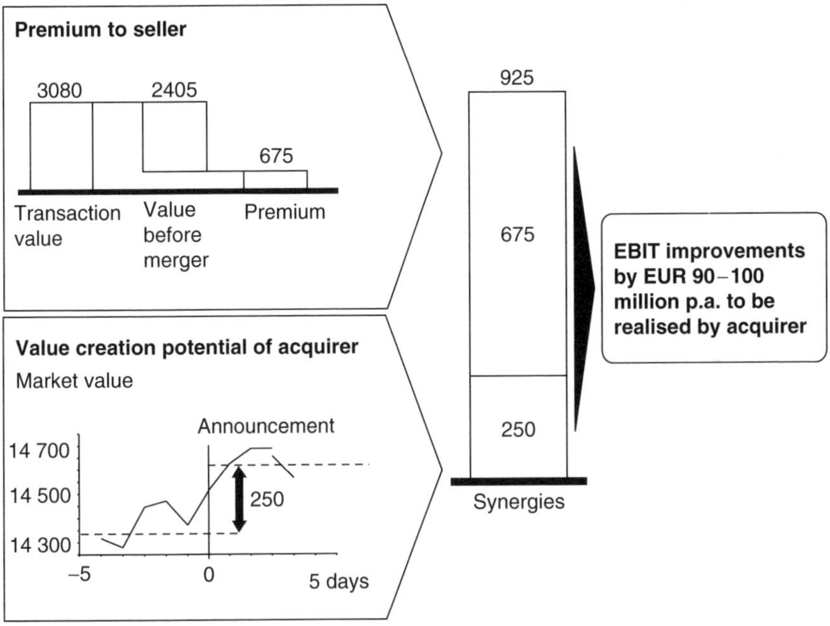

Figure 8.1 Market expectations of total synergies, EUR million
Notes: Simplified assumption: WACC of 10%, no growth, perpetuity. EBIT.
Source: McKinsey.

of view were generally below 50 per cent, both in the service sectors such as banking (approximately 44 per cent) and in manufacturing industries such as chemicals (approximately 50 per cent).[3] In the face of a challenge of such demonstrable proportions, the management team needs to gain a clear understanding of the key factors for success and the constraints at the start of the integration process, and use it as a basis for planning.

3 Key Factors for Success in Post-Merger Integration

According to studies of successful integration projects, there are essentially three decisive factors (see Figure 8.2).

Strong Leadership

Strong leadership is one crucial factor for success. The management team must be ready at all times to make clear and rapid decisions on fundamental issues, ranging from decisions on the organisational structure and the definition of areas of responsibility through to the appointment of key staff. As integration projects frequently take between one and two years, management must be very persistent in fostering integration and ensuring that all measures can be implemented in full and on time.

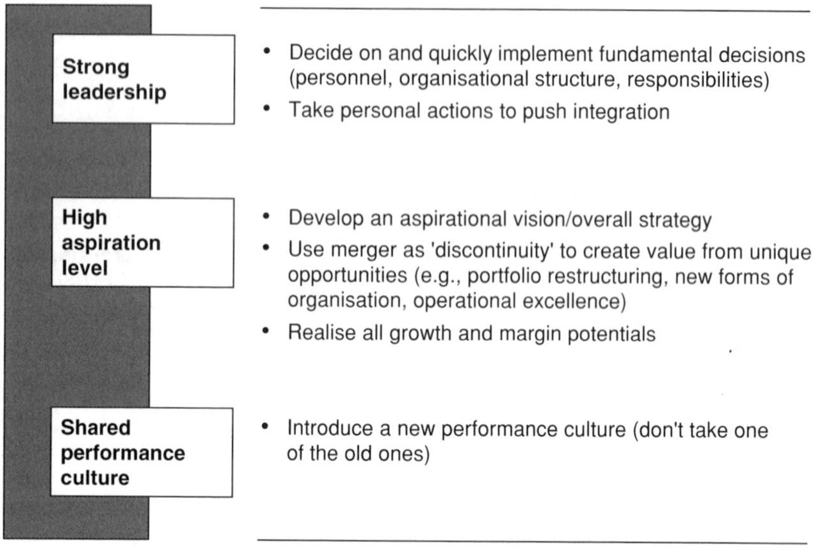

Figure 8.2 Key factors for successful post-merger integration (PMI)
Source: McKinsey.

High Aspiration Level

As a successful integration is ultimately measured by financial ratios, the company has to take full advantage of all the available synergy potentials and set ambitious goals for itself from the very beginning (see Figure 8.3).

Direct synergies will include, for example, reducing redundant costs in the area of administration or increasing revenues from the enlarged, combined customer base. In addition, the company should use integration as a unique opportunity to take a new direction – for example, by completely reorganising its businesses, introducing incentive systems and developing and communicating an inspiring vision and strategy for growth. The latter is particularly important as a motivator for the whole company, since it helps prevent employees from perceiving integration projects as a threat to their jobs.

Shared Performance Culture

One of the keys to success is *cultural integration*, a factor which is frequently underestimated and therefore not explicitly addressed. There are many reasons why this area is neglected. First of all, it is not something whose success is immediately quantifiable, so the need for it is not always perceived. Secondly, most companies still focus on 'assets', i.e. plants and structures, as a factor for success instead of on people and their individual skills and will. Nevertheless, a new, shared performance culture is crucial, based on a jointly established direction ('What are the targets we want to achieve together?') and a jointly established way of interaction ('How should we reach our targets?') (see Figure 8.4).

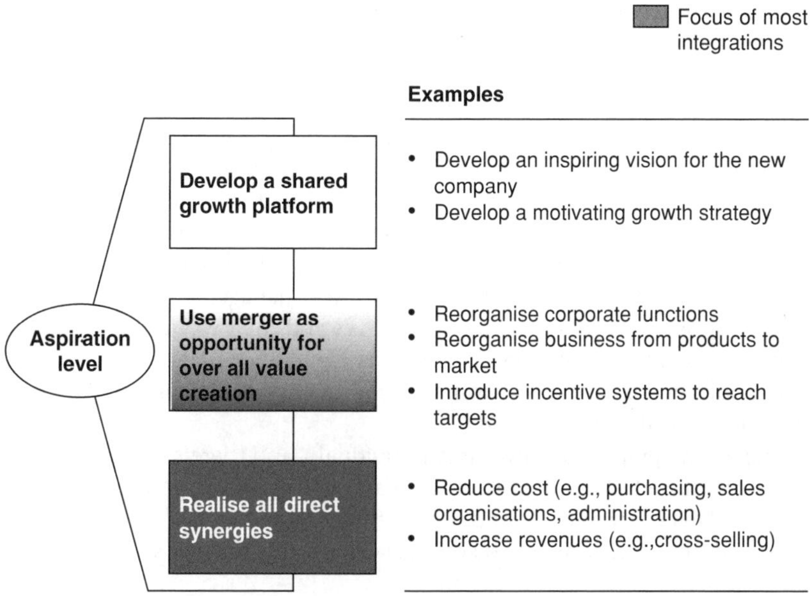

Figure 8.3 Aspiration level as a key factor for success
Source: McKinsey.

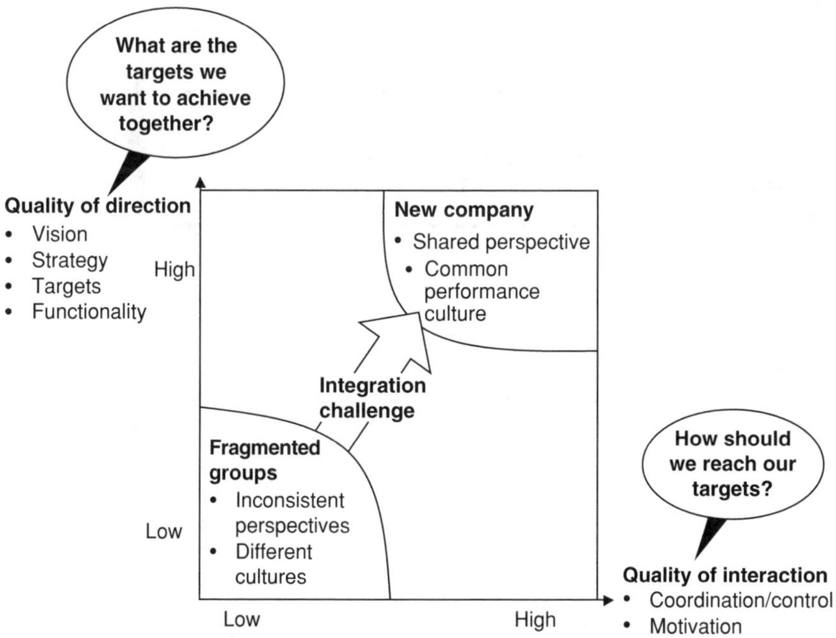

Figure 8.4 Performance culture as a key factor for success
Source: McKinsey.

Traditional integration strategies often focus only on defining new corporate structures, rules and processes in the hope that the two corporate cultures will merge of their own accord over time. This hope frequently proves false, and even a number of years later two distinct cultures can still be observed. Such integration strategies fail to consider *individual motivations and perspectives* such as personal goals, experiences, values and business interests, or even simply the employees' different ways of thinking. To induce the management team and other employees to believe in the company's goals, to pursue them and give them their personal support, the top managers have to do more than just write them down and announce them. In the example in Figure 8.5, the management team of a merged business unit were asked about their objectives and their way of interaction. The responses were all over the place: there was evidently no consensus within the group about the vision or, for example, the quality of the management information system (MIS) (see Figure 8.5).

During an integration process these individual – and therefore usually differing – viewpoints have to be brought into line and a new, shared performance culture developed. This is particularly important at the higher management levels, where direction-setting decisions are taken and where the tone is set for the whole organisation.

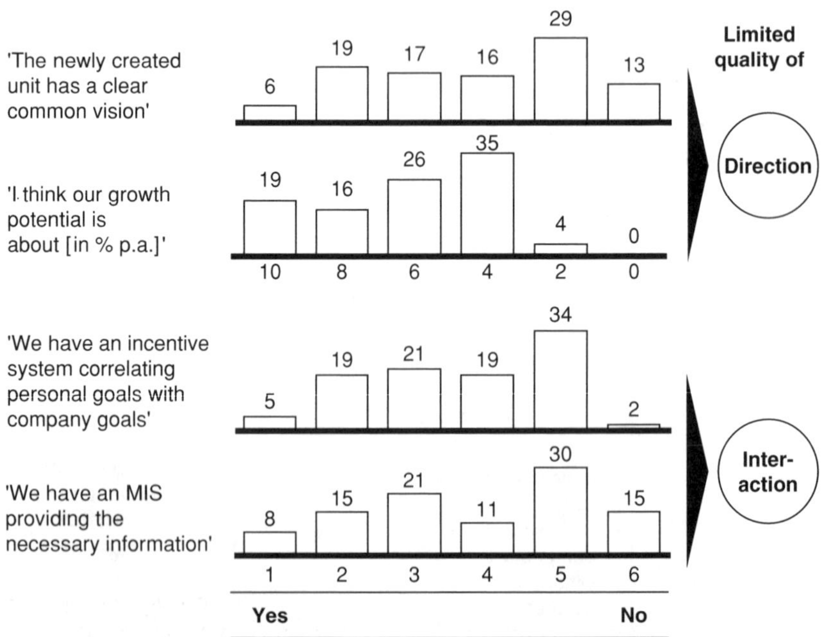

Figure 8.5 Alignment along quality of direction and interaction, result of management survey, per cent
Source: McKinsey.

4 Approach to Integration

The integration process as a whole can be divided into two phases (see Figure 8.6).

The first of these, which defines the cornerstones of the integration project, can take anything from two to three months depending on the scope and complexity of the merger. The second phase defines the specific actions required. Depending on the number and scope of the projects defined in the first phase it can take one to two years before implementation is completed. Though short, the *design phase* is the critical one for success, as this is where all the fundamental decisions about the new company are made. It is important for the management team to make all its decisions fast and jointly. In many cases the first phase is not carried out at all or is handled superficially, and companies get right down to implementation straight away. Experience shows, however, that all the problems which occur during the merger process can essentially be attributed to two causes: first, a lack of (clear) direction, and second, poorly defined interaction mechanisms, such as failure to assign responsibilities clearly.

Phase I: Design Integration

The main task of the first phase is to set a *challenging aspiration level*, which should be supported and subsequently realised by the entire management. Crucially, this process should also see the emergence of a new, homogeneous management team which is totally dedicated to the new company.

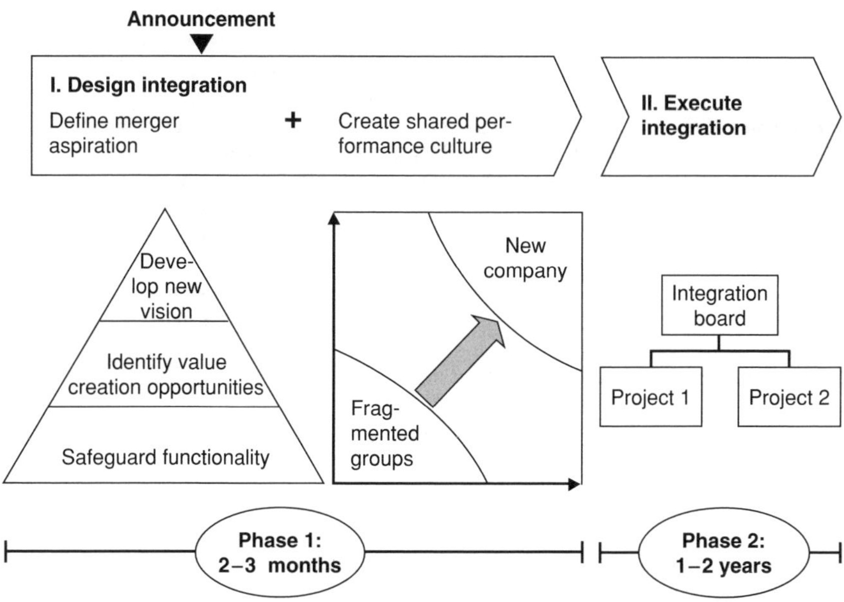

Figure 8.6 Integration approach
Source: McKinsey.

Set a Challenging Aspiration Level

Setting a high aspiration level is one of the fundamental success factors in any integration project. The three aspects involved of developing a vision, identifying value creation opportunities and ensuring the functionality of the new company should all be taken into account even at the planning stage. The most important one, however, is *ensuring functionality*. It is essential to avoid delays in implementing the merger and negative effects on the current business, especially in marketing and sales.

The entire process should be based on a positive attitude which considers the merger as a unique opportunity for corporate redesign, and realises that all current business processes are open to improvement.

The measures to be developed will, as a rule, consist of either general or industry-specific actions (see Figure 8.7). The general actions, based on universal management skills, relate to the areas of value creation (e.g. introduction of incentive systems), and functionality (e.g. stabilising the existing business, designing the corporate structure). The industry-specific actions – requiring industry knowledge – fall within the areas of the vision (e.g. developing an inspiring vision and strategy for growth) and, once more, of value creation (e.g. redesigning sales structures, transferring best practice through benchmarking in production).

	General actions	Industry-specific actions
Vision		• Develop/refine core-competence-based vision • Develop inspiring strategy for growth
Value creation	• Introduce value-based management and KPI systems • Introduce incentive systems	• Redesign marketing and sales structures • Develop site strategy • Introduce benchmarking and continuous improvement process in production • Develop 'customer-oriented' service units (e.g.,maintenance)
Functionality	• Stabilise current business (esp. marketing/sales) • Design corporate structure • Select personnel • Develop HR systems • Align IT systems	

Figure 8.7 Examples of general and industry-specific actions
Note: KPI = Key performances indicator.
Source: McKinsey.

Develop a shared vision and a value-creating strategy for growth. Announcing the *future direction* of the company at an early stage in the integration phase is important for two reasons: a clear, forward-looking vision prevents uncertainty in the organisation and ensures the motivation of the employees from day one, which contributes significantly towards ensuring that talent remains within the company. In addition, the firm intention of taking a new direction sends a very clear message to the capital markets. The merging companies should critically analyse their core competences and then develop an inspiring strategy for growth, which also means getting rid of businesses that do not fit.

An example of this clear separation of core business and those which do not fit in with the new strategy occurred in the merger of VEBA AG and VIAG AG. On the day that the merger was announced,[4] both the core businesses (energy and chemicals), and those which were being put up for sale (e.g. VAW, Stinnes), were named. Clear visions were laid out for the two core businesses. It was announced that the energy segment (consisting of oil, electricity, gas and water pre-merger) would be expanded in the long term into a multi-utility company that would operate right across Europe. The chemicals segment was to be streamlined to give a stronger focus on specialties.

Identify operational potential. Since the success of a merger is ultimately measured in terms of the *value generated* (the total return to shareholders, for example), two questions have to be addressed when formulating overall targets:

- Will the total synergies be sufficient to fulfil the owners' expectations?
- Are all value-creating opportunities (including 'stand-alone potentials') being taken into account?

The overall targets can be derived in one of two ways: they can either be developed 'top-down' by corporate management based on a comparison with the best companies in the industry, or 'bottom-up' by the individual project teams. A comparison of different integration programmes has shown that pure examples of these options are very rare in practice. Usually, a diluted form of the 'top-down' variety prevails, in which the companies' leadership team formulates targets in close cooperation with the management.

In some cases, particularly where the merger is not yet legally complete, the process of ascertaining synergy potentials is hampered by the fact that the companies cannot or do not want to exchange customer information (prices, for example). Bringing in neutral 'clean teams'[5] to prepare internal data for evaluation can save a significant amount of time here.

Once the targets have been finalised, they are often presented to the financial market in summary form right at the start of the merger (see Table 8.2).[6]

The value-creation potential can be divided into two categories: directly business-related opportunities and those created by new management systems. The former can be described easily along a simplified business system:

Table 8.2 Synergy Potentials: DaimlerChrysler merger, EUR million

Item	1999	From 2001
Purchasing	900	2700
Total integration of financial services	360	900
Research and technology, platform integration	180	900
Sales infrastructure	540	540
Increased sales volume	540	1350
Total	**2520**	**6390**

Increase purchasing competences: Not only the amount, but the speed with which purchasing potentials are realised is often of importance. The main levers here are to:

- Select the most *cost-effective supplier*
- Obtain *discounts* based on higher volumes
- *Redesign purchasing processes* and transfer best practice
- Get *management attention* during integration.

The savings potentials depend to a great extent on the category of material, the volumes purchased and the purchasing skills already available at the merging companies. In the case of companies of equal size with average purchasing skills, the total savings potential can be around 15–25 per cent of the purchasing volume. On the other hand, if the size of the companies differs greatly and both have highly developed purchasing skills, the total savings potential may be only around 4–6 per cent.

Optimise production and technology: There are essentially three types of savings levers in the operational areas:

- *Develop a long-term site strategy*: When companies of equal size merge the number of production sites generally doubles, and consequently so does complexity. The restructuring potential from site closures is therefore very important. Indicators of a high value-creation potential are similar production facilities with overcapacities, high administration costs for each site and redundant research facilities.
- *Optimise production facilities through know-how transfer*: A merger enables two former competitors to exchange their technical know-how. This can be particularly effective if they have comparable production facilities or processes, when benchmarking on the basis of a 'virtual plant' derived from the sum of cost leaders in each of the areas ('best of best') represents an excellent way of identifying performance potentials. With the help of the individual cost leaders, each production manager can develop ideas for improving operational performance along his or her particular process. Furthermore, a continuous improvement process should be introduced in which the future cost structure

is no longer orientated towards the 'achievable' but rather towards what is technically possible ('theoretical limit'). This means determining the *core costs* for each step of the process and setting them as the target parameter.

- *Introduce new service concepts*: When products and sites are restructured, the role of services is often considered as well. Do they form part of the core business, or can they be contracted out? In the chemical industry, for example, there has been a trend in recent years to bundle services – e.g. energy supply, maintenance, or logistics – within independent service companies (e.g. Infraserv at Hoechst, Infracor at Degussa). An integration project is the ideal time to introduce a new concept for services, because they are being consolidated and integrated as part of the process in any case. A new corporate infrastructure makes it possible for companies to focus on their actual core business and bundles competences while introducing a service mentality. Moreover, at some sites the infrastructure unit can also serve other companies, thus further 'diluting' fixed costs. Creating an independent service unit also makes it much easier to sell individual businesses in a tightly knit production structure such as that in the chemical industry. It is for this reason that a number of independent companies are always found at sites where chemical companies are clustered.

Strengthen marketing and sales: The combination of marketing and sales activities represents the most sensitive area of the entire merger, as these activities directly affect the customer:

- In the first few months following a merger, new companies are often observed to be losing market share. This is because the entire organisation has a strong inward focus at such times, competitors may well be enticing away top-performing sales staff and the resulting larger company may have gained a dominant supplier position for certain customers. To avoid losing revenues, the merged enterprise must act quickly to communicate openly with customers and employees.
- In order to realise the value-creation potentials, companies have to consolidate their customer bases and sales organisations worldwide and develop a new sales platform. Here, they should not be content to adopt the best of the existing systems but should also consider new sales structures – reorganising, for example, according to market and customer segments, developing consistent pricing tools, or introducing e-business.

Reduce administration/overhead functions: Creating slimmer corporate administration functions is probably where the most well-known value-creation potential lies. An important factor in reorganising and redimensioning corporate units is to define what they should *actually do*. It is essential to analyse the value the corporate centre should deliver in future. This is closely linked with the organisational structure, which can range from that of a financial holding company through to an 'operational' corporate centre at the other extreme. Redimensioning should always be based on a comparison with best industry practice.

In addition to business-related opportunities, the value-creation potential in new leadership and management systems has recently been gaining prominence. An important lever here is *value-based management*, which sets clear goals based on key performance indicators (KPIs) with a direct link to value improvement. An analysis of the different parameters has shown that the difference between the Return on Capital Employed (ROCE) and the Weighted Average Cost of Capital (WACC) as well as the growth potential are the decisive variables here. These need to be elaborated in detail for the individual businesses and linked to the parameters in everyday use in the business units (e.g. price, volume, conversion factors, inventory level) in a way which makes their own impact on the business clear to the employees concerned. The power of this controlling system can be enhanced by basing a new incentive system on achieving the targets for the individual levers.

Safeguard the existing business and future functionality. Among the many actions which have to be carried out without delay, safeguarding the functionality of the new company is the most important. The merging companies have to choose their new organisational form and appoint the managers at an early stage. Furthermore, all systems (e.g. information technology (IT), finance and accounting, personnel systems – in particular wages and salaries) need to be redesigned and implemented. Depending on the type and scope of the merger, this action programme will often comprise more than a thousand activities, starting with the legal completion of the merger and ranging from legal empowerment of managers to act for the company to the appointment of health, environment and safety officers.

Determine the new form of organisation: If both companies already have similar structures, as was the case with VEBA AG and VIAG AG (both of them financial holding companies), determining the new organisational form will not be a problem. In cases where the forms differ, the companies have to decide on which one will be best for the business. An example of this was the merger of Degussa AG and Hüls AG. Prior to the merger, Hüls AG was being run as a slim chemical holding group with 12 independent companies. Degussa, on the other hand, was running its three business segments under a single parent company supported by very strong corporate centre divisions. During the merger, both structures were evaluated and it was decided to operate the new company (Degussa-Hüls) as a decentralised parent company with four business segments and one service unit.

The question of the *organisational form* – i.e. how globally or regionally businesses should be run – also arises at the lower level of the business units. Here, depending on the type of business, all the functions within the business system (research and development (R&D), production, marketing and sales) have to be analysed for synergies across a number of business lines, and the question of whether the business activities can be run globally has to be examined. If they can, the relevant decisions for all business lines should be made on the business unit level.

This analysis can therefore lead to an ultimate organisational structure consisting of a wide variety of organisational forms for individual business units.

Select personnel: Once the organisational form and the corresponding positions have been defined, the managers have to be appointed. The entire managing board including the CEO are almost always appointed at the start of the merger. The second and subsequent levels are often not staffed at that point, and are also more difficult to fill as the board members are familiar only with the managers from their own companies. The aim here should be to build up a new 'high-performance organisation' as quickly as possible in order to reduce uncertainty within the companies. Depending on the management culture, the appointments can be made either by 'top-down' decisions by the managing board, or by using a structured selection process. To ensure that the latter is as fair and transparent as possible, it should be communicated openly. Each company should nominate two or three candidates for each position and these candidates should then be interviewed by their future supervisor and by the human resources director in a defined interview process. Candidates should be selected by the entire interview group. Ideally, the decision should be independent of the company to which the person previously belonged, and should be based on purely objective criteria. The involvement of an independent human resources consultant to increase neutrality in the decision-making process has also proved beneficial in many cases. The decision on the successful candidates should be made and announced within the company as soon as possible. The unsuccessful candidates should receive individual feedback with a personal strengths-and-weaknesses analysis, and if possible new positions should be found for them within the new company. Although this process creates 'runners-up', it is considered by all those involved to be fair and correct. As a by-product, this selection process creates a standardised database for assessing the top management team, in which the first 50 to 100 top performers are entered and appraised.

Create a Shared Performance Culture

The programmes and concepts described so far relate solely to the 'structural' side of the merger. They do not take into account the 'personal perspectives' of the managers affected on how the company should work and on the right style of interaction. The new enterprise has to bring together these very different perspectives, but take care not to achieve an excessively high level of consensus at the expense of its high aspirations.

Understand the individual perspectives. The concepts are as good only as the people who carry them out. Their success depends in essence on three factors: first, the individuals' own aspiration levels and goals; second, their interpretation of the existing opportunities and their freedom to act on them; and third, their identification with the task in hand. A useful practical technique for capturing and evaluating these factors for each individual is *deep structure interviewing*. Unlike the usual type of interview, this does not stick to purely factual questions but tries to uncover people's real motivation – i.e. not only the objective but also the often very personal reasons for their actions and attitudes. A typical example occurs when decisions have to be taken on business unit organisation and the business lines to be included in each unit. These are not always governed by pure 'business logic', but often also by an individual's personal need to integrate highly profitable areas into his or her own area of responsibility to cover up weaknesses in the overall portfolio.

The aim of the interview is to understand the individual's personal attitudes along the dimensions of 'what is to be done' (e.g. vision, value creation, functionality) and 'how to do it' (e.g. control, motivation).

Develop a shared perspective among the leadership team. By comparing the interview results, initial hypotheses can be formed about the strengths and weaknesses within the organisation and about those areas where the management team members might have different attitudes. These points should be made transparent in 'consensus workshops' with the leadership team and discussed to find solutions. One proven method to create transparency is the *consensor technique*, where each participant has the opportunity to answer questions anonymously. The answers to the questions are displayed immediately on a screen so that the workshop participants can see the group's opinions straight away. Depending on the scope of the question, the result is discussed in further depth by the whole group or by subgroups. At the end of the workshop the results of the discussion are presented again for discussion and agreement, once more using the consensor approach. If approved, they are adopted; if opinions still differ, they are passed on to a project team which attempts to find a solution. They are then reassessed at a later point in time.

Figure 8.8 shows this procedure for one business unit in a big merger. In preparation for the first consensus workshop, all managers were interviewed. The opinions of the group on critical points were then collected in the workshop using the consensor technique. In this case, there was no consensus in the group on the question of a shared vision. The subsequent discussions showed that no agreement could be reached at the first workshop. In the weeks that followed, a project team consisting of a selection of senior managers from the unit therefore went on working on this subject and presented the results to the entire management team at the second workshop. The convincing representation of the vision with a clearly formulated strategy for growth led to overwhelming acceptance within the management group. This procedure ensures full support from the management team throughout the entire integration phase.

Phase II: Execute Integration

At the end of the design phase, the new company will have created a framework with all the important targets as well as some major constraints, such as the time frame for integration. The projects needed to achieve these targets are started at the beginning of the phase II. A rough outline of the project's organisational structure – for example the integration board, the integration office and the main project clusters (e.g. communication) – is often drawn up as early as the design phase. This structure will be refined (i.e. divided into projects and subprojects) at the beginning of phase II.

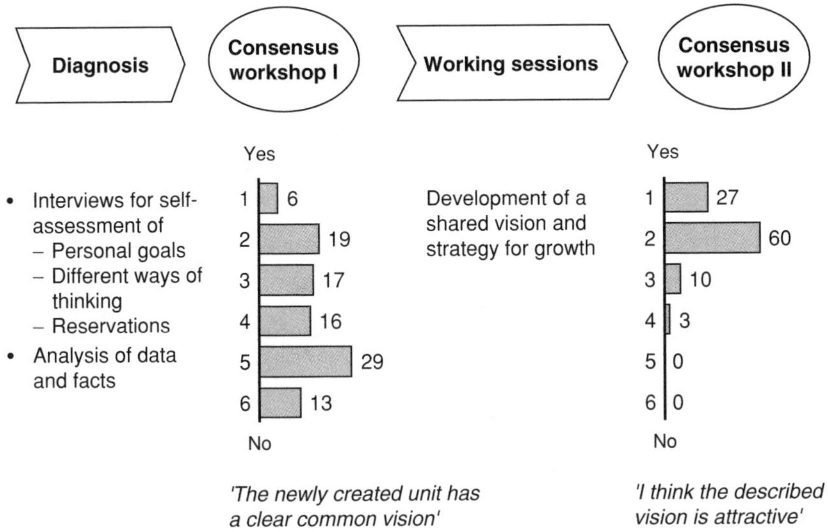

Figure 8.8 Procedure for achieving a shared perspective, result of management survey, in per cent
Source: McKinsey.

Prioritise the Project Portfolio

The project portfolio is prioritised and resources allocated on the basis of the targets set by the management team. Every project to develop the vision, realise the full value-generation potential and ensure the effective operation of the new business should be ranked on a matrix along the 'scope of the expected change' and 'expected value creation' axes (see Figure 8.9).

A dedicated, independent project team should be assigned by the management of those projects where high value-creation is combined with major change. The remaining projects should be supervised by the integration office.

Develop the Project Organisation

Controlling the number and complexity of the individual projects demands a structured project organisation with clearly defined roles and responsibilities. A *three-layer structure* has proved sufficient for smaller companies with a limited number of product groups and with revenues of around EUR 500 million. With the larger 'mega-mergers', however, a *four-layer structure* works better (see Figure 8.10).

In the case of a smaller integration project, the project organisation should consist of an *integration board* as the overall *steering committee* for the merger, an *integration office* to manage the project and *project teams* which work out the specific actions to be taken. Practical experience in mega-mergers has shown that the various actions developed by up to 250 project teams cannot be validated by the integration board alone. For this reason, *dedicated steering committees* are set

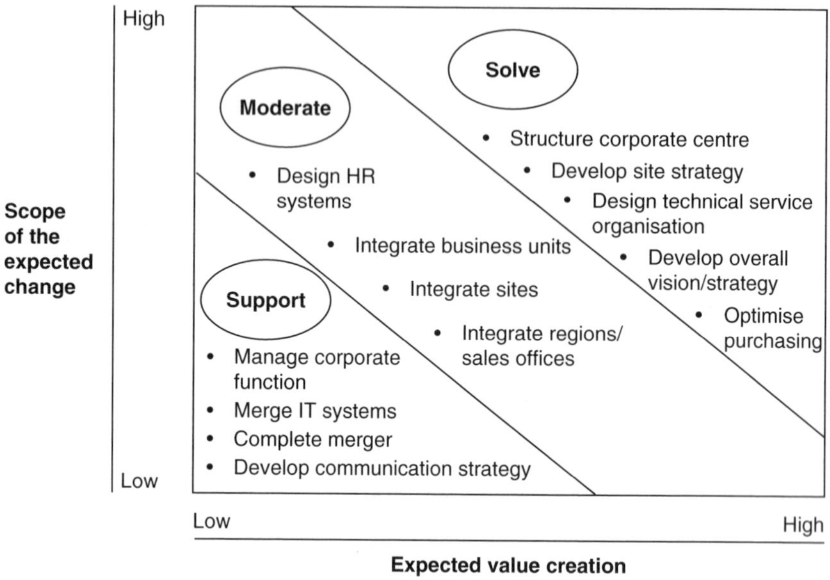

Figure 8.9 Prioritisation of project portfolio
Source: McKinsey.

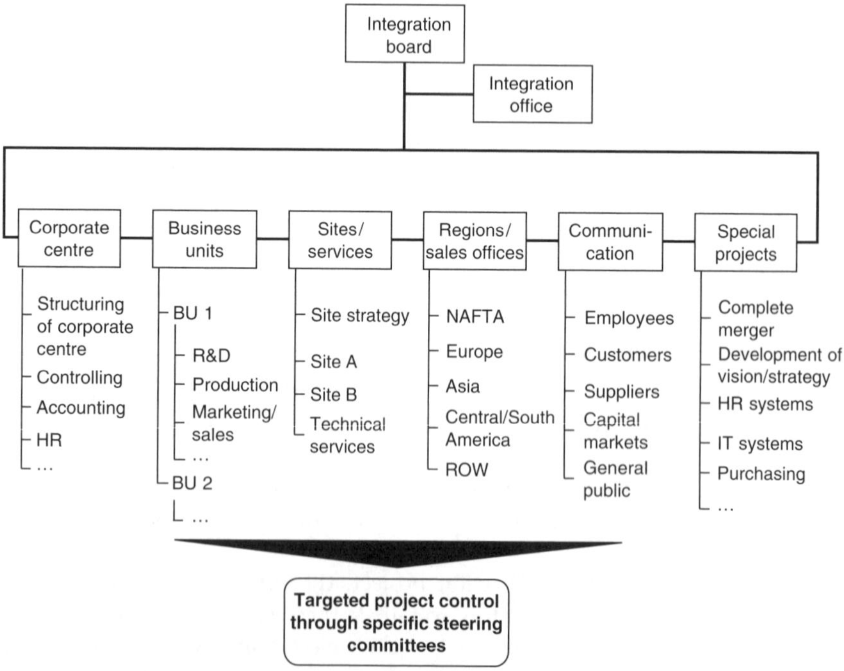

Figure 8.10 Project organisation
Note: BU = Business units
Source: McKinsey.

up to approve proposed sub-project actions, for example, ways to integrate individual business units or the purchasing function. The various projects should be clustered according to topics (project clusters) in order to make external and internal communication easier.

Role of the integration board: Depending on the scope of the integration activities, the integration board should consist of between two and four executive board members from the new company, staffed if possible in equal proportions by members of the pre-merger firms. The executive board members involved should be responsible for human resources, finance and some operational areas, to ensure that they cover a wide range. The fundamental task of the integration board is to set the direction and guidelines for the individual project teams, allocate the necessary human and financial resources and approve actions that will help achieve the objectives formulated in the design phase. It is important here to handle the project teams on the basis of hard facts, and to ensure that the same party does not always prevail. The integration board sessions should take place weekly in the first six months, with some unexpected meetings at short notice in the initial phase. The integration board and the CEO should be very actively involved in the whole integration process and represent a kind of role model. This includes actively participating in communication, e.g. by visiting sites and holding presentations or 'question-and-answer' sessions.

Role of the steering committees: In mega-mergers, steering committees are specifically assigned to individual projects. Two managing board members are sufficient here, one of whom should be responsible for the new area in the future. In contrast to the weekly meetings of the integration board, the steering committees need meet only once every three to five weeks to track the progress of the teams.

Role of the integration office: Again depending on the scope of the integration, the integration office should consist of four to six staff members who have been released to work on the project full-time. One of them should be appointed as the project leader. Here, too, appointments are made on the principle of equal proportions from the pre-merger companies if possible. The members of the integration office should be managers with a high standing within both organisations. The main task of this body is to control the merger overall and to prepare recommendations that will enable the integration board and the steering committees to take the best decisions. This involves the development and management of a master plan including the *critical path for the merger*, in which all the goals, responsibilities, the current status and the deadlines are set out. In addition to pure process control, the integration office frequently also assumes the function of a court of arbitration in moderating difficult questions such as finding a new form of organisation for individual areas. In the case of large, complex mergers the integration office can be supported by an additional integration team and external consultants.

Role of project teams: The individual project teams are the 'cells of the merger' (e.g. controlling, purchasing). They come up with the actions to safeguard functionality and create value, as well as ensuring that various areas such as research and development are aligned with the new company's vision. Project teams should consist of two to six staff members, again appointed in equal proportions from the former organisations, with the exact number depending on the complexity and urgency of the project. Each project team leader should be the future head of the division in question. Great demands are placed on the project teams over the course of the integration project, as their members have to handle their day-to-day work as well as their integration activities. Each team draws up a so-called 'team charter', on the basis of goals formulated in the consensus workshops and of the guidelines issued by the relevant steering committee and the integration board. This charter outlines the team members, the goals, current progress in the three areas of functionality, value-creation and vision as well as the deadlines and the problems which have arisen.

Project clusters: The following basic structure has proved useful when forming project clusters:

- *Corporate centre*: a structural project defines the design of the corporate centre and the associated processes regulating the interaction between the business units, the regional organisations and the corporate functions. The detailed design of the corporate functions (e.g. controlling, accounting) is carried out by the units themselves in accordance with general guidelines provided.
- *Business units*: all the business units affected by the merger are covered in these projects. The business units are further divided up along the business system into subprojects such as R&D, production, etc. where the actions to be taken in the areas of functionality, value-creation and vision are developed.
- *Sites/services*: the integration of neighbouring sites has to take place in close collaboration with the business units. Here, a strategic project with a long-term view should develop the site strategy and evaluate possible site closures. Targeted individual projects at neighbouring sites should identify the value-creation potentials which would result from shared services.
- *Regions/sales offices*: in addition to the production sites, all sales offices and distributors have to be consolidated in the various countries. It has proved useful to consolidate or redesign the sales structure country by country on a regional basis.
- *Communication*: particular attention should be devoted to overall project communication. A project team which is assigned specifically to this task should deal with all interest groups: employees, customers and suppliers, the capital markets, and the general public (see Figure 8.11).
- *Special projects*: these deal with the management of all overarching projects such as the legal execution of the merger, the development of the vision and strategies, the standardisation of systems (HR and IT) as well as the realisation of purchasing potentials at corporate level.

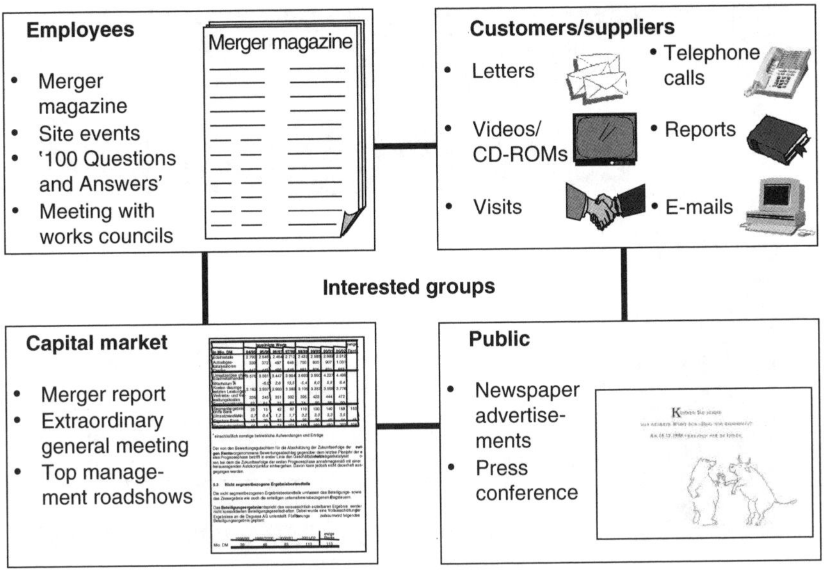

Figure 8.11 Communication strategy
Source: McKinsey.

Implement Project Control

The first task of project controlling is to track the goals and the current status of individual project teams ('team charter') individually in order to generate the merger's master plan. Its second task is to check on the actions taken, a process which brings together all the actions developed at corporate level and monitors in detail whether value-generation is on target in each project cluster at the individual project level. In large integration projects encompassing several thousand actions, it has proved useful to employ a team to monitor the implementation of the actions together with the subsections. Many companies nowadays have an *intranet platform* which can be used to make the status of action development and implementation at the individual project level accessible to a selected group of people within the company, to foster implementation through 'peer pressure' (see Figure 8.12). This also allows open communication within the management team on how well the goals are being achieved. The use of such a broad medium of communication, however, or even its extension to the Internet, should be critically examined and jointly approved in advance by the management team.

5 Basic Rules for Successful Integration

In summary, it can be said that although the procedure described above can be applied to all integration projects, each one has its own individual character. This

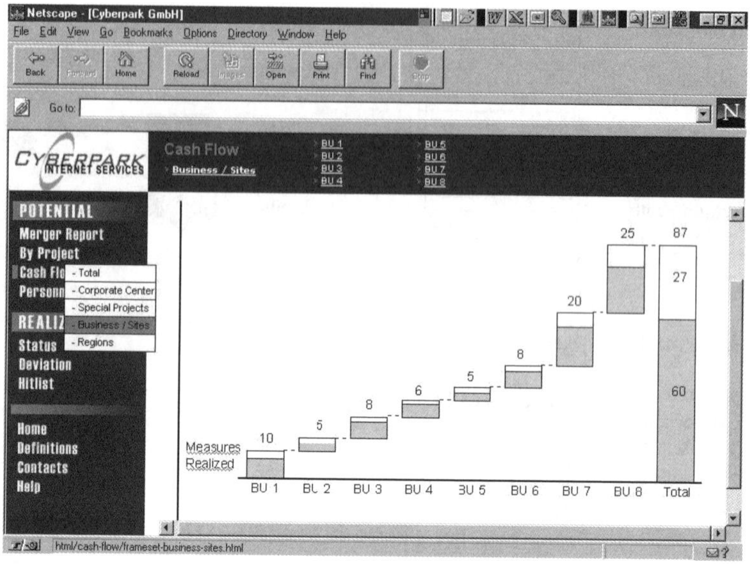

Figure 8.12 The intranet as a controlling medium
Source: McKinsey.

is partly determined by the context in which the merger takes place – such as the industry, the region, or the cultures of the companies concerned – but also partly by the new management team. Every company should therefore go its own way down the path to integration, but should always take the following principles into account:

1. Secure *functionality* to protect current business
2. Focus on *value-creation,* not just integration
3. Develop a *new, shared vision*
4. Develop a *new, shared performance culture*
5. Utilise the merger as an opportunity to *revive the company*
6. Exploit the *momentum* in the first 90 days after the announcement
7. Put *speed before perfection*
8. Do not make *personnel concessions* at the cost of *content*
9. Make *top management* drive the integration process
10. *Communicate openly and quickly.*

Notes

1 Comparison of development relative to the sector index or the competition three years before and three years after the merger.
2 Möller (1983)
3 Industry survey, McKinsey (1998, 1999)
4 Joint press conference by VEBA and VIAG (27 September 1999).
5 'Clean team': neutral team, without employees from the companies involved.
6 General meeting of shareholders of Daimler–Benz AG, (18 September 1998).

Bibliography

Möller, W.-P. (1983) Der Erfolg von Unternehmenszusammenschlüssen – Eine empirische Untersuchung, Dissertation Universität, Saarbrücken.

9

Restructuring with Mergers and Acquisitions

Gerhard Picot

1 General Aspects Concerning Implementation, Integration and Restructuring Measures

Nine aspects are of particular significance for implementation, integration, and restructuring measures during M.A activity:

- Determination of the *business goal* for the implementation, integration and restructuring measures
- Examination of the *formation possibilities* particularly considering their business and legal standards and effects
- Development of the implementation, integration and restructuring *strategies* necessary for business operations
- Determination of the conditions of the *legal framework* for the realisation of the transaction or restructuring concept
- Analysis of the *structure of the management* as well as the *affected personnel* and inclusion of all directly affected employees, in particular with regard to time in the business and age, family status, maternity rights, membership in the works council and severe handicap
- Determination of the *planning time period* and the necessary personnel, production and administrative capacity following the transaction or restructuring
- Calculation of the *internal and external costs* for the transfer or restructuring, including respective social compensation plan costs
- Drafting of a corporate *value-oriented compensation* model
- Drafting of a *detailed time and events plan* for the implementation, integration and restructuring, particularly considering conditions of the
  - Statutory framework for the rights of employees as well as
  - Service (members of management) and employment contracts, including individual and collective conditions under employment law,
  - Possible social measures necessary – such as, for example relocation, outplacement, etc.

2 Legal Basics regarding the Implementation of M&A

With M&As arise basic legal questions with the implementation of the transactions. Substantial explanations of the conversion-capable companies and conversion types (consolidation, splitting, asset transfer and change in form) as well as of the procedure for conversions are discussed in chapter 4.

3 Legal Obligation to Instruct, Inform and Consult

National Legislation

Under most national legislation, employers have to instruct, inform and consult with the representatives of the employees concerning the implementation, integration and (individual) restructuring measures.

European Law

Under European law, the obligation of the employers to inform employee representatives derives from Part III Article 6 of the Council Directive 98/50/EC of the European Union of 29 June 1998, amending Directive 77/187/EEC on the approximation of the laws of the member states relating to the safeguarding of employees' rights in the event of transfers of undertakings, businesses or parts of businesses.[1] The primary regulatory goal of this directive lies in the fact that, according to Part II, Article 3, the transferor's rights and obligations arising from a contract of employment or from an employment relationship existing on the date of a transfer shall be transferred to the transferee by reason of any transfer of an undertaking, business or part of an undertaking or business to another employer as a result of a legal transfer or merger, if there is a transfer of an economic entity which retains its identity, meaning an organised grouping of resources which has the objective of pursuing an economic activity, whether or not that activity is central or ancillary. Moreover, Part III Article 6 determines for members that information, consultation and participation for workers must be developed along appropriate lines, taking account of the practices in force in the various member states, and must be implemented in due time, particularly in connection with restructuring operations in undertakings or in cases of mergers having an impact on the employment of workers.

On the whole, the Directive holds that also for a simple transfer of ownership, in principal an obligation to inform exists. In member states in which employment contracts can call for a settlement committee or board of arbitration, according to Article 6 III of the Directive, the possibility exists to limit the information to the case in which the completed transfer causes a change in business that can have significant disadvantages for a considerable number of employees.

Aside from the question of information, concerning the implementation of a restructuring it is important to determine how much the employer must consult with the works' council on individual restructuring measures. An obligation of the employer for consultation again results from the applied Community Law, in particular from the European Council Directive 98/59/EC of 20 July 1998, amending Council Directive 75/129/EEC of 17 February 1975 on the approximation of the laws of the member states relating to collective redundancies, or from the national framework for employee rights.

4 Business Alterations

In regards to planned alterations in business under a number of national legislations it must fundamentally be differentiated

- Whether the business or part of the business that is to be transferred will *remain unchanged in its identity*, or
- Whether its *structure will be altered*.

Usually the transfer of a business that on the whole remains unchanged is not subject to the co-determination of the employees. With the transfer of a part of a business or with planned alterations to a business, in contrast, the company is obligated, under numerous national jurisdictions, to inform employee representatives in a timely and comprehensive manner about the planned alterations to the business or the restructuring, and to consult with them about the intended plans.

The goal of the consultation is to achieve a balance of interests and the conclusion of a social compensation plan. This concerns two different legal agreements between which, however, close interactions occur and which therefore must often be negotiated together.

The balance of interests concerns the questions of

- Whether
- When, and
- How

the planned measures will be implemented.

The social compensation plan should decrease economic disadvantages that can result for employees from the alterations in the business.

Types of Alterations in Business

The co-determination rights of the employees' representatives are to be observed with the implementation and integration measures if the intended plans present a change in business. For this reason during the planning of the transaction the question should be addressed whether considerable alterations in the existing operating structures are necessary for the integration or implementation. Such alterations include:

- *Limitation and shutdown* of the entire business or of significant parts of the business
- *Relocation* of the entire business or significant parts of the business
- *Merger* with other businesses or the splitting of businesses

- Basic changes to the business *organisation*, the *purpose* of the business or the *facilities*
- Introduction of *basic new working methods and production procedures*.

Limitation and Shutdown of the Entire Business or Significant Parts of the Business

The business purpose of a shutdown entails the dissolution of the organisational entity and the discharge of staff on the basis of a serious and final decision of the company. Such shutdown must occur for an undetermined and in terms of business a not insignificant period of time. If the business is reopened after a relatively not insignificant time by the current or new owner, no shutdown has occurred but rather a disruption in service as well as possibly a transfer of business, as defined by the Council Directive 98/50/EC of 29 June 1998, amending Directive 77/187/EEC on the approximation of the laws of the member states relating to the safeguarding of employees' rights in the event of transfers of undertakings, businesses or parts of businesses.[2]

A pure lay-off of the workforce while retaining business resources can also represent an alteration in business. This will always have to be assumed if the scope of the lay-off reaches certain proportions, because only in this case is a significant portion of staff affected.

Relocation of the Entire Business or of Significant Parts of the Business

A relocation of the business is understood if a significant change in geographical location is planned. The change is thus significant if substantial disadvantages can occur for the employees. It is insignificant whether the changes can be implemented under civil law on the basis of the right to give instructions or of the notice of a change. A relocation can also lead to a shutdown if the production department is dissolved and significant parts of the employees are not employed at the new location. Whether in this case a transfer of the enterprises, businesses or parts of businesses has occurred for the employees who wish to work at the new location is doubtful if the ownership changes simultaneously.

Merger with Other Businesses or the Splitting of Businesses

A merger or splitting of *businesses* cannot be compared to the merger (or combination/consolidation) or the splitting of *corporations*. If the identity of the businesses to which the consolidated or split corporations belong remains unchanged, there is no alteration in business.

Basic Changes in Business Organisation, Purpose or Facilities; Introduction of New Working Methods and Production Procedures

Situations of basic changes in business organisation, purpose or in facilities as well as the introduction of fundamentally new working methods and production procedures are, within the framework of transactions, usually of a subordinate nature. When changes in the organisational structure are executed, these are mostly only the consequence of the other above-mentioned kinds of alteration in business.

The Legal Consequences of Alterations in Business

Regarding the legal consequences of an alteration in business, as a rule, according to national jurisdictions, it is to be differentiated between the instruction and information of the employees' representatives and the consultation with the employees' representatives, in particular the negotiation and agreement on a balance of interests and a social compensation plan.

The Council Directive 98/50/EC of 29 June 1998, amending Directive 77/187/EEC on the approximation of the laws of the member states relating to the safeguarding of employees' rights in the event of transfers of undertakings, businesses or parts of businesses[3] contains under Section III Article 6 the obligation of the employers to inform and consult the representatives of the employees (see below):

The respective part of the Council Directive 98/50/EC of 29 June 1998 reads as follows:

Section III

Article 6

Information and Consultation

1. The transferor and transferee shall be required to inform the representatives of their respective employees affected by the transfer of the following:
   - the date or proposed date of the transfer,
   - the reasons for the transfer,
   - the legal, economic and social implications of the transfer for the employees,
   - any measures envisaged in relation to the employees.

   The transferor must give such information to the representatives of his employees in good time before the transfer is carried out and, in any event, before his employees are directly affected by the transfer as regards their conditions of work and employment.
2. Where the transferor or the transferee envisages measures in relation to his employees, he shall consult the representatives of his employees in good time on such measures with a view to reaching an agreement.
3. Member States whose laws, regulations or administrative provisions provide that representatives of the employees may have recourse to an arbitration board to obtain a decision on the measures to be taken in relation to employees may limit the obligations laid down in paragraphs 1 and 2 to cases where the transfer arried out gives rise to a change in the business likely to entail serious disadvantages for a considerable number of the employees.

   The information and consultations shall cover at least the measures envisaged in relation to the employees.

   The information must be provided and consultations take place in good time before the change in the business as referred to in the first subparagraph is effected.

4. The obligations laid down in this Article shall apply irrespective of whether the decision resulting in the transfer is taken by the employer or a company controlling the employer.
3. In considering alleged breaches of the information and consultation requirements laid down by this Directive, the argument that such a breach occurred because the information was not provided by a company controlling the employer shall not be accepted as an excuse.
5. Member States may limit the obligations laid down in paragraphs 1, 2 and 3 to enterprises or businesses that, in terms of the number of employees, meet the conditions for the election or nomination of a collegiate body representing the employees.
6. Member States shall provide that, where there are no representatives of the employees in an enterprise or business through no fault of their own, the employees concerned must be informed in advance of:
   - the date or proposed date of the transfer,
   - the reason for the transfer,
   - the legal, economic and social implications of the transfer for the employees,
   - any measures envisaged in relation to the employees.

SECTION IV

Article 7

Final Provisions

This Directive shall not affect the right of Member States to apply or introduce laws, regulations or administrative provisions which are more favorable to employees or to promote or permit collective agreements or agreements between social partners more favourable to employees.

Article 7a

Member States shall introduce into their national legal systems such measures as are necessary to enable all employees and representatives of employees who consider themselves wronged by failure to comply with the obligations arising from this Directive to pursue their claims by judicial process after possible recourse to other competent authorities.

With the instruments mentioned employee representatives are given the opportunity upon changes in business to influence the decision-making of the company. In the end the employer is left with the decision about the implementation, integration and restructuring and the employees' representatives cannot – in contrast to the conclusion of a social compensation plan – enforce a balancing of interests. Nevertheless, the employer may begin with the complete or only partial realisation of the changes in business only after he has concluded a (sincere) effort to reach a balance of interests. Such a sincere effort is given only if the employer has considered the entire legal process of the balancing of interests with all stages of negotiation – even if unsuccessfully.

5 Collective Redundancies

National Legislation

In the case of business-related notifications – and, in particular, of mass lay-offs – the relevant national legal system is first to be followed.

European Law

Moreover, the European Council Directive 98/59/EC of 20 July 1998 contains provisions on the approximation of the laws of the member states of the European Community relating to collective redundancies.[4]

This **European Council Directive 98/59/EC of 20 July 1998 reads as follows:**

THE COUNCIL OF THE EUROPEAN UNION,
Having regard to the Treaty establishing the European Community, and in particular Article 100 thereof,
Having regard to the proposal from the Commission,
Having regard to the opinion of the European Parliament (1),
Having regard to the opinion of the Economic and Social Committee (2),

(1) Whereas for reasons of clarity and rationality Council Directive 75/129/EEC of 17 February 1975 on the approximation of the laws of the Member States relating to collective redundancies (3) should be consolidated;
(2) Whereas it is important that greater protection should be afforded to workers in the event of collective redundancies while taking into account the need for balanced economic and social development within the Community;
(3) Whereas, despite increasing convergence, differences still remain between the provisions in force in the Member States concerning the practical arrangements and procedures for such redundancies and the measures designed to alleviate the consequences of redundancy for workers;
(4) Whereas these differences can have a direct effect on the functioning of the internal market;
(5) Whereas the Council resolution of 21 January 1974 concerning a social action programme (4) made provision for a directive on the approximation of Member States' legislation on collective redundancies;
(6) Whereas the Community Charter of the fundamental social rights of workers, adopted at the European Council meeting held in Strasbourg on 9 December 1989 by the Heads of State or Government of 11 Member States, states, inter alia, in point 7, first paragraph, first sentence, and second paragraph; in point 17, first paragraph; and in point 18, third indent:

7. The completion of the internal market must lead to an improvement in the living and working conditions of workers in the European Community (...).

   The improvement must cover, where necessary, the development of certain aspects of employment regulations such as procedures for collective redundancies and those regarding bankruptcies. (...)

17. Information, consultation and participation for workers must be developed along appropriate lines, taking account of the practices in force in the various Member States.

   (...)

18. Such information, consultation and participation must be implemented in due time, particularly in the following cases:

   (–...)

   – in cases of collective redundancy procedures;

   (–...);

(7) Whereas this approximation must therefore be promoted while the improvement is being maintained within the meaning of Article 117 of the Treaty;

(8) Whereas, in order to calculate the number of redundancies provided for in the definition of collective redundancies within the meaning of this Directive, other forms of termination of employment contracts on the initiative of the employer should be equated to redundancies, provided that there are at least five redundancies;

(9) Whereas it should be stipulated that this Directive applies in principle also to collective redundancies resulting where the establishment's activities are terminated as a result of a judicial decision;

(10) Whereas the Member States should be given the option of stipulating that workers' representatives may call on experts on grounds of the technical complexity of the matters which are likely to be the subject of the informing and consulting;

(11) Whereas it is necessary to ensure that employers' obligations as regards information, consultation and notification apply independently of whether the decision on collective redundancies emanates from the employer or from an undertaking which controls that employer;

(12) Whereas Member States should ensure that workers' representatives and/or workers have at their disposal administrative and/or judicial procedures in order to ensure that the obligations laid down in this Directive are fulfilled;

(13) Whereas this Directive must not affect the obligations of the Member States concerning the deadlines for transposition of the Directives set out in Annex I, Part B,

HAS ADOPTED THIS DIRECTIVE:

SECTION I

Definitions and scope

Article 1

1. For the purposes of this Directive:

   (a) 'collective redundancies' means dismissals effected by an employer for one or more reasons not related to the individual workers concerned where, according to the choice of the Member States, the number of redundancies is:

   (i) either, over a period of 30 days:
   - at least 10 in establishments normally employing more than 20 and less than 100 workers,
   - at least 10 per cent of the number of workers in establishments normally employing at least 100 but less than 300 workers,
   - at least 30 in establishments normally employing 300 workers or more,

   (ii) or, over a period of 90 days, at least 20, whatever the number of workers normally employed in the establishments in question;

   (b) 'workers' representatives' means the workers' representatives provided for by the laws or practices of the Member States.

   For the purpose of calculating the number of redundancies provided for in the first subparagraph of point (a), terminations of an employment contract which occur on the employer's initiative for one or more reasons not related to the individual workers concerned shall be assimilated to redundancies, provided that there are at least five redundancies.

2. This Directive shall not apply to:

   (a) collective redundancies effected under contracts of employment concluded for limited periods of time or for specific tasks except where such redundancies take place prior to the date of expiry or the completion of such contracts;

   (b) workers employed by public administrative bodies or by establishments governed by public law (or, in Member States where this concept is unknown, by equivalent bodies);

   (c) the crews of seagoing vessels.

SECTION II

Information and consultation

Article 2

1. Where an employer is contemplating collective redundancies, he shall begin consultations with the workers' representatives in good time with a view to reaching an agreement.
2. These consultations shall, at least, cover ways and means of avoiding collective redundancies or reducing the number of workers affected, and of mitigating

the consequences by recourse to accompanying social measures aimed, inter alia, at aid for redeploying or retraining workers made redundant.

Member States may provide that the workers' representatives may call on the services of experts in accordance with national legislation and/or practice.

3. To enable workers' representatives to make constructive proposals, the employers shall in good time during the course of the consultations:
   (a) supply them with all relevant information and
   (b) in any event notify them in writing of:
   (i) the reasons for the projected redundancies;
   (ii) the number of categories of workers to be made redundant;
   (iii) the number and categories of workers normally employed;
   (iv) the period over which the projected redundancies are to be effected;
   (v) the criteria proposed for the selection of the workers to be made redundant in so far as national legislation and/or practice confers the power therefore upon the employer;
   (vi) the method for calculating any redundancy payments other than those arising out of national legislation and/or practice.

   The employer shall forward to the competent public authority a copy of, at least, the elements of the written communication which are provided for in the first subparagraph, point (b), subpoints (i) to (v).
4. The obligations laid down in paragraphs 1, 2 and 3 shall apply irrespective of whether the decision regarding collective redundancies is being taken by the employer or by an undertaking controlling the employer.

   In considering alleged breaches of the information, consultation and notification requirements laid down by this Directive, account shall not be taken of any defence on the part of the employer on the ground that the necessary information has not been provided to the employer by the undertaking which took the decision leading to collective redundancies.

SECTION III

Procedure for collective redundancies

Article 3

1. Employers shall notify the competent public authority in writing of any projected collective redundancies.

   However, Member States may provide that in the case of planned collective redundancies arising from termination of the establishment's activities as a result of a judicial decision, the employer shall be obliged to notify the competent public authority in writing only if the latter so requests.

   This notification shall contain all relevant information concerning the projected collective redundancies and the consultations with workers' representatives provided for in Article 2, and particularly the reasons for the redundancies, the number of workers to be made redundant, the number of workers normally employed and the period over which the redundancies are to be effected.

2. Employers shall forward to the workers' representatives a copy of the notification provided for in paragraph 1.

   The workers' representatives may send any comments they may have to the competent public authority.

Article 4

1. Projected collective redundancies notified to the competent public authority shall take effect not earlier than 30 days after the notification referred to in Article 3(1) without prejudice to any provisions governing individual rights with regard to notice of dismissal.

   Member States may grant the competent public authority the power to reduce the period provided for in the preceding subparagraph.

2. The period provided for in paragraph 1 shall be used by the competent public authority to seek solutions to the problems raised by the projected collective redundancies.
3. Where the initial period provided for in paragraph 1 is shorter than 60 days, Member States may grant the competent public authority the power to extend the initial period to 60 days following notification where the problems raised by the projected collective redundancies are not likely to be solved within the initial period.

   Member States may grant the competent public authority wider powers of extension.

   The employer must be informed of the extension and the grounds for it before expiry of the initial period provided for in paragraph 1.

4. Member States need not apply this Article to collective redundancies arising from termination of the establishment's activities where this is the result of a judicial decision.

SECTION IV

Final provisions

Article 5

This Directive shall not affect the right of Member States to apply or to introduce laws, regulations or administrative provisions which are more favorable to workers or to promote or to allow the application of collective agreements more favorable to workers.

Article 6

Member States shall ensure that judicial and/or administrative procedures for the enforcement of obligations under this Directive are available to the workers' representatives and/or workers.

Article 7

Member States shall forward to the Commission the text of any fundamental provisions of national law already adopted or being adopted in the area governed by this Directive.

Article 8

1. The Directives listed in Annex I, Part A, are hereby repealed without prejudice to the obligations of the Member States concerning the deadlines for transposition of the said Directive set out in Annex I, Part B.
2. References to the repealed Directives shall be construed as references to this Directive and shall be read in accordance with the correlation table in Annex II.

Article 9

This Directive shall enter into force on the 20th day following its publication in the *Official Journal* of the European Communities.

Article 10

This Directive is addressed to the Member States.

Done at Brussels, 20 July 1998.
For the Council
The President
W. MOLTERER

(1) *OJ* C 210, 6. 7. 1998.
(2) *OJ* C 158, 26. 5. 1997, p. 11.
(3) *OJ* L 48, 22. 2. 1975, p. 29.
Directive as amended by Directive 92/56/EEC (*OJ* L 245, 26. 8. 1992, p. 3).
(4) *OJ* C 13, 12. 2. 1974, p. 1.

ANNEX I

PART A
Repealed Directives (referred to by Article 8)
Council Directive 75/129/EEC and its following amendment:
Council Directive 92/56/EEC.

PART B
Deadlines for transposition into national law (referred to by Article 8)

ANNEX II . . .

6 Corporate Value-Oriented Compensation Models

Introduction

In relation to cross-border and global takeovers and mergers, stock options and other corporate value-oriented employee compensation plans have taken on added meaning worldwide, especially since the discussion about the appropriateness of high earnings of former Chrysler managers and the required adaptation in income in the resulting DaimlerChrysler merger. Aspects of income such as company cars and security officers are today for the most part seen as normal. It is no wonder that an increasing number of mid-level and start-up companies give their employees incentives through performance-oriented compensation models, most of all in the competition for young, qualified and highly motivated college graduates.

Such compensation models demand not only motivation and creativity of the managers and other employees, but also their co-responsibility and identification with 'their' company, seeing that those benefiting are to a great degree naturally interested in an above-average development in the company's business. Many companies thus see the coupling of compensation with the efficiency of the employee and the company as an important stepping-stone in a partnership-oriented and future-oriented business culture.

Overview

In general, *employee participation* is understood as participation in the share of the capital of the employer company. Thereby, participation under corporation law or the law of obligations, on the one hand, is to be differentiated from profit-sharing participation in the form of revenue, profit or performance, on the other.

With employee participation under corporation law or the law of obligations (in the narrow sense), as a rule employees participate as shareholders, partners or lenders (e.g. silent partner, employee loan) in the capital of the employer company.

The other kinds of participation, in contrast, are paid to the employees as 'normal' additional income; for example, a percentage of profits or bonuses. The fixed income of the managers is thereby increasingly decreased to the benefit of higher variable participation.

Employee shares have long had their place with the variable income models. A disadvantage of this kind of participation is that the employees who have received the shares cannot evade the risks regarding the market price and can suffer losses in the case of a dip in the market price or in the case of insolvency.

It is different with so-called 'phantom stocks' (also stock appreciation rights or SAR), which treat the beneficiaries as if they were owners of stock in their company. This participation is thus designated as a virtual or synthetic share model. With this the employees benefiting receive no 'genuine' shares and therefore fundamentally also do not participate directly in losses. However, with a positive development in the market price they are paid in cash at a certain deadline the difference between the earlier determined strike price of the 'phantom stocks' and the actual value of the stock.

Stock Options

Among the variable income models for managers the (genuine) *stock option plan* is becoming more and more significant. Above all in the industries of telecommunications, information technology (IT) and biotechnology, managers are more tightly bound to the companies through stock option plans in which the right to exercise the option is coupled with a waiting period of many years or with membership in the company (e.g. cancellation without replacement of the option right upon resignation). In order to bind employees for longer periods of time companies accept the related high costs. Income systems with high option shares react most positively to young innovative companies that have only very thin capital covers and an increasing popularity in the competition for highly qualified managers, seeing as in this way during the initial period avoiding high fixed salaries that can burden the company. Within the framework of an initial public offering (IPO) it can be agreed upon with the issuing bank to reserve a part of the issue volume for employees.

Within the framework of a stock option plan the beneficiaries are granted options to draw a certain number of shares at a determined price (strike price) within a given time frame. The strike price is thereby often less than the value of the shares on the Stock Exchange at the time when the option is granted. The stock option plan can provide that the exercise of the option is permitted only during the existence of the contractual relationship between the employer and the employee and only after the passing of a certain binding period (vesting period) or a further waiting period. If the value of the quotation of the shares rises during the period, the beneficiary can realise the difference between the strike price and the actual value of the market price by realising shares as profits through a sale, or else refuse to sell.

Corporate Law

Most national legislations have comprehensive basic conditions under corporate law for the implementation of stock option plans and make it possible for the companies to obtain from members of management necessary financial resources by way of a conditional capital increase for the stock options.

The shareholders, according to national legislation, have comprehensive information and approval rights regarding the essential features of a stock option plan, in particular in terms of the purpose, circle of beneficiaries, strike price, division among management and employees, periods of time for success goals, acquisition and exercising of the right, as well as in terms of the determination of a waiting period. A contingent capital increase is advantageous for the company as long as its liquidity is not hurt by the stock option plan. Nevertheless, a diluation of capital stock can occur later if the value of the market price upon exercise of the option is higher than the given strike price – often below market value – when the option is granted.

Along with the conditional capital increase a company can regularly acquire its own shares in order to benefit the stock option programme.

Employment Law

Provisions of national employment law play an important role in the formation of option plans.

As a legal basis for such a compensation model voluntary business agreements in particular have to be taken into consideration as a measure of incentives for capital accumulation. For directors and managers to whom the business agreements do not apply, individual agreements are available. The company, as a rule, can make the fundamental decision without co-determination as to whether a participation model should be introduced, as well as the determination of its basic structure–i.e. circle of participants, time period and financial volume. It can, also without co-determination, agree upon compensation with the directors and managers. With the determination of the distribution principles (meaning the scope of the subscription rights of the different groups of employees), the employee representatives, according to a number of national legislations, have a right to co-determination, as long as it does not pertain to option plans for directors or managers.

In the individual case it is to be determined under national law whether forfeiture or repayment clauses (according to which employees are given no more rights from the stock option plan, should they resign), bind employees to an excessive degree to their employer and make it too difficult for them to change jobs. Such forfeiture or repayment clauses are permitted only if they are balanced according to a time limit, a credit proportionate to time, etc.

Through the repeated and unreserved granting of stock options a claim under employment law can result for the beneficiary on the basis of business practice. Furthermore, employees can receive rights from the principal of equal treatment under employment law. Such individual employees can be differentiated from employee groups only if this is pertinent and justified according to the goals of the participation model. For example, as a rule the differentiation according to hierarchical levels or a limitation on the acceptance of options at the managerial level are allowed if this acceptance – other than with the staff – represents a significant part of the income for management.

Insider Rules

Beneficiaries of stock option plans are often members of top management. These decision-makers are, on the basis of their prominent professional position, as a rule in possession of information that could be meaningful for the market price. Members of the board of directors and the supervisory board as well as other managers of a company, as much as they have attained insider information in accordance with requirements, are so-called 'primary insiders'. National directives broadly forbid such persons to acquire or sell stocks with the use of insider information.

With the formation of stock option plans the point in time for exercising the option is therefore to be determined so that any conflict with these Directives can be avoided right from the start. In this regard it is recommended that so-called 'trading windows' be established in order to make sure that the respective information that could be meaningful for the market price is available to not just managers but at the same time other market participants. In practice, the opening of these 'trading windows' two to three weeks after the respective periodical publishing of the reports on the company's quarterly or annual results has been proven successful. Such a time-limited exercise possibility prevents not only the occurrence of forbidden insider trading, but also the prohibited manipulation of market prices by managers and managers and simultaneously improves the public acceptance of stock option plans.

Tax Law

In terms of taxes stock option plans given to boards of directors or employees, under numerous national legislations, count as income from non-self-employed work and as such are to be taxed only at the time of receipt, meaning upon the actual enrichment of the beneficiary.

The inflow and thereby also the taxation therefore does not take place as a rule upon the granting of the option ('up-front taxation') because the beneficiary at this time, owing to the regularly planned binding and waiting period, does not yet have an economic asset free to be circulated and traded (fungibles); rather taxation occurs only upon the *exercise of the option* ('back-end taxation'). As a rule, with claims from an option right – as with other claims from the employment relationship that have not yet been fulfilled – the influx is to be terminated uniformly. The granting of an option right concerns, in the end, a possible chance for a later valuable acquisition of assets. The employer's agreement to grant certain services in the future is thus regularly to be seen as an influx even if the employer has met internal measures through which the right granted to the employee is financially secured. Given the use of an up-front taxation the danger arises that first of all the income tax or withholding tax on the option advantage would have to be paid, possibly also that the option would not be able to be exercised later at all because of a negative development in the market price. In regards to the strike price, advantageous developments in the market price are fundamentally to be taxed when the option is exercised. The value of the option right when it is granted is not subject to a withholding tax, but rather is to be taken as the basis of the difference between the value of the market price and the takeover price when the option is exercised. In addition, for this purpose national Directives should be tested as to whether further profits from sales (capital gains), which lie below a certain limitation or are realised only after a certain speculative period has lapsed, are completely tax-free.

Concerning the national contribution law of social security, as a rule, corresponding principles are to be applied.

Organisational possibilities under tax law usually exist with the introduction of a stock option plan not only in regard to the point in time of taxation, but rather also concerning the country responsible for taxation (e.g. in the case of options granted to a domestic company's management that has a service or employment relationship with a foreign parent company, or vice versa). Here, the regulations of a respective pertinent Double Taxation Treaty or the principle anchored in Article 15 of the OECD model treaty regarding taxation for the country where the business is taking place are to be taken into consideration. In general, it is recommended that given questions in regard to the taxation of a stock option plan, an appeal for information should be made to the responsible financial agency of the permanent establishment.

Conclusion

It remains a certainty that corporate value-oriented or performance-oriented compensation systems, such as, for example, stock option plans, motivate management and other employees in a special way and increase the value of the company in a sustained way. A tailor-made model of the respective company and its economic situation, is necessary, which takes into consideration the balanced interests of all participants.

Notes

1 Published in the *Official Journal* L 201, 17/07/1998 pp. 0088–0092. The Council Directive 77/187/EEC amended by the Council Directive 98/50/EC was replaced by the Council Directive 2001/23/EC of the European Union of 12 March 2001, published in the *Official Journal* L 82, 22/03/2001 p. 0016–0020.
2 Published in the *Official Journal* L 201, 17/07/1998 pp. 0088–0092.
3 Published in the *Official Journal* L 201, 17/07/1998 pp. 0088–0092.
4 Published in the *Official Journal* L 225, 12/08/1998 pp. 0016–0021.

10
Personnel and Cultural Integration

Peter H. Pribilla

1 Significance of Human Resources for M&A

Human resource (HR) strategy and policy play a strategic role in the success of M&A. Their significance is often overlooked, since decisions for or against a merger or acquisition are usually based on factors such as market share, market access, product strategy and financial considerations. Instead of including HR experts in the initial decision phase, the human aspect is often more closely examined only when integration issues begin to emerge. At that point, it is often too late. There is ample statistical evidence to show that 50 per cent of all alliances in the USA fail within five years (Kearney, 1999, p. 8). The reasons for failure in most cases are attitudes and behaviour of employees and management – in the acquiring as well as the acquired company. Resistance to change, often subliminal and therefore more dangerous, easily leads to cultural and organisational incompatibilities, decreasing productivity and even mass exodus of high calibre experts and managers to the competition.

Hubbard (1999) views personnel problems as one of the main reasons for the disappointing financial results of more than half of all M&A (1999, p. 16). Whether employees are paralysed into inaction because of fear, withdraw into 'internal resignation', or switch to the competition – the outcome is the same: customer focus suffers and productivity declines – with disastrous consequences.

Recent surveys show that 85 per cent of all US top executives believe that HR issues have a greater impact than financial issues on the success of acquisitions (Hubbard, 1999, p. 16). In other words, a merger has a chance to succeed only if employees accept the decision to merge and are willing to cooperate with their new colleagues.

The significance of the 'people' factor is even more evident in the market valuation of high-tech companies: financial assets often represent only a few per cent of the company's market value. Most of the company's value is determined by its structural capital – i.e. brand name, competitive position, customer base, patents, intellectual property etc. – and especially by its 'human capital' – the company's employees. 'Good' employees are hard to find, difficult to replace and are, in the end, the decisive factor for long-term competitive advantage. Maintaining competitive advantage and reaching business goals ultimately depends on employees' expertise and skills, their willingness to change, their motivation, competence and potential, as well as on management's leadership skills.

What makes human capital so valuable for maintaining a competitive edge is its *uniqueness*. It is difficult to imitate, as its effects appear in the daily interaction between individuals, for example between co-workers in different departments or areas of responsibility, between managers and employees and between employees and customers or suppliers. In this distributed network, human capital 'grows' and generates net value. For this growth process to be effective, however, everyone needs to understand, accept and realise their tasks, regardless of where these are in the global network.

A merger or acquisition brings two such networks together. Each network works according to its own rules and rituals, which have been established and proven successful over the years. These rules are not written down, but employees know what to do to reach their objectives – e.g. how directly or indirectly to raise issues, how openly to cooperate across hierarchies, how much freedom to act individuals have, how to deal with mistakes, or whether the customer is viewed as the most important partner. Grant (1991, pp. 114–35) views this '*tacit knowledge*' as the most strategic resource of every business because it makes a business unique and differentiates it from all others. The reasons are obvious: every business is a socio-technical system, where social factors like desire to achieve, motivation, cooperation and communication skills closely interact with technical factors as well as with work processes and organisational structure. Leadership style and corporate culture, therefore, play a key role in transforming business strategy into business success.

The 'knowledge factor' has long since surpassed traditional production factors like land, capital and labour. The growing service sector is creating more and more businesses whose entire market values are based on the knowledge of their employees. Software companies or consulting businesses are examples: such businesses cannot be managed using traditional hierarchies, and they are evolving their own management structures and corporate cultures.

2 Role of Corporate Culture for M&A

Every M&A results in a meeting of two formerly autonomous corporate cultures. Especially interesting are mergers that bring together traditional hierarchical structures with flat hierarchies, as is often the case when young start-up companies are acquired.

Often, employees initially perceive the other company's culture as 'external influence' – and frequently reject it, consciously or subconsciously, as a disruption. Usually, employees of the bigger company view their own culture as superior. To cite a negative example: A top manager of an acquiring company once told the employees of the acquired company: 'You're all frogs, and we're going to see if you can learn to be princes' (Hermsen, 1994, p. 79). The 'success' of this acquisition is predictable.

What does the term 'corporate culture' represent? Corporate culture is the *character or personality* of a business and differentiates a business from all others.

There are now infinite definitions for corporate culture, mostly based on sociological, behavioural or cultural–historical principles. Keller (1982), for example, defines culture as 'all collectively shared implicit and explicit behavioral norms, patterns, expressions and results learned by the members of a social group and transmitted from generation to generation using symbols' (1982, pp. 18 ff.). Such behaviour patterns are the basis for internal and external unity and for empowering employees to act (Figure 10.1).

Corporate culture contains *visible* and *invisible* elements. As with icebergs, visible elements represent only a small part of the whole. These elements are supported and characterised by what exists below the surface. This is where one finds the values, attitudes and ways of thinking that are shaped by the different stages of an individual's socialisation. It is also where one finds shared business experiences and action schemes that have been successful in different situations in the past. These success patterns influence, often subliminally, the current behaviour of employees or managers, which is expressed in the visible part of the iceberg. The following can be observed in every business:

- Certain *rituals* (for example, always greeting colleagues when walking down the hall; the way colleagues are treated even when one does not know them)
- *Shared symbols* (for example, dress codes such as dark suit and tie or jeans)
- *Shared work language* (each business develops its own jargon over time)
- *Unwritten rules* respected by everyone (such as not going over your boss's head).

Corporate culture, therefore, is holistic, historically developed, has a social structure and is difficult to change, because, from a sociological point of view, behaviour

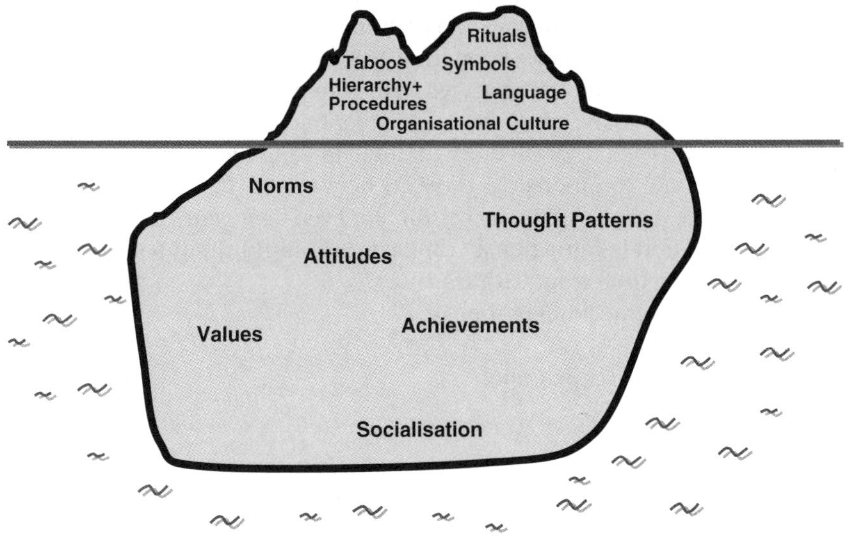

Figure 10.1 Corporate culture as an iceberg

patterns grow stronger the longer a group has employed them to achieve success. Hofstede (1997) talks about 'collective programming of the mind which distinguishes the members of one organization from another' (1997, p. 180). Such 'traditional behaviour' can handicap an organisation, especially when rapidly changing technology or economic factors require new behaviour patterns. Today, a company's success often depends on how quickly and flexibly it can respond to economic, political and other changes. Corporate cultures, therefore, are open systems that need to continuously evolve and adapt to new situations. These requirements are what make corporate culture so important.

Corporate cultures are important because:

- They provide *orientation* and therefore have a coordinating function
- They characterise the *interaction* of employees and management, the way they cooperate, leadership style and mutual trust
- Shared values are an important foundation for *employee identification*, their sense of 'Who we are', and job satisfaction.

Success factors for mergers – like cooperation, shared resource utilisation, transfer of management responsibility, or skills like development know-how or customer focus – are easier to realise the higher the degree of mutual trust, shared commitment and shared objectives.

All these factors are significantly influenced by corporate culture. If the cooperating partners share a similar culture (e.g. open, learning-oriented, cooperative), then there are few obstacles to success. Cultural differences, however, can easily become obstacles to cooperation, and their negative effects often take some time to appear. Experts refer to this as the 'hidden costs' of mergers.

For some new acquisitions, it may be desirable to maintain the differences in corporate culture if management expects cultural diversity to provide a stimulating effect. This can create tremendous opportunities for M&A, if the cultural differences are viewed as enriching and are managed well. Taking advantage of such opportunities, however, must not be left to chance and requires proactive, strategic planning and efficient management of HR during transaction and integration.

The more cultural commonalties there are between the merged companies, the more quickly the merger will be successful. But even divergent cultures are worth the integration effort because human capital is the only business resource that can renew and develop itself from within.

M&A go through three different phases:

- *Pre-acquisition* analysis/planning
- *Transaction*
- *Integration.*

HR management plays very different roles in each of these phases. Here 'HR management' is understood as everything that is managed 'around the employee', in each phase of M&A, by managers as well as by the HR organisation.

Each merger and each acquisition takes a different course and is unique in many aspects. There are, however, some recurring and predictable issues for which a company can prepare. What follows examines these issues in more detail and outlines solutions, with a focus on transaction and integration and with recommendations based on practical examples.

3 Developing an HR Strategy for a Merger

To develop a successful HR strategy for a merger, the responsible HR organisation requires timely access to all *relevant information*. Ideally, HR participates in the evaluation of the potential merger candidate and has an opportunity to perform HR due diligence (see Chapter 5) prior to the merger, when technologies, customers, markets and finances are being evaluated.

A common 'double handicap' often arises during this phase:

- First, the HR organisation of the acquiring company is often not involved in the evaluation until after a decision for a merger has been made. HR is then tasked with *executing the merger and handling all HR transactions*.
- Second, merger candidates rarely fully disclose *detailed personnel data*, with all its strengths and weaknesses. Often, small or medium size businesses do not have meaningful personnel reporting systems.

HR management is therefore often faced with the major challenge of developing an HR integration strategy without having a complete overview of all the facts. An effective way to address this situation is to form an HR integration team that brings together HR professionals from both companies as early as possible. This will enable the acquiring company to quickly gain a sound understanding of the HR potential for the merger. Joint HR teams can also develop a joint strategy for addressing the changes that every merger inevitably produces when organisational entities are merged or eliminated to optimise responsibilities and capacities. Such changes are managed most effectively by partners that understand the needs, attitudes and behaviour of the employees impacted by these changes.

Following a merger, two elements dominate the development of an HR strategy: *competence management* and *cultural management*.

These are prerequisites for leveraging optimisation potential and for efficiently and consistently employing human resources to reach business goals. The main goal of *competence management* is to optimise staffing, quantitatively as well as qualitatively. This requires systematic assessment and development of employee competencies and potential, which are measurable and can be influenced. *Cultural management* is more difficult, because corporate culture is not easily influenced, controlled or even dictated. The challenge for cultural management is to facilitate alignment of the strengths of the corporation with the strengths of employees as well as with societal demands.

Gut-Villa (1997, p. 123) describes the four main roles of HR professionals as follows:

- *Strategic partner* for top management
- *Administrative expert* for personnel administration
- *Employee champion* for the needs of employees
- *Change agent* for transformation processes (Figure 10.2).

What questions need to be considered when developing an HR strategy following a merger? There are four essential factors to be addressed by competence management and cultural management as well as for establishing efficient common HR business processes. These, in turn, influence strategy selection. They are:

1. *Basic business model*: this determines integration intensity and management philosophy
2. *Extent of international activities*: for international acquisitions, local culture influences values, thought processes and the behaviour of employees
3. *Intended cultural integration strategy*: this strongly impacts cultural management and leadership systems
4. *Anticipated pace of integration*: timely integration requires thorough examination and management of all HR issues.

How the Business Model Affects HR Strategy

Global corporations are faced with increasing complexities as they grow, because their output is generated in different locations, across departmental and geographic borders and time zones, and within a complex network of processes and decision paths. Where a task is handled within the global value-creation network is often determined by where the best know-how, the most suitable market access, sufficient capacities, efficient implementation and lowest costs can be realised.

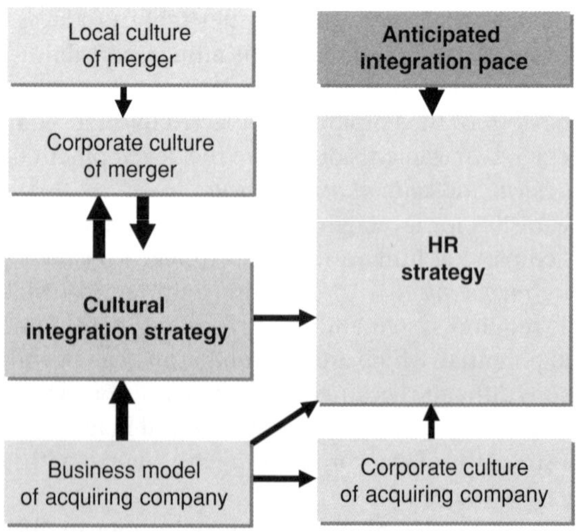

Figure 10.2 Developing an HR strategy for M&A

A global value-creation strategy integrates national and international subsidiaries and manufacturing sites, customers and suppliers, consultants, logistics providers and cooperation partners as well as employees and management.

Each merger and each acquisition carried out by a global corporation automatically becomes part of this worldwide network. Different corporate entities, however, have vastly different degrees of responsibility and freedom to act, and these influence integration intensity. Perlmutter (1969) developed three different business models to describe different levels of control exercised by the parent company (1969, p. 9 ff.) (Figure 10.3).

The *ethnocentric business model* is centralised and strongly headquarters-oriented. Headquarters allocates all resources worldwide and makes all relevant decisions. Corporate management is based on the principle of direction and control. 'Foreign entities' and subsidiaries have limited control over decision-making.

The *polycentric business model* is characterised by increased two-way interaction between headquarters and each corporate entity. HR strategy and day-to-day HR management reflect decentralised decision-making processes. Each business unit is largely autonomous. Leveraging global optimisation potential, however, requires a globally-applicable HR strategy and a global management system. These define worldwide standards while leaving the implementation largely up to the business units, which then can incorporate local requirements. These standards assure global benchmarking of skills and enhance international employee exchange. They also focus HR management consistently on accomplishing business goals.

The *geocentric business model* represents the ideal of a 'virtual corporation'. All decisions are made on a purely rational basis driven by optimisation objectives. Headquarters and peripheral business units are equal partners in all relevant decisions. Thirty years after Perlmutter first published his theory, this business model is still rarely implemented in its pure form. The trend, however, is clearly heading in this direction: decisions are made at the level and location where relevant information converges and where decisions can be implemented in the most effective way. Cooperation at all levels and distributed decision-making

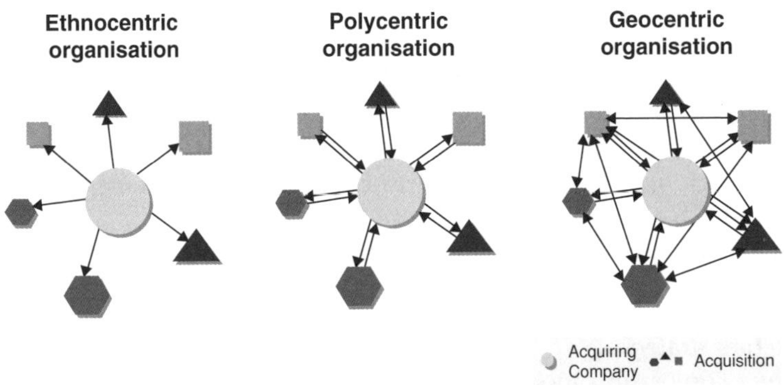

Figure 10.3 The decision-making process in different business models

enables geocentric corporations to profit from being both local and global and to systematically leverage synergies and integration advantages. Headquarters, in this model, becomes a communication centre that coordinates the various activities of the corporation.

How Local Culture Impacts a Merger's HR Strategy

International mergers and acquisitions need to consider the local cultures of the countries involved. These influence the thinking, behaviour, motivation and values of employees in those countries and need to be addressed by local HR strategies. While it is true that global corporations, over time, develop a global corporate culture, this culture will still exhibit country-specific characteristics. The differences are mainly in practices and not so much in values (Hofstede, 1997, p. 182), since global corporations will develop common values over time.

Hofstede (1997) points out five country-specific cultural dimensions that influence the behaviour of employees in a corporation:

- High/low power distance
- Individualism/collectivism
- Masculinity/femininity
- Strong/weak uncertainty avoidance
- Long-term/short-term orientation.

When a global company acquires a nationally focused company, it is always advisable to investigate any local cultural characteristics of the acquisition. Corporate as well as HR management can be successful only if they are in harmony with local behaviour patterns, which are often determined by local culture. Incentives need to consider existing local motivational structures. For international mergers, in particular, efficient cooperation and true integration can take place only if local characteristics are adequately addressed. Employees of the larger company need to be sensitised to the differences in local cultures and be motivated to achieve a common denominator. Only then can they appreciate 'strange' behaviour and act in a manner that will be accepted by their new colleagues. This is especially important when massive restructuring is required.

How Cultural Integration Strategy Affects HR Strategy

Each merger and each acquisition brings together two autonomous corporate cultures. The acquiring company can pursue three different cultural integration strategies, each of which has characteristic impacts on HR strategy, HR management and day-to-day HR practices (Figure 10.4).

Scholz (1993) outlines three different strategies for cultural integration (1993, pp. 807 ff.).

Monoculture strategy

The larger corporation more or less superimposes its corporate culture on the smaller corporation in a kind of 'cultural colonisation'. This approach is often

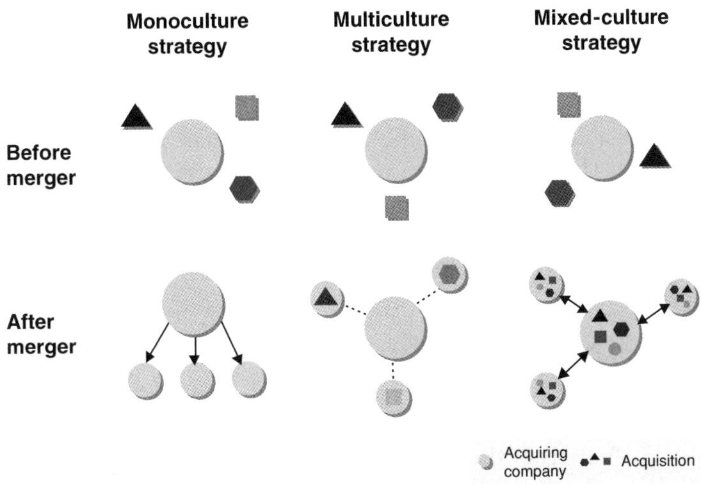

Figure 10.4 Types of cultural integration

resisted by employees of the acquired corporation, and requires a sensitive and intensive integration approach.

Multiculture strategy

The acquisition retains its own culture. The resulting peaceful coexistence is rated positively and viewed as an enrichment. This strategy requires a basic understanding of relevant interests and core values and is frequently employed for acquisitions of young, dynamic start-up companies.

Mixed-culture strategy

This strategy is often used for mergers of equals. Both corporations merge into one, and the workforce is combined. A new, joint culture develops that is supported by everyone.

Each of these strategies has specific *impacts on management systems* and leadership tools employed. The *monoculture* strategy will, inevitably, involve strong control by the acquiring company. The goal is usually a one-to-one transfer of control systems and management practices to the acquisition, usually by placing headquarters' employees in key positions. Headquarters makes all relevant decisions. If the acquisition is a foreign company, national cultural differences, as a rule, are ignored. This can lead to culture shock and persistent demotivation in the acquired company.

The *multiculture* strategy, on the other hand, involves agreeing on a focused 'umbrella culture' and encouraging the development of as much independence as possible. The challenge is to allow diversity and still achieve unity. The merger is granted large areas of autonomy. Decisions are decentralised and recruitment takes place locally in the respective countries. Management positions are filled with locals and their performance is evaluated using local criteria.

The biggest challenge for human resource management is the *mixed-culture* strategy. It requires constructive effort, since headquarters can carry out its coordinating function only if local conditions and characteristics are well understood and taken into account. Local HR management should participate in all relevant decisions, if possible from the beginning. International management teams best accomplish this. The mixed-culture strategy leverages the advantages of cultural diversity and transforms the strengths of each corporate entity into business success. Successfully employing this approach requires performance measurement criteria and management principles that are uniform worldwide. This necessitates the development of common management standards.

How Integration Pace Affects HR Strategy

The fourth factor that impacts a merger's HR strategy is the intended timeframe. Gradual and rapid integration both have advantages. *Gradual* integration allows for a thorough analysis of the acquired company's products, customers, markets, employee potential and personnel management systems. Employees and management are able to actively participate in the integration process and deal with impending changes. This enables a smooth transition to the new ownership situation. The disadvantage of gradual integration is that employees view this period as a time of extreme uncertainty and respond with reduced productivity.

Rapid integration counteracts this disadvantage. It takes advantage of employees' anticipation of changes and promptly sets things straight. Management positions are quickly reassigned, which establishes unequivocal leadership and avoids drawn-out power struggles. This enables the corporation speedily to refocus on market requirements and avoid energy loss due to friction.

4 Strategic and Operational HR Management

Each merger or acquisition requires the development of a new HR strategy to address different business models, local cultural requirements, selected integration strategy and projected timeframe. The central focus of integration after a merger or acquisition will, however, always be on HR management, with all its facets.

Management can be defined in many ways, ranging from brief to more complex:

- 'To set targets, plan, make decisions, implement and control.'
- 'To manage success factors for achieving higher targets by enlisting employee participation.'
- 'To set and communicate targets, develop processes, promote internal and external communication, motivate, provide feedback, communicate visions and shape corporate culture.'

Reichwald *et al.* (1998) gets straight to the point with his definition of management: 'to set targets and to coordinate tasks and relationships' (1998, p. 142). This definition combines the need to reach business goals with the resulting need for leadership. Guiding these two vectors so that they move in the same direction is what makes business management successful. The emphasis is on clear strategy, open communication, well-defined targets and measurement of results. Top management's primary task is to translate a company's vision into strategic business goals that are put into operation by a business unit's management and are realised together with the unit's staff. Against this backdrop, management is primarily business-oriented communication, regardless of the degree of responsibility. This applies equally to all business models, as they differ primarily in their degree of operational independence and the scope of decision making granted to employees in local subsidiaries.

In the past, industrial enterprises traditionally exhibited more or less rigid organisational structures and strict rules. Today, management of geocentric or polycentric companies is based on

- *visions* and *objectives*,
- *cultural management*, and
- *competence management*.

These three factors represent the core of HR management. In the following discussion, HR management stands for HR functions, HR processes, HR systems and HR tools that need to be developed, implemented and controlled in order to manage a business successfully. In this context, HR management and administration are of equal importance.

HR development plays a key role in every merger, because achieving employee commitment requires dialogue-oriented management. HR management's top objectives are to align

- long-term business goals,
- day-to-day business reality, and
- shared employee values.

Companies where every employee has internalised these objectives develop tremendous energy that can be transformed into business success.

Rosenstiel (1997, p. 123) emphasises four criteria that determine the productivity of every employee:

- Individual skills
- Personal desire
- Social empowerment
- Situational enabling by the organisation.

All four criteria are substantially influenced by HR management.

HR strategies for mergers, therefore, address the following questions:

- How many *employees* with which skills are needed to make the merger successful and to realise business objectives?

- How are *redundant employees* handled?
- How are *cultural differences* – either in corporate or local culture – between the acquirer and the acquisition managed?
- How can HR management develop *synergies* between both work forces?
- If *cultural integration* is planned, how can both workforces be merged into a unit?

Comprehensive answers to these questions require analytical assessment of the situation at hand. This usually takes place during the transaction phase.

Strategic HR During the Transaction Phase

HR Due Diligence

Pre-acquisition analysis and planning usually takes place 'behind closed doors'. Ideally, HR participates in this phase, but this is not usually the case. In most cases, decisions for or against a merger or acquisition are based on 'hard' facts like market position, product scope, regional market access or profitability. 'Soft' facts like human capital are considered during this phase only if the emphasis of the acquisition is on the know-how of the target company. This often applies to acquisitions of software companies.

For all other mergers and acquisitions general due diligence does not focus on HR. Research has shown that:

- Only one-third of all acquirers perform due diligence of HR – and, by and large, do so only in a cursory manner (Hubbard, 1999, p. 62).
- Fewer than 10 per cent of all buyers perform *serious* HR-related due diligence (Hubbard, 1999, p. 15).

Careful due diligence of the HR area, however, is essential if employee potential is to be realistically assessed because it provides important indicators for the *integration effort* that will subsequently be required. Timely HR due diligence will also point out potential issues related to anticipated employee fluctuation or 'friction loss' caused by incompatible cultures.

HR due diligence involves the following essential items:

- **Employee data** Number of employees in all locations, their qualification and potential, age levels, wage and salary costs, the levels of sick leave and employee fluctuation.
- **Working conditions** Compensation systems, incentives, pension systems and other voluntary employer benefits, retirement benefits, local legal requirements such as employee representation or union involvement.
- **Personnel administration** Electronic payroll systems, personnel information systems, skill databases or online recruitment.

Key items for analysis are the capabilities of the target company's management. Areas to investigate are strengths and weaknesses in management style and philosophy, leadership skills, competencies and development potential, team spirit and cross-cultural skills. These are especially important for international mergers and acquisitions. A quick screening of the target company's management enables pre-selection of suitable managers for staffing key positions immediately following closure.

Cultural Due Diligence

Comprehensive HR due diligence includes cultural due diligence, which takes a closer look at the corporate culture of the company to be merged or acquired. The more tightly both companies are to be merged, the more important the question of cultural fit: How big are the cultural differences? Are the two company cultures a good match? Are they compatible? This involves more than just evaluating corporate culture – for international M&A, it is also important to know how well the local cultures of acquirer and acquisition *harmonise*, because successful cultural integration is one of the most important factors of a successful merger (Hubbard, 1999, pp. 14–16). A survey of 200 European CEOs about the role of corporate culture showed the ability to integrate the target company and its culture to be a primary factor of overall acquisition success (Hubbard, 1999, p. 14).

Employees in every corporation have a particular way of communicating and interacting that differentiates them from people in other corporations. This applies to interaction with each other and across hierarchies as well as to interaction with customers and suppliers.

Indicators for corporate culture include:

- The role of *hierarchies* and *symbols*
- Management *style*
- *Career paths*
- Openness of *interaction*
- Freedom to act and scope of *decision-making powers*
- *Error tolerance*
- *Mutual trust*
- *Learning behaviour*
- *Customer focus*
- Aggressiveness towards *competition*
- *Social engagement*

Due diligence of a company's corporate culture is not an easy task because many facets are interrelated. Experience has shown the following methods to be effective. (However, at this point it must be mentioned that before the closure it is mandatory not to interfere with the other party's operational business.)

- **Standardised employee surveys** Employees of both the acquirer and acquisition complete a survey. The acquiring company designs the survey to focus on values and behaviours that it considers important – e.g. customer service, openness to new developments, learning behaviour and leadership style. One major advantage of this method is that it enables corporate cultures to be directly compared along the lines surveyed. Results are quickly translatable into *targeted measures*. Another advantage of this method is that repeated surveys can document cultural changes over time.

- **Individual interviews** with selected employees and management in the acquired company. This method has been referred also to as 'storytelling'. In open conversations, interviewees talk about their career path and their individual experience. Statements made in interviews allow conclusions to be drawn about corporate culture. Information about the way people interact, about corporate values and unwritten rules is revealed not only by what is said, but also by the choice of topics that are *not addressed*. This method is labour-intensive and is rarely employed during a merger phase. If it is used during that phase, it is not applied in a representative manner. Interviewed employees and managers, however, value this method highly because it sends the message that the acquirer is really interested in the acquisition's people. This can be a strong motivating factor during the phase after announcement of a merger.

'Merger Syndrome'

'Merger Syndrome' is a term often applied to how employees respond to a merger (Marks and Mirvis, 1992, p. 70 ff.). It reflects the mood of the workforce and significantly impacts integration success (Figure 10.5).

During a merger or acquisition, employees and management of the target company go through different emotional phases. Understanding these phases is important to prepare for their impact and to develop effective countermeasures. Most employees initially respond to the announcement with shock and strong emotional reactions. The merger is viewed as a *loss of identity*. Employees lose an environment of rules, tasks, hierarchies, structures and colleagues they have until now judged as secure and dependable. Their whole social fabric is thrown into question all at once, which usually leads to significant distress and fear.

Employees ask themselves:

- Is my job secure? Will I be reassigned to new tasks? Do I have to move? What about my retirement? Will benefits be cut? Who is my new boss? What about my career?
- Also: What happens to my colleagues? Will 'the others' take over and force their corporate culture on us?

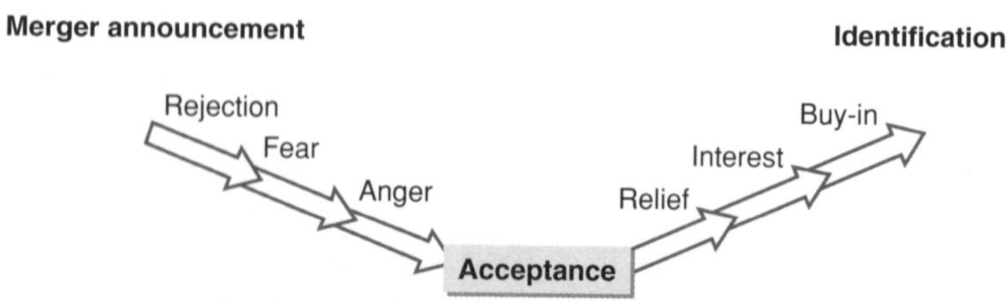

Figure 10.5 Emotional responses of target company employees to a merger

During this phase, the employee is not at all interested in management's pronouncements about the great opportunities presented by the acquisition or about new growth or new markets. Employees barely notice such statements because they are mostly focused on their own situation. Estimates show that during the first year following an acquisition, employees spend up to two hours a day at work dealing with rumours (Sewing, 1996, p. 158).

How strongly and in what manner individual employees respond to the announcement of a merger and how long the different phases of the merger syndrome last depend on individual character traits, personal circumstances and past experiences. Self-confidence, job options, career level and individual needs play an important role.

The distress caused by a merger or acquisition has psychological causes: employees not only have a legal contract with their employer, they also develop, over time, an unspoken 'social contract' that is non-material. This social contract encompasses expectations by the employee of the employer and forms the basis for an employee's trust in the employer. Many employees are not aware of this contract – until it is broken. When that happens, the contract has to be, in a sense, *renegotiated*. This renegotiation is a subconscious process and boils down to each individual having sooner or later to tolerate or accept the changes (Hubbard, 1999, p. 27) or leave the company.

Those who have been thinking about leaving the company all along will now intensify their search for a new position. This can lead to increased fluctuation, with disastrous consequences if important contributors and experienced managers leave. The well-known expression 'exit of the best and merger of the rest' may well presage the beginning of the end of a merger. A doomsday mood spreads quickly, causing resignation and withdrawal. In the acquired company, the merger produces stress and often a management vacuum. This is amplified when employees and management of the acquiring company act in an excessively dominant manner and results in imagined worst-case scenarios and rumours that fill all information gaps with half-truths and fabrications and paralyse the staff.

This destabilisation phase is not preventable. One can, however, attempt to keep it as brief as possible to minimise its negative effects and financial impact. Managing this turbulence and starting the real integration effort is a major challenge for HR management.

Cooperation with Works Councils

All staffing decisions must comply with legal requirements. This applies especially to job protection and regional or national requirements. It is highly advisable to involve legal experts during HR due diligence and to seek their advice throughout the entire process.

In Germany, for example, the acquiring company usually assumes all employment rights and obligations, and the individual employment contract does not change. If the acquired company is to remain a legally separate subsidiary, employment terms do not change. If the acquisition is to be integrated, then the acquiring company's wage agreements and employment terms supersede those of the acquisition. Larger companies usually offer better working conditions and benefits than small or medium-sized companies, which means that employees can expect more advantages than disadvantages from integration. Frequently, large corporations opt to keep the acquisition a separate legal entity to take advantage of cost savings resulting from lower pay scales and fewer benefits.

Whether the acquisition is integrated or maintained as a separate company, local employee representation should be involved in the planning as early as possible. Creating a partnership with works councils has many advantages. As 'multipliers' they have significant influence on employees and can reduce the stress and fear phases that employees experience as a result of the merger syndrome. Experience also shows that employees raise fewer objections to a merger if works councils are positively inclined towards the merger and are involved in integration planning. That is why transition employment agreements are developed to define future employment terms. In the USA, agreements are common at the senior management level.

Planning the Integration

Sound integration planning contributes to reducing employee distress and accelerates the integration process. During this very sensitive phase for all participants far-reaching decisions need to be made in an environment of relative uncertainty. This may explain why fewer than 20 per cent of all acquirers do sufficient pre-acquisition planning (Hubbard, 1999, p. 48). European executives, when surveyed about lessons learned from failed mergers, cite lack of adequate planning as the most frequent reason. However, such lessons rarely result in changes for subsequent mergers, most likely owing to time constraints.

The most critical event during the transaction phase is the *announcement of the merger*, which often produces intense reactions among the target company's employees. Ideally, the entire deal is kept confidential until the official announcement (one impressive example – at least in this regard – being the DaimlerChrysler deal). However, this is not always the case. The effect, in either case, is almost identical: the announcement, or even rumours of an announcement, has a profound impact on many employees.

Immediately after the announcement (respectively, the closure), employees of the acquiring and the target company, customers, suppliers and of course shareholders expect unequivocal information about objectives, reorganisations, restructuring plans and integration steps.

Integration planning provides answers to the following questions:

- Which steps are to be *implemented*, by when?
- How much *integration*, and how quickly?
- What are the *transition plans* for organisation, structure and composition of the target's management team?
- What is the process for *announcement, pre-briefing* of managers and *employee communication*?
- Who is responsible for *integration*, and who contributes to it?

HR management needs to be made an active part not only of due diligence but also of integration planning, because that is when important decisions are made about schedules, future management structure, integration of corporate culture, personnel systems and personnel processes, as well as about communication content and interaction between management and employees.

Effective Communication and Interaction

From the beginning of the negotiations the entire communication process should be carefully planned in a small, confidential group. Communication elements to be addressed are:

- Reasons and objectives for acquisition
- Long-term vision
- Integration strategy
- Schedule.

Information about the history and successes of both companies helps develop mutual trust and a 'we are in this together' spirit. Posting key questions and answers about the merger on the intranet has proven successful. This also enables electronic questions and answers (Q&As) to be updated on a daily basis. The main communication effort, however, needs to be focused on the personal communication of managers with their employees. It is important that managers understand the sentiments of the people impacted by the acquisition and are prepared for the different emotional phases their employees usually go through during changes of this kind.

The unfortunate reality, however, is that 86 per cent of all businesses do not adequately communicate about the new partnership (Kearney, 1999, p. 26). Reasons can include lack of preparation or the fact that managers in the target company often suffer from distress and fear themselves and, in the worst case, have a negative amplification effect on their employees. Communication must be fast, intense and unambiguous to reduce paralysing uncertainty as much as possible and to quickly achieve consensus about common goals. The following factors should be addressed:

- **Targeted communication** Managers and employees often have different perceptions about what is important to them during a merger. The information content needs to reflect these differences.
- **Rapid communication** Employees should be the first to hear about a merger – and not via the press, television or from agitated customers. This requires managers and works councils to be briefed in advance of the announcement so that they can provide competent answers to employees.
- **Direct communication** Immediately following disclosure, a direct dialogue between managers and employees needs to take place. This could be person-to-person dialogue, department meetings or information and discussion forums with all employees.

- **Explicitness and truth** Employees and managers impacted by a merger want explicit information to help them emerge from an environment of stifling uncertainty. It is important to address all relevant items openly and to conceal as little as possible, even if, owing to impending factory closures or layoffs, the news may not be positive for many. People can deal more effectively with explicit information, even if it is negative, than with uncertainty. Telling the truth improves credibility, which needs to be established quickly. A message like: 'We need to re-evaluate our resources and will make an announcement within 4 weeks' is better than trying to smooth things over and raising false hopes.
- **Credibility** Management should not say that there will be 'business as usual' after the merger. This is simply not true because changes are always to be expected. Those who talk about 'business as usual' simply demonstrate that they misjudge the situation and are out of touch with the mood of their employees. Employees judge the credibility of managers largely by the extent to which those managers empathise with employee concerns and needs, how openly they interact with employees and how actively they represent employee interests. Perception is reality: *how* answers are communicated to employees is even more important than what is communicated: 30 per cent of impact comes from what is said – 70 per cent from how it is said.
- **Welcoming attitude** To increase credibility, the acquirer should send the unequivocal message: '*We welcome you*!'. It is essential that key executives like the CEO or president of the acquiring company visit the target company and personally talk with its employees and answer their questions.

Personal communication needs to be complemented by intensive use of other merger-specific communication media such as personal welcome letters to the new employees, web pages with Q&As, merger newsletters, hotlines, workshops and press releases. The effectiveness of informal networks also should not be underestimated: whenever such informal networks can be identified, they should be utilised. They are an important enabler for efficient operational processes and strongly influence opinion-making and the general mood.

Retention

Experience shows that employee fluctuation rates will increase following a merger or acquisition, especially for exceptional employees and managers. Studies show that:

- Up to 50 per cent of a target's management leave the company in the first three to five years (Hermsen, 1994, p. 133).
- In US companies, a much higher number of managers leave during the first two to three years after an acquisition than before the acquisition or in comparable companies (Sewing, 1996, pp. 107 ff.).
- 'When no coordinated retention actions are taken, 47 per cent of all senior managers leave within the first year of the acquisition. But the exodus doesn't

stop there. Within the first three years, 72 per cent end up heading for the door' (Pritchett, 1997, p. 101).

Strong fluctuation of key employees can seriously impact and jeopardise a merger's success. The expertise and management know-how that are lost may be precisely the skills the buyer intended to acquire in order to reach its strategic goals. This 'brain drain' can become critical because the people leaving the company often take customers and supplier relationships with them. And it is an established fact that developing new customer relationships is difficult, time-consuming and expensive.

The departure of managers who are role models casts doubt in employees' minds about merger benefits and negatively impacts their motivation and attitudes. Also, managers who leave a company often take good employees with them (the 'domino effect'). Headhunters play a significant role in this process, for them, acquisitions and mergers in their unstable phase are ideal hunting grounds for top managers and experts.

How can employee fluctuation be stopped?

During due diligence, *important managers* and *key employees* with skills that are difficult to replace should be identified and evaluated. Conversations with these employees should take place as early as possible to reassure them and to make statements about new positions, changes, expectations, career opportunities and income. These measures should be complemented by financial incentives such as retention bonuses or stock options, and especially by involvement in challenging integration projects.

Operational HR Management During Integration

Leadership Role of Management

A successful merger requires managers with the necessary know-how and sensibility to be available in the acquiring and the acquired company. These managers need to motivate employees and lead them out of their emotional 'slump', create new organisational structures, fill positions with the right people, maintain customer relationships and develop new markets. Managers therefore play a pivotal role internally and externally, and the demands on their leadership skills are enormous.

Many acquisitions suffer when top management starts to lose interest after closing and assumes that 'it's done'. Such thinking is perilous. Leaning back and relaxing at this point amounts to gross negligence. Haspeslagh and Jemison (1991) clearly demonstrate that it is not the transaction itself that produces the expected results. It is the measures and actions taken by managers *after* closure that make or break a merger. The reasons are obvious: *net value* is created after the merger, when skills are transferred and employees of both companies are working together to realise the expected gain or to discover additional advantages (Haspeslagh and Jemison, 1991, pp. 24 ff.). Even more significant is the development of a *vision* that is supported by everyone. This visionary component is the definitive expression of leadership after a merger. The most important thing about a vision, however, is not its originality but how well it reflects the interests of the relevant decision-makers – customers, employees, shareholders – and how easily it can be translated into a realistic competitive strategy. In this context, Senge talks about the challenge to develop the 'creative tension' that serves as an integrating factor. 'Creative tension comes from seeing clearly where we want to be, our "vision", and telling the truth about where we are, our "current reality". The gap between the two generates a natural tension' (Senge, 1998, p. 297). This tension in turn builds tremendous motivational momentum.

Financial success requires leading all employees and managers in the same direction. This is a leadership task of the highest order and requires top management to have both great powers of persuasion and motivational skills. True leadership starts with good management and goes far beyond it in critical situations (Table 10.1).

Employees are very adept at sensing whether their managers stand behind the organisational changes taking place. That is why the management of the company to be integrated needs to be informed early on about the objectives, reasons and benefits of the merger. Joint workshops involving the management of both companies are one possible approach. At the same time, operational business must be stabilised, for example with short-term objectives, strict performance monitoring and renewal of customer focus. Employees are not the only ones in a state of uncertainty. Many customers are asking: 'What is my supplier's future? Will it continue to offer the same products or services? Will I continue to receive good service? Will my contacts stay the same?' Distressed employees do not provide good customer service and instead spread rumours externally, which is bad for business.

The following rule applies in this situation: better to challenge employees and ask more of them rather than too little. The objective is to produce *early wins*, even if these wins are smaller ones. Goals and results that can be reached in the short term are a good way to restore the acquired employees' bruised self-esteem.

Integration Management

Operational integration is certainly the most critical phase of the entire merger process: different organisations, corporate cultures, management styles, systems,

Table 10.1 Management vs. leadership

Management	**Leadership**
Targets and control	Inspiring, direction-setting vision
Managing by objectives (MBO)	Leading by motivation
Dealing with complexity	Dealing with change
Working within the system	Working on the system
Passive goal orientation	Active goal-setting
Focus on requirements	Focus on creative process
Organising people	Aligning people

processes and structures need to be brought together to allow the expected synergies to emerge. Studies show that companies that place a strong emphasis on post-merger integration (PMI) surmount cultural differences more easily and manage the entire integration process more efficiently (Kearney, 1999, p. 11).

Some recommendations based on experience:

- Establishing a *project-based organisation* with integration teams that are responsible for the integration of business functions such as sales, production, IT systems, human resources and core processes.
- Integration teams should include employees from *both* companies. This reduces the 'us vs. them' attitudes and shows consideration for the acquired company. Also, the acquired company's *know-how* must be used.
- Involving, as much as possible, not only managers of the acquisition in the integration process but also 'ordinary' employees. Managers know their area of responsibility very well and may also be important opinion leaders. The more employees of the acquirer and the acquisition jointly gather *positive project experience*, the faster mutual trust will develop and barriers will decrease.
- Establishing an *integration headquarters* that is responsible for the entire integration process, preferably headed by two people, one from the acquisition and one from the acquiring company. This integration headquarters manages the entire process, is a member of the steering committee and has a high level of authority, including *vis-à-vis* top management. It is the first point of contact as well as the driving integration force and it is empowered to make significant decisions.
- Applying the principles of *organisational justice* to the entire integration process (Hubbard, 1999, p. 136 ff.). This prevents employees from feeling that they or their own group are not being treated as well as others. The perception of fairness is critical for a successful merger, since it is often not the extent of changes but the way in which changes are introduced that frustrates employees. When employees feel unfairly treated, they will question not only the credibility of management, but also its decisions and the entire process.
- *Consistent, honest and open communication* throughout integration is critical. Information gaps are filled in by speculation and rumour, with serious consequences. Even if there is nothing new to communicate, state when new developments and decisions are expected. Also repeat previously communicated statements. This makes sense because employees continue to discover new facets of information each time, which helps them to see the 'big picture' and to understand decisions. In addition, keep communicating the objectives of the merger or acquisition and its schedule, and keep reporting on integration progress – especially early wins.
- *Uniform HR management* in the merging companies helps to level differences between corporate cultures and creates a basis for mutual trust. Therefore the extent to which the two personnel systems are to be brought into alignment should be decided early on for every merger. This includes salaries, incentives, personnel management, employee development and personnel administration

systems. Divergent systems tend to create friction and may foster envy, especially regarding financial aspects. Employees quickly develop a sense of inequity, especially if direct comparisons can be drawn when employees of the acquirer and the acquisition work closely together and gain insight into potentially striking differences in salaries and other company benefits.

Optimal Staffing After a Merger

The merger strategy determines long-term staffing requirements and the resulting personnel planning process, which defines qualitative and quantitative staff composition. Ideas about staffing of key positions, preliminary organisational structure and possible process changes should be developed during due diligence or shortly thereafter. These ideas form the basis for the personnel planning process.

Selection and appointment of the new management team should be completed at the latest within 100 days of the merger announcement. This only happens in 39 per cent of all cases (Kearney, 1999, p. 16).

A dialogue with key employees about their future with the company usually takes place during the transaction phase. During integration, this selection process needs to be expanded to the majority of employees.

A systematic *personnel planning process* best accomplishes this (Figure 10.6).

Personnel planning starts with developing *job descriptions* and *roles* that identify goals, tasks and skills for each function. These requirements are then compared with existing skill profiles. Large corporations often have developed *skill databases* for this purpose that can be especially useful for large mergers of equals or for international mergers. Personal data is input into these databases and updated by employees, and performance-related data is handled by human resources. HR usually updates the database annually following performance reviews. In addition to skills, these databases also document qualifications and performance.

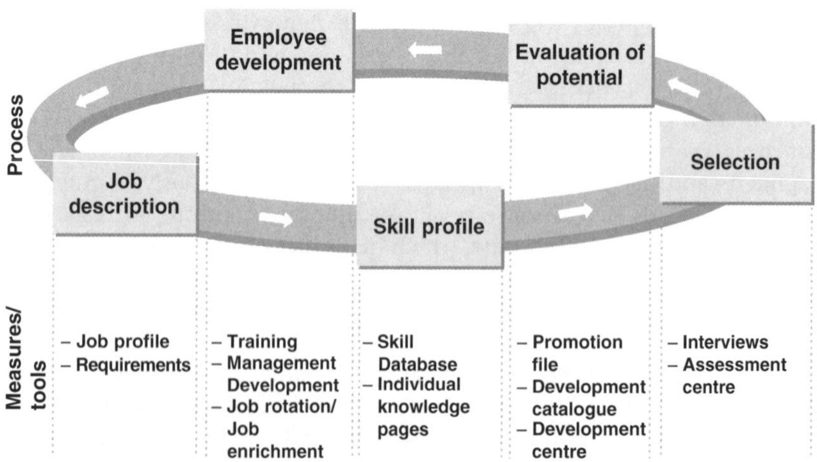

Figure 10.6 The staffing process after a merger

A second method for systematically recording skill profiles is to maintain *individual knowledge pages*. Employees input their own work experience, skills and career development interests into a standardised electronic form. This enables employees to communicate to a large audience their personal desires and ideas for career development or changes. Knowledge pages primarily serve as a 'career bulletin board' and increase an individual's opportunities for career changes.

The advantage of both methods is the ability to record skill profiles for a large number of employees. By providing international standardisation, both methods also assure international transparency.

Local management usually handles staffing selection. Two interesting variants are:

- *Every* employee can re-apply. The issue here is to determine who can perform a truly neutral appraisal of the employee. The employee's former managers are not neutral, and management in the acquiring company is not in a position to make the right choices from existing performance reviews.
- *Structured interviews* with the applicant's (former) managers, complemented by background interviews of the employee by an external, professional HR consultant (Pritchett, 1997, p. 91 ff.).

Assessment of individual potential plays a crucial role in staffing decisions. In a business environment characterised by completely new technologies and services every three to five years, employee potential and flexibility is essential. The higher the individual's position in the organisational hierarchy, the more carefully their potential must be assessed to prevent staffing mistakes that can be very costly down the road. Potential is usually assessed during annual performance reviews and also by development centres, and is recorded in promotion files and development catalogues. These define long-term career targets for each employee and are the basis for individual employee development measures. HR development is a business process that translates employee skills into measurable business results and successes. Measures can include job rotation, individual training and development or systematic management development.

During integration, employee development aspects usually take a back seat or are even completely neglected. Efforts are focused on finding new jobs for every employee as quickly as possible or on laying off employees whose jobs have become redundant. Nearly every merger will result in job redundancies. This necessitates a *separation process* that is difficult not only for the impacted employees but also for management and HR professionals. What are the selection criteria for individual employees? Who informs the employees subject to separation? How are employees told that they need to look for a new job? What monetary and non-monetary support do they receive? It is highly advisable to perform this separation process with the utmost fairness. A fair separation leaves open the opportunity in the future to rehire good people who cannot be employed at the current time. This aspect should not be underestimated, especially for experts.

Assignment Policy

The assignment policy is also part of personnel planning during integration. By assigning employees from their own companies, acquirers seek to improve not only their connections and integration with the acquired company but also their level of control. This approach is certainly appropriate, especially during the period immediately following announcement when relationships with the acquisition need to be stabilised and aligned with the direction of the parent company.

However, problems arise when the newly acquired company is flooded with managers, coaches, experts and other 'advisers' from the acquiring company, as is often the case (Hermsen, 1994, p. 145). This can quickly produce cultural rejection, and labels like 'buyers' mafia' for assignees represent only the tip of the iceberg.

Especially problematic are the 'self-important hicks' below top management who, according to Leichsenring, 'fly in and out . . . like vultures . . . and act . . . as if they are the mental health police' (Leichsenring, 1999, p. 98).

The following US example illustrates that buyers need to adopt a sensitive approach and accommodate the corporate culture of the 'other' company if an acquisition is to be successful. Before the communications company ROLM became part of Siemens, ROLM had been acquired by IBM – at that time still the 'old' IBM, strict, very centrally organised and data processing-oriented. IBM sent its managers in blue suits and starched shirts into a typical Silicon Valley startup whose employees wore sneakers and thought more in terms of networks than hierarchies and therefore had developed a completely different corporate culture than IBM. Before long, a 'two-tier society' developed: IBM management came and announced what headquarters wanted, and the employees – those who were still around – tried more or less successfully to meet those demands. The end of the story: within a few years many of the highly qualified ROLM employees had left the company.

To prevent such a 'brain drain' it is highly advisable, before a merger, to perform cultural due diligence and to develop a *cultural integration strategy* in order to purposely manage cultural integration and to prevent unintended results.

5 Corporate Culture and the Integration Process

Developing Cultural Integration

How intensively the cultures need to be brought together and how cultural integration is achieved depends on the intended degree of integration. Of course, corporate cultures and the process of cultural integration cannot be managed in the same way that, for example, manufacturing processes, finance or distribution channels can be managed. Corporate culture has too many facets and drivers that are difficult to control because they are rooted in the past and, in part, even outside the company. What is possible is *'culture-conscious' management* that focuses on HR management and handles cultural differences very sensitively. In most cases, the problem is not cultural differences, but the fact that these differences are not sufficiently considered and appropriately managed. Culture-conscious management requires cultural analysis to determine the cultural differences between the companies. This analysis goes further than the preliminary 'culture check' performed during due diligence.

After every merger, employees initially perceive the influence of the other culture as interference because its ways of thinking and behaviours are different from what they are used to. Over time, however, as employees have to deal with the other company's culture in their daily work, an adjustment process is bound to happen, regardless of the cultural integration strategy employed (monoculture, multiculture or mixed-culture strategy). During integration, there is also a tendency for employees of the acquiring company increasingly to question their own corporate culture, especially in areas where they prefer the 'foreign' culture. Therefore, every merger will create a 'new' corporate culture. This culture is characterised by the interaction between both cultures and the desired degree of harmony. Successful cultural integration is likely when there is a good relationship between the acquiring and acquired companies – or, in case of a bad relationship, if the acquisition subordinates its culture to that of the acquirer.

Cultural integration is considered successful when any differences, however big or small, between parent and subsidiary can remain without creating substantial conflict (Sewing, 1996, p. 166).

The success and pace of cultural integration depend primarily on the

- *Dominating behaviour* of the stronger company
- Attitudes of *employees and managers* toward the merger
- Desired degree of *harmony*
- Degree of *cultural freedom* conferred upon the merger.

The organisational environment also plays an important role. Critical situations develop if the stronger company strongly asserts its dominance over the acquisition. This is likely if there are strong networks in the acquiring company that uses this period of change to secure advantageous positions for their members.

Such 'social networks' exist in every company. They develop from a basic human desire for bonding, comfort, friendship and security, and they comprise the *informal structure* of every company. Social networks are also a key element of successful acquisitions. They are expressed as mutual social obligations combined with a high potential for sanctions. Every company has countless social networks, some tightly knit and some more loosely linked.

Successful integration requires identifying the opinion leaders in the most important social networks, because they have a strong guiding role. This role is not to be underestimated during periods of uncertainty when positions have to be reassigned and other changes need to be implemented. Insufficient inclusion of these opinion-making leaders can easily create cultural resistance and cause the merger to fail (Figure 10.7).

The critical success factors for cultural integration are the relationship between the acquiring and the acquired company as well as the individual attitudes of employees and management towards integration. The four most frequently observed results of cultural integration are:

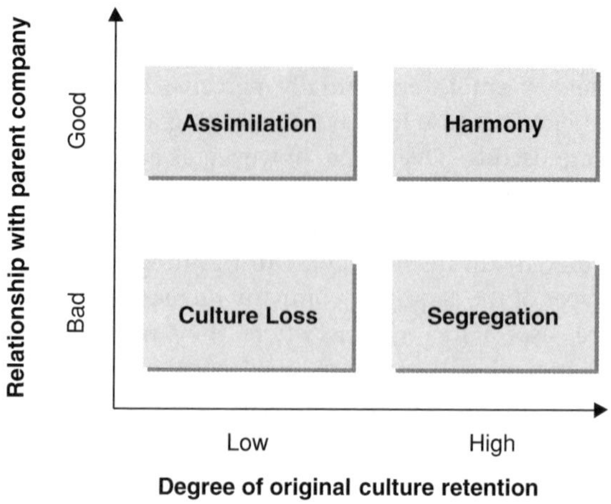

Figure 10.7 Results of cultural integration
Source: Sewing (1996, p. 168).

At best, a *harmonious relationship* develops between acquirer and acquisition. This is to be expected when the employees of both companies strongly embrace the merger or acquisition. A new culture develops that combines the best elements of both. This form of cultural integration works especially well for mergers of equals and for geocentric business models.

Assimilation also characterises a good relationship between the two companies, but with little desire by the acquired company to retain its own cultural elements. Instead the new acquisition easily integrates into the acquiring company and adjusts to its values and cultural characteristics. Relationships between the employees of both companies are good. This result works well for ethnocentric and polycentric business models.

Cultural integration is more difficult if the relationship between both companies and their employees is strained – for example, during an unfriendly takeover or when a merger was not well communicated. This can lead to *segregation* and *culture loss*. In the case of segregation, the acquired company clings to its culture. In the case of culture loss, employees of both companies submit to the new situation without a strong interest in cooperating. Mergers like this are at high risk of failure, and cultural integration must be very carefully planned and implemented.

Successful cultural integration has many advantages:

- Several studies show that the stronger a company's corporate culture, the less management effort, policy-making and control is required (Hofstede, 1997, p. 179).
- In companies with a strong corporate culture, employees at all levels know what is expected of them in most situations because they share the same basic values, pursue the same goals and head in the same direction.

One major challenge for the integration team is to create excitement about coming together, because that is what is required for synergies to develop. The best tool to achieve this excitement is a *joint vision* that everyone can identify with. Therefore, it is extremely important to develop a joint direction and to create a basic set of shared values as quickly as possible following a merger. These form the foundation for a shared identity, strengthen cooperation and orient the organisation towards joint goals.

HR management and leadership tools play a key role in culture-conscious management. Employee development and performance management as well as compensation systems need to be designed to reward desired behaviour and sanction undesired behaviour. Symbolic measures like joint events – for example, a picnic, a memento or a new corporate design – complement this.

Often, minor issues turn out to be handicaps to cultural integration if they are not resolved to everyone's satisfaction. For example, during a merger of two US companies, two different 'picnic' cultures were discovered: one company invited its employees' partners to the picnic, the other did not. To resolve this difficult dilemma, the two companies agreed that in even years the picnic would include partners and in odd years partners would stay home.

The following four steps towards cultural integration have proven successful:

Building Trust and Mental Networking

This is best accomplished by involving as many employees and managers as possible in the change process and by forming *integration teams* that include employees from both companies. This facilitates getting to know each other, creates shared experiences and reduces prejudices. At the same time, creativity, readiness to learn and tolerance for 'different' ideas increases, and willingness to share information readily and voluntarily improves. This forms the basis for 'mental networking', which is achieved when all partners within a network think and act along the same lines. Success factors for mental networking are shared goals, similar values and behaviours, and decision patterns that are aligned with long-term business goals.

Developing Shared Values/Joint Vision

People who share the same values also assess situations in a similar manner and understand each other better. This minimises friction loss and coordination effort – especially for cooperation between partners who are distributed around the globe. Joint visions are the basis for development of trust in an organisation because similar values offer a basic measure of stability and continuity and are an essential prerequisite for company loyalty. They provide a 'home base' during the constant changes that members of virtual teams are subjected to.

The actual content of the vision is less important than how firmly a company believes in it and aligns all its actions towards it. Collins and Porras (1994) have shown convincingly that companies which consistently live their visions are more successful than others. This success can be seen primarily in excellent financial returns over long periods. Such companies also possess astounding *regenerative capabilities* that enable them to survive even serious crises.

A company's vision is incorporated in all its goals, strategies, operations and processes. It affects workflow and performance management. This creates a company-specific environment that, in turn, shapes the behaviour and motivation of employees. Such a 'total environment... envelops employees' and exposes them to a set of signals that – and this is crucial – are consistent and mutually reinforcing (Collins and Porras, 1994, p. 202).

When a large corporation acquires a smaller company, as a rule the larger company's vision also permeates the acquisition.

Comparing Intended Values with Everyday Business Reality

If cultural due diligence has been performed, which is not usually the case, the results can be used here. This comparison can set off a very painful and momentous process. The acquiring company usually has specific objectives for the acquisition and expects the acquisition's employees and management to internalise and accept these objectives. If, in working together on a daily basis, ways of thinking and behaviour patterns emerge that run counter to the values of the acquiring company, appropriate steps must be taken to address them. *Integration workshops* with employees and managers from both companies who are to work together more closely in the future are one successful approach. In these groups, specific behaviours and individual ideas can be discussed together. In most cases, these workshops result in tangible action plans for what is to be accomplished jointly, by what date, and who will contribute which part. Such commitment is the first step towards effective cooperation.

Creating Consistent Management Models

Performance management offers very effective instruments for cultural integration of both companies. Leveraging international synergy and optimisation potential requires a globally applicable HR strategy and a global leadership model. Different business models employ different degrees of control. Ethnocentric businesses tend to regulate every detail of their management system and apply it to the acquisition. Polycentric and geocentric businesses create a few global standards that each country and the acquisition then adapt to its local requirements. The motto is: *as local as possible and as global as necessary*. This creates local autonomy and, at the same time, a shared foundation for international cooperation within the company, which enables international performance comparisons and international employee exchange.

The Siemens Way of Integration

In a large corporation like Siemens, with more than 450 000 employees in 190 countries around the globe, acquisition and integration of smaller companies, as well as joint ventures with domestic and foreign companies are the order of the day. One of the key tools used by the corporation to quickly integrate partners into the Siemens group of companies is its statement of corporate principles (Figure 10.8).

The Siemens corporate principles were redrawn in 1997. By defining focus areas such as 'customers', 'innovation', 'excellent leadership', 'learning', 'corporate

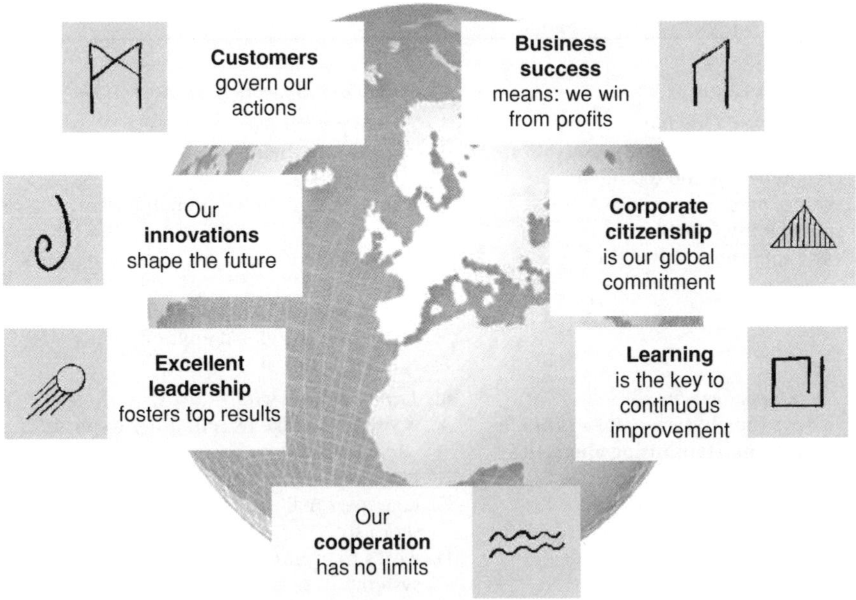

Figure 10.8 Siemens' corporate principles
Source: Siemens.

citizenship' and 'business success' the corporation sets clear standards for its employees and managers as well as for its business partners, customers, suppliers and future employees.

These corporate principles were derived from attitudes and values shared by its employees worldwide, as determined by a comprehensive value analysis. The analysis was based on a model by Hall (1995) and employed a survey to assess the values held by employees. A similar approach can be used for cultural analysis during mergers. Cultural analysis can provide interesting insights into which areas need additional focus in order to minimise differences.

A simple method for measuring corporate culture is an electronic *'value quick check'*. This quick check presents 60 questions that employees answer onscreen. These questions are grouped into categories such as 'long-term goals' and 'talents and skills'. From a list of multiple choices, employees select the answer that best fits their individual personality and attitudes. Redundancies in different combinations of answers allow accurate evaluation. This quick check reveals the degree to which the values of individual employees match corporate principles. This method highlights areas that require specific measures to make progress towards achieving the intended corporate culture (Table 10.2).

Cultural integration in general is about establishing comprehensive contacts between both 'worlds' to enable and support employees getting to know each other. There are limits, of course: it is not possible for entire development departments to visit the acquisition and get to know their new colleagues. Project-oriented

Table 10.2 Excerpts from Siemens' quick check of attitudes and values

Section One **Long-Term Goals**	***Please choose answers that most fit the present***
1: ***I am a person who:*** A. puts a priority on self preservation B. is competent and confident C. values personal security D. puts family first E. not applicable at this time	3: ***I am a person who:*** A. can be overwhelmed by the wonder and awe of life B. wants to develop my human potential to the fullest C. by my presence adds meaning to people's lives D. is involved with and has influence in preserving the global environment E. not applicable at this time
2: ***I am a person who:*** A. enjoys the physical comforts of life B. spends time fantasising about the good life C. enjoys work but prefers play D. contemplates or meditates regularly E. is not applicable at this time	4: ***I am a person who:*** A. is willing to take risks in order to pursue a personal goal B. is proud to work hard for a living C. takes personal equality and freedom very seriously D. works to promote human dignity in the system E. not applicable at this time

Source: Siemens.

cooperation offers a useful alternative to site visits. During integration there are many projects that require cooperation, which quickly creates shared experience and – most importantly – *mutual trust*.

Siemens has developed a standard approach to adapting the cultures of newly acquired companies to its corporate principles:

- *A joint integration team* charged with 'corporate culture' with members from both partner companies is formed. This is followed by the cultural analysis of target company values described earlier.
- Results of the cultural analysis are presented in a *workshop* with the acquisition's top management. This includes core values, special skills and readiness to change. Differences with the Siemens' corporate principles, the principles that constitute the culture to which Siemens aspires, are outlined.
- This is followed by an intense discussion, sometimes a very emotional process, during which an attempt is made to develop understanding and commitment. It goes without saying that this is not always achieved at the first try, which is why the workshop is *repeated* after a while.
- The next step is *communication with employees*. This includes meetings and team workshops to discuss how the values outlined by the corporate principles can be implemented, using practical examples. These measures are complemented by joint projects and training related to the corporate principles.

The most effective lever for implementing corporate principles and timely integration, however, is *performance management*. Siemens has created worldwide standards to consistently align its HR development system with its vision.

- Individual *objectives* define the specific contributions each employee is expected to make to the company's business success. They provide individual orientation and define the necessary scope of action and decision making. Subsequent performance reviews enable concrete performance appraisals.
- *Standardised employee surveys* regularly assess corporate culture. The goal is to increase every department's productivity by identifying the need for action and improvement potential.
- Annual *upward feedback* enables employees to provide positive feedback to managers and to identify areas requiring individual management improvements. Managers compare this feedback with their self-evaluation and, together with their employees, develop management goals to be implemented within one year.
- The *Siemens leadership framework* enables all managers to clearly assess their own performance. It specifies business requirements derived from the corporate principles and compares them with actual management performance. The results are then used to determine measures for improving management performance.
- In annual *performance reviews*, employees discuss their performance and personal potential with their manager. Manager and employee then jointly agree on specific employee development measures.
- *Flexible compensation systems* relate income to business success and reward both individual and group results. They tie management incentives, annual bonuses and stock options to achievement of business goals.
- *Management learning* embeds the goals defined by the corporate principles into the consciousness of managers. By participating in international training teams, competent employees with leadership potential are systematically prepared for management and executive responsibilities. Self-study using the latest media tools, workshops and interdisciplinary business projects are used to develop skills required for business success and to promote cooperation within the company.

Efficient, world-wide HR management requires a human resource organisation that views itself as a global network of HR professionals and that makes decisions jointly. To this purpose, Siemens has established a 'Personnel Council World' where headquarters, regional and operating group HR representatives are equally represented. This council makes all HR decisions of world-wide relevance and manages the implementation of these decisions, thus ensuring that personnel and cultural integration for international mergers and acquisitions is performed expeditiously and according to uniform criteria.

6 Summary

What are the key success factors for personnel and cultural integration with mergers and acquisitions?

- No successful M&A without employee participation
- Involvement of HR experts as strategic partners during pre-acquisition planning, due diligence and integration planning
- Comprehensive communication planning with detailed scheduling
- Continuous, honest and timely communication and feedback
- Preparing management for employee reactions and how to deal with them
- Preventive risk management to deal with declines in productivity and rising employee fluctuation
- An integration office that drives and is responsible for success of integration
- Consistent application of organisational justice
- Targeted measures to achieve cultural integration
- Clear understanding of compatibility and degree of cultural integration of the two corporate cultures.

If the assumption that people create business success is valid, then the 'human factor' plays a decisive role in mergers and acquisitions. HR management's role is to actively guide a company and its employees through all phases of integration.

Bibliography

Collins, J. C. and Porras, J. I. (1994) *Built to Last. Successful Habits of Visionary Companies* (New York).

Gertsen, M. C., Soderberg, A.-M. and Torp, J. E. (1998) *Cultural Dimensions of International Mergers and Acquisitions* (New York).

Grant, R. M. (1991) The Resource-Based Theory of Competitive Advantage: Implications for Strategy Formulation, *California Management Review*, Spring.

Gut-Villa, C. (1997) *Human Resource Management bei Mergers & Acquisitions* (Bern).

Hall, B. (1995) *Values Shift* (Rockport, MA).

Haspeslagh, P. C. and Jemison, D. B. (1991) *Managing Acquisitions: Creating Value Through Corporate Renewal* (New York).

Hermsen, C. (1994) *Mergers & Acquisitions – Integrationsmanagement von Akquisitionsobjekten* (Hallstadt).

Hofstede, G. (1997) *Cultures and Organizations: Software of the Mind; Intercultural Cooperation and Its Importance for Survival* (New York).

Hubbard, N. (1999) *Acquisition – Strategy and Implementation* (London).

Kearney, A. T. (1999) *Integration nach Unternehmenskauf – Ihr Weg zur Post-Merger-Excellence* (Unpublished presentation slides).

Keller, E. von (1982) *Management in fremden Kulturen* (Bern).

Kraillinger, J. (1997) *M&A – Managing the Transition* (New York).

Leichsenring, V. (1999) Corporate Vulture – über den Umgang mit fremden Unternehmenskulturen, *Wirtschaftswoche*, 25.

Marks, M. L. and Mirvis, P. H. (1992) Track the Impact of Mergers and Acquisitions, *Personnel Journal*, 4.

Perlmutter, H. V. (1969) The Tortuous Evolution of the Multinational Corporation, *Columbia Journal of World Business*, 4.

Pritchett, P. (1997) *After the Merger* (New York).

Reichwald, R., Möslein, K., Sachenbacher, H., Englberger, H. and Oldenburg, S. (1998) *Telekooperation – Verteilte Arbeits-und Organisationsformen* (Berlin).

Rosenstiel, L. (1997) Human Resource Management bei Mergers & Acquisitions, in Gut-Villa, C., *Human Resource Management bei Mergers & Acquisitions* (Bern).

Scholz, C. (1993) *Personalmanagement. Informationsorientierte und verhaltenstheoretische Grundlagen* (Munich).

Senge, P. (1998) The Leader's New Work: Building Learning Organizations, in Segal-Horn, S. (ed.), *The Strategy Reader*, (Oxford and Malden, MA).

Sewing, N. (1996) *Akquisitionserfolg durch Integration der Mitarbeiter* (Wiesbaden).

11
Internal and External Communications

Rainer Zimmermann

1 Introduction

Mergers and acquisitions (M&A) make demands on communications which can be described with a total of seven basic functions. Not all of these basic functions are necessarily required in all cases. The first task of communications planning prior to an M&A, which is described in this chapter, is to create an awareness of, and give priority to the basic functions.

Communications as Stakeholder Value

The industrial logic of M&A is, to great extent, determined by the concept of *shareholder value*. Mergers or acquisitions are intended to improve the competitiveness of business divisions, with the aim of raising values over the medium term to ensure a competitive rate of return on investment. Higher values, owing to mergers, arise, for example, from a broader customer base, from extended access to new markets, from sales optimisation, from a bundling of resources, from economies of scale and synergetic effects and from the complementary combination of the best practice areas of the merger candidates to form new process chains.

The general focus of all arguments found by communications in all M&A cases thus inevitably relates to a higher benefit and higher acceptance among shareholders, partners and the financial community. Leading up to an M&A, there is, at best, only a vague idea of the value that can be derived for customers and employees of the merging companies from a proposed merger or integration of one company into the other. *An added value for customers and employees is naturally not the motivation for an M&A*.

Corporate communications, on the other hand, basically serve the function of documenting and demonstrating the performance and economic value of a company to all of its stakeholders (see Figure 11.1).

A comprehensive consideration of all reference groups of a company immediately raises a conflict between target group-specific information and messages for the four reference groups in Figure 11.1 and a consistent and fully plausible story. Thus, it is generally a compulsory exercise to describe to the financial community what synergetic effects, and thus profit maximisation, will result

Stakeholders Financial community	**Employees** Employee representatives
Customers Brokers Trade	**Society** Opinion leaders

Figure 11.1 Stakeholders

from the consolidation of cross-sectional functions or the reduction of sites. What produces confidence in the meaningfulness of an investment, or even fantastic price movement expectations, on the one hand, causes, on the other, employees to be demotivated or frustrated.

Moreover, the M&A concepts presented to the supervisory boards would then hardly sound like a greater degree of appreciation to customers, but more like a marginalisation or standardisation of their personal customer relations. As a consequence of the M&A logic, they would have benevolently to take note of the fact that the cost–income ratio per customer will improve in the future, and that the company intends to earn Euro *XY* per year with each customer. In the case of service companies, M&A frequently involve re-defining and standardising the process of rendering services, through an increase in the number of customers handled by each consultant or a reduction of the range of services offered. Manufacturing businesses also experience a loss of proximity, continuity of contact partners or tailor-made customer demands owing M&A, e.g. because of platform strategies, global sourcing measures or integrated logistics.

The examples mentioned above illustrate that the second task of communications in the case of M&A must be to develop a *communicative logic* from the given parameters of the intended M&A, rather than to translate or transport facts and messages. The aim of such communicative logic is to determine, with a plausibility test, the (increased or reduced) economic value of the proposed M&A for all four reference groups in Figure 11.1, and whether this economic value portfolio can be communicated. Acceptance and sympathy for the corporate strategy and the performance of the company after the M&A are intended effects of communications which can be achieved from the substance of the economic values.

Communications as a Plausibility Test

The benefit analysis described above for all four reference groups of the companies involved is ideally made in the form of a SWOT analysis (Strength/Weaknesses, Opportunities/Threats), determining the direct advantages and disadvantages for all four reference groups as well as indirect opportunities and risks involved in the proposed M&A. The communications consultants must put themselves into the position of the reference group examined in each case, and describe their perception and potential of criticism in worst-case and best-case scenarios.

Thus, this communicative analysis frequently has the function of a *load test* or a *plausibility test* for the proposed M&A. The implications for the employees, the customers and the company, the national economy and the opinion leaders are generally not fully thought out in the planning and decision-making phase for an M&A. For example, insufficient benefits for customers would be delegated at a later time as a problem to the marketing department in the course of a reactive M&A implementation. The response to this would presumably be greater marketing investments or a call for help in the form of product or service innovations. If the plausibility test is made prior to the announcement, it is possible to either better balance the economic value portfolio within the four reference groups or to present the counteractive measures as an inherent element of the M&A strategy.

Whoever fails to understand or leave unclear the scope and implications of the M&A strategy for the reference groups in the announcement phase will risk having to make improvements at a later time, or to even change a part of the M&A strategy, possibly even at the request of a reference group. This would have to be seen as a communications failure because it can hardly be done subtly. On the other hand, being able to show the benefits of the M&A for stakeholders, customers and employees at the time of the announcement is a first and clear communications success. This is especially important since the high publicity and public influence involved in the announcement should be used to send the proper internal signals and also to set the proper course for communications with the customers. An essential factor which is critical to the success of an M&A is the optimal use of *momentum* – i.e. of 'creative self-destruction' according to Schumpeter (1949), which can release enormous forces in the organisation and in relation to the market. It is the function of communications to maintain this momentum, beginning with the announcement up to the final conclusion of the post-merger integration (PMI). Any deficit in the envisaged benefit will diminish the momentum. A *communicative plausibility test* should therefore always be done in the pre-merger phase.

Communications as a Driving Force

In view of the stakeholder value and the plausibility test for the benefit for all reference groups, one important basic function of corporate communications has been described: to ensure coherence, without regard to the later segmentation and creation of content and messages depending on the target groups. The strategic programme of a company and its vision of the future are indivisible at first. It is important that this strategy as an indivisible whole can be conveyed to all reference groups. In addition to this coherence function, there is especially for M&A the function of corporate communications as a 'driving force'. Thus driving force can be described as ensuring the implementation of the projects, for example of the integration teams, within defined deadlines and to have an organisation adjust to procedural thinking. Naturally, the driving forces of communication must be seen in combination with the pulling forces connected to the stakeholder value and the plausibility test. The employees are 'pulled' and 'attracted' by the plausibility of the entire story, by the benefit determined for the reference group of the employees (migration possibilities within the group, international horizon, career perspectives, context of competitiveness and job security), by the positive force of the corporate vision and the momentum in change management. Where speed is desired, and that is always the case in an M&A, it is better not to rely only on the pulling forces, but to employ additional driving forces. In detail, the 'driving' communication steps in Table 11.1 should be made within the organisation.

Empirical comparisons with M&A projects by European Communications Consultants show that communicative driving forces contribute not only to accelerating the processes, but primarily to providing orientation to the intended direction of the change and the actual and intended positions at any particular time. Especially for the middle management and the employees as a whole, these explanations are of great value, because they raise the degree of identification with the defined aims and relieve the top management of the task of giving redundant explanations and continuously answering questions. However, process tracking should, like any measure of internal communications, not be limited to something owed by corporate management in the sense of 'top-down information', but should likewise be something sought by dedicated employees. The point is not so much to regularly distribute all essential information and to take measures to involve everyone, but rather to create opportunities to gain access and to participate. Intranet and extranet, call centres and open events can serve not only to offer access and participation possibilities, but also to measure how often they are used, and by whom.

Apart from the integration function and the partial projects defined therein, the function of communications as a driving force for a great number of other strategic

Table 11.1 Communicative driving forces in seven steps

Information	Process cycle definition for PMI
Information	The milestones in the process, criteria for measuring plan achievement
Argumentation	Why these milestones, why these criteria?
Argumentation	Significance of the time factor for M&A success
Motivation	Incentive for plan achievement
Involvement	Process tracking, quick transparency of the process steps already made and still to be made for all employees concerned
Involvement	Accompanying measures (such as games), infotainment

corporate projects is indispensable. For example, the introduction of *balanced score cards* or other *benchmark* or *control* systems is simply impossible without the clarifying and stimulating effect of the communicative driving forces.

Communications as a Centripetal Force

The function of communications as a centripetal force was first recognised in the early 1980s and has been used by most companies in the context of corporate identity or corporate culture programmes. However, without any doubt, the centripetal forces have become stronger in recent years. Decentralisation and globalisation processes, faster growth, rapid changes in the portfolios of companies, the elimination of 'old' business segments and the creation of 'new' business segments, the segmentation of former product groups, plants, business divisions, forming new profit centres, the destruction of traditions and of traditional decades-old company names, as well as the establishment of new, mostly synthetic and frequently computer-generated names – all these are factors which tear apart the common denominator of a company and make the socio-cultural binding forces more diffuse. The stronger the centrifugal forces act, the more necessary it is to counteract with communicative centripetal forces. For this, it is by no means sufficient to provide a logo to all employees or to design directives which are distributed by interoffice mail and then shelved. Especially in an M&A, and even more so in the case of bi-national M&A, cultural identities are not only endangered, but sometimes deliberately exposed to review. The hectic action which occasionally opens new identity accounts and closes old ones quite recklessly in connection with an M&A far too often lacks any reflection on desired 'home feelings' on the part of the employees.

As a matter of principle, it is necessary to determine how many and which identity accounts are possible and feasible within the group. The *identity offers* within multistage companies are often not coordinated. Employees receive letters, staff magazines, invitations to events or intranet connections or access to corporate missions not only of the group (the umbrella brand name), but also of the divisional companies or their microcosm GmbH or profit centre. The effort of making the synthesis by reconciling these different identity offers generally remains the task of the employee himself. Such identity shopping almost always results in greatly differing affiliation and loyalty feelings. Especially those who have been employed for many years tend to feel attached to a particular site, whereas employees who have joined a company only recently think in terms of divisions.

M&A additionally cause a wealth of fears and acquired rejection patterns to arise. It is not easy to suddenly see a former competitor as an ally. For this reason, drafting corporate identity concepts as a theoretical exercise can hardly achieve the desired results. If one regards cultural coherence and identification with the company as an important factor in competition, one is well advised to plan the developments in a *participative manner* and as a *process*. A suitable figure of speech for identity-creating concepts is the 'fleet' which carries out holistic joint operations under the leadership of a 'flagship' with, however, clearly definable tasks for each 'ship'.

Communications as a Theme Generator

'If the company knew what the company knows' is a popular *bon mot* to illustrate the potential in concealed and undiscovered skills. Especially in the case of an M&A, the knowledge of management as a basis for positioning the company is of crucial importance. Even if M&A do not basically change the core competence of the company, they tend in most cases to be more deeply verticalised or to be extended. After the diversification period in the 1970s and 1980s, refocusing or focusing concepts have come to dominate, seeking to agglomerate volumes and appropriate core competences in preferred fields of business. Within the industrial logic of an M&A, the defined core fields of business are always *theme fields*.

Two examples may be mentioned here: the theme field of life sciences has triggered a whole series of M&A among chemical companies. This term is an attempt to reconcile the activities in the classical health care and pharmaceutical sector with the activities in the agricultural and veterinary sector to create a uniform focus and business concept. For a variety of reasons which begin in research and end in distribution, it made sense to the chemical companies to no longer present themselves in the future as a two-column model with two divisions, but to place a uniform basic concept above the former concept of separate fields of business. But life sciences are initially not a market, but only an abstract idea which must first create its own market in a self-fulfilling prophecy. Substantial positioning arises when the idea of life sciences is thematically filled with life. A further example is the considerations or already complete plans of utility companies to focus on the future as utilities or suppliers of basic requirements. Utility companies pursued a diversification strategy for decades and are now reorganising a part of their business based on the new concept of becoming an integrated supplier of electricity, gas, or water. In some cases, the formerly separate electricity and gas businesses are made subordinate to a supposedly graphic, but in reality abstract, heat. In both cases, the industrial logic requires focusing over diversification and suggests that focusing is honoured by the Stock Exchange with higher multiples. To cut back the business while achieving calculable advantages for shareholder value, it is necessary to relate the organisational structures and business systems to the idea of focusing.

In both cases, the industrial logic gave rise to a core competence which is not genuinely, but is regarded as, new. There is no demand for life sciences or utilities: customers (at least for the time being) wish to purchase either headache tablets or pesticides, rarely both at the same time. The idea of buying electricity, gas or water and maybe even waste disposal in a package from one service provider will succeed only if those areas that are to belong together are allowed to grow together thematically.

This is where communications – and, within communications, especially journalism – must begin and develop stories from ideas. For this, a great deal of work must first be done: research within the group as to what thinking, studies and data are available in relation to the newly chosen theme field; external research on the publications concerning the theme field or related theme fields, and which universities or institutes, think tanks or competitors have commented on this;

retrospective media analyses, internal demoscopic studies. In a second step, different divisions from the two merged companies are to be joined together in order to give them as much substance as possible. In a third step, the positioning substance that has been won can be extrapolated and developed into a *theme career.*

The systematic handling of the theme by communications promotes the intellectual consideration of the *field of business*. New trends, aspects previously not considered, interesting application examples or culmination points of public interest in this theme are revealed, and by means of this input also increase the output. Communications thus have the function of generating themes where opinion leadership or at least an important role in the share of voice are possible. At the same time, communications cause an experienceable interpretation power to unfold from the newly defined competence of the company, turning lonely concepts into interesting stories on a strategy chart and laying the foundation stone for an intellectual consideration of the new business orientation.

Communications as an Added Value

As already seen every company must convey and argue economic values to its stakeholders. Communications are the medium in which this happens. But at the same time, communications are a supplier of information which is regarded as a fourth production factor and becomes increasingly appreciated within the *information and knowledge society.* The accessibility, availability and preparation of information on themes, branches of business, markets, target groups, consumers and trends are consequently a service which not only gives the company a profile as the holder and sender of this information, but are also a service as such, provided the quality of the information or the ease of access and of selection represents a value for the receiving target group.

All information which is not specifically related to a particular company and is disseminated or made available by a company represents a *communicative added value* in that the products and services of the company are supplemented by an information service. This realisation is of course not new and has, in the past, caused companies – especially companies which depend on products which are not easily distinguishable – to offer their customers (or business partners/or the company on the whole) added value. A prominent example is BAT Freizeitforschungsinstitut, which has for many years conducted and published studies on the leisure and recreation conduct of Germans. The added value arises here for the company as a whole. Advisers and orientation help represent added value for existing and potential customers. Market information or trade directories create added value either for the brokers or trading partners or for the journalists and opinion leaders.

In an M&A, existing added value functions must be reviewed and compared with the intended position of the 'NewCo' and with its target group orientation. Here an obviously appropriate strategy is to underpin the high degree of market knowledge and capability of interpretation, the market presence and the market-influencing ambition of the company with added information values addressed primarily to the business community and the opinion leaders.

Communications as a Differentiation

Every M&A is a hard blow for the differentiation theory because it demonstrates that, at the end of the day, other things are more important than the (communicative) distinctiveness of two companies or brands. With one blow, the M&A equalises or even eliminates differentiations which may have been carefully built up over decades. Whatever may have been different, setting the company apart from others and distinguishing them, is now the same. In view of this, differentiation incantations look like empty promises which are financially worthless. To merge first means to eliminate distinctions and is thus a contradiction of differentiation.

To aggravate matters, the old names are maintained only rarely, for political reasons, and new names come up which signify no more than a naked projection screen and are therefore a far cry from any effort to differentiate. M&A candidates first face the task of making clear that their companies or parts of their companies have taken on a form which is an expression of the new contents. At the same time, a mathematical impossibility must be conveyed, namely that on the one hand $A + B = C$, but on the other hand $C > A + B$ in the sense of 'added value'.

The significance of differentiation strategies grows with the maturity of companies and the lack of distinctiveness of their products and services. M&A candidates are a very young company after the merger. Moreover, this company has captured new differentiating potential through the merger – for example, cost advantages which can be passed on to the customers, an improved global reach, which has a favourable effect on service, or stronger research resources, which will ensure product innovations. The significance of differentiation from competitors in communications is accordingly low.

It can generally be said that communications as a differentiating factor must apparently assume the function of a stopgap, because metaphors are used to create the impression of differences which do not exist in product reality. This is normal and inevitable in the area of fast moving consumer goods (fmcg), but also always demonstrate that there is no superior business concept. In the area of business-to-business (B2B) communications and also in relation to opinion leaders, differentiation by communications plays a minor role in any case. If the functions 'communications as stakeholder value' and 'communications as theme generator' are persistently exercised, differentiation is automatically achieved by virtue of profiling, as a consequence of an autonomous theme policy. Differentiation strategies which choose competition as their starting point always have only one extrapolating value and cannot make any quantum leaps.

2 Communications Management

Conduct

The question of how communications are conducted cannot be answered in a standardised way in view of the governing practices in the companies. Surprisingly, the organisational charts for communications departments differ greatly between companies which are comparable in size, international alignment or branch of business. Whereas organisational optimisation processes began no later than in the 1980s in practically all other corporate divisions as a result of benchmarking, reengineering and best-practice aspects, resulting in a higher degree of *similarity* between structures in a global comparison, communications departments grew organically, unhindered and individually. Companies organise their responsibilities and management tasks in the field of communications according to communication disciplines (advertising, public relations, sponsoring, sales promotion, direct marketing, online relations, event marketing), in some cases according to target groups (financial community, end consumers, trade, opinion leaders, journalists), but also in accordance with generic terms which are difficult to define, such as 'investor relations', 'corporate communications', 'public relations', 'public affairs', 'environment and society', 'culture and society', 'marketing', 'marketing services', or 'brand management'. The traditional abstention in relation to changes within communications departments frequently leads to 'special cultures' and a lack of transparency. The difficulties begin with the comparison between two communications departments in the case of a proposed merger: organisational charts are not always available; the same functional designations do not always mean the same; job profiles exist only rarely. Basic organisational decisions such as the separation between marketing communications and corporate communications were taken in many cases as long as 20 years ago; the reaction to new developments was a escalation. Younger fields of communications such as multimedia, evaluation or online-interactive find themselves 'docked' with some other department.

The wealth of organisational unclarities and delimitation difficulties continues in the management question. Disciplinary management and departmental management are frequently in different hands, many employees report to several executives. Traditionally, several management board members are also involved. For example, internal communications are sometimes handled by the chairman of the management board, but frequently also by the personnel director. Opinions differ already about the question as to what belongs in fact to the field of communications. For example, does a foundation established years ago belong to it? Is the promotion of the local tennis club a part of the CEO's representation budget, or is it communication? Accordingly, budgeting processes can be chaotic. Only few communications chiefs can answer the question as to how much money they spend on communications every year. They find it even more difficult to answer the question how much money they have already spent on 1 January of every year because of committed budget items.

The definition problems referred to here always grow in an M&A and become unmanageable and uncontrollable conglomerates where both companies have large communications departments (i.e. employ more than about 80 persons for this purpose). At the same time, an apparently natural *beauty contest* develops with the M&A information between the communications departments of both companies, which frequently begin an immediate armament race with special budgets, agencies and measures (Figure 11.2). To achieve a proper personnel balance, the positions in 'NewCo' are gladly filled twice – or, even worse, ghost positions are created which sediment and form a paralysing layer in the company.

A clear recommendation for the organisation and conduct of communications results from all these reasons in an M&A: the 'green meadow' principle. As described in Figure 11.2, ideally a task force is set up to drive the process of change. From it, a new communications department arises after the end of the integration period. This manner of proceeding offers only advantages. The new communications department can be defined in its structures and functions in a task-oriented manner and benefits from the opportunity to get rid of redundant structures. The task force operates in a process-oriented rather than structure-oriented manner and need not take complex reporting lines into account. It puts its projects on track quickly. Finally, 'NewCo' is given a *voice and face* for its communications in one go, and the rivalries between the two departments end even before they begin.

Task Force

A task force (for communications) is the only meaningful instrument to plan and implement communications tasks in an M&A. The task force is the interface to the management of the company, the investment bankers involved, management consultants, auditors and lawyers and to the existing resources in both companies. The task force should be led by the individual who has been designated as the communications chief for 'NewCo'. Individual employees from the communications

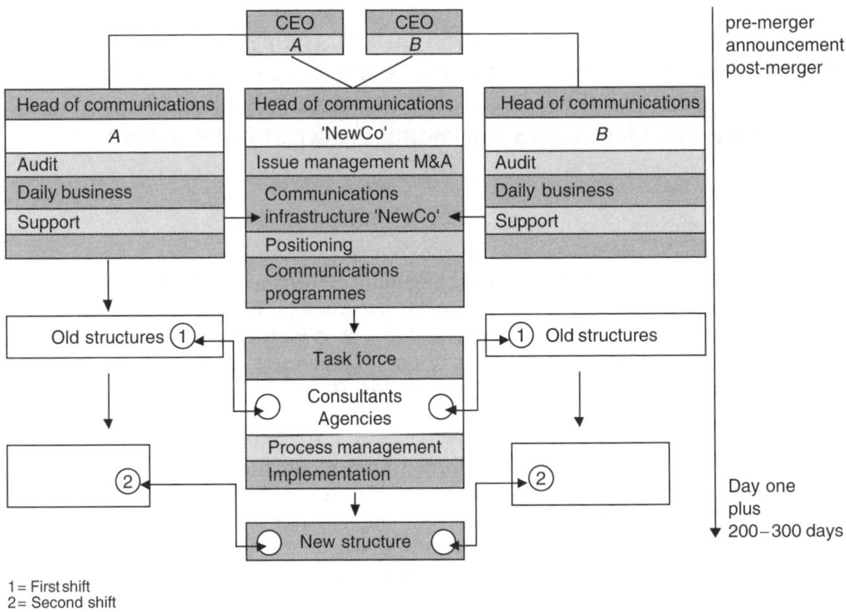

Figure 11.2 Communications management in M&A

departments of both M&A companies can be chosen and work immediately 100 per cent for the task force. Membership of the task force must be understood as a distinction. Experienced consultants from consultancy companies for communications or from agencies can support the task force. For this, only consultants with experience with M&A should be chosen. Moreover, it is necessary to ensure that the external members of the task force are entirely free from any other tasks during the process and are 100 per cent available to the task force. Depending on the complexity of the task and the number of countries involved, the task force should consist of 6 to 12 persons at the beginning. It delegates some project tasks to teams from both companies within the 'old' structures. For reasons of confidentiality and especially speed in the starting phase, a greater part will have to be delegated to external teams. It is therefore advisable to integrate two principals or senior consultants from external consultancy companies into the task force. The task force can control resources in their regular organisations from within.

After the beginning of the post-merger phase, tasks can successively be 'in-sourced' again. The speed of this in-sourcing depends on the shifting of resources from the 'old' structures to the task force or to the 'new' structures arising from this. The intensity of in-sourcing is a managerial and political question which must be decided as a matter of principle. Of course, all employees and also all external staff must sign specific confidentiality statements. The standard operation guidelines, course of conduct, technological safety standards and confidentiality guarantees of the consulting and advisory business must be checked.

Audit

The planning of future structures and activities should be preceded by a careful analysis of the actual current situation in both companies. For this purpose a *communications audit* is conducted in the companies to be merged. It looks into the following questions through desk-top research methods and interviews with the staff of the communications and controlling departments (Table 11.2).

Table 11.2 Communications

Resources	Organisational chart of the communications department/functions
Resources	Advisers, agencies, service providers (contracts and agreements)
Resources	Data, distribution structure, contacts, cooperation partners
Methods	Planning cycles, target orientation, market research, evaluation
Values	Mission statements, CI (Corporate Identity)/CD (Corporate Design) manuals, guidelines
Duties	Defined service functions
Duties	Commitments undertaken, orders placed, bookings
Resonance	Data supported/unsupported, brand awareness, brand features, quantitative/qualitative media resonance, customer satisfaction, expectance data, target groups, awards, ranking positions, image meters
Budget	Structure/committed/uncommitted budgets
Routines	On-going measures
Output	Publications, websites, campaigns, magazines, etc.

Both overlapping audits then show a complete picture of the strength and weaknesses, the starting points for restructuring and points of contact, existing target group ties as well as planning bases and tasks with medium-term deadlines already fixed. The audits also help to make one's own objectives and activities transparent for colleagues in the other communications department. Decisions as to which work and services should be performed in the future and on what technical platform and with which systems, are easier because the two audits make the basis and performance of the two departments comparable.

Management Information Systems

Management information systems for the communications staff and the overall executive staff are crucial especially for decentralised multinationally operating companies, not only to ensure that headquarters will be informed about the entire range of activities, but also to provide information to all decentralised employees in the field of communications. The technical basis for these systems now exists in an ideal form through intranets or extranets. However, quality depends to a great extent on the nature of the data fed in centrally and decentrally and on the homogeneity of the reporting levels.

Monitoring

- Does media observance, tracking, web watch follow the same principles in all countries and are they documented in uniform reporting formats?
- Who feeds reporting into the databases with what frequency, or who distributes them?
- Are there decentralised access possibilities?
- Can issues be raised quickly and internationally, are there daily quick reports or press reviews?
- Are the code words for media observation standardised, can topical code words quickly be integrated into the monitoring routine?
- Is the reporting frequency acceptable?
- Are there retrospective search functions and documentation possibilities – for example, electronic press archives?
- Do the questions raised fit together with the defined targets and benchmarks?
- How is the user behaviour of the communications people in the company?
- Are the monitoring data used for planning purposes?
- Is learning satisfactory?

Controlling

- Are there project databases or budget control tools?
- How quickly can budget funds be spent and open budgets be documented?
- Are the status reports by the different partners made in accordance with uniform principles?
- Is information transferred exclusively for the purposes of 'bottom-up' information – or, for example, do individual countries also benefit bilaterally from the data from other countries?

- Does reporting help to optimise the technical use of funds and to organise budget changes in accordance with current requirements?
- How are the decision-making processes between the various departments and the purchasing department regulated?
- Is the number of budget decision-makers properly defined?
- Does budget planning function as a strategic controlling instrument or as a subsequent adjustment to programme decisions already taken?

Planning

- Are the proposed projects, dates, campaigns documented in advance?
- Is it possible to obtain an overview of all communications activities in the group within one calendar week?
- Are the contents of communications means – for example texts – accessible to all communications employees prior to publication?
- Are contents used across borders or produced through a division of tasks?
- Who maintains and edits the planning data, who has the possibility to review them?
- How quickly are data updated?
- How much time does the maintenance of planning data take, are the effort and benefits disproportionate?

Documentation

- Are there any databases or collected information on preferred service providers, authors, ghost writers, artists, speakers, locations?
- Are the means of communications and campaigns that are produced documented and retrospectively retrievable?
- Can individual departments or countries benefit from the know-how or work already done in the past?
- Are best-practice processes described and documented so that comparable projects can be optimally structured from the beginning?
- Are checklists readily available?
- Are the evaluation data or efficiency reviews from earlier activities retrievable, can experience from successes and failures be used for future planning of measures?
- Are the data usefully organised and retrievable by keywords, is desired information quickly and easily obtainable?

Agenda-Setting

- Can topical information be quickly distributed to management?
- Are there possibilities to access basic materials – for example board members' speeches, positioning bases, guidelines, theme research, key messages?
- Is the orientation of those responsible for communications by contents centrally controlled?
- How quickly do communications follow the corporate strategy?

- Does important information reach the communications staff before it reaches other staff; is the communications staff sufficiently qualified to answer internal and external questions?
- Are questions and answers papers relating to key themes distributed?
- Can the communication of topical key issues be quickly and simultaneously organised internationally?

In an M&A, the flow of information and the frequency of new and changed information is traditionally high. To guarantee a consistent information policy free from any contradictions throughout the group, the communications staff must be ideally incorporated into the process and used as multipliers. In addition to the HR departments, they are the preferred contact persons for employees in the case of a change, and must also be able to answer external questions. Accordingly, it is necessary to define the distribution channels for all information relevant to an M&A, classified according to confidentiality and relevance, both for those responsible for communications and for management and subsequently for the employees as a whole.

Investment Planning

If the management of communications is approached as described on pp. 342 ff., the investments for communications within 'NewCo' will fall over the medium term compared to the original budgets of the merger candidates. In the first three years, comparatively high but non-recurrent investments must be made, especially for internal communications, which can be partially absorbed if the old infrastructure in the communications departments is reduced in a determined manner. For internal communications, it can generally be said that about 500 Euro per employee of 'NewCo' must be invested in the first year of the PMI, and approximately 300 Euro in the second year. External communications can be determined only individually and depending on the size of the company, the degree of internationalisation and the branch of business, but will generally amount at least to the same level as the expenses for internal communications. The communications budgets can be classified as special expenses for communications in the context of M&A restructuring costs and, even if they are generously fixed, they will be hardly be noticeable among the many exponentially higher restructuring costs in other areas. It is also true that from the point of view of practically all PMI studies, communications are regarded as a crucial factor for the success of a merger, which it is why it is not advisable to save money on an item which is crucial for success. Nevertheless, the necessary investments can be reduced by, for example, preventing the costly 'beauty contest' between the communications departments after the announcement or before the legal effectiveness of the M&A, or by using budget items already earmarked for projects which are in any case no longer useful in view of the M&A as quickly as possible to finance new M&A projects.

'Top-down'/'Bottom-Up' Dynamics

Anyone who views communications as a dialogue and not as a one-way street will face the difficulty, especially in large, decentralised, and international corporations, of gaining a complete and correct picture of the thinking and feeling of the employees, because it is rare to find a path on which this thinking and feeling can move from the bottom to the top. Naturally attempts are made everywhere to fill this gap with 'letters to the editor' in employee magazines, a chatroom on the intranet, and an email domain of the CEO which is accessible to all, or similar measures. All the same: The emotional conviction and credibility potential of medial communications is low, especially if something that is held together only by spot welding is intended to grow together quickly. Also to be viewed sceptically are the classical reporting lines through established hierarchical levels which often see and hear only what they choose to see and hear.

Moreover, communications simply serve more tasks in an M&A than in the normal course of business. A large amount needs to be *learned* within an extremely short period of time about the motives for the M&A, new strategies, new processes, new colleagues, new rules and products, new names and forms, new responsibilities for each individual and new expectations to be met. The abstract definition of these changes in the hierarchical structure and for advisers is difficult enough. Things then generally become unexpectedly complex in the course of the implementation, which cannot work if it is planned only *deductively*. It must also be *inductive* – i.e. thought out as a process moving from the specific to the general – and for this practically all employees are needed. Everything which must be learned must also be conveyed and understood, it must be possible to make corrections or modifications from the top to the bottom if instructions from the top cannot be put into effect at the bottom or can be implemented better and faster in some other way. For all of these coordination processes, communications are the *transmission belt*. Moreover, they then also serve the classic functions of cultural integration and to open up perspectives and provide motivation.

Consequently systems calculated for a lower load are not sufficient for this workload. Supplementary action must be taken to make the 'top-down' and 'bottom-up' dynamics possible at all. A tested and proven interim instrument for a duration of 9 to 18 months for an M&A are *scouts* or *messengers*. They are found among the employees and are entrusted with special functions.

Scouts are released from their regular work for a limited period of time for 25 per cent of their working time. This time is to be used by them to collect opinions, misunderstandings, comments and suggestions from their colleagues and to pass them on in weekly reporting sessions to the communications managers. The procedure is totally open. The point of the exercise is not to 'spy' on the employees, but better to transport opinions in the context of an opinion-forming process. Employees thus see the serious interest of the management of the company in their thinking. This enables management much better to localise and react faster to problems. At the same time, the scouts have a transmission function for all 'top-down' messages. These can be conveyed not only medially, but also personally in workshops or through presentations and in this interactivity they reach a higher degree of efficiency. The scouts are regularly given chart presentations, questions and answers (Q&As) and materials, they meet for training and an exchange of ideas and also discuss matters directly with the management. Beside the regular reporting lines, an independent and very fast communications instrument is thus established. The number of employees who can be reached by a scout is approximately 100. Working in this relation, one obtains an excellent multiplies effect.

Insourcing/Outsourcing Ratio

The insourcing/outsourcing culture differs greatly between companies, extreme forms in similar companies are quite common. Moreover the subject is ideologically preconceived. Agency representatives tend traditionally to argue for outsourcing and expose themselves to the suspicion of *pro domo* (partial) thinking. However, independently of these fields of discussion, the dominant opinion is out of 100 per cent communication costs including all in-house costs (salaries, overheads), at least 70 per cent should be freely disposable and not earmarked. This rough rule should be changed in favour of flexibility in times of intensive corporate transformation. It is thus advisable for a company first to figure out what percentage of its communications budget is tied down for employees in communications departments. As soon as this figure has been determined, many companies feel that their investment freedom is threatened and look around for outsourcing possibilities.

Although communications do not form a part of the core competence of a company (unless it operates in the communications branch of business), they do constitute a central competence to support and further the corporate success. For this reason all companies should take care that communications managers and their support staff are as qualified as possible – both in terms of training and intellect and in view of their management powers. Apart from this small and very select team, it is quite adequate to have 10 per cent of the heads and hands needed on board. Experience shows that other heads and also other hands will be needed the following year to solve the tasks arising.

In any case, it is advisable in every M&A to plan for a high outsourcing ratio. The immense need for flexibility, mobility and time cannot be frequently demanded even of one's own employees.

3 Creation of Names and Image Accounts

In most companies there are several image accounts into which the company activities and communications activities pay. These are, for example, the name of the company, the names of brands and subsidiaries, the names of the most important individuals acting, and also generic terms associated with the company. In an M&A, the number of these image accounts doubles. Because communications always constitute a *perception contest*, a concentration policy is always preferable in principle and the number of accounts should be minimised. The fewer image accounts there are, the better the investments can be reflected in the absolute amount of the account balance. Many image accounts are useful whenever the diversification of risks or crises communications are involved. For example, there is the popular attempt to keep a crisis of a subsidiary away from the umbrella brand name. However, this rarely succeeds because the attribution mechanisms of the media do not function as assumed in somewhat academic marketing presentations. For example, it is very difficult for a big and established, even paradigmatic brand such as Deutsche Bank to establish subsidiaries or participations whose activities do not all the same pay into the image account of Deutsche Bank (or debit from it). DB Investor or Deutsche Bank 24 are examples of this. The half-life period of image accounts long since closed lingers in consumers' heads; new accounts have a very long start-up phase. Many conglomerates tried for several years to teach the world that they consist of so many divisions with their respective names. Success was not overwhelming and even further negatively affected by subsequent portfolio adjustments. In the field of corporate issues, journalists prefer to remember the names where decisions are made, and they are hardly impressed by further subsumptions of business under new names.

It is therefore advisable to take clear decisions at an early time in an M&A. 'NewCo' needs a name, at the time of the announcement. Unpleasant decisions which should maybe still posted in (old) name accounts must therefore be taken before the announcement. It is often better if the new name is one of the old ones. If new names arise from another motive than the inability of two M&A candidates to agree on one of the two names, for reasons of vanity, and a new name which both can live with is chosen only as a matter of balance between the two companies, then the name is in most cases as weak as the motive. People will very easily identify a bogus name, and they correctly consider a useless change of name to be an untrustworthy labelling swindle. If the new name is then created in a synthetic laboratory and deprived of any semantic reference, it is very difficult to turn a meaningless jumble of vowels into a flag for the new company. This is aggravated by the fact that the word creations are frighteningly confusable ('Aventis' vs. 'Avanza') and that the burial of the old names destroys many hundreds of millions of dollars in terms of brand equity in consumers' heads.

In principle there is nothing to be said against new names, on the contrary. It is a great and free act of self-determination to give oneself a name. Boys during puberty have a great liking for choosing secret names for themselves, or for the Indian custom of dreaming up one's own name upon reaching manhood. But such a name is also always a programme meant to unfold. In this way new names bring about a high degree of momentum and identification with the programme of the future. Naturally it is not easy to find names not yet being used which at the same time express one's own programme. Modern highwaymen have specialised in obtaining protection for names which they do not need: especially popular for this purpose are domain addresses for the internet. But in general it can be said that it always makes sense to acquire the rights to an optimal name, even if a high initial investment is needed. The investment pays off easily. The example of 'Yello', a spin-off of the power supply company EnBW, shows how it is possible within three months to become the best-known brand in a segment where others have toiled for decades. The inspired idea to give colour to an invisible electricity corresponds with the presence and transparency of this service provider in an abstract low-interest and low-involvement market. All other competitors will have to invest manifold amounts in communications for years in order to make up for the distance which they fell behind because of their poor name value.

4 Positioning

Core Competence and Profiling Themes

Core competence is the most important positioning basis. However, as popular as this term is in strategic vocabulary, as difficult it is to fill it with life. As soon as a core competence is presented as such to outsiders, it should fulfil two conditions: self-identity and competition distinctiveness. Claiming a core competence which cannot stand the test of time and is not covered by corporate realities can quickly turn into an Achilles' heel, earning the company ridicule, scorn and a lack of credibility for years. A core competence which can be found elsewhere by the dozen is exchangeable and hardly attractive. In this dilemma between the self-identity and competitive distinctiveness, one's own ability to perform is often pushed to the limits in order to generate comparative competitive advantage. But competitors do exactly the same thing, a spiral quickly develops and one moves away communicatively from the actual focus: the real core competence.

For communications, the point is thematically to grasp what is regarded as the core competence in production or service. For example, a company which regards logistics as its core competence should know everything about logistics – and, what is more, should be able to convey this knowledge to others. It is not sufficient just to do something – publications are also important and knowledge and thinking should be presented. Many companies have the problem that they have highly specialised experts on board who have many interesting ideas and a lot of information about the core competence of the company and its fields of application. Unfortunately they cannot or do not want to reduce them to paper. Usually institutions, ghost writers and agencies then search for gripping themes around the field of competence, write texts and formulate forecasts. The real experts remain silent, and the core competences are cultivated by others.

The thematic sovereignty of the air is gained only by someone who is able to combine both resources. As valuable as the time of the brains in the company is for its business, as important it is for the purposes of marketing this business to involve these brains in the briefing processes for positioning. It is indispensable for the purpose of securing the core competences that they be documented and presentable. This intersubjective control also ensures that no excessively large gap opens up between images and realities. In the long term such gaps always turn out to be an acceptance trap. Therefore, especially in an M&A, it is essential to bring together the brains, the representatives of the defined core competences in both companies, with the communications experts so that their knowledge will flow into the positioning process.

Innovative Power and Future Interpretation

Innovation is regarded as a valuable asset and has come to be seen as an indispensable key qualification for every successful company. In addition to 'responsibility' it might well be the most commonly used term in positioning papers. But the management reports for most companies show that innovation is frequently spoken about after the fact, in incantations and claims, but only very rarely in the form of *forecasts for the future*. Anyone who wishes to demonstrate his ability to survive in the future will not be able to avoid interpreting the future, not in the style of trend researches, but certainly with scientific care and in cooperation with the leading heads in the field of application of one's own services. Thinking about the future and expressing substantial thoughts about the future opens up this future for one's reference groups and is in this sense *perceivably and understandably* innovative. The interpretation of the future is always the first step towards new standards which can be set by a company. Accordingly, sources outside the company must be used for the positioning process of 'NewCo': sources which can make statements on the development of technology, customers' expectations, social and cultural framework conditions and other factors which concern the positioning of the company. University professors, institutions and authors must be researched and observed. Contract research, paid publications or joint projects further networking and one's reputation, not to mention the valuable impulses for the actual business. Here, too, it can thus be said that one should have thematic sovereignty, even if it is only the dwarf which climbs onto the shoulders of a virtual global giant of knowledge. Nothing is less credible than, for example, a bank which calls itself the 'bank of the future' or 'tomorrow's bank' but fails to give its target groups any idea of what banking will or should be like in 10 years from its point of view.

In the case of an M&A, a forecast of medium-term market developments is certainly key element of industrial logic. If these industrial forecasts are tied together with a serious social cultural extrapolation, one gains not only positioning substance but at the same time arguments for the absolute inevitability of the M&A. Generally it is desirable not to have to view the M&A as a forced reaction to omissions in the past or competitive disadvantages in the present, but instead as a preparation for the future and its framework conditions.

Market Definition, Market Position and Market Interpretation

The third thematic research and substantive anchor for positioning concerns the market, competition and thus the economic framework conditions. M&A take place to improve market positions. If this is wanted, one must have an idea of what this market is, and be able to describe and interpret it. Once that has been achieved, one's own position and future position in this market can be made clear. One can credibly claim to play a market-defining role only if the market with its mechanisms, framework conditions and perspectives can also be interpreted by the company claiming to be able to define it. Many companies make the mistakes of keeping their reflections on the market secret because they fear that competitors could benefit from their considerations. However, anyone who chooses not to interpret publicly will quickly be perceived as a hanger-on who only floats along in the tide without setting standards and defining focal points. Moreover, market interpretation must always be seen in the context of 'communications as an added value', i.e. it creates a perceivable (information) added value for the business community and the opinion leaders and journalists, and gives the sender a profile as a source of information and interpretation. The establishment of a competent image within a certain market is possible in this way.

Especially in an M&A, prospective market terms are frequently a basis or even motivation for mergers and acquisition. Because it must become clear that 'NewCo' is positioning itself in view of future market constellations, it is indispensable also to present the dynamics of market change to outsiders. A part of this context is the relational positioning and rule definition in relation to the most important competitors.

Concept and Vision

Once the initial basic substantive work has been done in view of 'core competences', 'innovation and future' as well as 'market and market definition', this must flow into a *conceptual model*. Such models as guidelines are frequently regarded as static descriptions of an existing condition or as a definition of unshakeable basic cultural values in the company. Visionary processes are then organised as a parallel process and flow into a corporate vision. However, a more modern view is that such guidelines have a dynamic orientation function and must therefore be updated. Naturally the new definition of values and rules in respect to 'NewCo' is necessary in an M&A (Figure 11.3).

The development of a guideline is a *dynamic and participative process* – in relation to the company rollout of such guidelines and also to external reference groups. If such guidelines are not to become a silent grave for aesthetic prose, they must be directly implemented into action and measures. They thus constitute the scaffolding for the planning of communications. Figure 11.4 shows the exemplary guideline process where, in addition to the research steps already mentioned above, further studies on one's perception of oneself and of others are taken into account.

For multilevel companies or multibrand companies, the task orientation of the different parts of the company must already be taken into account for the purposes of such guidelines. The primary responsibility to a reference group should be clearly defined with one legal entity or one brand. The allocation of functions to the holding and the operative companies also follows the regular allocation of business with respect to communications. Here, given the aspect of stakeholder value of communications, the merger strategy is to be translated into the different currencies 'profitability and growth', 'career and perspectives', 'proximity, service and quality' as well as 'jobs and public benefit'.

Corporate Story

The corporate story comprises all parts of the model which can be published – i.e. those statements about the company programme not only for executives and their management functions, but which can be and should be conveyed to all employees and all external reference groups. In the corporate story, the role model (Figure 11.5) takes on the form of messages. Accordingly, considerations regarding the transmission and transmittability first arise here, not substantively, but in a logical, causal and semantic manner. Before the corporate story is written, the entire content of what is to be said has become clear. But it has not yet been defined how and in what

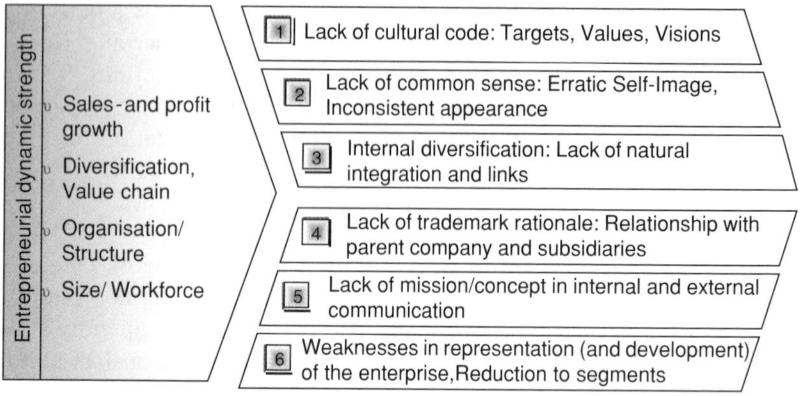

Figure 11.3 New definition of values and rules

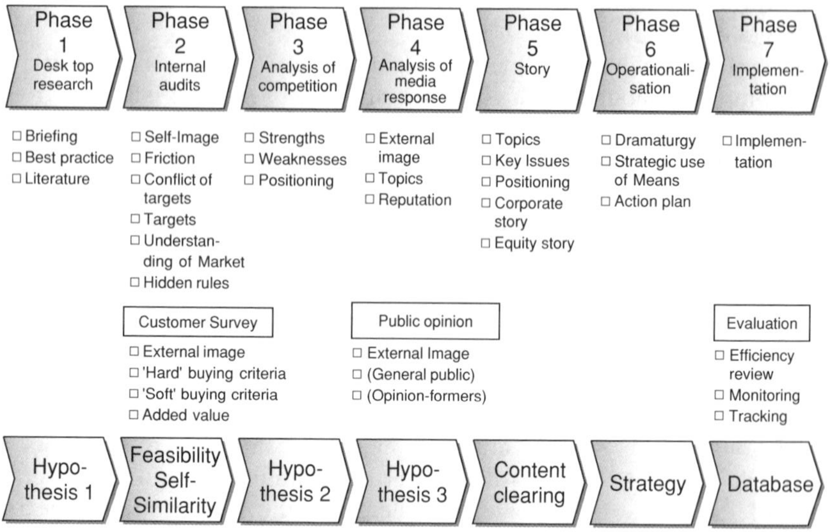

Figure 11.4 The guideline process

order it is to be said, what terms are to be chosen, and what arguments are to be weighted in what way, depending on the reference group to be targeted.

The corporate story generally breaks down the basic outlines of what has been written by the investment bankers, into the *equity story*. It must present quantitative arguments to the financial community and arouse visions for the future. It is made primarily for the analysts and consequently must be oriented by the criteria and terminology important to them.

The *management story* personalises the corporate strategy and illustrates the sources and drivers of the desire to change. It must make clear which individuals (board members) represent which programmes and tasks, and in which way they

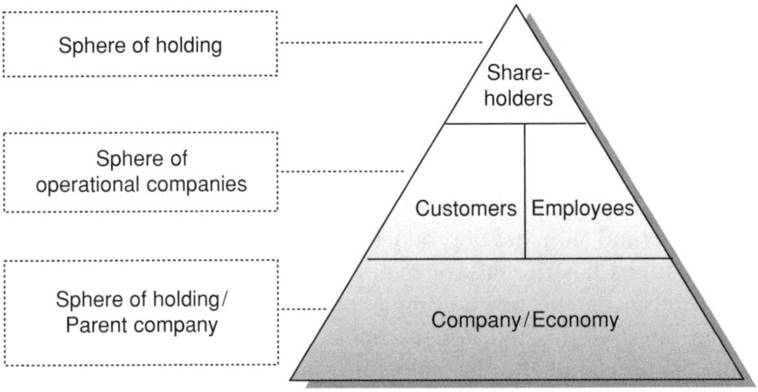

Figure 11.5 Role sort

are approached. The quality of management is well known to be a crucial factor for attractiveness and credibility in relation to investors and employees. Moreover, a strategy is not worth much if it is not wholly represented by the people who will implement it. The anonymity of stock corporations and the high degree of abstractness of complex undertakings call for more visibility and a personal touch. Especially the media – and, in particular, the opinion-leading press in the area of commercial journalism – personalise their reports to a great extent. Accordingly, the management story and its conveyability must be oriented by the customs and usages of journalism and news factors. *Change management needs management of change.* Who does this and hows he does it is an interesting piece of news value which pays high amounts into the image account.

The *customer story* addresses all benefits for customers which directly or indirectly arise from the M&A and must be written together with the marketing staff. It then constitutes a basis both for the product-related press and media work and for briefings concerning the activities of all sales-supporting communications.

The *employee story* discusses all aspects of the internal changes as well as the opportunities for employees which arise from improved competitiveness. It is the basis for programme planning for internal communications, which must transport not only the messages of the employee story, but also all other stories. Employees should know and understand the arguments and their presentation to customers and the external opinion-leading public before they are asked about them by outsiders.

5 Dramaturgy

Imminent Milestones

Time is a factor critical to the success of M&A because the synergetic potential must quickly be raised in order to compensate for lost goodwill, the acquisition premium exceeding the market price. For this reason, there is a time schedule for every M&A which defines the milestones for the change process on the basis of industrial logic, and determines which steps must be taken within which deadlines. Before Day Zero for 'NewCo', there are regulatory and legal milestones, dates for supervisory board meetings, merger reports, general meetings, cartel office decisions, or EU permits to be dealt with. After the start of 'NewCo', milestones are generally defined which concern the closure or establishment, migration or integration of departments and divisions, there are subsequent divestments or IPOs of parts of the company, turning points in the restructuring of processes, or new sales systematics and launches of products, services and programmes.

Communications has the task of maintaining the momentum in the change process and ensuring the quick completion of the defined process steps. It is therefore an effective method not to choose an separate campaign dramaturgy for communications, but to orient oneself from the beginning to the imminent milestones based on a 'staged-course' dramaturgy. This has the advantage of process transparency and also creates a feeling of success within the company as each stage is successfully completed. Here it depends on internal communications to form an overall, uniform and illustrative imagery from the different PMI stages, which make overall sense only at the industrial logic level and can easily appear disconnected if regarded individually. Such an imagery also makes the interdependence of the stages plausible for a common observer.

External Milestones

In the case of an M&A not requiring a stringent internal time schedule and having no long pauses between its milestones and turning points, it is advisable to favour momentum by voluntary time pressure and to set target deadlines selected from the calendar of the market or opinion market. The 100-day period of grace for the CEO is an example of an arbitrary external milestone which exerts a deliberate time pressure on internal processes and breaks down the path of change into a first stage. Carly Fiorina, the CEO of Hewlett Packard, announced when she was nominated that this period would be shortened to 90 days and that she intended to present the future HP strategy at the end of this stage. This pressure sends out a strong signal within the company and outside, has a driving function and illustrates the sense of urgency for the company. Seasonal dates, trade exhibitions, celebrity events or quantifiable stages provide further opportunities for external deadlines.

6 External and Internal Communications

Interaction

External and internal communications can hardly be separated from each other, especially in an M&A. The substantive overlaps are extremely large because practically all information conveyed externally to customers or society must first be transmitted internally to prevent one's own employees from being unprepared or uninformed when they are approached by outsiders. This applies especially to employees with customer contact, in the sense of equal treatment and as a cultural gesture, but it of course applies in the same way for all employees. Also in view of the processes, the time schedules for external and internal communications hardly differ. They are oriented by the defined milestones and give internal communications only a small time lead, if any. However, because of the communication leaks in large organisations, too much of a time lead is not advisable. Internal arguments or first drafts of brochures easily find their way to the press and water down the intended actual launch date. In this respect internal and external communications are synchronous – not only substantively, but also in their timing.

Moreover, it cannot be overemphasised that external communications more effectively form perceptions in the minds of employees than information addressed only internally. An article in the *FAZ* or the *Handelsblatt* presenting the new corporate strategy has a higher degree of objectivity and commitment than an identical text which, for example, is distributed as a letter from the chairman of the board. The evaluation of understanding and acceptance of an M&A strategy among employees has clearly proven that external prophets are more highly regarded than the company's own, both in terms of power of recollection and in terms of their own convincing power. It should not be underestimated that a high potential for mistrust can break out in the process of a merger, even if the corporate culture is healthy, causing suspicions and doubts as the existence of a hidden agenda. Because employees apparently consider journalists to be better informed and to be more competent than themselves for the evaluation of strategies, they trust analysts and published performance forecasts more than the announcements of their own management. Internal medial information frequently also suffers from the 'overfeeding' effect which frequently counteracts the information policy for an M&A. Honourable motives lie behind the efforts to inform the employees about all details, one wishes to avoid the impression of having a hidden agenda. But because this causes an excessive mass of information which could overwhelm too many people for whom this information is irrelevant, the entire internal M&A communications can easily run into a relevancy problem. Truly relevant messages can no longer be identified and are overlooked in the confusing wealth of irrelevant information. This is true especially if such information reaches the employees through routine channels – for example, in-house mail. A letter sent to the employee's private address is read twice as often and produces three times as much resonance and enquiries as the same letter sent through the in-house mail service. The difference between the (supposedly) individual approach of a serial letter to a private address and the (supposed) mass mail-approach is clearly measurably reflected by its reception.

Public interest and public opinion have a significant *self-confirming* effect and additionally the advantage of *intersubjective verifiability*. The internal announcement that no jobs will be lost can, in most employees' opinion, always be revised. They expect that they will then hear something about changed conditions. If this promise is made publicly, the board cannot then take it back without losing face – this is how simple logic functions.

For this reason, corporate advertising, the press and media work and publishing should be given high priority also for internal persuasion efforts. Especially for smaller companies, M&A are frequently a publicity peak compared to their earlier media presence. Pride and identification are promoted if the employees feel that the world and the business community is looking at 'their' company. It has been observed repeatedly in smaller and medium-sized companies that, for example, an ad which had appeared in a foreign business journal (e.g. *Financial Times, Fortune, Wall Street Journal*) with a report on 'NewCo' and was distributed internally for the information of the employees generated more merger acceptance and optimism in the future than the five-fold investment in internal information material. Reports appearing in the media should also be distributed internally as a matter of principle and as a part of PMI to an extended circle of addressees. Separate budgeting for internal and external communications may be formally necessary, but plays no role in effectiveness.

Instruments

The question of the use of communications instruments is technical and practical. Standard recommendations are not possible here. Generally it can be said that the number of instruments or communication channels which transport or interactively convey contents from the sender to the recipient is structurally limited. The choice of instruments and of the mix of channels is to be made based on efficiency considerations (see Figure 11.6). Depending on the clustering, between 15 and 24 communication channels are available; in Figure 11.6 there are 21. In the four media groups Print, TV, Radio and Online, advertising or editorial work is possible. Intranets and extranets are subcategories of the editorial online channel. Own publications, whether periodicals, brochures, CD-ROMs or films, can be distributed through one's own distribution channels or through established distribution channels. For example, a customers' magazine can be sent in parallel

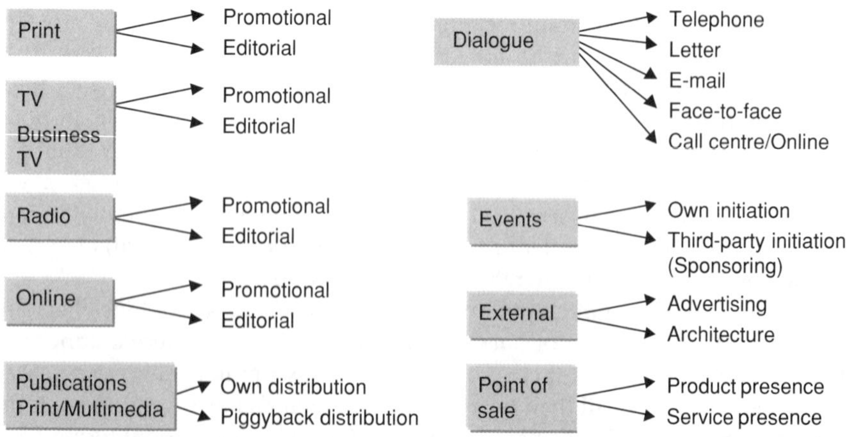

Figure 11.6 Communication channels

through the mail to existing customer addresses and simultaneously distributed as a supplement to an economic magazine. In the area of dialogue communications, a structural distinction can be made between letters, email, telephone and face-to-face conversations. The conversation can have a high intensity within a workshop or create only minimal personal ties in promotion campaigns or an approach on the street. The integrated use of websites and call centres, for example to advise customers or for technical after-sales services, is a separate path.

Events are either initiated by the company itself or under the full control of the host, or already existing events (tennis tournaments, art exhibitions, Olympia, etc.) are instrumentalised for one's own purposes by way of sponsoring. In the external area not only posters, campaigns, but also the communicative functions of architecture must be taken into account. Finally, at the point of sale, the brand itself is represented by the sales staff or the product by its packaging and presentation.

For any M&A, the most important communication carriers with external and internal effects are found in the press and media work as well as advertising campaigns, publishing and a professional online presence. With internal communications, examples of these would be the events, personal conversations and presentations in workshops as well as intranets and magazines.

7 Control of Processes

IBM was pleased. The star in the PMI of DaimlerChrysler was called Klara and is a think pad. On it, Jürgen E. Schrempp can see at any time, as *ManagerMagazin* and many other papers have reported with fascination, whether the processes in the integration teams are proceeding and are doing so to schedule. A quick overview is obtained by the boss by means of the popular McKinsey traffic-light indication, as simple as a kindergarten tool and immensely practical in view of the overpowering complexity of mergers. Green means 'everything OK', yellow means 'better watch out and possibly intervene', red means 'there is trouble here'. This smart tool was like a reccurring theme in the press, signalling as it did to all who were sceptical about spot welding large companies together that DaimlerChrysler not only has control over its processes, but can direct them effortlessly. Deutsche Post Worldnet AG, one of the biggest McKinsey clients overall, also uses this system, as the *Spiegel* noted: 'Thanks to a carefully thought out computer system, CEO Zumwinkel can at any time obtain a precise overview over the planning status. If a predefined goal such as, for example, a new paint job for a truck in a Spanish subsidiary has not been completed in time, a little red traffic light lights up on Zumwinkel's computer.'

It is no great surprise that this cute little system has found so many friends as it appears to provide the maximum reduction of complexity with the integrated instructions: 'Don't interfere', 'Check', 'Hit them hard'. Without any doubt the *controllability of processes* is becoming a focal point of the change mania. Many business consultants have long admitted, albeit not publicly, that the processes can hardly be controlled any more. Although the processes are still set in motion with strategic direction, tough time schedules and refined bottleneck management methods, step-by-step management triumphs after three weeks, if not earlier. This is often called 'inductive management', because this term is not quite as evocative as 'improvisation'. Nobody is responsible for this state of affairs, it is immanent in the system.

Communications management faces similar problems as companies and business consultants do. The processes are becoming more complicated and at the same time they must be completed within increasingly shorter deadlines. What must be done to keep up with these requirements? First: one needs *task forces* in communications as it is not possible for a communications team which is not process-oriented, but structurally-oriented, to support a project team consisting of staff units and advisers. The usual processes of concepts with an allocation of work between the corporate communications department and the advisory teams in the agencies do not function. In such cases, it is necessary to be able to distinguish immediately between such in-house staff and agency employees who handle the day-to-day business and those who together and exclusively drive the defined change project. Secondly: in the case of strategic changes or change projects, it must be possible to quickly make *short-term communication investment decisions*. For this it is of great advantage if as few long-term investment decisions as possible have been taken, and as many budget items as possible are uncommitted. Thirdly: the number of decision makers must be kept small, because otherwise one would drown in consultation and coordination processes. Fourthly: an efficient management information system (MIS) for communications is necessary to keep one's own staff and all service providers and advisers updated as quickly as possible. Fifthly: stand-by resources are needed which can be deployed 100 per cent for the project randomly and are free from other tasks. Sixthly: employees are needed in the communications department who are flexible and open, free from their regular duties to work on something completely different in the coming weeks and months, and are also prepared to work up to 12 hours a day in the critical phase (which can take up to 9 months). Seventh: service providers, agencies and advisers are needed who have the ability to work in a task force and to move to the customer for weeks and months if necessary.

8 Evaluation

M&A provide an opportunity to put future evaluation standards on to a new basis. Companies often do not change the design of their questionnaires in demoscopic studies or their search words for media observation because they want to ensure the compatibility of the data over the years. 'NewCo' therefore provides the welcome opportunity to close old image accounts and to open new ones. Accordingly, the entire evaluation system can be set up in accordance with the latest information available and the most modern methods.

In the area of the evaluation of advertising activities, the interest in acquiring information has increasingly shifted in recent years. Key success factors were supplemented or replaced by qualitative ones. The quality of the specific target groups reached and their affinity to the themes of the company play a greater role than the mass market does. A good example to be observed is n-tv, the TV station, which can hardly compete in the area of mass television, but on the other hand has a homogeneous and socio-culturally describable public.

In the evaluation of media reporting, differentiating methods have existed for some time which go beyond the mere collection and classification of clippings by keywords. Qualitative media resonance analysts offer a precise analysis of published opinions, whether by regions, nationally or internationally.

In market research there has also been great progress, especially in view of the collection of European and international sample surveys. For example, there are now internationally staffed call centres with native speakers who, from one central location, make consumer or opinion leader research by telephone throughout Europe, making it possible to avoid the aggregation of different national panels and to ensure time advantages and improved methodical transparency.

Especially in the integrated analysis of public opinion with the means of empirical social research and the analysis of published opinions through content analysis, there are much better bases today which, however, are used only rarely. In many companies, the responsibilities for brand research and media research are divided up into different departments; demoscopic studies and media resonance analysis are commissioned independently of each other, and interest in such information is uncoordinated. Whereas market research generally inquires with or without support about brand awareness or the memory and association of brand attributes, media research seeks information about themes, messages and opinions published about the company. However, the path of opinion and image-building is complex and can be of value in planning future communication measures only if a uniform overall and long-term approach is used. For example, a comparable study design is necessary for demoscopy and media resonance in order to find out whether the published opinion is at all relevant to the target group – and, if so, with how much of a time delay and loss.

Especially important for M&A is the rapid tracking of internal views and feelings. This can be done through *focus groups*, with the help of the scouts already mentioned, on the basis of the intranet, in writing, by telephone or in one-to-one interviews. An approximate rule claims that about 5 per cent of the annual communications budget should be invested in evaluation and market research.

9 The Future

M&A communications, especially in the PMI phase, are communications in an exceptional state. This means not only that other rules apply as long as this state continues, but also that a number of rules will be changed forever as a consequence of the natural revolutionary implications of this state. Things will never be as before, the state of exception is logically always the legitimisation for a fundamental change. This fact provides an opportunity to companies to redefine the content, concepts, methods and structure of their communications, to make revolutionary changes within 9 to 12 months, instead of having to set tedious optimisation processes in motion. Such processes must always unfold against the resistance of existing customs, 'old boy' networks and structures. The understanding of communications in the M&A process is thus a dual one. On the one hand, current and extraordinary requirements must be met quickly. This goal suggests that the best approach might be a short-term intervention mentality pragmatism instead of visions and solutions with a short half-life. On the other hand, communications aim not only at a limited time of exceptional conditions, but at a basic change of the company's own foundation, which is why they should be designed as long-term and visionary tools. The great art of communications management in an M&A therefore is to reconcile short-term requirements with long-term meaningful structures and processes. The best possible advice is to use the window of opportunity during the short PMI phase to revise one's own communications policy in its entirety in order to meet the demands and requirements of the next 10 years. What was not fulfilled during the revolution must be remedied afterwards with a long march through the institutions. As we all know, this can take time.

Bibliography

Schumpeter, Joseph A. (1949) [1912, 1934] *The Theory of Economic Development* Cambridge, Mass.: Harvard University Press.

12

Pre- and Post-Merger Integration in Cross-Border Transactions: Trends, Tools, Theses, and Empirical Tests of Old and New Economy Deals

Stephan A. Jansen

1 The Starting Point: New Integration Paradigm Because of Changed Industrial Condtions

Five Waves on the M&A Market

Mergers are not an invention of recent times. Since the first appearance of business mergers in high frequency at the end of nineteenth century, cyclic waves have been observable. All waves emerged due to very different strategic motivations with very specific integration demands (Figure 12.1).

In spite of concrete integration activities it is conspicuous – albeit not to prove monocausal – that each merger wave was followed by an economic recession. The economic crises – or, rather, stock market crashes – shown in the Figure 12.1 lead us to assume a correlation between these gigantic investment amounts for acquisitions and the overall economic situation. In the USA, the value of all transactions in comparison with the total market capitalisation in the year 2000 has increased by 12 per cent and, thus, again more than the average growth rate of 10 per cent in the last 15 years. This number might corroborate the thesis that merger waves are followed by recessions for the reason that the premiums already distributed to the shareholders of the target company in the closing of the transaction – as discounted future proceeds – cannot be realised in the subsequent phase of integration.

Six Trends with Integration Effects of the Fifth Merger Wave

In 2000 a worldwide a total of 36 700 business mergers were counted, which added up to a value of 3.49 trillion dollars. Compared to 1999 this was a sharp rise in the number of the transactions, whereas *announcement value* was nearly constant (the volume of closed transactions in 1999 was only 2.74 trillion dollars). In the actual transaction waves, different trends are revealed, which are of decisive relevance for the M&A market:[1]

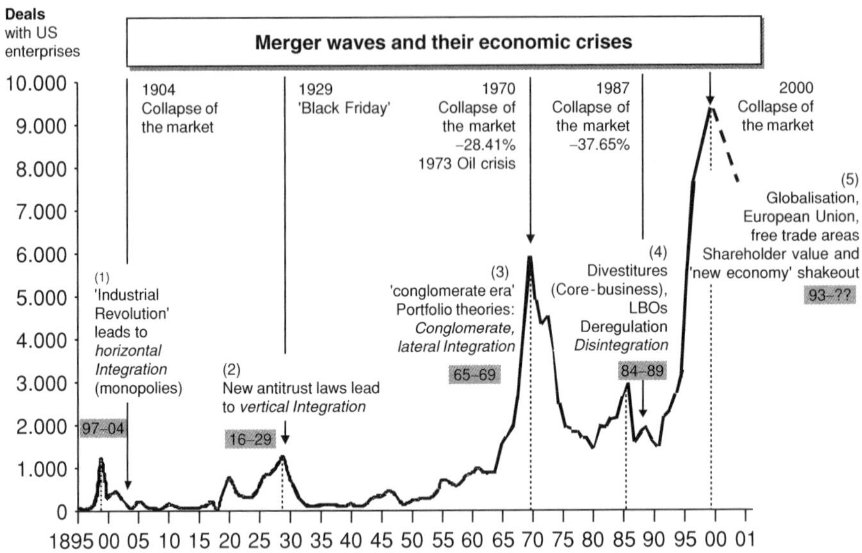

Figure 12.1 Merger waves, their specific integration logics and economic turmoil, 1895–2001
Source: Jansen and Müller-Stewens (2000).

Cross-Border Transactions

The share of cross-border transactions in the total number of world-wide transactions increased from 35 to 40 per cent in 2000. After a long period of stagnation in the 1990s at a level of about 25 per cent, a clear increase could be observed in 1997. The development of the volume of cross-border transactions parallels the development of the total volume: Here also, a slight increase from about 33 per cent in 1999 to 37 per cent in 2000 could be noticed (Figure 12.2). Altogether a cross-border volume of about 1.165 trillion dollars was calculated. The tendency is still for volumes to rise, especially in Europe. With a deal volume of 421 billion dollars, European buyers were the most active.

Industry Change: New Economy Shakeout

In recent years the 'New Economy' replaced the classic production companies in the field of merger activity. Telecommunication, media and technology (TMT) in particular again became the most important driver of the current M&A wave. So TMT mergers accounted for more than 20 per cent of the total market. The world-wide technology stock market crashes created the phrase 'shakeout'. The consolidation in the sector was already clearly observable in 2000, particularly affiicting the Internet businesses. One of the main information providers in this field, Webmergers, announced an increase of 85 per cent in M&A activities of Internet company transactions. Altogether Dotcoms were acquired for an amount of 87 billion dollars – compared to 48 billion dollars in 1999. The number of deals

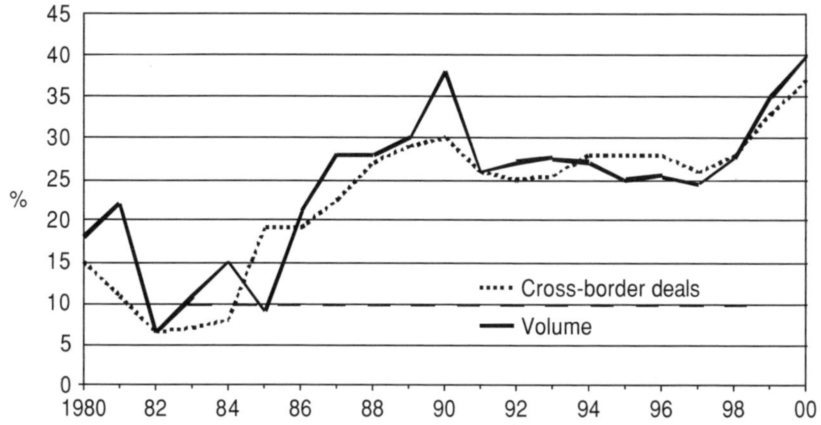

Figure 12.2 Number of cross-border deals and their volume as a fraction of total M&A activity, 1980–2000
Source: UNCTAD (2000), estimation for 2000.

doubled to 910 between 1999 and 2000. Interestingly, the 'fourth-quarter year' has also struck here: in the first quarter (the pre-crash-period), 60 per cent of the total transaction volume of the year was realised, whereas the fourth quarter accounted for just 6 per cent. However, the transaction figures were different: here the second quarter was the most powerful, with 244 deals, and the fourth quarter followed, closely with 211 deals.

Hostile Take-Overs

In 1999, hostile takeovers caused a great stir. Takeover laws aiming at the legal prevention of such transactions were discussed. This excitement was not persistent: hostile takeovers were not established on the market as a successful instrument for companies. While three of the five largest transactions in 1999 were could be regarded as to be hostile – i.e. against the will of top management – there was only one successful hostile takeover among the 30 largest transactions in 2000: the acquisition of Bestfoods by Unilever. The volume of hostile takeovers went down from 705 to 127 billion dollars in 2000. The rate of success was also significantly lower: only 32 per cent of the announced hostile takeovers were actually carried out, compared to the average of 41 per cent in the years 1995–9. The defence strategies and the defence audit measures implemented in 1999 seemed to have taken effect.

Demergers

One trend, however, again seems to have been corroborated during 2000: divestitures and demerger – i.e. separation in the course of a restructuring. Especially within the telecomunication industry, numerous spin-offs were carried out. But there are other examples, which seem to emphasise the present need for a divestiture policy – e.g. the well-known BMW and Rover case with its considerable increase in market prices following the demerger or the renewed restructuring at

Aventis leading it away from its life science strategy. Compared with the USA and England, Germany is still clearly at a disadvantage. The actual figures in the framework of an A.T. Kearney study conducted in 1998 show that in the USA the number of divestitures was 10.8 times higher, and England was 4.3 times more active in the field of divestitures than Germany.[2]

Premiums

The average premium paid in corporate acquisitions in respect of goodwill increased again in 2000. The takeover premium for companies listed at a Stock Exchange reached an average as high as 50 per cent (Goldman Sachs, 2001); in the 1990s premiums were about 40 per cent.

Transaction Financing

The way of financing business mergers also shows some development. Whereas only 45 per cent of all transactions were provided with a cash offer, the share as 'currency' lost its purchasing power: in the last months of 2000 and the first quarter of 2001, cash offers accounted for 52 per cent of all offers.

For Practice and Research: A New Paradigm of Integration

From the evidence of the different merger waves, figures and current trends, it becomes clear that a considerable change in integration demands, integration depth and integration competence has to take place (Table 12.1). First, it may be surprising that only a few pieces of research concerning post-merger activities exist. The reason for this is that the subject of 'integration' was of hardly any relevance in the first waves, as integration competence was not the decisive factor for the success of a transaction. In accordance with the trends displayed in the current wave, six clear influences on these specific integration demands can now be identified:

(1) Cross-border transactions demand a new *region-and nation-based* integration competence in nearly all areas – e.g. corporate governance, production, marketing, sales and corporate finance.
(2) Owing to the importance of intellectual, human and social capital, mergers in the *'New Economy' and in the services industries* are very different in their integration activities from mergers among traditional production companies with their higher deployment of financial and material resources.
(3) Following hostile takeovers, enormous efforts have to be made in *operational synergy tracking* – regardless of their usual friendly outcome – because of the strongly negative emotional atmosphere between the two or three organisations involved.
(4) The significant speeding up of competition leads to ever-faster *strategic reorientation*, so that company parts (such as business units) become more fungible than they were a few years ago. Strategic divestitures – even within just-acquired activities – will be entrepreneurial normalcy during the next years, with all the risks involved. This looser alignment has immediate consequences for integration intensity.

(5) The high premium distribution to the target shareholders ties down the newly merged company for years with respect to rationalisation results. Goodwill amortisations specifically determine the next strategic decisions (path dependency), so that a *detailed post-merger management* including synergy tracking has to be drafted to recover purchase price and integration costs.
(6) Owing to the renaissance of *cash offers* post-merger failures cannot any longer be disguised by the positive performance of the Stock Exchanges.

Table 12.1 Challenges for integration in five merger waves, 1880–Y2K+

Period	Strategic background	Integration competence
1880–1904	*1st Wave* **Strategy:** Realisation of monopoly rents by horizontal takeovers **Challenge for Integration:** Pooling of market power	■□□□□
1916–29	*2nd Wave* **Strategy:** Vertical integration to gain control of the complete value chain **Challenge for integration:** Optimisation of the interface management	■■□□□
1965–9	*3rd Wave* **Strategy:** Anti-cyclical portfolio building to harmonise different industry-driven economic downturns **Challenge for integration:** No challenges due ouring unrelated acquisitions	□□□□□
From 1981	*4th Wave* **Strategy:** 'Back to core business' through divestitures and carve-outs **Challenge for integration:** No great challenges ouring to consolidation with very few horizontal acquisitions	■□□□□
1985–9	**Strategy:** Speculative gains for financial acquirers (e.g. LBO)[1] **Challenge for Integration:** No challenges owing to mainly financial motives	■□□□□
From 1993	*5th Wave* **Strategy:** Increasing shareholder value and globalisation **Challenge for integration:** High owing to horizontal acquisitions for core competencies and owing to cross-border deals	■■■■■
Y2K+	**Strategy:** Talents technology and consolidation of the 'New Economy' **Challenge for integration:** High owing to specific start-up cultures and an innovation/HR-driven approach	■■■■□

Note: LBO = Leveraged buy-out.

In summary, a completely new entrepreneurial core competence in acquisition management can be observed, which has – against the background of the prospects of success shown below – to appear clearly in the pre- as well as in the post-merger phase. This competence cannot count on and trust in scientific results, because up to now the research has been at best based on individual cases only. In the management philosophy, there can also only be found references that are highly contradictory.

Licence to Kill: The Success Rate of Mergers

Are mergers a licence to kill? Even more spectacular than the last merger waves, with regard to their constantly increasing volumes and the shorter intervals between them, are the failure rates of business mergers. How to assess the success of mergers precisely adequacy cannot be determined with scientific adequacy, because all methods employed so far to measure it show systematic weaknesses and take into account only quantitative criteria.[3] Figure 12.3 attempts to show the general tendency without approaching these problems in detail.

These general failure rates have, however, very different implications for the target shareholders and the shareholders on the buying side: The shareholders of the target company can reckon on an average an increase in share prices of almost 20 per cent. In 2000 an average takeover premium of easily 50 per cent was paid; in the 1990s, the average comprehensive premium was 40 per cent.[4] On the side of the shareholders of the buying company, however, these numbers look different: for all transactions of companies carried out at the NYSE/AMEX between 1995 and 1997 a statistically significant value loss of 10.26 per cent in the five years

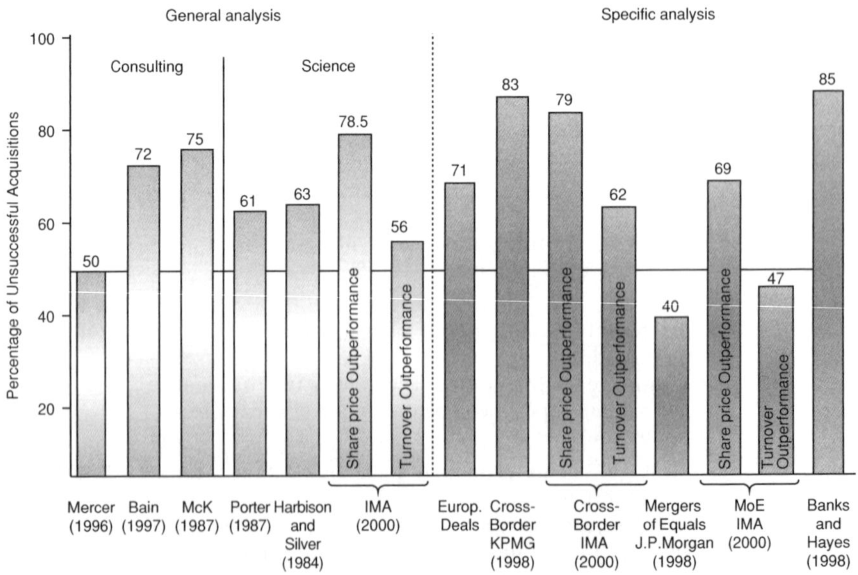

Figure 12.3 Overview of M&A failure rates, by consulting firms and scientific studies, 1984–2000

following the closure can be observed.[5] According to other studies, the value loss for the buyers amounts to about 7 per cent in the first six months.[6]

2 Basic Model and Instruments of Post-Merger Management

The 7C Model of Integration

The previous debates on post-merger management have only been very superficial and abundantly selective so far. In nearly all textbooks concerning M&As the post-merger process has not found appropriate consideration.[7] Here, the 7C Model, which integrates all essential aspects of post-merger management in an overall strategy and which helps to determine the resulting integration costs, will be the basis for all further consideration in this section (Figure 12.4).

In this article, the seven Cs can only be outlined very brietly to get an impression of the complexity of the whole process. The intention and one of the main advantages of this model is the determination of the integration costs, which are very rarely considered in the valuation process. The essential types of capital of an organisation – market capital, human capital, intellectual capital and social capital – are focused by the model.

Costs of Integration: Cost Synergies Cost!

Within this model the reflection of all perspectives is fundamental for determination of integration costs, which have not been included systematically in the valuation so far – in contrast to the synergies! Whereas valuation has created floods of consultation products,[8] no far-reaching approach to calculating integration costs has been developed. Figure 12.5 displays the fundamental logic.

It is evident that the costs of *synergy tracking* must be included. In the past these costs were higher than the synergies to be achieved in many mergers!. Therefore, Porter's (1987) partially disproved thesis of excessive purchasing prices can be revitalised as a reason for failure. This calculus can be presented as in Figure 12.6.

The future efforts in research as well as in entrepreneurial practice, therefore, aim at estimating these cost drivers correctly. As shown in the 7C Model, all seven Cs of integration have already to be considered with regard to their cost effect in the pre-merger management. Whereas all managers of the five highest hierarchy levels inform themselves about the stock value continuously, the three original capitals of the organisation remain unobserved: mergers have a direct influence on the *human* capital (the core staff and attractiveness in the 'war for talents'), on the *intellectual* capital (knowledge, innovations and other intangible assets) and on the *social* capital (market reputation, brand equity, relations). The direct influence of mergers on the destruction of these capitals will be clarified.

Coordination: Architectures

A merger calls into question nearly all routines, all communication and decision rules in the operative business. This complexity of organisational re-establishing

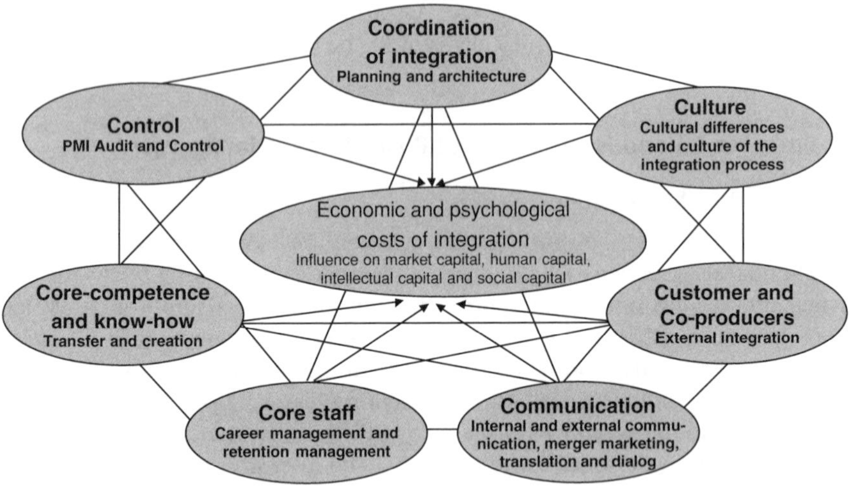

Figure 12.4 The 7C Model of post-merger management
Source: Jansen 1999 and 2000c.

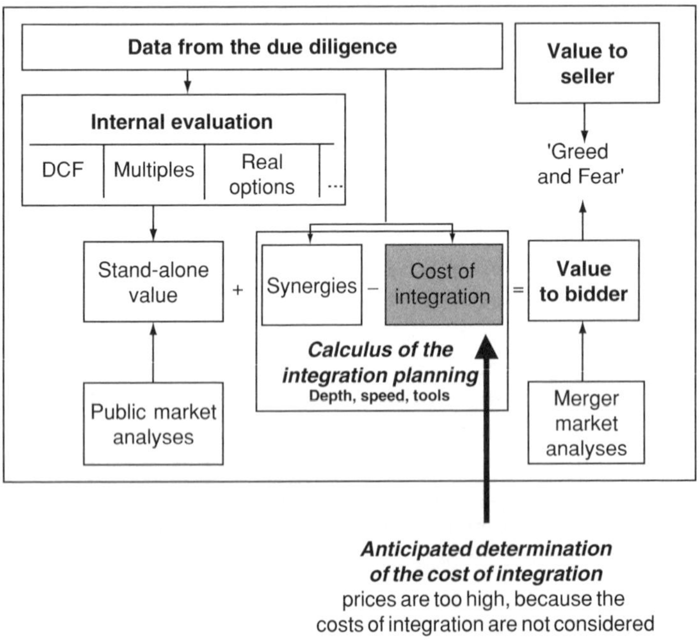

Figure 12.5 Calculus of synergies and costs of integration
Source: Jansen (2001a, p. 193).

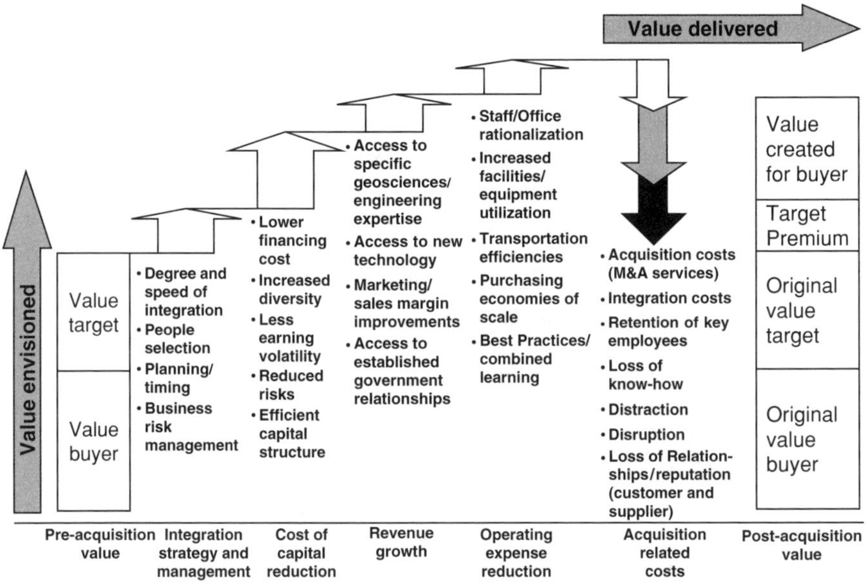

Figure 12.6 Sources of synergies and costs of integration
Source: Jansen (2001a, p. 193).

('novation') becomes possible only through a complex structure of integration architecture, which functions as temporary *parallel organisation* (see also Chapter 8 in this book).

The coordination and architecture of the integration activities is basically determined by the type of transaction and by its strategic objective, from which decisions with regard to integration necessities, integration bans – and, hence, also to integration intensity – can be derived. The ideal typical differentiation of three merger types in Figure 12.7 gives a first attempt to answers question of coordinating the integration challenge.

Following this determination of merger type, different integration attempts can be distinguished with regard to their requirements for the organisational change (Figure 12.8).

Basically, centralised and decentralised post-merger architectures can be observed, such as the symbiotic approaches frequently seen in cross-border transactions (Morosini, 1999). Whereas the *centralised* types often suffer from surrender and failure of consideration of decentralised intelligence, *decentralised* integration architectures often tend to delays in the synergy tracking. *Symbiotic* architectures are used in complex integration processes – e.g. in great mergers of equals and especially in cross-border transactions (e.g. Price WaterhouseCoopers, Figure 12.9). In these, a central perspective with a rough definition of integration activities and a reporting system is deployed, while self-defined decentralised issues teams are staffed within the organisation which work directly on the market (e.g. the frequently used organisation blueprint of DaimlerChrysler).

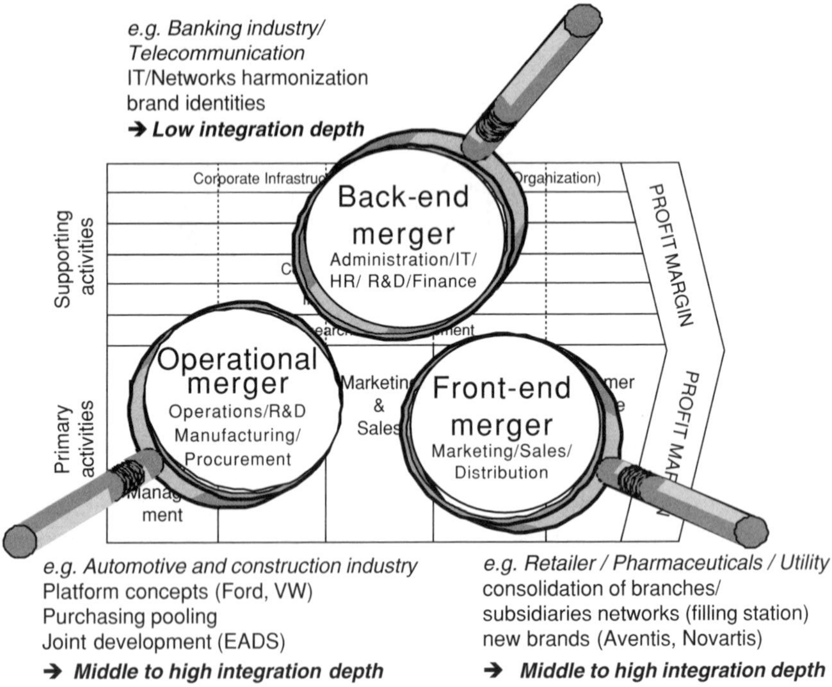

Figure 12.7 Three merger types with different integration depths
Source: Jansen (2001b, Figure 13).

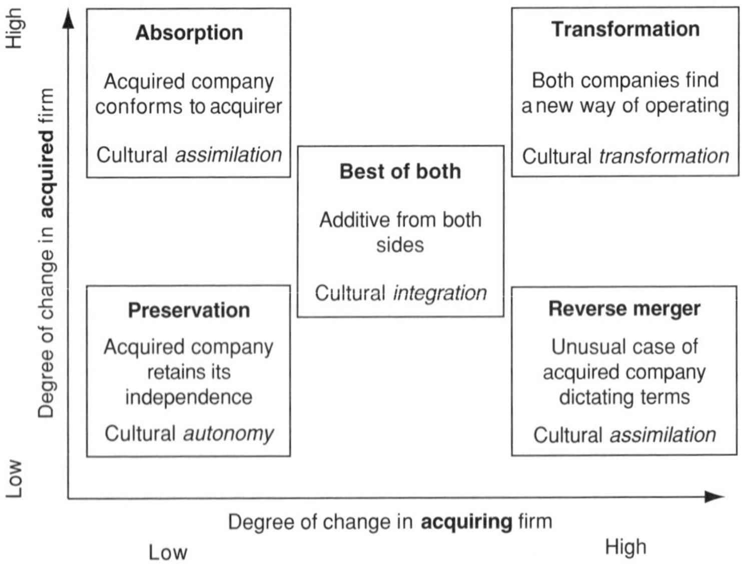

Figure 12.8 Integration typologies and their 'integration culture'
Source: Marks and Mirvis (1998, p. 73).

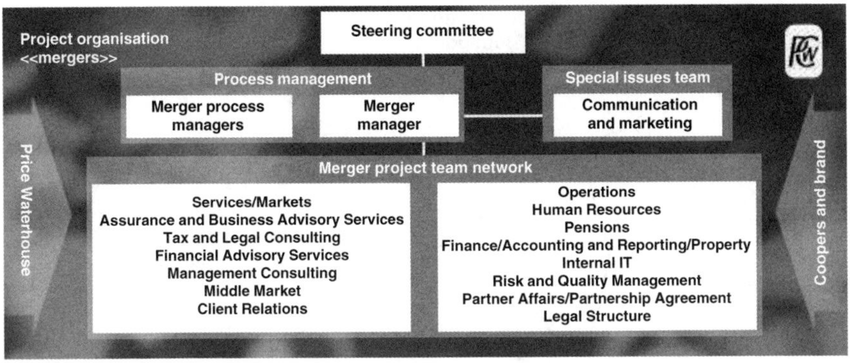

Figure 12.9 Integration architecture of PriceWaterhouseCoopers
Source: UBS (2000).

Nonetheless, the present practice shows that each merger needs a highly specific architecture, orienting on industry logic, related to the merger strategy and also to previous experiences in other change management projects.

Culture: Due Diligence and Merger Culture

One of the constant subjects in mergers seems to be that of *culture*. Especially in cross-border mergers, culture is named as a substantial factor of success or failure. In scientific as well as in management-oriented literature, the subject is predominant. The large variety of different attempts to explain the phenomenon of 'culture' is conspicuous, however, they have all in common that culture is recognised as a substantial problem. As we cannot imagine consultancies without covering this subject, since the 1980s, in view of the merger wave own-products are now offered which directed substantially to the pre-merger phase. The so-called 'cultural due diligence' is such a attempt to identify corresponding culture profiles that permit statements about the post-merger phase (Figure 12.10).

The basic problems of this instrument are the assumptions that must be made. Therefore, it cannot be stated clearly if a cultural fit has corresponding positive or negative consequences for the post-merger performance in an individual case. The cultural clash is typically named as a prominent reason for failure.

Nahavandi and Malekzadeh (1988) summarised the constellations that can appear in different business cultures (Figure 12.11). The interest in preserving the own culture on the one hand and the attractiveness of the new culture on the other have a significant impact here.

A multitude of studies have dealt with the differences in national cultures in cross-border transactions, and have come to very different results.[9] Similar to the assumptions made regarding corporate cultures, it is not clear in how far different national cultures have correspondingly positive or negative influences on post-merger experiences. Figure 12.12 from Morosini (2000) focuses on the differences in national cultures that are, in his opinion, obviously full of conflicts: dealing

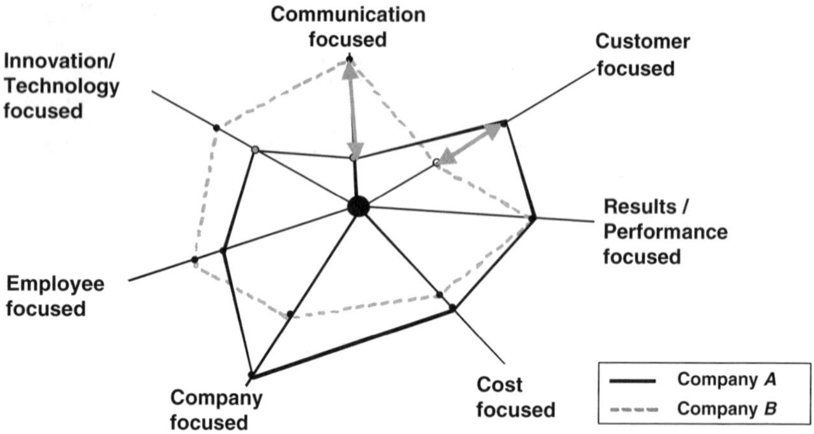

Figure 12.10 Cultural due diligence of two companies
Source: Vgl. Jung (1993, p. 22).

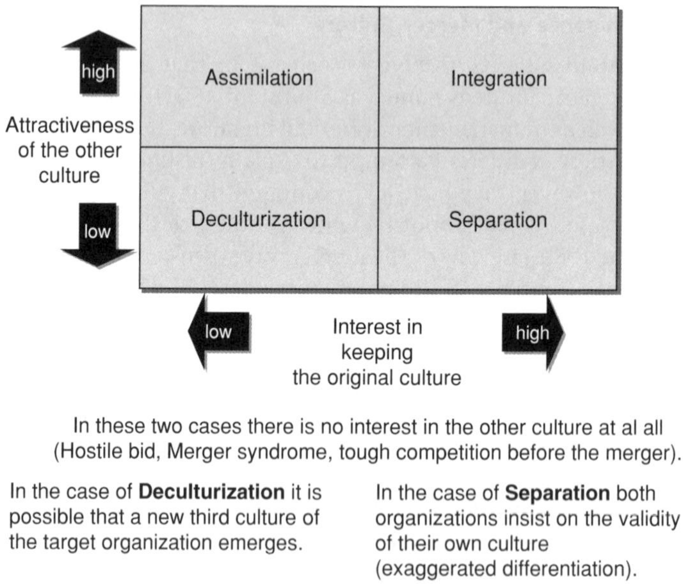

Figure 12.11 Four modes of intercultural relationships
Source: Modified from Nahavandi and Malekzadeh (1988).

uncertainty with decisions on the one hand, and power or hierarchy as a crucial-means for leadership on the other.

Within the scope of the theses and our own studies, these aspects of national and organizational cultures will be dealt with in more detail.

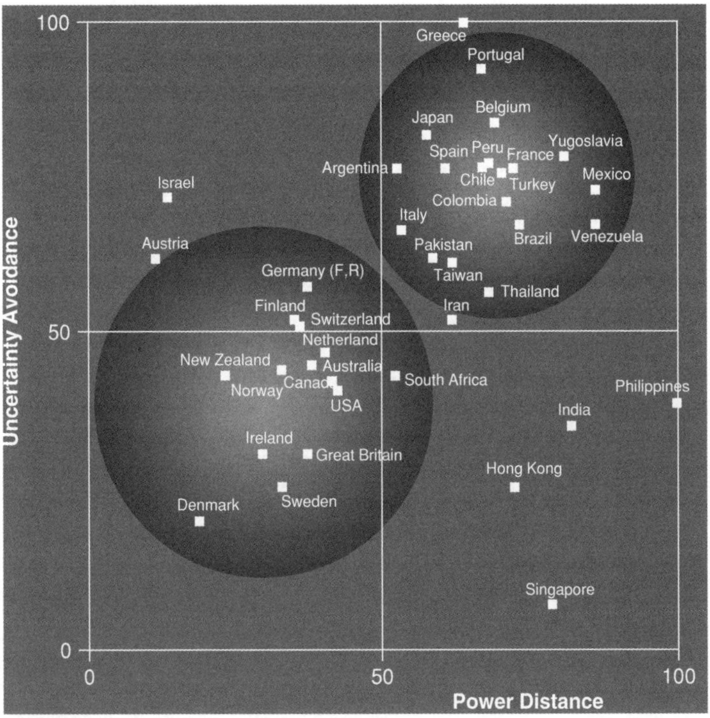

Figure 12.12 Differences in national cultures
Source: Morosini (2000).

Customers and Co-Producers: Integrate the Externals!

Mergers are surrounded by a myth: the customer does not realise mergers and the supplier just has to accept them. 'Under new management!' Myth because the loss of turnover and the customer movements after mergers are symptomatic. On average, merging companies lose about 5 to 10 per cent of their customer base immediately after the merger. Suppliers at the same time face the cost synergies, especially on their own side. It thus looks like a zero-sum game as it is all about a redistribution of the suppliers' profits to the merging companies. Therefore anticipative direct or indirect price increases by suppliers can be observed. The well-timed integration of external stakeholders – before Day One – is an urgent task to avoid problems. A backward and a forward integration for the whole supply chain management as well as customer integration are therefore necessary (Figure 12.13).

Communication: Communicate to Stakeholder for Shareholder Value

The aspect of corporate communication has been recognised as the most important challenge both at the time of the announcement of mergers and during the post-merger phase. The challenge lies in the necessity to address *very different target groups* simultaneously (Figure 12.14).

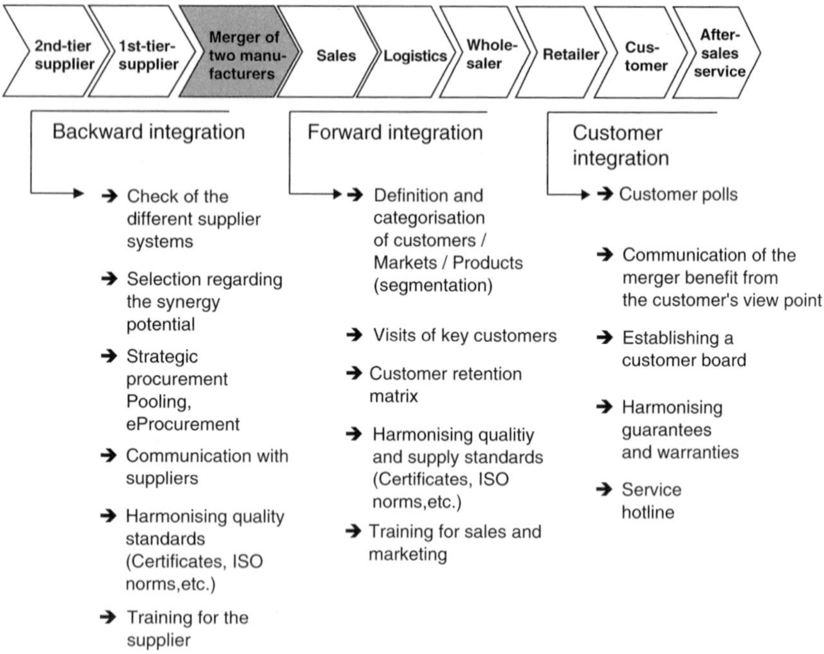

Figure 12.13 External integration as post-merger supply chain management

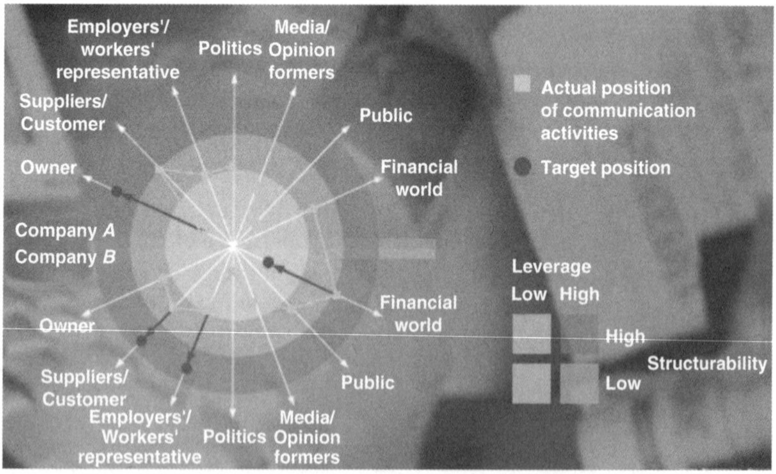

Figure 12.14 The communication radar
Source: UBS (2002).

The systematic *gap in communication*, owing to the confidential negotiations up to the *MA* announcement, creates a distrust that is hard to overcome. According to current studies, the internal as well as the external communication to all stakeholders are crucial aspects for the success of mergers. Figure 12.14 visualises the corresponding communication activities in regard to their current and necessary intensity. Pure *information* activities are not enough to avoid the spreading of destructive rumours. Therefore the principle for top management is: bad news first! Only through honesty can confidence be restored, so that the good news is believed to be true, too. What is also interesting here is the well-known insight of the corporate communication departments: external communication is internal communication – and vice versa. External communication, however, is challenged by a stabilisation of the respective brand equity, the merger marketing and by an intensive stakeholder communication (see Chapter 11).

Core Staff: Identification and Incentives

John Chambers, CEO of Cisco Systems, answered the question 'How do you measure success in your acquisitions?' clearly and precisely for his industry: 'Retention of people and... short-term wins for acquired employees.' Indeed: in the 'Old Economy', the rate of fluctuation of employees increases up to twelve-fold the normal rate after mergers. Therefore HR management is confronted with a lot of challenges in the post-merger phase – often without being involved in the pre-merger phase (Figure 12.15).

All these aspects need to be included in the framework of a HR due diligence, since here especially can substantial cost drivers for integration costs be found (see Chapter 10).

Core Competence Management: Pool Your Knowledge

The increased premiums on the stock market price that acquirers pay for the target company are to be seen against the background of the *implicit knowledge* embedded in the target company. If a buyer pays so much money for something that is as little tangible as 'knowledge', she must have a great interest in changing this success potential immediately into a business success during the integration process. A failure at this point in time – i.e. the draining away of knowledge – jeopardises profitability of the investment. The successful use of the knowledge potentials in the integration process – and in the following operative business – is facilitated by means of a structured process in the handling of knowledge, the so-called 'knowledge management'.

In the 1990s, knowledge management became one of the most important trend concepts in management education. Still, it is notable that this subject has almost no meaning in MAs in practice as well as in scientific analysis. And yet, the reasons for knowledge losses after mergers are numerous:

- Staff fluctuation – loss of knowledge holders
- A lot of routines are discussed (uncertainty)
- Fear of expressing tacit knowledge (rationalisation of their own jobs)
- Insufficient harmonisation of information and communication technologies (knowledge management systems and Intranet applications)
- Problems with different languages

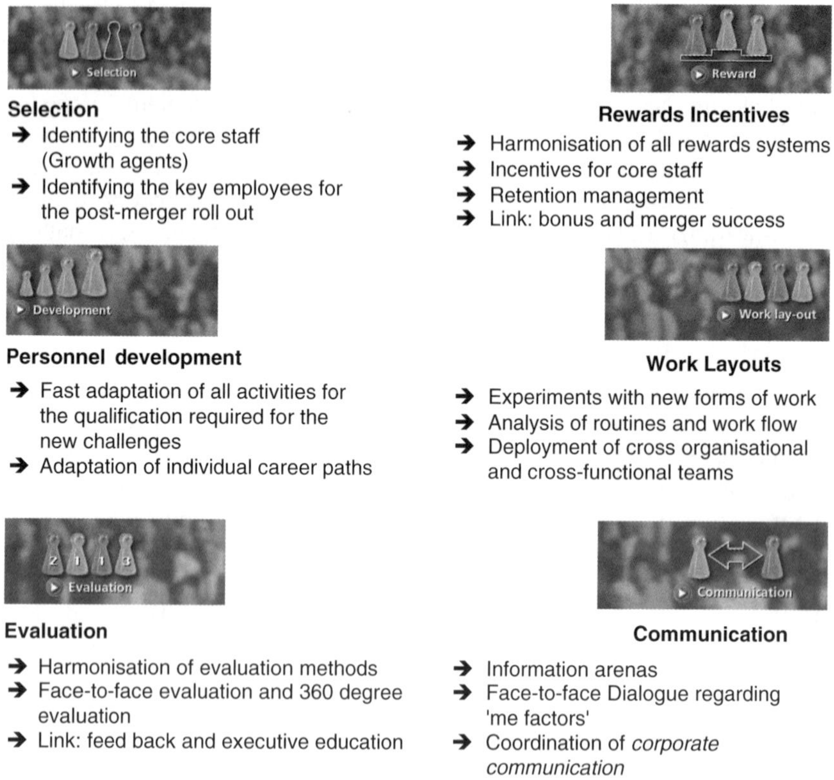

Figure 12.15 HR management in mergers

- Research and development (R&D) departments particularly suffering from the 'merger syndrome'.

Two motivations can be distinguished in knowledge management: knowledge *transfer* and knowledge *genesis*. Whereas most economic theories, such as the resource dependence theory, are aimed at knowledge transfer between both organisations, knowledge genesis is directed at the requirements for an increased *innovation power* of companies. Here, cross-functional and cross-organisational teams from *both* organisations are used as an appropriate structure for the development of new products. Further, the corporate universities, which emerged in the 1990s, are useful in the linking-up of knowledge holders (but not so much for the imparting of knowledge). We need to outline in more detail in the following thesis what kind of effect knowledge and its management have on the long-term success of mergers. The innovation-driven 'New Economy' can give some information about this.

Control: The Integration Balanced Scorecard

In mergers there is a high demand for *process auditing*. The need for intensive communication with all stakeholders is enormous and comes with the difficult communication tasks of merging companies. The post-merger phase is the most complex reorganisation activity, with consequences for nearly all stakeholders – especially customers and suppliers, but also shareholders and analysts. But this information basis is relevant also for the own-learning curve in a merger and, hence, for the own-decisions. Therefore, a compact overview becomes necessary to introduce correction measures (define responsibilities and give rise to commitment). A lot of attempts to check these mergers are gathered under the byword 'Post-Merger Audit'. It is almost exclusively a matter of *profitability checks* (good will amortisation calculations). However, a meaningful post-merger audit also requires considerations of further aspects:

- The post-merger audit must facilitate the *integration of different dimensions of objectives*, in other words means to include a financial evaluation of the transactions as well as an evaluation of all further qualitative aims.
- Post-merger audits must also consider the measures and interventions of the *post-merger management itself.*

It should be the aim of these efforts that frequent acquirers reach a better learning curve while they observe their merger management in a reflective way, because they survey their own skills in respect to the implementation. The Balanced Scorecard[10] concept is a first attempt to operationalise these different dimensions of objectives in a post-merger audit (Figure 12.16).

3 Theses and Tests Concerning Merger Management of National and International Mergers in the 'Old Economy' and 'New Economy'

The main problem for practice in post-merger management is the management handbooks. Owing to the lack of broad databases, myths about the 'right' integration management have emerged, which, of course, should not be taken as valid. But against the background of these aspects and the almost unchanged failure rates in recent years, there are many unanswered questions in practice as well as in the very painstaking scientific research that will how be presented and discussed using selected hypotheses within the framework of the 7C Model.

Using two of our own studies as well as other specialised analyses, we will present some initial clues to support the selected hypotheses. Our own studies can be characterised as follows in Table 12.2.

Even if a relatively broad overview of current post-merger problems is given here, some of the hypotheses cannot be analysed or assessed precisely because of the inadequate research material available at present.

The following theses are partially connected with an analysis of critical success factors. Because of the very different measurement possibilities it is essential to explain the definition of 'success':[11] in our own empirical analyses success was

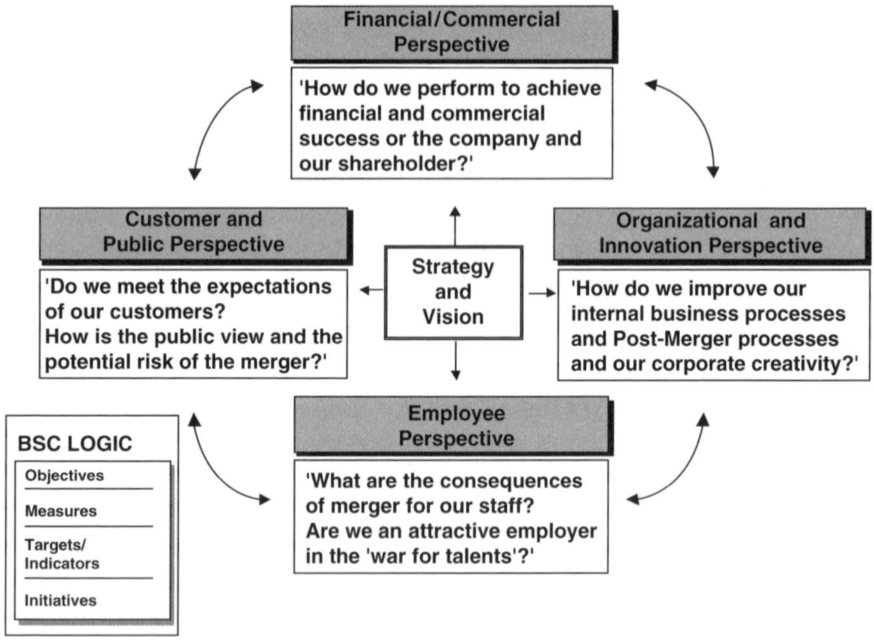

Figure 12.16 The post-merger balanced scorecard
Source: Kaplan and Norton (1996).

measured by outperformance in turnover and stock market value in comparison to the industry. Consequently, only quantifiable sizes are taken into account, and thus a simple measure can be provided, which at least facilitates certain comparability. For cross-border transactions the success rates in Figure 12.17 can be presented.

Theses Concerning Coordination in Mergers

Thesis 1: *The speed of integration is not a criterion for a successful merger. Cross-border transactions take longer. In the 'New Economy', however, integration will be carried out faster.*

Speed! Speed! Speed! One of the most incessant myths in merger management is the myth of speed. One of the driving forces behind this myth is the 'Rapid Integration Approach' of General Electric, which is still accepted by many people as standard for the integration process (Ashkenas, 1998). According to that, speed is mainly of use for the creation of clear leading and communication structures, for change anticipation, the breaking down of uncertainty and the achieving 'quick hits'. Against this stands the approach 'Go slow!'. Here, emphasis is especially laid on aspects of better preparation, on the consideration of the merger syndrome with all its psychological consequences as well as on a higher participation of all stakeholders.[12]

Table 12.2 Sample and research design of the empirical analysis

General analysis on merger management

Sample:	800 transactions with the highest volumes in Germany (one German company)
Source:	'M&A Review Database', St Gallen
Period:	Deals announced and closed between 1994 and 1998
Participants:	103 transactions (13% return rate)
Research design:	Comprehensive questionnaires and selected Interviews
Differentiated analysis:	

Type of M&A	Nationality	Industries	Size
Merger of equals vs. Acquisitions	National transactions vs. Cross-border	Service and retailing companies vs. Manufacturing	'Giants' vs. 'Mittelstand' (<1 billion Euro sales)

Type:	58% acquisitions and 42% mergers of equals
Nationality:	63% national transactions and 37% cross-border transactions
Industry:	30% service economy and retailing 70% manufacturing
Size:	62.5% giants
Consolidation:	86% of the transactions were either in the late phase of consolidation or completed → high validity of the sample

Specific analysis of new economy deals

Sample:	Frequent acquirers in Silicon Valley ('Early New Economy')
Criteria:	Frequent acquirers (at least 10 transactions per year with an M&A approach for external growth
Participants:	5 Buyers (Adobe, Cisco, Exite@Home, Quantum, Veritas)
Research design:	Semi-structured qualitative interviews with top managers (board positions or vice presidents 'post-merger')
Research period:	December 1999, Stanford University

Notes: *Mittelstand* = Medium-sized companies. The comprehensive results of the studies are in Jansen (2000b, 2000c); Jansen and Körner (2000).

But in the empirical analyses, no significant correlation could be found between the length from closure up to the start of integration activities and the corresponding development of turnover and market value in the aftermath of the merger. In only one-fifth of the analysed mergers that started integration process directly in the first month was an increase in value achieved. The results in mergers that started the integration process after three months were slightly better – 40 per cent achieved an increase in value. A period of time efficiently used for a thorough planning and analysis of the future integration activities is seemingly more successful than quick and thus possibly hasty activities. Even if the speed of such activities is not necessarily decisive for a successful merger, the speed of necessary decisions – e.g. the decisions about new management and adjustment of wages – is obviously a success factor for integration management.

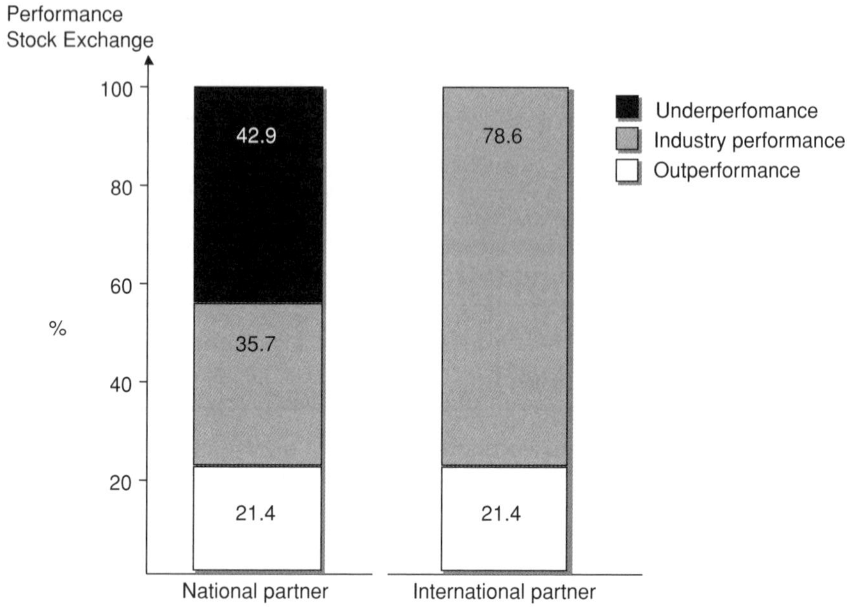

Figure 12.17 Outperformance of the two firms involved in cross-border transactions

Two interesting empirical results for the cross-border transactions and 'New Economy' deals were that: in the general sample, there were no significant differences in the speed of integration of national or international transaction (Gerds, 2000, p. 185). Contrary to expectations, however, were the results in the 'New Economy' deals: the speed of integration was far less high than assumed. A major reason lies in the change management in the 'New Economy' transactions that are basically mergers of growth with a focus on innovation, in contrast to the rationalisation mergers with a focus on costs.

Thesis 2: *Integration architecture and integration typologies are too static in theory and have to be differentiated for practice on the business-unit level. Integration teams are crucial for the success of transformation in the post-merger phase.*

As mentioned above, integration architectures can be differentiated into centralised (hierarchical), decentralised (non-hierarchical) and symbiotic architectures. The empirical analysis shows that the symbiotic arrangements are more successful because of the delay of activities in decentralised architectures and because of the management surrender in centralised architectures. It is similar if we look at the integration typologies: in practice, a significant deviation from the ideal types can be observed. There are thus sequential successive types of integration. Particularly in the 'New Economy', very loose connections (stand-alone) were built at the beginning and gradually either integrated more intensely (symbiosis or absorption) or even disinvested. We also have to differentiate the integration planning at

Theses Concerning Communication in Mergers

Thesis 7: *After the announcement, an inevitable communication paradox arises. Failures of communication are the most central faults in mergers.*

As a consequence of merger announcements a so-called 'merger syndrome' arises (Marks and Mirvis, 1985). The dominance of 'me-factors' leads to a gossip factory. As nearly everything seems to be in question in a single moment there is an enormous stress level in the organisation. Additionally, mistrust arises from the generally secret negotiation of the management board before the transaction. The communication paradox appears as follows: because of the information gap in the framework of the negotiations, fast information and communication becomes the most important task for top management and this urgency is precisely the reason why communication are not taken and accepted, or are not believed. From the empirical results of the self-assessment communication is the second most-quoted fault with, 27 per cent and communication concepts are seemed the most necessary instruments for communication strategy, with 72 per cent. In international mergers, attention has clearly been paid more to this even though language does not play the central role here. As the experiences of the 'New Economy' transactions have also shown, there is only one way to gain credibility: bad news first and pure.

Thesis 8: *External communication is internal communication – and vice versa. External support through an external communication agency is more authentic and more relevant to stock value than merely internal public relations work.*

Because of the spread of rumours, all investigated companies have led the experience that internal communication believed only what was reported about the deal externally – the internal becomes the external communication. In Müller-Stewens and Salecker's (1991) analysis, the effectiveness of internal and external public relations work was investigated. External support in public relations work proved more successful than a merely internal communication strategy.

Theses Concerning Core Staff and Career Management in Mergers

Thesis 9: *After mergers, the staff fluctuation rate increases significantly. This is a substantial reason for the failure of mergers. Therefore, a focus should be made on retention management.*

Different analyses show that the fluctuation rate increases to twelve times the normal level. On average, about 70 per cent of higher management leave the company within five years – often they are switching to competitor.[13] The correlation between fluctuation and the success of mergers remains scientifically unclarified. No significant correlation in an analysis of fluctuation rates could be found (Gerpott, 1993). It is intuitively reasonable, that, especially in pure acquisitions, a bad management performance of the target company is the main motive for the deal. Change management according to 'change the management' strategies can thus be planned and can fit the merger logic. Providing a definition particularly of the core staff and their corresponding incentives becomes very important. Particularly in the case of a high integration depth, nothing is more demotivating than insufficiently harmonised salary and incentive structures.[14] In the framework of a HR due diligence, this definition and the corresponding costs should be considered. Service companies, and more especially the 'New Economy' companies, have placed the retention management first on the post-merger agenda.

Thesis 10: The two HR departments as well as inhouse consultancies should work largely separately, so that 'merger syndrome' does not affect the important multipliers.

This thesis has not been analysed empirically as yet. But it is assumed that the HR departments and the inhouse consultancies involved should not be integrated immediately. Especially in this phase, much higher demands for their activities in the field of individual staff coaching as well as the 'multipliers' in the change management process arise. Through the first parallel structures in this early stage, an individualisation of staff and more frictionless post-merger advice become possible, without merger stress, but with a corresponding focus on the core business and not just on the internal structures and positions.

Theses Concerning Core Competence Management in Mergers

Thesis 11: The merged companies have innovation problems because of their own activities.

Regarding the strategic motives for mergers, cost synergies on the production and on the distribution side were seemed are most important, with 39 per cent and 31 per cent, respectively. The increase in innovation power was named last, with only 4 per cent, and the realisation of growth synergies was in the middle, with 16 per cent. Most of the horizontal mergers are *cost mergers*. This is also reflected in the innovation power after mergers: to give an example in the German sample, expenses for research and development (R&D) remained constant, but the number and the quality of patents dropped significantly after the merger. The own-activities concerning the integration of research areas lead to the problem that the product pipeline fails in a lot of innovation fields (e.g. the pharmaceutical industry) and therefore drops in turnovers can arise, with persisting effects. In 'New Economy' deals, the opposite is true: whereas no cost synergies were fixed at all in business valuations, the knowledge capital systematically left its mark.

Thesis 12: Mergers happen because of the implicit knowledge and networks of relations. But mergers lead to destruction of intellectual and social capital.

In a many mergers good will is paid for the implicit knowledge, relationships and reputation. It is amazing that in mergers only occasional activities in knowledge management are considered, and this aspect is also still extensively ignored in research. However, there are indications that the very cursory intellectual and social capital is destroyed very fast through mergers. High losses in organisational knowledge bases are particularly to be noted. Reasons for the losses are the fear of rationalism, uncertainty concerning the future of existing projects, staff fluctuation and technological harmonisation of the different knowledge management systems.

Theses Concerning Control in and of Mergers

Thesis 13: Post-merger audits are important instruments of process control and should evaluate the profitability of the investments from a financial and social perspective, as well as the post-merger management itself.

Post-merger audits, which are taken for granted in the investment calculation concerning the amortisation analysis, are almost never carried out empirically. Only 7 per cent of the participants considered this to be an important task for merger success. The result that there was 16 per cent demand for further instruments can be interpreted as an indication of the insufficiency of current ones. The Balanced Scorecard sketched on p. 346 can contribute a reflection on financial and non-financial results as well an evaluation and correction of process controls for the intervention applied during post-merger management.

Thesis 14: There is a learning curve for the frequent acquirers. They achieve a better performance than acquirers with the experience of only few transactions.

This intuitive thesis could not be confirmed. A first analysis on this issue suggested a U-curve relationship between the number of transactions of the company and its success. That means that first-time buyers are more successful than companies that have already carried out some transactions (Haleblian and Finkelstein, 1999). According to these results, the success of the following deals will decline owing to management hubris but after some more deals the post-merger performance increases again, slowly.

It is interesting that in our sample, no correlation between the number of transactions made before and post-merger performance could be identified. Against the background of the 'New Economy' deals it can be noted that the acquisition strategy is based on smallest acquisitions, like Cisco or the myth of General Electric. Huge mergers of equals, however, change the organisation so fundamentally that the experiences can hardly be applied to later transactions.

Notes

1 For figures and trends, see Jansen (2001a, pp. 38ff.).
2 Cf. Müller-Stewens, Schäfer and Szeless (2001, p. 13).
3 See for the procedures, problems, and potentials of evaluating the success of mergers Jansen and Petersen (2000). For an overview of the different approaches and studies, see also Jansen (2001a, p. 244).
4 Müller-Stewens (2000, p. 54; figures from Goldman Sachs).

5 Agrawal, Jaffe and Mandelker (1992).
6 Müller-Stewens (2000, p. 54).
7 For example Weston, Chung and Hoag (1990) or Gaughan (1999).
8 For an overview, see Jansen (2001a, pp. 190–223).
9 Examples for several studies with M&A focus: Olie (1994); Morosini (1999); Gertsen, Søderberg and Torp (1998).
10 See, for the general logic of the Balanced Scorecard, Kaplan and Norton (1996).
11 Jansen and Petersen (2000).
12 For example Yunker (1983), cited in Buono and Bowditch (1989, p. 15).
13 Figures in Jansen and Pohlmann (2000).
14 For empirical tests, see Datta (1991).

Bibliography

Agrawal, A., Jaffe, J. F. and Mandelker, G. N. (1992) The Post-Merger Performance of Acquiring Firms: A Re-Examination of an Anomaly, *Journal of Finance*, 47, 4, pp. 1605–21.

Ashkenas, R. N., DeMonaco, L. J. and Francis, S. C. (1998) Making the Deal Real: How GE Capital Integrates Acquisitions, *Harvard Business Review*, January–February, pp. 165–78.

Bleeke, J. and Ernst, D. (1991) The Way to Win in Cross-Border Alliances, *Harvard Business Review*, Nov.–Dec., pp. 127–35.

Bleeke, J. and Ernst, D. (1994) *Rivalen als Partner. Strategische Allianzen und Akquisitionen im globalen markt* (Frankfurt: Campus).

Bleeke, J. and Ernst, D. (1995) Is Your Strategic Alliance Really a Sale?, *Harvard Business Review*, Jan.–Feb., pp. 97–105.

Boston Consulting Group (BCG) (2000) Crossing Borders – European Mergers and Acquistions, *BCG-Report*, September.

Bühner, R. (1992) Aktionärsbeurteilung grenzüberschreitender Zusammenschlüsse, *Zeitschrift für betriebswirtschaftliche Forschung*, 5.1992, pp. 445–59.

Buono, A. F. and Bowditch, J. L. (1989) *The Human Side of Mergers and Acquisitions – Managing Collisions Between People, Cultures, and Organizations* (San Francisco: Jossey-Bass).

Datta, D. K. (1991) Organizational Fit and Acquisition Performance: Effects of Post-Acquisition Integration, *Strategic Management Journal*, 12, pp. 281–97.

Down, J. W. (1995) The M&A Game is Often Won or Lost After the Deal, *Management Review Executive Forum*, 10, pp. 10–11.

Galpin, T. J. and Herndon, M. (2000) *The Complete Guide to Mergers and Acquisitions – Process Tools to Support the M&A Integration at Every Level* (San Francisco: Jossey-Bass).

Gaughan, P. (1999) *Mergers, Acquisitions and Corporate Restructuring*, 2nd edn (New York: John Wiley).

Gerds, J. (2000) *Post Merger Integration – Eine Empirische Untersuchung zum Integrationsmanagement* (Wiesbaden: Giabler).

Gerpott, T. J. (1993) Ausscheiden von Top-Managern nach Akquisitionen: Segen oder Fluch?, *Zeitschrift für Betriebswirtschaftslehre*, 63, 12, pp. 1271–94.

Gertsen, M. C., Soderberg, A. -M. and Torp, J. E. (eds) (1998) *Cultural Dimensions of International Mergers and Acquisitions* (Berlin and New York: de Gruyter).

Goldman Sachs (2001) Internal study (Frankfurt).

Hayes, J. (1998) 'After the wedding: Avoiding Post-Merger Pitfalls', in *Antitrust Law and Economics Review*, 25, 2, pp. 98–110.

Jansen, S. A. (1999) Mergers and Acquisitions optimal managen: Die Härte der weichen Faktoren: Post Merger Management, *Handelsblatt*, 6 August, p. K3.

Jansen, S. A. (2000a) Post Merger Management in Deutschland Teil I, *M&A Review*, 9, pp. S334–9.

Jansen, S. A. (2000b) Post Merger Management in Deutschland Teil II, *M&A Review*, 10, pp. 388–92.

Jansen, S. A. (2000c) 10 Thesen gegen Post Merger Integration Management, *Organisationsentwicklung*, 1/2000, pp. 16–32.

Jansen, S. A. (2001a) *Mergers & Acquisitions: Unternehmensakquisition und kooperation – Eine strategische organisatorische und kapitelmarkttheoretische Einführung*, 4th edn (Wiesbaden: Gabler).

Jansen, S. A. (2001b) DaimlerChrysler Post-Merger Management, *Case Study* N9-701-051, Harvard Business School 2002.

Jansen, S. A. and Körner, K. (2000) Fusionsmanagement in Deutschland – Eine empirische Analyse von 103 Zusammenschlüsse mit deutscher Beteiligung zwischen 1994 and 1998 unter spezifischer Auswertung der Erfolgswirkungen des Typus der Fusion, der (Inter-) Nationalität, der Branche und der Unternehmensgröβe, *Discussion Paper*, Witten/Herdecke University, 2nd edn, November.

Jansen, S. A. and Müller-Stewens, G. (2000) Endet die fünfte Welle auf dem Markt für Unternehmensübernahmen in einer neuer Rezession? Geschichte, Trends und Erfolgsfaktoren von Zusammenschlüssen, *Franfurter Allgemeine Zeitung*, 230, 4 October, p. 49.

Jansen, S. A. and Petersen, J. (2000) Mythos 'Merger-Misserfolg'? Prozedere, Probleme und Potentiale der Erfolgsmessung von Unternehmenszusammenschlüssen, *M&A Review*, 12/2000, pp. 470–5.

Jansen, S. A. and Pohlmann, N. (2000) Herausforderungen und Zumutungen: Das Human Resource Management bei Firmenszusammenschlüssen, *Personalführung*, 2/2000, pp. 30–9.

Jung, H. (1993) *Erfolgsfaktoren von Unternehmensakquisitionen* (Stuttgart: M&P).

Kaplan, R. S. and Norton, D. P. (1996) Using the Balanced Scorecard as a Strategic Management System, *Harvard Business Review*, January–February, pp. 75–85.

Lajoux, A. R. (1998) *The Art of M&A Integration: A Guide to Merging Resources, Processes and Responsibilities* (New York *et al.*: McGraw-Hill).

Lubatkin, M., Calori, R., Philippe, V. and Vega, J. F. (1998) Managing Mergers Across Borders: A Two-Nation Exploration of a Nationally Bound Administrative Heritage, *Organization Science*, November–December, 9, 6, pp. 670–84.

Marks, M. L. and Mirvis, P. (1985) Merger Syndrome: Stress and Uncertainty, *Mergers and Acquisitions*, 20, 2, pp. 50–5.

Marks, M. L. and Mirvis, P. (1998) *Joining Forces: Making One Plus One Equal Three in Mergers, Acquisitions, and Alliances* (San Francisco: Jossey-Bass).

Morosini, P. (1999) *Managing Cultural Differences – Effective Strategy and Exeustion Across Cultures in Global Corporate Alliances* (Oxford: Pergamon).

Morosini, P. (2000) *Managing Cultural Differences*, Presentation '2nd Executive M&A Congress', Institute for Mergers and Acquisitions (IMA), Witten/Herdecke University.

Morosini, P., Shane, S. and Singh, H. (1998) National Culture Distance and Cross-Border Acquisition Performance, *Journal of International Business Studies*, 29, 1, pp. 137–58.

Müller-Stewens, G. (2000) Akquisitionen und der der Markt für Unternehmenskontrolle: Entwicklungen und Erfolgsfaktoren, in Picot, A., Nordmeyer, A. and Pribilla, P. (eds), *Management von Akquisitionen* (Stuttgart: Schäffer-Poeschel), pp. 41–62.

Müller-Stewens, G. and Salecker, J. (1991) Kommunikation – Schlüsselkompetenz im Akquisitionsprozeβ, *Absatzwirtschaft*, 10, pp. 104–13.

Müller-Stewens, G., Schäfer, M. and Szeless, G. (2001) Wertschaffung durch strategische Desinvestititionen, *M&A Review*, 1/2001, pp. 13–18.

Nahavandi, A. and Malekzadeh, A. R. (1988) Acculturation in Mergers and Acquisitions, *Academy of Management Review*, 13, 1, pp. 79–90.

Olie, R. (1994) Shades of Culture and Institutions in International Mergers, *Organization Studies*, 15, 3, p. 381–405.

Porter, M. E. (1987) From Competitive Advantage to Corporate Strategy, *Harvard Business Review*, May–June, pp. 43–59.

Pritchett, P. with Robinson, D. and Clarkson, R. (1997) *After the Merger: The Authoritative Guide for Integration Success*, revised edn (New York and London: McGraw-Hill).

Schleifer, A. and Summers, L. H. (1987) Breach of Trust in Hostile Takeovers, in Auerbach, A. J. (ed.), *Mergers and Acquisitions* (Cambridge, UP Chicago), pp. 7–20.

Schmidt, R. (1999) Cross Border Mergers and Corporate Governance – An Empirical Analysis from 1988 to 1999, *Betriebswirtschaftliche Diskussionsbeiträge Martin-Luther-Universität Halle-Wittenberg*, 36/99.

UBS (2000) *Mergerland*, CD-ROM, in cooperation with G. Müller-Stewens.

Weston, F. J., Chung, K. S. and Hoag, S. E. (1990) *Mergers, Restructuring, and Corporate Control* (Englewood Cliffs, NJ: Prentice Hall).

Yunker, J. A. (1983) *Integrating Acquisitions: Making Corporate Marriages Work* (New York: Praeger).

Index

Note: f = figure; n = endnote; t = table.